ANTON CHEKHOV'S
SHORT STORIES

TEXTS OF THE STORIES
BACKGROUNDS
CRITICISM

W. W. NORTON & COMPANY
also publishes

THE NORTON ANTHOLOGY OF AFRICAN AMERICAN LITERATURE
edited by Henry Louis Gates Jr. and Nellie Y. McKay et al.

THE NORTON ANTHOLOGY OF AMERICAN LITERATURE
edited by Nina Baym et al.

THE NORTON ANTHOLOGY OF CONTEMPORARY FICTION
edited by R. V. Cassill and Joyce Carol Oates

THE NORTON ANTHOLOGY OF ENGLISH LITERATURE
edited by M. H. Abrams et al.

THE NORTON ANTHOLOGY OF LITERATURE BY WOMEN
edited by Sandra M. Gilbert and Susan Gubar

THE NORTON ANTHOLOGY OF MODERN POETRY
edited by Richard Ellmann and Robert O'Clair

THE NORTON ANTHOLOGY OF POETRY
edited by Margaret Ferguson et al.

THE NORTON ANTHOLOGY OF SHORT FICTION
edited by R. V. Cassill

THE NORTON ANTHOLOGY OF WORLD MASTERPIECES
edited by Maynard Mack et al.

THE NORTON FACSIMILE OF
THE FIRST FOLIO OF SHAKESPEARE
prepared by Charlton Hinman

THE NORTON INTRODUCTION TO LITERATURE
edited by Jerome Beaty and J. Paul Hunter

THE NORTON INTRODUCTION TO THE SHORT NOVEL
edited by Jerome Beaty

THE NORTON READER
edited by Linda H. Peterson, John C. Brereton, and Joan E. Hartman

THE NORTON SAMPLER
edited by Thomas Cooley

THE NORTON SHAKESPEARE, BASED ON THE OXFORD EDITION
edited by Stephen Greenblatt et al.

1893
$ 8.00

A NORTON CRITICAL EDITION

ANTON CHEKHOV'S SHORT STORIES

TEXTS OF THE STORIES
BACKGROUNDS
CRITICISM

Selected and Edited by

RALPH E. MATLAW

THE UNIVERSITY OF CHICAGO

W · W · NORTON & COMPANY

New York · London

Library of Congress Cataloging in Publication Data
Chekhov, Anton Pavlovich, 1860–1904.
    Anton Chekhov's short stories.
    (A Norton critical edition)
    Bibliography: p.
    1. Chekhov, Anton Pavlovich, 1860–1904—Criticism
and interpretation—Addresses, essays, lectures.
I. Matlaw, Ralph E.   II. Title.
PZ3.C3985Cg   1979   [PG3456.A15]   891.7'3'3   78–17052

ISBN 0-393-04528-5
ISBN 0-393-09002-7 pbk.

Printed in the United States of America.

All Rights Reserved

W. W. Norton & Company, Inc., 500 Fifth Avenue, New York, N.Y. 10110

7 8 9 0

ACKNOWLEDGMENTS

Anton Chekhov: The following translations by Constance Garnett are reprinted by arrangement with Macmillan Publishing Co., Inc.; Chatto and Windus Ltd.; and David Garnett: from *"The Darling" and Other Stories* (© 1916 by Macmillan Publishing Co., Inc.; renewed 1944 by Constance Garnett), "Anyuta" and "The Darling"; from *"The Lady with the Dog" and Other Stories* (© 1917 by Macmillan Publishing Co., Inc.; renewed 1945 by Constance Garnett), "A Doctor's Visit"; from *"The Party" and Other Stories* (© 1917 by Macmillan Publishing Co., Inc.; renewed 1945 by Constance Garnett), "The Teacher of Literature" and "Anna on the Neck"; from *"The Wife" and Other Stories* (© 1918 by Macmillan Publishing Co., Inc.; renewed 1946 by Constance Garnett), "About Love"; from *"The Witch" and Other Stories* (© 1918 by Macmillan Publishing Co., Inc.; renewed 1946 by Constance Garnett), "The Student" and "The Huntsman"; from *"The Chorus Girl" and Other Stories* (© 1920 by Macmillan Publishing Co., Inc.; renewed 1948 by David Garnett), "A Gentleman Friend"; from *"The Schoolmistress" and Other Stories* (© 1921 by Macmillan Publishing Co., Inc.; renewed 1949 by David Garnett), "Misery," "The Requiem," "In Exile"; from *"The Cook's Wedding" and Other Stories* (© 1922 by Macmillan Publishing Co., Inc., renewed 1950 by David Garnett), "Oysters," "Sleepy," "Whitebrow." The following translations by Marian Fell are reprinted with the permission of Charles Scribner's Sons: from *Stories of Russian Life* (© 1914 by Charles Scribner's Sons), "Agatha," "Dreams," "At Home"; from *Russian Silhouettes: More Stories of Russian Life* (© 1915 by Charles Scribner's Sons), "Grisha," "The Chorus Girl," "Rothschild's Fiddle," "The Pecheneg," "A Journey by Cart," "The Bishop." The following translations by Ivy Litvinov are reprinted from A. P. Chekhov, *Short Novels and Stories* (Moscow: Foreign Languages Publishing House, n.d.): "Chameleon," "Vanka," "The Man in a Case," "Gooseberries," "The House with the Mansard," "The Grasshopper," "The Lady with the Dog," "The Betrothed."

A. B. Derman: from *O Masterstve Chekhova* (On Chekhov's Craftsmanship), pp. 74–88. Moscow, 1959. Translated by Ralph E. Matlaw.

Karl Kramer: from *The Chameleon and the Dream*. The Hague: Mouton Publishers, 1970. Reprinted by permission of the publishers.

D. S. Mirsky: from *A History of Russian Literature: From Its Beginnings to 1900* by D. S. Mirsky, edited by Francis T. Whitfield. Copyright © 1926, 1927, 1949, © 1958 by Alfred A. Knopf, Inc. Reprinted by permission of Alfred A. Knopf, Inc.

Nils Åke Nilsson: from *Studies in Chekhov's Narrative Technique: "The Steppe" and "The Bishop."* Stockholm: Almqvist and Wiksell, 1968 (Stockholm Slavic Studies, 2). Reprinted by permission of the author.

Renato Poggioli: "Storytelling in a Double Key," reprinted by permission of the publishers from *The Phoenix and the Spider* by Renato Poggioli. Cambridge, Mass.: Harvard University Press. Copyright © 1957 by the President and Fellows of Harvard College.

Donald Rayfield: from *Chekhov: The Evolution of His Art* by Donald Rayfield, pp. 152–155. Copyright 1975. Reprinted by permission of Barnes & Noble Books (Div. of Harper & Row Publishers, Inc.) and Paul Elek Ltd.

Virginia Llewellyn Smith: from *Anton Chekhov and the Lady with the Dog* by Virginia Llewellyn Smith, pp. 96–97, 212–218. © 1973 Oxford University Press. Reprinted by permission of Oxford University Press.

Gleb Struve: "On Chekhov's Craftsmanship: The Anatomy of a Story," *Slavic Review*, vol. 20, no. 3 (October 1961), pp. 465–476. Reprinted by permission of the author and the publisher.

Contents

Backgrounds

Criticism

Preface

A professor's view: "It's the commentaries on Shakespeare that matter, not Shakespeare."
—from Chekhov's *Notebooks*

A selection of Chekhov's stories is also a critical judgment, an evaluation, and therefore a distortion. It is difficult today to appreciate Chekhov's technical innovations in the shorter forms of fiction, since they have become standard practice. Yet technique and length concerned Chekhov deeply from the very beginning of his career, when he was limited to one hundred lines per story, and may be used as one of the bases of choice. This edition is restricted to the short stories, eliminating such masterpieces of the longer story or short novel as *The Steppe, A Dreary Story, Ward No. 6, Three Years, My Life,* and *In the Ravine,* which at the moment are conveniently available in other collections. Stories of an intermediate length, like *The Nameday Party* or *The Murder,* were also omitted, not as any particular entity of narrative fiction but in order to accommodate more of Chekhov's stories. The stories chosen from the hundreds that remain present a variegated yet inadequate or incomplete spectacle of human behavior and thought depicted by Chekhov. Several large topics are missing: among the earlier stories, many of Chekhov's humorous pieces devoted to human foibles in general and to the theater in particular; in the middle phase, stories concerned more immediately with reactions to contemporary problems and ideas, to a quest for meaning, as in *A Nervous Breakdown, The Bet, Gusev, An Anonymous Story;* in the late period, those dealing with the rise of huge factories and the change in the rural population that create so grim a social picture when grouped together (*A Woman's Kingdom, At Home* [1897], *The New Villa*); and throughout his career, stories revolving around sex: *A Misfortune, Slime, Ariadne,* and many others. Yet the general picture of Chekhov's work that emerges from this selection reflects his major concerns, techniques, and attitudes, and includes most of his best and most popular stories. Some things have necessarily been left out even among the late stories (*Ionych, At Christmas Time*), as less rewarding than others (*The Lady with the Dog,* my favorite among Chekhov's stories, and *The Student,* his own); the earlier stories again reflect within the broader categories some personal preferences, to the point of my having translated two stories (*A Living Chronology* and *The Siren's Song*) that did not seem to convey quite the right tone in existing translations. A good case could be made out for a different choice, and I hope the reader will be provoked into making it after reading all those stories translated into English that could not be included here.

Chekhov the man and Chekhov's art have given rise to many contradictory legends. The first is presented briefly through Gorky's memoirs of Chekhov during the last years of his life. Although that picture omits many details, moods, attitudes, and phases of Chekhov's life, it captures much of the essence of the man. The second has been by and large ignored. There are famous essays on Chekhov as a pessimist, the portrayer of gloom and hopelessness, futility, "the voice of twilight Russia," of isolation, the process of vulgarization, and the constant failure of communication among people, just as there are essays on the hopeful Chekhov foreseeing a new era and a glorious future. There are good and valid historical reasons for such views, but these essays do little to advance our understanding of Chekhov's work. Chekhov was not given to generalities like these, but rather insisted on honesty and truth, on depicting what existed rather than what one hoped to see because one saw in automatic, ordinary, and unthinking ways. The selection from his letters amply demonstrates this, and a fuller selection would have documented and elaborated attitudes that may be gleamed in his work. Yet like all art the work is far richer than the attitudes and circumstances that provided the impulse to create it. The attempt to draw a message or moral or lesson from Chekhov's stories always turns out unsatisfactory and simplistic. Pasternak's Dr. Zhivago says of Chekhov's (deceptive) simplicity that it has a "modest reticence in such high-sounding matters as the ultimate purpose of mankind or its salvation. It's not that [he] didn't think of such matters, and to good effect, but to talk about such things seemed to [him] pretentious, presumptuous." The picture is there, fully; what it means, what can be done about it, and whether anything should be done about it, and at what cost, is something else again. The essays chosen, therefore, tend to emphasize the methods and scope of the stories, rather than some normative conclusion, and to present the humorist and satirist as well as the depictor of "more serious" existence. I have purposely omitted expatiations on *poshlost'* (the banal, trivial, specious, vulgar) that Chekhov depicted so masterfully, as on recurrent motives like obesity, slovenliness, concern for food, and the like as an indicator of such *poshlost'*, because they merely label (whether correctly or not) and thereby seem to obviate the necessity for considering the passages themselves. I have also found it difficult to use much of the material that studies Chekhov's dialogue, descriptions, and narrators, and their relationship to Chekhov's predecessors and the Russian tradition, since the subtleties of Chekhov's style are lost in translation. Moreover, much of this material is devoted to the longer works or to stories not reprinted here, and relies greatly on extensive quotations. It is a minor revelation to find out that a large portion of the extensive critical literature on Chekhov seems to be irrelevant once specific stories have been selected. There are, of course, innumerable articles dealing with one phase or another of particular stories: Chekhov himself has an interesting notation in his *Notebooks*: " 'Dmitri the Pretender and Actors,' 'Turgenev and Tigers'—it is possible to write such articles and people do write them." No such essays have been included.

D. S. Mirsky's essay, characteristically opinionated, incisive, and lively, still serves as an excellent introduction to Chekhov, although some of its "correctives" to opinion prevalent in the 1920's no longer seem necessary. Renato Poggioli's consideration of the early work indicate Chekhov's range and originality, while his treatment of the *The Darling* may serve (in conjunction with Karl Kramer's view), among other things, as an indicator of the multiplicity of interpretations possible for a single story. There are remarks on form by A. Derman, on the technique of a particular story (*Sleepy*) by Gleb Struve, on the relationship between biography and a story in a view of *The Lady with a Dog* by Virginia Llewellyn Smith, and, in a very different and more suggestive sense, in *The Bishop*. Many technical considerations, critical insights, and interpretations abound in these and the other essays, which have been arranged to follow the chronological order of the stories.

The translations, with the exception of *A Living Chronology* and *The Siren's Song*, were made by three women during different parts of this century: Ivy Litvinov, Marian Fell, and Constance Garnett. Chekhov may be easier to translate than other Russian writers, as Mirsky suggests, but the difference in quality from the original nevertheless is very marked. The translations have been revised, wherever necessary, in accordance with contemporary usage; where I have noticed mistakes I have corrected them without further ado. There is a minimum of explanatory footnotes. The stories do not need a more elaborate apparatus to convey their meaning, and a more refined reading cannot in any case depend upon a translation.

RALPH E. MATLAW

The Texts of
The Stories

Chameleon

Police Inspector Ochumelov[1] crossed the marketplace in a new greatcoat holding a bundle in his hand. After him strode a red-haired constable carrying a sieve filled to the brim with confiscated gooseberries. All around was silence.... There was not a soul in the marketplace.... The open doors of small shops and taverns gaped drearily out at God's world, like so many hungry jaws. There were not even any beggars standing near them.

All of a sudden the sound of a voice came to Ochumelov's ears. "So you'd bite, would you, you cur! Don't let it go, lads! Biting is not allowed nowadays. Hold it! Ow!"

A dog's whine was heard. Ochumelov glanced in the direction of the sound and this is what he saw: a dog came running out of the timberyard of the merchant Pichugin on three legs, pursued by a man in a starched print shirt and an unbuttoned waistcoat, his whole body bent forward; the man stumbled and caught hold of the dog by one of its hind legs. There was another whine, and again a shout of: "Don't let it go!" Drowsy faces were thrust out of shops, and in no time a crowd which seemed to have sprung out of the earth had gathered around the timberyard.

"Looks like a public disturbance, Your Honor!" said the constable.

Ochumelov turned, and marched up to the crowd. Right in front of the gate of the yard he saw the above-mentioned individual in the unbuttoned waistcoat, who stood there with his right hand raised, displaying a bleeding finger to the crowd. The words: "I'll give it to you, you devil!" seemed to be written on his tipsy countenance, and the finger itself looked like a banner of victory. Ochumelov recognized in this individual Khryukin,[2] the goldsmith. In the very middle of the crowd, its forelegs well apart, sat the culprit, its whole body a-tremble—a white borzoi pup, with a pointed nose and a yellow spot on its back. In its tearful eyes was an expression of misery and horror.

"What's all this about?" asked Ochumelov, shouldering his way through the crowd. "What are you doing here? Why are you holding up your finger? Who shouted?"

"I was walking along, Your Honor, as quiet as a lamb," began Khryukin, coughing into his fist. "I had business about some wood with Mitri Mitrich here, and suddenly, for no reason whatever, that

---

1. From the word *ochumely*, "crazed." 2. *Khryu-khryu*—pig's grunt. [*Translator.*] [*Translator.*]

nuisance bit my finger. Excuse me, but I'm a working man. . . . Mine is a very intricate trade. Make them pay me compensation— perhaps I won't be able to move this finger for a week. It doesn't say in the law, Your Honor, that we have to put up with ferocious animals. If everyone's to start biting, life won't be worth living. . . "

"H'm . . . well, well," said Ochumelov severely, coughing and twitching his eyebrows. "Well, well . . . whose dog is it? I shan't leave it at this. I'll teach people to let dogs run about! It's time something was done about gentlemen who are not willing to obey the regulations! He'll get such a fine, the scoundrel—I'll teach him what it means to let dogs and cattle of all sorts rove about! I'll show him what's what! Eldirin," he continued, turning to the constable, "find out whose dog it is, and draw up a statement. And the dog must be exterminated without delay. It's probably mad . . . whose dog is it, I ask?"

"I thing it belongs to General Zhigalov," said a voice from the crowd.

"General Zhigalov! H'm. Help me off with my coat, Eldirin. . . . Phew, how hot it is! It must be going to rain." He turned to Khryukin: "One thing I don't understand—how did it happen to bite you? How could it have got at your finger? Such a little dog, and you such a strapping fellow! You must have scratched your finger with a nail, and then taken it into your head to get paid for it. I know you fellows! A set of devils!"

"He burned the end of its nose with a lighted cigarette for a joke, Your Honor, and it snapped at him, it's nobody's fool! That Khryukin's always up to some mischief, Your Honor!"

"None of your lies, Squinty! You didn't see me do it, so why lie? His Honor is a wise gentleman, he knows who's lying and who's telling a God's truth. May the justice of the peace try me if I'm lying! It says in the law . . . all men are equal now. I have a brother in the police myself, if you want to know. . . ."

"Don't argue!"

"No, that isn't the General's dog," remarked the constable profoundly. "The General hasn't got a dog like that. All his dogs are pointers."

"Are you sure?"

"Quite sure, Your Honor."

"And you're right! The General's dogs are expensive, breed-dogs, and this one—just look at it! Ugly, mangy cur! Why should anyone keep a dog like that? Are you crazy? If a dog like that were to find itself in Moscow or Petersburg, d'you know what would happen to it? Nobody would worry about the law, it would be got rid of in a minute. You're a victim, Khryukin, and mind you don't leave it at that. He must be taught a lesson! It's high time. . . ."

"Perhaps it is the General's after all," said the constable, thinking aloud. "You can't tell by looking at it. I saw one just like it in his yard the other day."

"Of course it's the General's!" came the voice from the crowd.

"H'm! Help me on with my coat, Eldirin. . . . I felt a gust of wind. I'm shivery. Take it to the General's and ask them. Say I found it, and sent it. And tell them not to let it into the street. Perhaps it's an expensive dog, and it'll soon get spoiled if every brute thinks he can stick cigarettes into its nose. A dog's a delicate creature. And you put down your hand, blockhead! Stop showing everyone your silly finger. It's your own fault. . . ."

"Here comes the General's chef, we'll ask him. . . . Hi, there, Prokhor! Come here, old man! Have a look at this dog . . . is it yours?"

"What next! We've never had one like that in our lives!"

"No need to make any more inquiries," said Ochumelov. "It's a stray. What's the good of standing here talking. You've been told it's a stray, so a stray it is. Destroy it and have done with the matter."

"It isn't ours," continued Prokhor. "It belongs to the General's brother, who came a short time ago. Our General takes no interest in borzois. His brother now, he likes . . ."

"What, has the General's brother come? Vladimir Ivanich?" exclaimed Ochumelov, an ecstatic smile spreading over his features. "Fancy that! And I didn't know. Come to stay?"

"That's right."

"Just fancy! Wanted to see his brother! And I didn't know. So it's *his* dog? Very glad! Take it . . . it's a nice little doggie! Snap at his finger! Ha-ha-ha! Come now, don't tremble! Gr-gr . . . the little rascal's angry. . . . What a pup!"

Prokhor called the dog and walked out of the timberyard with it. The crowd laughed at Khryukin.

"I'll have you yet!" Ochumelov threatened him, and, wrapping his greatcoat around him, he continued his way across the marketplace.

1884

Oysters

I need no great effort of memory to recall, in every detail, the rainy autumn evening when I stood with my father in one of the more frequented streets of Moscow, and felt that I was gradually being overcome by a strange illness. I had no pain at all, but my legs were giving way under me, the words stuck in my throat, my head slipped weakly on one side. . . . It seemed as though, in a moment, I must fall down and lose consciousness.

If I had been taken into a hospital at that minute, the doctors would have had to write over my bed *Fames*,[1] a disease which is not in the manuals of medicine.

Beside me on the pavement stood my father in a shabby summer overcoat and a serge cap, from which a bit of white wadding was sticking out. On his feet he had big heavy galoshes. Afraid, vain man, that people would see that his feet were bare under his galoshes, he had drawn the tops of some old boots up round the calves of his legs.

This poor, foolish, queer creature, whom I loved the more warmly the more ragged and dirty his smart summer overcoat became, had come to Moscow, five months before, to look for a job as copying-clerk. For those five months he had been trudging about Moscow looking for work, and it was only on that day that he had brought himself to go into the street to beg for alms.

Before us was a big house of three stories, adorned with a blue signboard with the word "Restaurant" on it. My head was drooping feebly backwards and to one side, and I could not help looking upwards at the lighted windows of the restaurant. Human figures were flitting about at the windows. I could see the right side of the orchestrion, two oleographs, hanging lamps. . . . Staring into one window, I saw a patch of white. The patch was motionless, and its rectangular outlines stood out sharply against the dark, brown background. I looked intently and made out of the patch a white placard on the wall. Something was written on it, but what it was, I could not see. . . .

For half an hour I kept my eyes on the placard. Its white attracted my eyes, and, as it were, hypnotized my brain. I tried to read it, but my efforts were in vain.

At last the strange disease got the upper hand.

The rumble of the carriages began to seem like thunder, in the stench of the street I distinguished a thousand smells. The restaurant lights and the lamps dazzled my eyes like lightning. My five senses were overstrained and sensitive beyond the normal. I began to see what I had not seen before.

"Oysters . . ." I made out on the placard.

A strange word! I had lived in the world eight years and three months, but had never come across that word. What did it mean? Surely it was not the name of the restaurant-keeper? But signboards with names on them always hang outside, not on the walls indoors!

"Papa, what does 'oysters' mean?" I asked in a husky voice, making an effort to turn my face towards my father.

My father did not hear. He was keeping a watch on the movements of the crowd, and following every passer-by with his eyes. . . . From his eyes I saw that he wanted to say something to the passers-by, but the fatal word hung like a heavy weight on his trembling lips

1. "Hunger," in Latin.

and could not be flung off. He even took a step after one passer-by and touched him on the sleeve, but when he turned round, he said, "I beg your pardon," was overcome with confusion, and staggered back.

"Papa, what dose 'oysters' mean?" I repeated.

"It is an animal . . . that lives in the sea. . . ."

I instantly pictured to myself this unknown marine animal. . . . I thought it must be something midway between a fish and a crab. As it was from the sea they made of it, of course, a very nice hot fish soup with savory pepper and laurel leaves, or broth with vinegar and fricassee of fish and cabbage, or crayfish sauce, or served it cold with horse-radish. . . . I vividly imagined it being brought from the market, quickly cleaned, quickly put in the pot, quickly, quickly, for everyone was hungry . . . awfully hungry! From the kitchen rose the smell of hot fish and crayfish soup.

I felt that this smell was tickling my palate and nostrils, that it was gradually taking possession of my whole body. . . . The restaurant, my father, the white placard, my sleeves were all smelling of it, smelling so strongly that I began to chew. I moved my jaws and swallowed as though I really had a piece of this marine animal in my mouth. . . .

My legs gave way from the blissful sensation I was feeling, and I clutched at my father's arm to keep myself from falling, and leant against his wet summer overcoat. My father was trembling and shivering. He was cold. . . . .

"Papa, are oysters a Lenten dish?" I asked.

"They are eaten alive . . ." said my father. "They are in shells like tortoises, but . . . in two halves."

The delicious smell instantly stopped affecting me, and the illusion vanished. . . . Now I understood it all!

"How nasty," I whispered, "how nasty!"

So that's what "oysters" meant! I imagined to myself a creature like a frog. A frog sitting in a shell, peeping out from it with big, glittering eyes, and moving its revolting jaws. I imagined this creature in a shell with claws, glittering eyes, and a slimy skin, being brought from the market. . . . The children would all hide while the cook, frowning with an air of disgust, would take the creature by its claw, put it on a plate, and carry it into the dining-room. The grown-ups would take it and eat it, eat it alive with its eyes, its teeth, its legs! While it squeaked and tried to bite their lips. . . .

I frowned, but . . . but why did my teeth move as though I were munching? The creature was loathsome, disgusting, terrible, but I ate it, ate it greedily, afraid of distinguishing its taste or smell. As soon as I had eaten one, I saw the glittering eyes of a second, a third. . . . I ate them too. . . . At last I ate the table-napkin, the plate, my father's galoshes, the white placard. . . . I ate everything that caught my eye, because I felt that nothing but eating would take away my illness. The oysters had a terrible look in their eyes and were loathsome. I shuddered at the thought of them, but I wanted to eat! To eat!

"Oysters! Give me some oysters!" was the cry that broke from me and I stretched out my hand.

"Help us, gentlemen!" I heard at that moment my father said, in a hollow and shaking voice. "I am ashamed to ask but—my God!— I can bear no more!"

"Oysters!" I cried, pulling my father by the skirts of his coat.

"Do you mean to say you eat oysters? A little chap like you!" I heard laughter close to me.

Two gentlemen in top hats were standing before us, looking into my face and laughing.

"Do you really eat oysters, youngster? That's interesting! How do you eat them?"

I remember that a strong hand dragged me into the lighted restaurant. A minute later there was a crowd round me, watching me with curiosity and amusement. I sat at a table and ate something slimy, salt with a flavor of dampness and moldiness. I ate greedily without chewing, without looking and trying to discover what I was eating. I fancied that if I opened my eyes I should see glittering eyes, claws, and sharp teeth.

All at once I began biting something hard, there was a sound of a scrunching.

"Ha, ha! He is eating the shells," laughed the crowd. "Little silly, do you suppose you can eat that?"

After that I remember a terrible thirst. I was lying in my bed, and could not sleep for heartburn and the strange taste in my parched mouth. My father was walking up and down, gesticulating with his hands.

"I believe I have caught cold," he was muttering. "I've a feeling in my head as though someone were sitting on it. . . . Perhaps it is because I have not . . . er . . . eaten anything to-day. . . . I really am a queer, stupid creature. . . . I saw those gentlemen pay ten rubles[1] for the oysters. Why didn't I go up to them and ask them . . . to lend me something? They would have given something."

Towards morning, I fell asleep and dreamt of a frog sitting in a shell, moving its eyes. At midday I was awakened by thirst, and looked for my father: he was still walking up and down and gesticulating.

1884

1. In the 1880's a ruble (one hundred kopeks) was worth about fifty cents, but its purchasing power was much greater: for two rubles one could have a decent dinner.

A Living Chronology

Councilor-of-State Sharamykin's living room is bathed in pleasant semi-darkness. A large bronze lamp with a green shade casts a green light *à la* "Ukrainian Nights"[1] on the walls, furniture, and faces. Now and then a smoldering log bursts into flame in the fireplace and for a moment sheds the color of a conflagration on the faces, but that does not spoil the general harmony of the illumination. The general tone, as artists say, is sustained.

Sharamykin himself, an elderly man with the gray side-whiskers of a bureaucrat and gentle light-blue eyes sits, in an armchair in front of the fireplace, in the pose of someone who has just dined. Tenderness spreads over his face, his lips are composed into a sorrowful smile. At his feet Vice-Governor Lopnev, a dashing man of forty, sits on a footstool, lazily stretching out and sticking his feet toward the fireplace. Sharamykin's children, Nina, Kolya, Nadya, and Vanya, are playing near the piano. A light timidly darts through the slightly open door leading to Mrs. Sharamykin's study. There, behind the door, Sharamykin's wife, Anna Pavlovna, the president of the local ladies' committee, a lively and piquant little lady, aged thirty and a touch, sits at her desk. Her dark alert eyes run over the pages of a French novel through a pince-nez. Under the novel lies the disarranged annual report of the committee.

"Our town used to be more fortunate in that respect in previous years," says Sharamykin, blinking his gentle eyes at the smoldering fire. "Not a single winter passed without the visit of some star. There used to be famous actors and singers, while today, God only knows! Nobody visits except magicians and organ-grinders. No esthetic satisfaction whatsoever. We live in a wilderness. Yes, sir. . . . But do you remember that Italian tragedian, Your Excellency . . . what was his name? That dark-haired, tall . . . if I can just . . . Ah, yes! Luigi Ernesto de Ruggiero. . . . A remarkable talent . . . powerful! Sometimes he would utter a single word, and the whole theatre would shake. My Anyutochka took great interest in his talent. She went to a lot of trouble to get him a theatre, and sold enough tickets for ten performances. In return he taught her declamation and mime. A splendid man! He came here . . . if I'm not mistaken . . . about twelve years ago. . . . No, I'm off. . . . Less, maybe ten years ago. . . . Anyutochka, how old is our Nina?"

"She was nine on her last birthday!" Anna Pavlovna shouts from her study. "Why?"

"Nothing, dearest, I just asked. . . .—And good singers used to come. . . . Do you remember the *tenore di grazia*[2] Prilipchin? What

---

1. Green dominates A. I. Kuindzhi's painting by that name (1876).

a splendid man! What a figure! Blonde . . . such an expressive face,
Parisian manners. . . . And what a voice, Your Excellency! He only
had one shortcoming: he forced some notes and sang high B
falsetto, but all the rest was fine. He said that he had studied with
Tamberlick. . . . Anyutochka and I managed to get him a hall in the
Assembly and out of gratitude he used to sing entire days and nights
for us in return. . . . He taught Anyutochka to sing. . . . He came
here, I remember it distinctly, during Lent in . . . in . . . twelve
years ago. No, more. . . . Oh, God! There's memory for you!
Anyutochka, how old is our Nadechka?"

"Twelve!"

"Twelve . . . if you add ten months. . . . Well, there you have
it . . . thirteen! . . . There used to be more life in town formerly, too,
somehow. . . . Take the benefit nights for example. What marvelous
evenings we used to have. What a delight! There was singing, and
acting, and recitations. . . . I remember after the war, when the
Turkish prisoners were kept here. Anyutochka organized an evening
for the benefit of the wounded. They collected eleven hundred
rubles. . . . The Turkish officers were crazy about Anyutochka's
voice, I remember, and kept kissing her hand. Hee, hee, hee. . . .
They're a grateful nation, even if they are Asiatics. The evening was
so successful that I put it down in the journal, would you believe it.
That was, I remember it distinctly, in seventy-six . . . no! in seventy-
seven. . . . No! Excuse me, when were the Turks here? Anyutochka,
how old is our Kolechka?"

"I'm seven years old, Papa!" says Kolya, a swarthy kid with a
dark complexion and hair black as coal.

"Yes, we've gotten old, and no longer have the energy we used to
have! . . ." Lopnev agrees, heaving a sigh. "That's the reason. . . .
Old age, my friend! There are no new people to take the initiative,
and the old have gotten old. . . . They no longer have the old fire.
When I was younger I didn't want anyone to have a tedious
time. . . . I was your Anna Pavlovna's right-hand man. . . . Whether
it was arranging a benefit night, or a lottery, or to entertain a
visiting celebrity—I'd give up everything and start busying myself
about arrangements. One winter, I remember, I fussed and rushed
around so much that I even fell ill. . . . I'll never forget that winter!
Do you remember what a show your Anna Pavlovna and I put on
for the benefit of those who got burned out?"

"What year did that take place?"

"Not long ago. . . . In seventy-nine. . . . No, I think in eighty.
Excuse me, how old is your Vanya?"

"Five!" Anna Pavlovna shouts from the study.

"Well, that was six years ago then. . . . Yes, sir, my friend, there
were lots of things afoot then! It's not the same anymore! The old
spark is missing!"

---

2. Or *tenore leggiero*: "lyric tenor."

Lopnev and Sharamykin become pensive. The smoldering log bursts into flame for the last time and becomes coated with ashes.

1885

The Huntsman

A sultry, stifling midday. Not a cloudlet in the sky. . . . The sun-baked glass had a disconsolate, hopeless look: even if there were rain it could never be green again. . . . The forest stood silent, motionless, as though it were looking at something with its tree-tops or expecting something.

At the edge of the clearing a tall, narrow-shouldered man of forty in a red shirt, in patched trousers that had been a gentleman's, and in high boots, was slouching along with a lazy, shambling step. He was sauntering along the road. On the right was the green of the clearing, on the left a golden sea of ripe rye stretched to the very horizon. He was red and perspiring, a white cap with a straight jockey peak, evidently a gift from some open-handed young gentleman, perched jauntily on his handsome flaxen head. Across his shoulder hung a game-bag with a blackcock lying in it. The man held a double-barreled gun cocked in his hand, and screwed up his eyes in the direction of his lean old dog who was running on ahead sniffing the bushes. There was stillness all round, not a sound . . . everything living was hiding away from the heat.

"Yegor Vlassich!" The huntsman suddenly heard a soft voice.

He started and, looking round, scowled. Beside him, as though she had sprung out of the earth, stood a pale-faced woman of thirty with a sickle in her hand. She was trying to look into his face, and was smiling diffidently.

"Oh, it is you, Pelagea!" said the huntsman, stopping and deliberately uncocking the gun. "H'm! . . . How have you come here?"

"The women from our village are working here, so I have come with them. . . . As a laborer, Yegor Vlassich."

"Oh . . ." growled Yegor Vlassich, and slowly walked on.

Pelagea followed him. They walked in silence for twenty paces.

"I have not seen you for a long time, Yegor Vlassich . . ." said Pelagea looking tenderly at the huntsman's moving shoulders. "I have not seen you since you came into our hut at Easter for a drink of water . . . you came in at Easter for a minute and then God knows how . . . drunk . . . you scolded and beat me and went away. . . . I have been waiting and waiting. . . . I've tired my eyes out looking for you. Ah, Yegor Vlassich, Yegor Vlassich! you might look in just once!"

"What is there for me to do there?"

"Of course there is nothing for you to do . . . though to be sure

. . . there is the place to look after. . . . To see how things are going. . . . You are the master. . . . I say, you have shot a blackcock, Yegor Vlassich! You ought to sit down and rest!"

As she said all this Pelagea laughed like a silly girl and looked up at Yegor's face. Her face was simply radiant with happiness.

"Sit down? If you like . . ." said Yegor in a tone of indifference, and he chose a spot between two fir-trees. "Why are you standing? You sit down too."

Pelagea sat a little way off in the sun and, ashamed of her joy, put her hand over her smiling mouth. Two minutes passed in silence.

"You might come for once," said Pelagea.

"What for?" sighed Yegor, taking off his cap and wiping his red forehead with his hand. "There is no object in my coming. To go for an hour or two is only waste of time, it's simply upsetting you, and to live continually in the village my soul could not endure. . . . You know yourself I am a pampered man. . . . I want a bed to sleep in, good tea to drink, and refined conversation. . . . I want all the niceties, while you live in poverty and dirt in the village. . . . I couldn't stand it for a day. Suppose there were an edict that I must live with you, I should either set fire to the hut or lay hands on myself. Since childhood I've had this love for ease; there is no help for it."

"Where are you living now?"

"With the gentleman here, Dmitry Ivanich, as a huntsman. I furnish his table with game, but he keeps me . . . more for his pleasure than anything."

"That's not proper work you're doing, Yegor Vlassich. . . . For other people it's a pastime, but with you it's like a trade . . . like real work."

"You don't understand, you silly," said Yegor, gazing gloomily at the sky. "You have never understood, and as long as you live you will never understand what sort of man I am. . . . You think of me as a foolish man, gone to the bad, but to anyone who understands I am the best shot there is in the whole district. The gentry feel that, and they have even printed things about me in a magazine. There isn't a man to be compared with me as a sportsman. . . . And it is not because I am pampered and proud that I look down upon your village work. From my childhood, you know, I have never had any calling apart from guns and dogs. If they took away my gun, I used to go out with the fishing-hook, if they took the hook I caught things with my hands. And I went in for horse-dealing too, I used to go to the fairs when I had the money, and you know that if a peasant goes in for being a sportsman, or a horse-dealer, it's good-bye to the plough. Once the spirit of freedom has taken a man you will never root it out of him. In the same way, if a gentleman goes in for being an actor or for any other art, he will never make an official or a landowner. You are a woman, and you do not understand, but one must understand that."

"I understand, Yegor Vlassich."

"You don't understand if you are going to cry. . . ."

"I . . . I'm not crying," said Pelagea, turning away. "It's a sin, Yegor Vlassich! You might stay a day with luckless me, anyway. It's twelve years since I was married to you, and . . . and . . . there has never once been love between us! . . . I . . . I am not crying."

"Love . . ." muttered Yegor, scratching his arm. "There can't be any love. It's only in name we are husband and wife; we aren't really. In your eyes I am a wild man, and in mine you are a simple peasant woman with no understanding. Are we well matched? I am a free, pampered, profligate man, while you are a working woman, going in bast shoes and never straightening your back. The way I think of myself is that I am the foremost man in every kind of sport, and you look at me with pity. . . . Is that being well matched?"

"But we are married, you know, Yegor Vlassich," sobbed Pelagea.

"Not married of our free will. . . . Have you forgotten? You have to thank Count Sergey Pavlovich and yourself. Out of envy, because I shot better than he did, the Count kept giving me wine for a whole month, and when a man's drunk you could make him change his religion, let alone getting married. To pay me out he married me to you when I was drunk. . . . A huntsman to a herd-girl! You saw I was drunk, why did you marry me? You were not a serf, you know; you could have resisted. Of course it was a bit of luck for a herd-girl to marry a huntsman, but you ought to have thought about it. Well, now be miserable, cry. It's a joke for the Count, but a crying matter for you. . . . Beat yourself against the wall."

A silence followed. Three wild ducks flew over the clearing. Yegor followed them with his eyes till, transformed into three scarcely visible dots, they sank down far beyond the forest.

"How do you live?" he asked, moving his eyes from the ducks to Pelagea.

"Now I am going out to work, and in the winter I take a child from the Foundling Hospital and bring it up on the bottle. They give me a ruble and a half a month."

"Oh. . . ."

Again a silence. From the strip that had been reaped floated a soft song which broke off at the very beginning. It was too hot to sing.

"They say you have put up a new hut for Akulina," said Pelagea. Yegor did not speak.

"So she is dear to you. . . ."

"It's your luck, it's fate!" said the huntsman, stretching. "You must put up with it, poor thing. But good-bye, I've been chattering long enough. . . . I must be at Boltovo by the evening."

Yegor rose, stretched himself, and slung his gun over his shoulder; Pelagea got up.

"And when are you coming to the village?" she asked softly.

"I have no reason to, I shall never come sober, and you have little to gain from me drunk; I am spiteful when I am drunk. Goodbye!"

"Good-bye, Yegor Vlassich."

Yegor put his cap on the back of his head and, clicking to his dog, went on his way. Pelagea stood still looking after him. . . . She saw his moving shoulder-blades, his jaunty cap, his lazy, careless step, and her eyes were full of sadness and tender affection. . . . Her gaze flitted over her husband's tall, lean figure and caressed and fondled it. . . . He, as though he felt that gaze, stopped and looked round. . . . He did not speak, but from his face, from his shrugged shoulders, Pelagea could see that he wanted to say something to her. She went up to him timidly and looked at him with imploring eyes.

"Take it," he said, turning round.

He gave her a crumpled ruble note and walked quickly away.

"Good-bye, Yegor Vlassich," she said, mechanically taking the ruble.

He walked by a long road, straight as a taut strap. She, pale and motionless as a statue, stood, her eyes seizing every step he took. But the red of his shirt melted into the dark color of his trousers, his step could not be seen, and the dog could not be distinguished from the boots. Nothing could be seen but the cap, and . . . suddenly Yegor turned off sharply into the clearing and the cap vanished in the greenness.

"Good-bye, Yegor Vlassich," whispered Pelagea, and she stood on tiptoe to see the white cap once more.

1885

Misery

"To whom shall I tell my grief?"[1]

Twilight. Big flakes of wet snow are whirling lazily about the street lamps, which have just been lighted, and lie in a thin soft layer on roofs, horses' backs, shoulders, caps. Iona Potapov, the sleigh-driver, is all white like a ghost. He sits on the box without stirring, bent as double as the living body can be bent. If a regular snowdrift fell on him it seems as though even then he would not

1. From "Joseph's Lament" ("Plach Iosifa"), in *Spiritual Verse* (*Dukhovnye stikhi*), a series of oral poems thought to have been written between the fifteenth and seventeenth centuries.

think it necessary to shake it off. . . . His little mare is white and motionless too. Her stillness, the angularity of her lines, and the stick-like straightness of her legs make her look like a halfpenny gingerbread horse. She is probably lost in thought. Anyone who has been torn away from the plough, from the familiar gray landscapes, and cast into this slough, full of monstrous lights, of unceasing uproar and hurrying people, is bound to think.

It is a long time since Iona and his nag have budged. They came out of the yard before dinnertime and not a single fare yet. But now the shades of evening are falling on the town. The pale light of the street lamps changes to a vivid color, and the bustle of the street grows noiser.

"Cabby, to the Vyborgskaya!" Iona hears. "Cabby!"

Iona starts, and through his snow-plastered eyelashes he sees an officer in a military overcoat with a hood over his head.

"To the Vyborgskaya," repeats the officer. "Are you asleep? To the Vyborgskaya!"

In token of assent Iona gives a tug at the reins, which sends cakes of snow flying from the horse's back and shoulders. The officer gets into the sleigh. Iona clicks to the horse, cranes his neck like a swan, rises in his seat, and, more from habit than necessity, brandishes his whip. The mare cranes her neck, too, crooks her stick-like legs, and hesitatingly sets off.

"Where are you shoving, you devil?" Iona immediately hears shouts from the dark mass shifting to and fro before him. "Where the devil are you going? Keep to the r-right!"

"You don't know how to drive! Keep to the right," says the officer angrily.

A coachman driving a carriage swears at him; a pedestrian crossing the road and brushing the horse's nose with his shoulder looks at him angrily and shakes the snow off his sleeve. Iona fidgets on the box as though he were sitting on thorns, jerks his elbows, and turns his eyes about like one possessed, as though he does not know where he is or why he is there.

"What rascals they all are!" says the officer jocosely. "They are simply doing their best to run up against you or fall under the horse's feet. They must be doing it on purpose."

Iona looks as his fare and moves his lips. Apparently he means to say something, but only a sniff comes out.

"What?" inquires the officer.

Iona gives a wry smile and, straining his throat, brings out huskily: "My son . . . er . . . my son died this week, sir."

"H'm! What did he die of?"

Iona turns his whole body round to his passenger and says:

"Who can tell! It must have been from fever. . . . He lay three days in the hospital and then he died. . . . God's will."

"Turn round, you devil!" comes out of the darkness. "Have you gone off your head, you old dog? Look where you are going!"

"Drive on! drive on!" says the officer. "We won't get there till tomorrow at this rate. Hurry up!"

Iona cranes his neck again, rises in his seat, and with heavy grace swings his whip. Several times he looks round at the officer, but the latter keeps his eyes shut and is apparently disinclined to listen. Putting his fare down at the Vyborgskaya, Iona stops by a restaurant, and again sits huddled up on the box. . . . Again the wet snow paints him and his horse white. One hour passes, and then another.

Three young men, two tall and thin, one short and hunchbacked, come up, railing at each other and loudly stamping on the pavement with their galoshes.

"Cabby, to the Police Bridge," the hunchback shouts in a cracked voice. "The three of us . . . twenty kopeks!"

Iona tugs at the reins and clicks to his horse. Twenty kopeks is not a fair price, but he has no thoughts for that. Whether it is a ruble or whether it is five kopeks does not matter to him now so long as he has a fare. . . . The three young men, shoving each other and using bad language, go up to the sleigh, and all three try to sit down at once. The question remains to be settled: Which are to sit down and which one is to stand? After a long altercation, ill-temper, and abuse, they come to the conclusion that the hunchback must stand because he is the shortest.

"Well, drive on," says the hunchback in his cracked voice, settling himself and breathing down Iona's neck. "Cut along! What a cap you've got, my friend! You wouldn't find a worse one in all Petersburg. . . ."

"He-he! . . . he-he! . . ." laughs Iona. "It's nothing to boast of!"

"Well, then, nothing to boast of, drive on! Are you going to drive like this all the way? Eh? Shall I give you one in the neck?"

"My head aches," says one of the tall ones. "At the Dukmasovs' yesterday Vaska and I drank four bottles of brandy between us."

"I can't make out why you talk such stuff," says the other tall one angrily. "You lie like a brute."

"Strike me dead, it's the truth! . . ."

"It's about as true as that a louse coughs."

"He-he!" grins Iona. "Me-er-ry gentlemen!"

"Tfoo! the devil take you!" cries the hunchback indignantly. "Will you get on, you old plague, or won't you? Is that the way to drive? Give her one with the whip. Hang it all, give it her well."

Iona feels behind his back the jolting person and quivering voice of the hunchback. He hears abuse addressed to him, he sees people, and the feeling of loneliness begins little by little to be less heavy on his heart. The hunchback swears at him, till he chokes over some elaborately whimsical string of epithets and is overpowered by his cough. His tall companions begin talking of a certain Nadezhda Petrovna. Iona looks round at them. Waiting till there is a brief pause, he looks round once more and says:

"This week . . . er . . . my . . . er . . . son died!"

"We shall all die, . . ." says the hunchback with a sigh, wiping his lips after coughing. "Come, drive on! Drive on! My friends, I simply cannot stand crawling like this! When will he get us there?"

"Well, you give him a little encouragement . . . one in the neck!"

"Do you hear, you old plague? I'll make you smart. If one stands on ceremony with fellows like you one may as well walk. Do you hear, you old dragon? Or don't you care a hang what we say?"

And Iona hears rather than feels a slap on the back of his neck.

"He-he! . . ." he laughs. "Merry gentlemen. . . . God give you health!"

"Cabman, are you married?" asks one of the tall ones.

"I? He-he! Me-er-ry gentlemen. The only wife for me now is the damp earth. . . . He-ho-ho! . . . The grave that is! . . . Here my son's dead and I am alive. . . . It's a strange thing, death has come in at the wrong door. . . . Instead of coming for me it went for my son. . . ."

And Iona turns round to tell them how his son died, but at that point the hunchback gives a faint sigh and announces that, thank God! they have arrived at last. After taking his twenty kopeks, Iona gazes for a long while after the revelers, who disappear into a dark entry. Again he is alone and again there is silence for him. . . . The misery which has been for a brief space eased comes back again and tears his heart more cruelly than ever. With a look of anxiety and suffering Iona's eyes stray restlessly among the crowds moving to and fro on both sides of the street: can he not find among those thousands someone who will listen to him? But the crowds flit by heedless of him and his misery. . . . His misery is immense, beyond all bounds. If Iona's heart were to burst and his misery to flow out, it would flood the whole world, it seems, but yet it is not seen. It has found a hiding-place in such an insignificant shell that one would not have found it with a candle by daylight. . . .

Iona sees a house-porter with a parcel and makes up his mind to address him.

"What time will it be, friend?" he asks.

"Going on for ten. . . . Why have you stopped here? Drive on!"

Iona drives a few paces away, bends himself double, and gives himself up to his misery. He feels it is no good to appeal to people. But before five minutes have passed he draws himself up, shakes his head as though he feels a sharp pain, and tugs at the reins. . . . He can bear it no longer.

"Back to the yard!" he thinks. "To the yard!"

And his little mare, as though she knew his thoughts, falls to trotting. An hour and a half later Iona is sitting by a big dirty stove. On the stove, on the floor, and on the benches are people snoring. The air is full of smells and stuffiness. Iona looks at the sleeping figures, scratches himself, and regrets that he has come home so early. . . .

"I have not earned enough to pay for the oats, even," he thinks. "That's why I am so miserable. A man who knows how to do his work, . . . who has had enough to eat, and whose horse has had enough to eat, is always at ease. . . ."

In one of the corners a young cabman gets up, clears his throat sleepily, and makes for the water-bucket.

"Want a drink?" Iona asks him.

"Seems so."

"May it do you good. . . . But my son is dead, mate. . . . Do you hear? This week in the hospital. . . . It's a queer business. . . ."

Iona looks to see the effect produced by his words, but he sees nothing. The young man has covered his head over and is already asleep. The old man sighs and scratches himself. . . . Just as the young man had been thirsty for water, he thirsts for speech. His son will soon have been dead a week, and he has not really talked to anybody yet. . . . He wants to talk of it properly, with deliberation. . . . He wants to tell how his son was taken ill, how he suffered, what he said before he died, how he died. . . . He wants to describe the funeral, and how he went to the hospital to get his son's clothes. He still has his daughter Anisya in the country. . . . And he wants to talk about her too. . . . Yes, he has plenty to talk about now. His listener ought to sigh and exclaim and lament. . . . It would be even better to talk to women. Though they are silly creatures, they blubber at the first word.

"Let's go out and have a look at the mare," Iona thinks. "There is always time for sleep. . . . You'll have sleep enough, no fear. . . ."

He puts on his coat and goes into the stables where his mare is standing. He thinks about oats, about hay, about the weather. . . . He cannot think about his son when he is alone. . . . To talk about him with someone is possible, but to think of him and picture him is insufferable anguish. . . .

"Are you munching?" Iona asks his mare, seeing her shining eyes. "There, munch away, munch away. . . . Since we have not earned enough for oats, we will eat hay. . . . Yes, . . . I have grown too old to drive. . . . My son ought to be driving, not I. . . . He was a real cabman. . . . He ought to have lived. . . ."

Iona is silent for a while, and then he goes on:

"That's how it is, old girl. . . . Kuzma Ionich is gone. . . . He said good-by to me. . . . He went and died for no reason. . . . Now, suppose you had a little colt, and you were own mother to that little colt. . . . And all at once that same little colt went and died. . . . You'd be sorry, wouldn't you? . . ."

The little mare munches, listens, and breathes on her master's hands. Iona is carried away and tells her all about it.

1886

The Requiem

In the village church of Verkhny Zaprudy mass was just over. The people had begun moving and were trooping out of church. The only one who did not move was Andrey Andreyich, a shop-keeper, intellectual,[1] and old inhabitant of Verkhny Zaprudy. He stood waiting, with his elbows on the railing of the right choir. His fat and shaven face, covered with indentations left by pimples, expressed on this occasion two contradictory feelings: resignation in the face of inevitable destiny, and stupid, unbounded disdain for the smocks and striped kerchiefs passing by him. As it was Sunday, he was dressed like a dandy. He wore a long cloth overcoat with yellow bone buttons, blue trousers not thrust into his boots, and sturdy galoshes—the huge clumsy galoshes only seen on the feet of practical and prudent persons of firm religious convictions.

His torpid eyes, sunk in fat, were fixed upon the icon stand. He saw the long familiar figures of the saints, the verger Matvey puffing out his cheeks and blowing out the candles, the darkened candle-stands, the threadbare carpet, the sacristan Lopukhov running impulsively from the altar and carrying the holy bread to the church-warden. . . . All these things he had seen for years, and seen over and over again like the five fingers of his hand. . . . There was only one thing, however, that was somewhat strange and unusual. Father Grigory, still in his vestments, was standing at the north door, twitching his thick eyebrows angrily.

"Who is it he is winking at? God bless him!" thought the shop-keeper. "And he is beckoning with his finger! And he stamped his foot! What next! What's the matter, Holy Queen and Mother! Whom does he mean it for?"

Andrey Andreyich looked round and saw the church completely deserted. There were some ten people standing at the door, but they had their backs to the altar.

"Do come when you are called! Why do you stand like a graven image?" he heard Father Grigory's angry voice. "I am calling you."

The shopkeeper looked at Father Grigory's red and wrathful face, and only then realized that the twitching eyebrows and beckoning finger might refer to him. He started, left the railing, and hesitat-ingly walked towards the altar, tramping with his heavy galoshes.

---

1. Chekhov's irony is obvious.

"Andrey Andreyich, was it you asked for prayers for the peace of Marya's soul?" asked the priest, his eyes angrily transfixing the shopkeeper's fat, perspiring face.

"Yes, Father."

"Then it was you wrote this? You?" And Father Grigory angrily thrust before his eyes the little note.

And on this little note, handed in by Andrey Andreyich before mass, was written in big, as it were staggering, letters:

"For the peace of the soul of the servant of God, the harlot Marya."

"Yes, certainly I wrote it, . . ." answered the shopkeeper.

"How dared you write it?" whispered the priest, and in his husky whisper there was a note of wrath and alarm.

The shopkeeper looked at him in blank amazement; he was perplexed, and he, too, was alarmed. Father Grigory had never in his life spoke in such a tone to a leading resident of Verkhny Zaprudy. Both were silent for a minute, staring into each other's face. The shopkeeper's amazement was so great that his fat face spread in all directions like spilled dough.

"How dared you?" repeated the priest.

"Wha . . . what?" asked Andrey Andreyich in bewilderment.

"You don't understand?" whispered Father Grigory, stepping back in astonishment and clasping his hands. "What have you got on your shoulders, a head or some other object? You send a note up to the altar, and write a word in it which it would be unseemly even to utter in the street! Why are you rolling your eyes? Surely you know the meaning of the word?"

"Are you referring to the word harlot?" muttered the shopkeeper, flushing crimson and blinking. "But you know, the Lord in His mercy . . . forgave this very thing, . . . forgave a harlot. . . . He has prepared a place for her, and indeed from the life of the holy saint, Marya of Egypt, one may see in what sense the word is used— excuse me. . . ."

The shopkeeper wanted to bring forward some other argument in his justification, but took fright and wiped his lips with his sleeve.

"So that's what you make of it!" cried Father Grigory, clasping his hands. "But you see God has forgiven her—do you understand? He has forgiven, but you judge her, you slander her, call her by an unseemly name, and whom! Your own deceased daughter! Not only in Holy Scripture, but even in worldly literature you won't read of such a sin! I tell you again, Andrey, you mustn't be over-subtle! No, no, you mustn't be over-subtle, brother! If God has given you an inquiring mind, and if you cannot direct it, better not go into things. . . . Don't go into things, and hold your peace!"

"But you know, she, . . . excuse my mentioning it, was an actress!" articulated Andrey Andreyich, overwhelmed.

"An actress! But whatever she was, you ought to forget it all now she is dead, instead of writing it on the note."

"Just so, . . ." the shopkeeper assented.

"You ought to do penance," boomed the deacon from the depths of the altar, looking contemptuously at Andrey Andreyich's embarrassed face, "that would teach you to give up being so clever! Your daughter was a well-known actress. There were even notices of her death in the newspaper. . . . Philosopher!"

"To be sure, . . . certainly," muttered the shopkeeper, "the word is not a seemly one; but I did not say it to judge her, Father Grigory, I only meant to speak spiritually, . . . that it might be clearer to you for whom you were praying. They write in the memorial notes the various callings, such as the infant Ivan, the drowned woman Pelagea, the warrior Yegor, the murdered Pavel, and so on. . . . I meant to do the same."

"It was foolish, Andrey! God will forgive you, but beware another time. Above all, don't be subtle, but think like other people. Make ten bows and go your way."

"Yes, sir," said the shopkeeper, relieved that the lecture was over, and allowing his face to resume its expression of importance and dignity. "Ten bows? Very good, I understand. But now, Father, allow me to ask you a favor. . . . Seeing that I am, anyway, her father, . . . you know yourself, whatever she was, she was still my daughter, so I was, . . . excuse me, meaning to ask you to sing the requiem today. And allow me to ask you, Father Deacon!"

"Well, that's good," said Father Grigory, taking off his vestments. "That I commend. I can approve of that! Well, go your way. We will come out immediately."

Andrey Andreyich walked with dignity from the altar, and with a solemn, requiem-like expression on his red face took his stand in the middle of the church. The verger Matvey set before him a little table with the memorial food upon it, and a little later the requiem service began.

There was perfect stillness in the church. Nothing could be heard but the metallic click of the censer and slow singing. . . . Near Andrey Andreyich stood the verger Matvey, the midwife Makaryevna, and her one-armed son Mitka. There was no one else. The sacristan sang badly in an unpleasant, hollow bass, but the tune and the words were so mournful that the shopkeeper little by little lost the expression of dignity and was plunged in sadness. He thought of his Mashutka, . . . he remembered she had been born when he was still a servant in the service of the owner of Verkhny Zaprudy. In his busy life as a servant he had not noticed how his girl had grown up. That long period during which she was being shaped into a graceful creature, with a little flaxen head and dreamy eyes as big as kopek-pieces, passed unnoticed by him. She had been brought up like all the children of favorite servants, in ease and comfort in the company of the young ladies. The gentry, to fill up their idle time, had taught her to read, to write, to dance; he had had no hand in her bringing up. Only from time to time, casually meeting her at the gate or on the landing of the stairs, he would remember that she was his daughter, and would, so far as he had leisure for it, begin teaching her prayers and the Scripture. Oh, even then he had the reputation of an authority on the church rules and the Holy Scriptures! Forbidding and stolid as her father's face was, yet the girl listened readily. She repeated the prayers after him yawning, but on the other hand, when he, hesitating and trying to express himself elaborately, began telling her stories, she was all attention. Esau's pottage, the punishment of Sodom, and the troubles of the boy Joseph made her turn pale and open her blue eyes wide.

Afterwards when he gave up being a servant, and with the money he had saved opened a shop in the village, Mashutka had gone away to Moscow with his master's family. . . .

Three years before her death she had come to see her father. He had scarcely recognized her. She was a graceful young woman with the manners of a young lady, and dressed like one. She talked cleverly, as though from a book, smoked, and slept till midday. When Andrey Andreyich asked her what she was doing, she had announced, looking him boldly straight in the face: "I am an actress." Such frankness struck the former servant as the acme of cynicism. Mashutka had begun boasting of her successes and her stage life; but seeing that her father only turned crimson and threw up his hands, she ceased. And they spent a fortnight together without speaking or looking at one another till the day she went away. Before she went away she asked her father to come for a walk on the bank of the river. Painful as it was for him to walk in the light of day, in the sight of all honest people, with a daughter who was an actress, he yielded to her request.

"What a lovely place you live in!" she said enthusiastically. "What ravines and marshes! Good heavens, how lovely my native place is!"

And she had burst into tears.

"The place is simply taking up room, . . ." Andrey Andreyich had thought, looking blankly at the ravines, not understanding his daughter's enthusiasm. "There is no more profit from them than milk from a billy-goat."

And she had cried and cried, drawing her breath greedily with her whole chest, as though she felt she had not a long time left to breathe.

Andrey Andreyich shook his head like a horse that has been bitten, and to stifle painful memories began rapidly crossing himself. . . .

"Be mindful, O Lord," he muttered, "of Thy departed servant, the harlot Marya, and forgive her sins, voluntary or involuntary. . . ."

The unseemly word dropped from his lips again, but he did not notice it: what is firmly imbedded in the consciousness cannot be driven out by Father Grigory's exhortations or even knocked out by a nail. Makaryevna sighed and whispered something, drawing in a deep breath, while one-armed Mitka was brooding over something. . . .

"When there is no sickness, nor grief, nor sighing," droned the sacristan, covering his right cheek with his hand.

Bluish smoke coiled up from the censer and bathed in the broad, slanting patch of sunshine which cut across the gloomy, lifeless emptiness of the church. And it seemed as though the soul of the dead woman were soaring into the sunlight together with the smoke. The coils of smoke like a child's curls eddied round and round, floating upwards to the window and, as it were, holding aloof from the woes and tribulations of which that poor soul was full.

1886

Anyuta

In the cheapest room of a big block of furnished apartments Stepan Klochkov, a medical student in his third year, was walking to and fro, zealously cramming anatomy. His mouth was dry and his forehead perspiring from the unceasing effort to learn it by heart.

In the window, covered by patterns of frost, sat on a stool the girl who shared his room—Anyuta, a thin little brunette of five and twenty, very pale, with mild gray eyes. Sitting with bent back she was busy embroidering with red thread the collar of a man's shirt. She was working against time. . . . The clock in the passage struck two drowsily, yet the little room had not been put to rights for the morning. Crumpled bedclothes, pillows thrown about, books, clothes, a big filthy slop-pail filled with soapsuds in which cigarette ends were swimming, and the litter on the floor—all seemed as though purposely jumbled together in one confusion. . . .

"The right lung consists of three parts . . ." Klochkov repeated. "Boundaries! Upper part on anterior wall of thorax reaches the fourth or fifth rib, on the lateral surface, the fourth rib . . . behind to the *spina scapulæ*. . ."

Klochkov raised his eyes to the ceiling, striving to visualize what he had just read. Unable to form a clear picture of it, he began feeling his upper ribs through his waistcoat.

"These ribs are like the keys of a piano," he said. "One must familiarize oneself with them somehow, if one is not to get muddled over them. One must study them in the skeleton and the living body. . . . I say, Anyuta, let me pick them out."

Anyuta put down her sewing, took off her blouse, and straightened herself up. Klochkov sat down facing her, frowned, and began counting her ribs.

"H'm! . . . One can't feel the first rib; it's behind the shoulder-blade. . . . This must be the second rib. . . . Yes . . . this is the third . . . this is the fourth. . . . H'm! . . . yes. . . . Why are you wriggling?"

"Your fingers are cold!"

"Come, come . . . it won't kill you. Don't twist about. That must be the third rib, then . . . this is the fourth. . . . You look such a skinny thing, and yet one can hardly feel your ribs. That's the second . . . that's the third. . . . Oh, this is muddling, and one can't see it clearly. . . . I must draw it. . . . Where's my crayon?"

Klochkov took his crayon and drew on Anyuta's chest several parallel lines corresponding with the ribs.

"First-rate. That's all straightforward. . . . Well, now I can sound you. Stand up!"

Anyuta stood up and raised her chin. Klochkov began sounding her, and was so absorbed in this occupation that he did not notice how Anyuta's lips, nose, and fingers turned blue with cold. Anyuta shivered, and was afraid the student, noticing it, would stop drawing and sounding her, and then, perhaps, might fail in his exam.

"Now it's all clear," said Klochkov when he had finished. "You sit like that and don't rub off the crayon, and meanwhile I'll learn up a little more."

And the student again began walking to and fro, repeating to himself. Anyuta, with black stripes across her chest, looking as though she had been tattooed, sat thinking, huddled up and shivering with cold. She said very little as a rule; she was always silent, thinking and thinking. . . .

In the six or seven years of her wanderings from one furnished room to another, she had known five students like Klochkov. Now they had all finished their studies, had gone out into the world, and, of course, like respectable people, had long ago forgotten her. One of them was living in Paris, two were doctors, the fourth was an artist, and the fifth was said to be already a professor. Klochkov was the sixth. . . . Soon he, too, would finish his studies and go out into the world. There was a fine future before him, no doubt, and Klochkov probably would become a great man, but the present was anything but bright; Klochkov had no tobacco and no tea, and there were only four lumps of sugar left. She must make haste and finish her embroidery, take it to the woman who had ordered it, and with the quarter ruble she would get for it, buy tea and tobacco.

"Can I come in?" asked a voice at the door.

Anyuta quickly threw a woollen shawl over her shoulders. Fetisov, the artist, walked in.

"I have come to ask you a favor," he began, addressing Klochkov, and glaring like a wild beast from under the long locks that hung over his brow. "Do me a favor; lend me your young lady just for a couple of hours! I'm painting a picture, you see, and I can't get on without a model."

"Oh, with pleasure," Klochkov agreed. "Go along, Anyuta."

"The things I've had to put up with there," Anyuta murmured softly.

"Rubbish! The man's asking you for the sake of art, and not for any sort of nonsense. Why not help him if you can?"

Anyuta began dressing.

"And what are you painting?" asked Klochkov.

"Psyche; it's a fine subject. But it won't go, somehow. I have to keep painting from different models. Yesterday I was painting one with blue legs. 'Why are your legs blue?' I asked her. 'It's my stockings stain them,' she said. And you're still cramming! Lucky fellow! You have patience."

"Medicine's a job one can't get on with without grinding."

"H'm! . . . Excuse me, Klochkov, but you do live like a pig! It's awful the way you live!"

"How do you mean! I can't help it. . . . I only get twelve rubles a month from my father, and it's hard to live decently on that."

"Yes . . . yes . . ." said the artist, frowning with an air of disgust; "but, still, you might live better. . . . An educated man is in duty bound to have taste, isn't he? And goodness knows what it's like here! The bed not made, the slops, the dirt . . . yesterday's porridge in the plates. . . . Tfoo!"

"That's true," said the student in confusion; "but Anyuta has had no time today to tidy up; she's been busy all the while."

When Anyuta and the artist had gone out Klochkov lay down on the sofa and began learning, lying down; then he accidentally dropped asleep, and waking up an hour later, propped his head on his fists and sank into gloomy reflection. He recalled the artist's words that an educated man was in duty bound to have taste, and his surroundings actually struck him now as loathsome and revolting. He saw, as it were in his mind's eye, his own future, when he would see his patients in his consulting-room, drink tea in a large dining-room in the company of his wife, a real lady. And now that slop-pail in which the cigarette ends were swimming looked incredibly disgusting. Anyuta, too, rose before his imagination—a plain, slovenly, pitiful figure . . . and he made up his mind to part with her at once, at all costs.

When, in coming back from the artist's, she took off her coat, he got up and said to her seriously:

"Look here, my good girl . . . sit down and listen. We must part! The fact is, I don't want to live with you any longer."

Anyuta had come back from the artist's worn out and exhausted. Standing so long as a model had made her face look thin and sunken, and her chin sharper than ever. She said nothing in answer to the student's words, only her lips began to tremble.

"You know we should have to part sooner or later, anyway," said the student. "You're a nice, good girl, and not a fool; you'll understand. . . ."

Anyuta put on her coat again, in silence wrapped up her embroidery in paper, gathered together her needles and thread: she found the screw of paper with the four lumps of sugar in the window, and laid it on the table by the books.

"That's . . . your sugar . . ." she said softly, and turned away to conceal her tears.

"Why are you crying?" asked Klochkov.

He walked about the room in confusion, and said:

"You are a strange girl, really. . . . Why, you know we shall have to part. We can't stay together forever."

She had gathered together all her belongings, and turned to say good-bye to him, and he felt sorry for her.

"Shall I let her stay on here another week?" he thought. "She really may as well stay, and I'll tell her to go in a week"; and, vexed at his own weakness, he shouted to her roughly:

"Come, why are you standing there? If you are going, go; and if you don't want to, take off your coat and stay! You can stay!"

Anyuta took off her coat, silently, stealthily, then blew her nose also stealthily, sighed, and noiselessly returned to her invariable position on her stool by the window.

The student drew his textbook to him and began again pacing from corner to corner. "The right lung consists of three parts," he repeated; "the upper part, on anterior wall of thorax, reaches the fourth or fifth rib. . . ."

In the passage some one shouted at the top of his voice: "Grigory! The samovar!"

1886

Agatha

During my stay in the province of S——— I spent much of my time in the company of Sava Stukach, or Savka for short, the watchman of the communal vegetable gardens of the village of Dubovka. These gardens on the bank of the river were my favorite spot for what may be called fishing "in general"—when you leave home without knowing the hour or day of your return and take with you a supply of provisions and every conceivable article of fishing-tackle. To tell the truth, I cared less for the fishing than I did for the peaceful idling, the chatting with Savka, the eating at all hours, and the long watches in the quiet summer nights.

Savka was a young fellow of twenty-five, tall, handsome, and hard as a brick. He had a reputation for cleverness and good sense, could read and write, and seldom drank vodka; but, powerful and young as he was, as a workman he was not worth one copper kopek. Though as tough as whipcord, his strong muscles were impregnated with a heavy, invincible indolence. Like everyone else in the village, he had formerly lived in a hut of his own and had had his own share of the land, but he had neither ploughed nor sowed nor followed any trade. His old mother had gone begging from door to door while he lived like the birds of the air, not knowing in the morning what he would eat at noon. It was not will, nor energy, nor pity for his mother that were lacking; he simply felt no inclination for toil and did not see the necessity for it. A sense of peace and an inborn, almost artistic, passion for an idle, disorderly life emanated from his whole being. When his healthy young body craved muscular exercise the lad would abandon himself completely for a short time to some untrammelled but absurd occupation such as sharpening a lot of useless stakes or running races with the women. His favourite state was one of concentrated immobility. He was capable of remaining for hours in one place, motionless, and with his eyes fixed on the same spot. He moved when the fancy seized him, and then only when he saw a chance for some swift, impetuous action such as catching a running dog by the tail, snatching the kerchief from the head of a woman, or leaping across a broad ditch.

It follows that, being so stingy of movement, Savka was as poor as Job's turkey and lived worse than a vagabond. As time went on his arrears had accumulated and, young and strong as he was, he had been sent by the commune to take an old man's place as watchman and scarecrow in the village communal gardens. He did not care a snap of his finger how much he was laughed at for his untimely old age. This occupation, so quiet and so well adapted for motionless contemplation, exactly suited his tastes.

I happened to be visiting Savka one beautiful evening in May. I lay, I remember, on a worn, tattered rug near a shed from which came the thick, choking smell of dried grass. With my hands behind my head I lay staring before me. At my feet was a wooden pitchfork; beyond that a dark object stood out sharply—it was Savka's little dog Kutka—and not more than fifteen feet beyond Kutka the ground fell away abruptly to the steep bank of the river. I could not see the water from where I lay, only the tops of the bushes crowding along the bank and the jagged and winding contours of the opposite shore. Beyond the river, on a dark hill, the huts of the village where my Savka had lived lay huddled together like startled young partridges. The evening light was fading behind the hill, only a pale strip of crimson remained, and across this little clouds were gathering as ashes gather on dying embers.

To the right of the garden lay a dark alder wood whispering softly and shivering sometimes as a sudden breeze wandered by. A bright little fire was twinkling in the dusk, there, where the eye could no longer distinguish the fields from the sky. At a short distance from me sat Savka, cross-legged, his head bowed, thoughtfully gazing at Kutka. Our hooks had long since been baited and dropped into the stream, and there was nothing for us to do but surrender ourselves to the repose so much loved by the never-weary but eternally resting Savka. Though the sunset had not faded entirely the summer night had folded the world in its soothing, sleep-giving embrace.

Nature had sunk into her first profound slumber; only in the wood some night-bird unknown to me uttered a slow, lazy cry which sounded like, "Is that Ni-ki-ta?" and then answered himself: "Nikita! Nikita! Nikita!"

"Why aren't the nightingales singing this evening?" I asked.

Savka turned slowly toward me. His features were large but well formed and expressive and gentle as a woman's. He looked with kind, pensive eyes, first at the wood and then at the thicket, then quietly took out a little pipe from his pocket, put it to his lips, and blew a few notes like a hen nightingale. At once, as if answering his call, a rail-bird "chucked" from the opposite shore.

"There goes a nightingale for you!" laughed Savka. "Chuck-chuck! chuck-chuck! as if it were jerking at a hook, and yet it thinks it is singing!"

"I like those birds," I said. "Do you know that when the time for migrating comes the rail doesn't fly but runs along the ground? It only flies across rivers and the ocean and goes all the rest of the way on foot."

"The little monkey!" murmured Savka, gazing with respect in the direction of the calling rail.

Knowing how much Savka loved listening, I told him all I had learned about rails from my sportsman's books. From rails we slipped imperceptibly into migration. Savka listened with rapt attention, not moving an eyelash, smiling with pleasure.

"In which country are the birds most at home, in ours or over there?" he asked.

"In ours, of course. They are hatched here and here they raise their young. This is their native land, and they only fly away to escape being frozen to death."

"How strange!" Savka sighed, stretching. "One can't talk of anything but what it is strange. Take that shouting bird over there, take people, take this little stone—there's a meaning in everything. Oh, if I had only known you were going to be here this evening, sir, I wouldn't have told that woman to come! She asked if she might."

"Oh, you mustn't mind me!" I said. "I won't interfere. I can go and lie in the wood."

"What an idea! It wouldn't have killed her to wait till tomorrow. If she were sitting here now and listening, we could do nothing but drivel. One can't talk sense when she is around."

"Are you expecting Darya?"

"No, a new one asked to come here this evening; Agatha, the switchman's wife."

Savka uttered this in his usual impassive way, in a dull voice, as if he were speaking of tobacco or porridge, but I jumped with astonishment. I knew Agatha well. She was still very young, not more than nineteen or twenty, and less than a year ago had married a railway switchman—a fine, bold young peasant. She lived in the village, and her husband came home to her every night from the railway.

"These affairs of yours with women will end badly some day," I said sadly.

"Never mind!"

Then, after a moment's reflection, Savka added:

"So I have told the women, but they won't listen; the idiots don't care."

Silence fell. The shadows deepened, the outlines of all objects faded into the darkness. The streak of light behind the hill was altogether extinguished, and the stars shone ever clearer and brighter. The mournful, monotonous chirping of the crickets, the calling of the rail-bird, and the whistling of the quail seemed not to break the nocturnal silence but rather to add to it a still greater depth. It was as if the stars, and not the birds and insects, were singing softly and charming our ears as they looked down from heaven.

Savka broke silence first. He slowly turned his gaze from Kutka's black form to me, and said:

"This is tedious for you, sir, I can see. Let's have supper."

Without waiting for my consent, he crawled on his stomach into the shed, rummaged about there until the whole building shook like a leaf, and crawled back with a bottle of vodka and an earthenware bowl, which he placed before me. In the bowl were baked eggs, fried cakes of rye flour, some pieces of black bread, and a few other things. We each had a drink out of a crooked glass that refused to stand up, and began our meal. Oh, that coarse, gray salt, those dirty, greasy cakes, those eggs as tough as India-rubber, how good they all tasted!

"You live the life of a tramp, and yet you have all these good things!" I exclaimed, pointing to the bowl. "Where do you get them?"

"The women bring them," grunted Savka.

"Why?"

"Oh, out of pity."

Not only the bill of fare but Savka's clothes, too, bore traces of feminine "pity." I noticed that he wore a new woolen belt that evening and that a little copper cross was suspended round his grimy neck by a bright crimson ribbon. I knew the weakness of the fair sex for Savka, and I knew, too, how unwilling he was to speak of it, so I did not pursue the subject. Besides, I had no time to say more. Kutka, who had been sitting near by in patient expectation of scraps, suddenly pricked up his ears and growled. We heard an intermittent splashing of water.

"Someone is crossing the ford," said Savka.

In a few minutes Kutka growled again and emitted a sound like a cough.

"Here!" cried his master.

Light footsteps rustled in the night, and a woman's form came out of the wood. I recognized her in spite of the darkness; it was Agatha.

She came forward timidly, stopped, and breathed heavily. It was probably more fear at fording the river by night than her walk which had robbed her of breath. When she saw two men by the shed instead of one she gave a faint cry and fell back a step.

"Oh, is that you?" asked Savka, thrusting a cake into his mouth.

"I—I—" she faltered, dropping a little bundle she carried and glancing at me. "Yakov sent you his greetings, and told me to give you this—this——"

"Why do you tell a story? Yakov, indeed!" Savka laughed at her. "No fibbing! Sit down and pay us a visit."

Agatha cast another glance at me and irresolutely sat down.

"I had already given you up this evening," said Savka after a long pause. "What makes you sit there like that? Eat something. Or is it a drink of vodka you want?"

"What are you thinking about?" cried Agatha. "Am I a drunkard?"

"Drink it! It warms the heart. Come on!"

Savka handed Agatha the crooked glass. She drank the vodka slowly, without eating anything after it, and only blew noisily through her lips.

"So you have brought something with you?" Savka continued as he undid the bundle. His voice took on a playfully indulgent tone. "She can't come without bringing something. Aha! A pie and potatoes! These people live well," he sighed, facing me. "They are the only ones in the village who still have potatoes left over from winter."

It was too dark to see Agatha's face, but from the movement of her shoulders and head I thought that she kept her eyes fixed on Savka's face. I decided to take a stroll so as not to make the third at a tryst, and rose to my feet. But at that moment a nightingale in the wood suddenly gave out two deep contralto notes. Half a minute later it poured forth a fine, high trill and, having tried its voice thus, began to sing.

Savka leaped up and listened. "That is last night's bird!" he exclaimed. "Wait ——"

"Let it alone!" I called after him. "What do you want with it?"

Savka waved his hand as much as to say, "Don't shout!" and vanished into the darkness. He could be a splendid hunter and fisherman when he liked, but this gift was as much wasted as his strength. He was too lazy to turn it to account, and his passion for the chase he expended on idle feats. He loved to seize nightingales in his hands, or to shoot pike with birdshot, or to stand by the river for hours at a time trying with all his might to catch a little fish on a large hook.

When she was left with me Agatha coughed and drew her hand several times across her brow. The vodka was already beginning to go to her head.

"How have you been, Agatha?" I asked after a long silence, when it seemed awkward not to say something.

"Very well, thank you—you won't tell anyone, will you, master?" she added suddenly in a whisper.

"No, no," I reassured her. "But you are very brave, Agatha. What if Yakov should find out?"

"He won't find out."

"He might."

"No, I shall get back before he does. He works on the railway now and comes home when the mail-train goes through, and I can hear it coming from here."

Agatha again drew her hand across her brow and looked in the direction which Savka had taken. The nightingale was still singing. A night-bird flew by close to the ground; as it caught sight of us it swerved, rustled its wings, and flew away across the river.

The nightingale soon ceased, but still Savka did not return. Agatha rose to her feet, took two or three restless steps, and sat down again.

"Where is he?" she burst out. "The train won't wait till tomorrow! I must go at once!"

"Savka!" I shouted. "Savka!"

Not even an echo answered. Agatha stirred uneasily and rose once more.

"It is time to go!" she cried in a troubled voice. "The train will be here in a moment. I know when the trains come."

The poor girl was right. In less than ten minutes we heard a distant noise. Agatha looked long at the wood and impatiently wrung her hands.

"Oh, where is he?" she cried with a nervous laugh. "I am going; indeed I am going!"

Meanwhile, the rumbling grew louder. The clanking of the wheels was distinguishable now from the deep panting of the engine. A whistle blew and the train thundered across a bridge. Another minute and all was still.

"I'll wait one second more," sighed Agatha, sitting down resolutely. "I don't care what happens, I'll wait."

At last Savka appeared in the gloom. He was humming softly and his bare feet fell noiselessly on the mellow earth of the garden.

"Let me tell you the bad luck," he cried with a merry laugh. "Just as I reached the bush and stretched out my hand he stopped singing! Oh, you little rat! I waited and waited for him to begin again and finally snapped my fingers at him——"

Savka dropped awkwardly down beside Agatha and caught her round the waist with both arms to keep his balance.

"Why, you're as black as a thundercloud! What's the matter?" he asked.

For all his warmhearted simplicity, Savka despised women. He treated them carelessly, in an offhand way, and even sank so low as to laugh with contempt at their feeling for himself. Heaven knows if this careless disdain may not have been one of the secrets of his charm for the village Dulcineas.[1] He was graceful and comely, and a quiet caress always shone in his eyes even when they rested on the women he despised, but his outward appearance alone could not account for the fascination he exercised. Beside his happy exterior and his odd ways, it seems as if the touching role played by Savka must also have exerted its influence over the women. He was known to everyone as a failure, an unfortunate exile from his native hut.

"Ho-ho!" he cried. "Let's have another drink, Friend Agatha!"

I rose and walked the length of the garden, picking my way among the beds of vegetables. They lay like large, flat graves, and an odor rose from them of fresh earth and moist, tender leaves newly wet with dew. The little red fire still gleamed and seemed to wink a smiling greeting.

I heard a blissful laugh. It was Agatha.

---

1. Dulcinea was Don Quixote's fair lady, in fact a coarse village lass.

"And the train?" I remembered. "It came long ago!"

I waited a little while and then went back to the shed. Savka was sitting motionless, with his legs crossed, softly, almost inaudibly, humming a monosyllabic song that sounded like:

"Oh, you—come you—you and I——"

Overpowered by the vodka, by Savka's careless caresses, and by the sultry heat of the night, Agatha lay on the ground with her head against his knees.

"Why, Agatha, the train came in long ago!" I cried.

Savka seized the suggestion. "Yes, yes, it's time for you to go!" he said, raising his head.

Agatha started up and looked at me.

"It's long past the time!" I said.

Agatha turned and raised herself on one knee. She was suffering. For a minute her whole figure, as well as I could see in the darkness, expressed struggle and vacillation. There was a moment when she drew herself up to rise, as if she had summoned her strength, but here some irresistible, implacable force smote her from head to foot and she dropped again.

"Oh, what do I care?" she cried with a wild, deep laugh, and in that laugh rang reckless determination, impotence, pain.

I walked quietly into the wood and from there went down to the river. The stream lay asleep. A soft flower on a high stem brushed my cheek like a child who tries to show that he is still waking. Having nothing to do, I felt for one of the lines and pulled it in. It resisted feebly and then hung limp. Nothing had been caught. The village and the opposite shore were invisible. A light flashed in one of the huts but quickly went out. I searched along the bank and found a hollow which I had discovered in the daytime, and in this I ensconced myself as if in an easy chair. I sat for a long time. I saw the stars begin to grow misty and dim; I felt a chill pass like a light sigh over the earth, stirring the leaves of the dreaming willows.

"A-ga-tha!" cried a faint voice on the other shore.

It was the frightened husband searching for his wife through the village. At the same moment a burst of laughter came from the garden, from the wife who was trying, in a few hours of happiness, to make up for the torture that awaited her on the morrow.

I fell into a doze.

When I awoke, Savka was sitting beside me lightly tapping my shoulder. The river, the wood, both shores, the green, newly washed trees and fields were flooded with bright morning light. The rays of the rising sun beat on my back from between the slender trunks of the trees.

"So you are fishing," chuckled Savka. "Get up!"

I rose, stretched myself blissfully, and my awakening lungs greedily drank in the moist, scented air.

"Has Agatha gone?" I asked.

"There she is." Savka pointed in the direction of the ford.

I looked and saw Agatha. Disheveled, her kerchief slipping from her hair, she was holding up her skirts and wading across the river. Her feet scarcely moved.

"She feels the shoe pinching," murmured Savka, gazing at her with half-closed eyes. "She is hanging her tail as she goes. They are as silly as cats and as timid as hares, those women. The idiot wouldn't go when she was told to last night, and now she will catch it, and I'll be called in! There'll be another row about women."

Agatha stepped out onto the bank and started across the fields to the village. At first she walked boldly, but emotion and terror soon had their way with her; she looked back fearfully and stopped, panting.

"She is frightened," Savka smiled sadly, with his eyes on the bright-green ribbon that stretched across the dewy grass behind Agatha. "She doesn't want to go on. Her husband has been standing there waiting for her for an hour. Do you see him?"

Savka smiled as he spoke the last words, but my heart stood still. In the road, near one of the huts on the outskirts of the village, stood Yakov with his eyes fixed on his returning wife. He did not stir from one spot but stood as still as a post. What were his thoughts as he looked at her? What words had he prepared to receive her with? Agatha stood still for some time, looked back again as if expecting succour from us, and went on. Never have I seen anyone, whether drunk or sober, walk with such a gait. Agatha seemed to be writhing under her husband's gaze. First she zigzagged, and then stopped and trampled the ground in one spot, throwing out her arms, her knees bending under her, and then staggered back. After she had gone a hundred paces she looked back once more and sat down.

I looked at Savka's face. It was pale and drawn with that mixture of pity and aversion that men feel at the sight of a suffering animal.

"What is joy for the cat is tears for the mouse," he sighed.

Suddenly Agatha jumped up, threw back her head, and advanced with firm footsteps toward her husband. She was resolved now, one could see, and had plucked up her courage.

1886

Grisha

Grisha, a chubby little boy born only two years and eight months ago, was out walking on the boulevard with his nurse. He wore a long, padded snowsuit, a large cap with a furry knob, a muffler, and wool-lined galoshes. He felt stuffy and hot, and, in addition, the waxing sun of April was beating directly into his face and making his eyelids smart.

Every inch of his awkward little figure, with its timid, uncertain steps, bespoke a boundless perplexity.

Until that day the only universe known to Grisha had been square. In one corner of it stood his crib, in another stood Nurse's trunk, in the third was a chair, and in the fourth a little icon-lamp. If you looked under the bed you saw a doll with one arm and a drum; behind Nurse's trunk were a great many various objects: a few empty spools, some scraps of paper, a box without a lid, and a broken jumping-jack. In this world, besides Nurse and Grisha, there often appeared Mama and the cat. Mama looked like a doll, and the cat looked like Papa's fur coat, only the fur coat did not have eyes and a tail. From the world which was called the nursery a door led to a place where people dined and drank tea. There stood Grisha's high-chair and there hung the clock made only in order to wag its pendulum and strike. From the dining-room one could pass into another room with big red chairs; there, on the floor, glowered a dark stain for which people still shook their forefingers at Grisha. Still farther beyond lay another room, where one was not allowed to go, and in which one sometimes caught glimpses of Papa, a very mysterious person! The functions of Mama and Nurse were obvious: they dressed Grisha, fed him, and put him to bed; but why Papa should be there was incomprehensible. Aunty was also a puzzling person. She appeared and disappeared. Where did she go? More than once Grisha had looked for her under the bed, behind the trunk, and under the sofa, but she was not to be found.

In the new world where he now found himself, where the sun dazzled one's eyes, there were so many Papas and Mammas and Aunties that one scarcely knew which one to run to. But the funniest and oddest things of all were the horses. Grisha stared at their moving legs and could not understand them at all. He looked up at Nurse, hoping that she might help him to solve the riddle, but she answered nothing.

Suddenly he heard a terrible noise. Straight toward him down the street came a squad of soldiers marching in step, with red faces and sticks under their arms. Grisha's blood ran cold with terror and he looked up anxiously at his nurse to inquire if this were not dangerous. But Nursie neither ran away nor cried, so he decided it must be safe. He followed the soldiers with his eyes and began marching in step with them.

Across the street ran two big, long-nosed cats, their tails sticking straight up into the air and their tongues lolling out of their mouths. Grisha felt that he, too, ought to run, and he started off in pursuit.

"Stop, stop!" cried Nursie, seizing him roughly by the shoulder. "Where are you going? Who told you to be naughty?"

But there sat a sort of nurse with a basket of oranges in her lap. As Grisha passed her he silently took one.

"Don't do that!" cried his fellow wayfarer, slapping his hand and snatching the orange away from him. "Little stupid!"

Next, Grisha would gladly have picked up some of the slivers of glass that rattled under his feet and glittered like icon-lamps, but he was afraid that his hand might be slapped again.

"Good-day!" Grisha heard a loud, hoarse voice say over his very ear, and, looking up, he caught sight of a tall person with shiny buttons.

To his great joy this man shook hands with Nursie; they stood together and entered into conversation. The sunlight, the rumbling of the vehicles, the horses, the shiny buttons, all struck Grisha as so amazingly new and yet unterrifying, that his heart overflowed with delight and he began to laugh.

"Come! Come!" he cried to the man with the shiny buttons, pulling his coat tails.

"Where to?" asked the man.

"Come!" Grisha insisted. He would have liked to say that it would be nice to take Papa and Mamma and the cat along, too, but somehow his tongue would not obey him.

In a few minutes Nurse turned off the boulevard and led Grisha into a large courtyard where the snow still lay on the ground. The man with shiny buttons followed them. Carefully avoiding the puddles and lumps of snow, they picked their way across the courtyard, mounted a dark, grimy staircase, and entered a room where the air was heavy with smoke and a strong smell of cooking. A woman was standing over a stove frying chops. This cook and Nurse embraced one another, and, sitting down on a bench with the man, began talking in low voices. Bundled up as he was, Grisha felt unbearably hot.

"What does this mean?" he asked himself, gazing about. He saw a dingy ceiling, a two-pronged oven fork, and a stove with a huge oven mouth gaping at him.

"Ma-a-m-ma!" he wailed.

"Now! Now!" his nurse called to him. "Be good!"

The cook set a bottle, two glasses, and a pie on the table. The two women and the man with the shiny buttons touched glasses and each had several drinks. The man embraced alternately the cook and the nurse. Then all three began to sing softly.

Grisha stretched his hand toward the pie, and they gave him a piece. He ate it and watched his nurse drinking. He wanted to drink, too.

"Give, Nursie! Give!" he begged.

The cook gave him a drink out of her glass. He screwed up his eyes, frowned, and coughed for a long time after that, beating the air with his hands, while the cook watched him and laughed.

When he reached home, Grisha explained to Mama, the walls, and his crib where he had been and what he had seen. He told it less with his tongue than with his hands and his face; he showed how the sun had shone, how the horses had trotted, how the terrible oven had gaped at him, and how the cook had drunk.

That evening he could not possibly go to sleep. The soldiers with their sticks, the great cats, the horses, the bits of glass, the basket of oranges, the shiny buttons, all this lay piled on his brain and oppressed him. He tossed from side to side, chattering to himself, and finally, unable longer to endure his excitement, he burst into tears.

"Why, he has fever!" cried Mama, laying the palm of her hand on his forehead. "What can be the reason?"

"The stove!" wept Grisha. "Go away, stove!"

"He has eaten something that has disagreed with him," Mama concluded.

And, shaken by his impressions of a new life apprehended for the first time, Grisha was given a spoonful of castor-oil by Mama.

1886

A Gentleman Friend

The charming Vanda, or, as she was described in her passport, the "Honorable Citizen Nastasya Kanavkin,"[1] found herself, on leaving the hospital, in a position she had never been in before: without a home to go to or a farthing in her pocket. What was she to do?

The first thing she did was to visit a pawnbroker's and pawn her turquoise ring, her one piece of jewelry. They gave her a ruble for the ring, but what can you get for a ruble? You can't buy for that sum a fashionable short jacket, nor a big hat, nor a pair of bronze-color shoes, and without those things she had a feeling of being, as it were, undressed. She felt as though the very horses and dogs were staring and laughing at the plainness of her dress. And clothes were all she thought about: the question what she should eat and where she should sleep did not trouble her in the least.

"If only I could meet a gentleman friend," she thought to herself, "I could get some money. . . . There isn't one who would refuse me, I know. . . ."

But no gentleman she knew came her way. It would be easy enough to meet them in the evening at the Renaissance, but they

1. The name suggests "gutter," "ditch."

wouldn't let her in at the Renaissance in that shabby dress and with no hat. What was she to do?

After long hesitation, when she was sick of walking and sitting and thinking, Vanda made up her mind to fall back on her last resource: to go straight to the lodgings of some gentleman friend and ask for money.

She pondered which to go to. "Misha is out of the question; he's a married man. . . . The old chap with the red hair will be at his office at this time. . . ."

Vanda remembered a dentist, called Finkel, a converted Jew, who six months ago had given her a bracelet, and on whose head she had once emptied a glass of beer during supper at the German Club. She was awfully pleased at the thought of Finkel.

"He'll be sure to give it me, if only I find him at home," she thought, as she walked in his direction. "If he doesn't, I'll smash all the lamps in the house."

Before she reached the dentist's door she thought out her plan of action: she would run laughing up the stairs, dash into the dentist's room and demand twenty-five rubles. But as she touched the bell, this plan seemed to vanish from her mind of itself. Vanda began suddenly feeling frightened and nervous, which was not at all her way. She was bold and saucy enough at drinking parties, but now, dressed in everyday clothes, feeling herself in the position of an ordinary person asking a favor, who might be refused admittance, she felt suddenly timid and humiliated. She was ashamed and frightened.

"Perhaps he has forgotten me by now," she thought, hardly daring to pull the bell. "And how can I go up to him in such a dress, looking like a beggar or some working girl?"

And she rang the bell irresolutely.

She heard steps coming: it was the porter.

"Is the doctor at home?" she asked.

She would have been glad now if the porter had said "No," but the latter, instead of answering ushered her into the hall, and helped her off with her coat. The staircase impressed her as luxurious, and magnificent, but of all its splendors what caught her eye most was an immense looking-glass, in which she saw a ragged figure without a fashionable jacket, without a big hat, and without bronze-color shoes. And it seemed strange to Vanda that, now that she was humbly dressed and looked like a laundress or sewing girl, she felt ashamed, and no trace of her usual boldness and sauciness remained, and in her own mind she no longer thought of herself as Vanda, but as the Nastasya Kanavkin she used to be in the old days. . . .

"Walk in, please," said a maidservant, showing her into the

consulting-room. "The doctor will be here in a minute. Sit down."

Vanda sank into a soft armchair.

"I'll ask him to lend it to me," she thought; "that will be quite proper, for, after all, I do know him. If only that servant would go. I don't like to ask before her. What does she want to stand there for?"

Five minutes later the door opened and Finkel came in. He was a tall, dark Jew, with fat cheeks and bulging eyes. His cheeks, his eyes, his chest, his body, all of him was so well fed, so loathsome and repellent! At the Renaissance and the German Club he had usually been rather tipsy, and would spend his money freely on women, and be very long-suffering and patient with their pranks (when Vanda, for instance, poured the beer over his head, he simply smiled and shook his finger at her): now he had a cross, sleepy expression and looked solemn and frigid like a police captain, and he kept chewing something.

"What can I do for you?" he asked, without looking at Vanda.

Vanda looked at the serious countenance of the maid and the smug figure of Finkel, who apparently did not recognize her, and she turned red.

"What can I do for you?" repeated the dentist a little irritably.

"I've got toothache," murmured Vanda.

"Aha! . . . Which is the tooth? Where?"

Vanda remembered she had a hole in one of her teeth.

"At the bottom . . . on the right . . ." she said.

"Hm! . . . Open your mouth."

Finkel frowned and, holding his breath, began examining the tooth.

"Does it hurt?" he asked, digging into it with a steel instrument.

"Yes," Vanda replied, untruthfully.

"Shall I remind him?" she was wondering. "He would be sure to remember me. But that servant! Why does she stand there?"

Finkel suddenly snorted like a steam-engine right into her mouth, and said:

"I don't advise you to have it filled. That tooth will never be worth keeping anyhow."

After probing the tooth a little more and soiling Vanda's lips and gums with his tobacco-stained fingers, he held his breath again, and put something cold into her mouth. Vanda suddenly felt a sharp pain, cried out, and clutched at Finkel's hand.

"It's all right, it's all right," he muttered; "don't you be frightened! That tooth would have been no use to you, anyway . . . you must be brave. . . ."

And his tobacco-stained fingers, smeared with blood, held up the tooth to her eyes, while the maid approached and put a basin to her mouth.

"You wash out your mouth with cold water when you get home, and that will stop the bleeding," said Finkel.

He stood before her with the air of a man expecting her to go, waiting to be left in peace.

"Good-day," she said, turning towards the door.

"Hm! . . . and how about my fee?" enquired Finkel, in a jesting tone.

"Oh, yes!" Vanda remembered, blushing, and she handed the Jew the ruble that had been given her for her ring.

When she got out into the street she felt more overwhelmed with shame than before, but now it was not her poverty she was ashamed of. She was unconscious now of not having a big hat and a fashionable jacket. She walked along the street, spitting blood, and brooding on her life, her ugly, wretched life, and the insults she had endured, and would have to endure to-morrow, and next week, and all her life, up to the very day of her death.

"Oh! how awful it is! My God, how fearful!"

Next day, however, she was back at the Renaissance, and dancing there. She had on an enormous new red hat, a new fashionable jacket, and bronze-color shoes. And she was taken out to supper by a young merchant up from Kazan.

1886

The Chorus Girl

One day while she was still pretty and young and her voice was sweet, Nikolai Kolpakov,[1] an admirer of hers, was sitting in a room on the second floor of her cottage. The afternoon was unbearably sultry and hot. Kolpakov, who had just dined and drunk a whole bottle of vile port, felt thoroughly ill and out of sorts. Both he and she were bored, and were waiting for the heat to abate so that they might go for a stroll.

Suddenly a bell rang in the hall. Kolpakov, who was sitting in his slippers without a coat, jumped up and looked at Pasha with a question in his eyes.

"It is probably the postman or one of the girls," said the singer.

Kolpakov was not afraid of the postman or of Pasha's girl friends, but nevertheless he snatched up his coat and disappeared into the next room while Pasha ran to open the door. What was her astonishment when she saw on the threshold, not the postman nor a girl friend, but an unknown woman, beautiful and young! Her dress was distinguished and she was evidently a lady.

1. The name suggests "nightcap."

The stranger was pale and was breathing heavily as if she were out of breath from climbing the stairs.

"What can I do for you?" Pasha inquired.

The lady did not reply at once. She took a step forward, looked slowly around the room, and sank into a chair as if her legs had collapsed under her from faintness or fatigue. Her pale lips moved silently, trying to utter words which would not come.

"Is my husband here?" she asked at last, raising her large eyes with their red and swollen lids to Pasha's face.

"What husband do you mean?" Pasha whispered, suddenly taking such violent fright that her hands and feet grew as cold as ice. "What husband?" she repeated beginning to tremble.

"My husband—Nikolai Kolpakov."

"N-no, my lady. I don't know your husband."

A minute passed in silence. The stranger drew her handkerchief several times across her pale lips, and held her breath in an effort to subdue an inward trembling, while Pasha stood before her as motionless as a statue, gazing at her full of uncertainty and fear.

"So you say he is not here?" asked the lady. Her voice was firm now and a strange smile had twisted her lips.

"I—I—don't know whom you mean!"

"You are a revolting, filthy, vile creature!" muttered the stranger looking at Pasha with hatred and disgust. "Yes, yes, you are revolting. I am glad indeed that an opportunity has come at last for me to tell you this!"

Pasha felt that she was producing the effect of something indecent and foul on this lady in black, with the angry eyes and the long, slender fingers, and she was ashamed of her fat, red cheeks, the pockmark on her nose, and the lock of hair on her forehead that would never stay up. She thought that if she were thin and her face were not powdered, and she had not that curl on her forehead, she would not feel so afraid and ashamed standing there before this mysterious, unknown lady.

"Where is my husband?" the lady went on. "However it makes no difference to me whether he is here or not, I only want you to know that he has been caught embezzling funds entrusted to him, and that the police are looking for him. He is going to be arrested. Now see what you have done!"

The lady rose and began to walk up and down in violent agitation. Pasha stared at her; fear rendered her uncomprehending.

"He will be found today and arrested," the lady repeated with a sob full of bitterness and rage. "I know who has brought this horror upon him! Disgusting, abominable woman. Horrible, corrupt creature! (Here the lady's lips curled and her nose wrinkled with aversion.) I am powerless. Listen to me, you low woman. I am powerless and you are stronger than I, but there is One who will avenge me and my children. God's eyes see all things. He is just. He will call you to account for every tear I have shed, every sleepless night I have passed. The time will come when you will remember me!"

Once more silence fell. The lady walked to and fro wringing her hands. Pasha continued to watch her dully, uncomprehendingly, dazed with doubt, waiting for her to do something terrible.

"I don't know what you mean, my lady!" she suddenly cried, and burst into tears.

"That's a lie!" screamed the lady, her eyes flashing with anger. "I know all about it! I have known about you for a long time. I know that he has been coming here every day for the last month."

"Yes—and what if he has? Is it my fault? I have a great many visitors, but I don't force anyone to come. They are free to do as they please."

"I tell you he is accused of embezzlement! He has taken money that didn't belong to him, and for the sake of a woman like you—for your sake, he has brought himself to commit a crime! Listen to me," the lady said sternly, halting before Pasha. "You are an unprincipled woman, I know. You exist to bring misfortune to men, that is the object of your life, but I cannot believe that you have fallen so low as not to have one spark of humanity left in your breast. He has a wife, he has children, oh, remember that! There is one means of saving us from poverty and shame; if I can find nine hundred rubles today he will be left in peace. Only nine hundred rubles!"

"What nine hundred rubles?" asked Pasha feebly. "I—I don't know—I didn't take——"

"I am not asking you to give me nine hundred rubles; you have no money, and I don't want anything that belongs to you. It is something else that I ask. Men generally give presents of jewelry to women like you. All I ask is that you should give me back the things that my husband has given you."

"My Lady, he has never given me anything!" wailed Pasha beginning to understand.

"Then where is the money he has wasted? He has squandered in some way his own fortune, and mine, and the fortunes of others. Where has the money gone? Listen, I impore you! I was excited just now and said some unpleasant things, but I ask you to forgive me! I know you must hate me, but if pity exists for you, oh, put yourself in my place! I implore you to give me the jewelry!"

"H'm—" said Pasha shrugging her shoulders. "I should do it with pleasure, only I swear before God he never gave me a thing. He didn't, indeed. But, no, you are right," the singer suddenly stammered in confusion. "He did give me two little things. Wait a minute, I'll fetch them for you if you want them."

Pasha pulled out one of the drawers of her bureau, and took from it a bracelet of hollow gold and a narrow ring set with a ruby.

"Here they are!" she said, handing them to her visitor.

The lady grew angry and a spasm passed over her features. She felt that she was being insulted.

"What is this you are giving me?" she cried. "I'm not asking for alms, but for the things that do not belong to you, for the things that you have extracted from my weak and unhappy husband by your position. When I saw you on the wharf with him on Thursday you were wearing costly brooches and bracelets. Do you think you can play the innocent child with me? I ask you for the last time: will you give me those presents or not?"

"You are strange, I declare," Pasha exclaimed, beginning to take offense. "I swear to you that I have never had a thing from your Nikolai, except this bracelet and ring. He has never given me anything, but these and some little cakes."

"Little cakes!" the stranger laughed suddenly. "His children are starving at home, and he brings you little cakes! So you won't give up the things?"

Receiving no answer, the lady sat down, her eyes grew fixed, and she seemed to be debating something.

"What shall I do?" she murmured. "If I can't get nine hundred rubles he will be ruined as well as the children and myself. Shall I kill this creature, or shall I go down on my knees to her?"

The lady pressed her handkerchief to her eyes and burst into tears.

"Oh, I beseech you!" she sobbed. "It is you who have disgraced and ruined my husband; now save him! You can have no pity for him, I know; but the children, remember the children! What have they done to deserve this?"

Pasha imagined his little children standing on the streetcorner weeping with hunger, and she, too, burst into tears.

"What can I do, my lady?" she cried. "You say I am a wicked creature, who has ruined your husband, but I swear to you before God I have never had the least benefit from him! Mota is the only girl in our chorus who has a rich friend, the rest of us all live on bread and water. Your husband is an educated, pleasant gentleman, that's why I received him. We can't pick and choose."

"I want the jewelery; give me the jewelery! I am weeping, I am humiliating myself; see, I shall fall on my knees before you!"

Pasha screamed with terror and waved her arms. She felt that this pale, beautiful lady, who spoke the same refined language that people did in plays, might really fall on her knees before her, and for the very reason that she was so proud and high-bred, she would exalt herself by doing this, and degrade the little singer.

"Yes, yes, I'll give you the jewelry!" Pasha cried hastily, wiping her eyes. "Take it, but it did not come from your husband! I got it from other visitors. But take it, if you want it!"

Pasha pulled out an upper drawer of the bureau, and took from it a diamond brooch, a string of corals, two or three rings, and a bracelet. These she handed to the lady.

"Here is the jewelry, but I tell you again your husband never gave me a thing. Take it, and may you be the richer for having it!" Pasha went on, offended by the lady's threat that she would go down on her knees. "You are a lady and his lawful wife—keep him at home then! The idea of it! As if I had asked him to come here! He came because he wanted to!"

The lady looked through her tears at the jewelry that Pasha had handed her and said:

"This isn't all. There is scarcely five hundred rubles' worth here."

Pasha violently snatched a gold watch, a cigarette-case, and a set of studs out of the drawer and flung up her arms, exclaiming:

"Now I am cleaned out! Look for yourself!"

Her visitor sighed. With trembling hands she wrapped the trinkets in her handkerchief, and went out without a word, without even a nod.

The door of the adjoining room opened and Kolpakov came out. His face was pale and his head was shaking nervously, as if he had just swallowed a very bitter draught. His eyes were full of tears.

"I'd like to know what you ever gave me!" Pasha attacked him vehemently. "When did you ever give me the smallest present?"

"Presents—they are a detail, presents!" Kolpakov cried, his head still shaking. "Oh, my God, she wept before you, she abased herself!"

"I ask you again: what have you ever given me?" screamed Pasha.

"My God, she—a respectable, a proud woman, was actually ready to fall on her knees before—before this—wench! And I have brought her to this! I allowed it!"

He seized his head in his hands.

"No," he groaned out, "I shall never forgive myself for this—never! Get away from me, wretch!" he cried, backing away from Pasha with horror, and keeping her off with outstretched, trembling hands. "She was ready to go down on her knees, and before whom? —Before you! Oh, my God!"

He threw on his coat and, pushing Pasha contemptuously aside, strode to the door and went out.

Pasha flung herself down on the sofa and burst into loud wails.

She already regretted the things she had given away so impulsively, and her feelings were hurt. She remembered that a merchant had beaten her three years ago for nothing, yes, absolutely for nothing, and at that thought she wept louder than ever.

1886

Dreams

Two soldiers are escorting to the county seat a vagrant who refuses to give his name. One of them is black-bearded and thick-set, with legs so uncommonly short that, seen from behind, they seem to begin much lower down than those of other men; the other is long, lank, spare, and straight as a stick, with a thin beard of a dark-reddish hue. The first waddles along, looking from side to side and sucking now a straw and now the sleeve of his coat. He slaps his thigh and hums to himself, and looks, on the whole, lighthearted and carefree. The other, with his lean face and narrow shoulders, is staid and important-looking; in build and in the expression of his whole person he resembles a priest of the Old Believers[1] or one of those warriors depicted on antique icons. "For his wisdom God has enlarged his brow," that is to say, he is bald, which still more enhances the resemblance. The first soldier is called Andrey Ptakha, the second Nikander Sapozhnikov.

The man they are escorting is not in the least like what everyone imagines a tramp should be. He is small and sickly and feeble, with little, colorless, absolutely undefined features. His eyebrows are thin, his glance is humble and mild, and his whiskers have barely made their appearance though he is already past thirty. He steps timidly along, stooping, with his hands thrust into his sleeves. The collar of his threadbare, unpeasantlike little coat is turned right up to the brim of his cap, so that all that can venture to peep out at the world is his little red nose. When he speaks, it is in a high, obsequious little voice, and then he immediately coughs. It is hard, very hard to recognise in him a vagabond who is hiding his name. He looks more like some impoverished, godforsaken son of a priest, or a clerk discharged for intemperance, or a merchant's son who has essayed his puny strength on the stage and is now returning to his home to play out the last act of the parable of the prodigal son. Perhaps, judging from the dull patience with which he battles with the clinging autumn mud, he is a fanatic; some youth trained for a monk who is wandering from one monastery to another all over Russia, doggedly seeking "a life of peace and freedom from

1. A religious sect that refused to accept the church reforms of 1682 and practiced its own rites.

sin," which he cannot find.

The wayfarers have been walking a long time, but for all their efforts they cannot get away from the same spot of ground. Before them lie ten yards of dark-brown, muddy road, behind them lies as much; beyond that, wherever they turn, rises a dense wall of white fog. They walk and walk, but the ground they walk on is always the same; the wall comes no nearer; the spot remains a spot. Now and then they catch glimpses of white, irregular cobblestones, a dip in the road, or an armful of hay dropped by some passing wagon; a large pool of muddy water gleams for a moment, or a shadow, vaguely outlined, suddenly and unexpectedly appears before them. The nearer they come to this, the smaller and darker it grows; they come nearer still, and before them rises a crooked mile-post with its numbers effaced, or a woebegone birch-tree, naked and wet, like a wayside beggar. The birch-tree is whispering something with the remains of its yellow foliage; one leaf breaks off and flutters sluggishly to the ground, and then again there come fog and mud and the brown grass by the roadside. Dim, evil tears hang on these blades—not the tears of quiet joy that the earth weeps when she meets and accompanies the summer sun, and with which at dawn she quenches the thirst of quail and rails and graceful, long-billed snipe! The feet of the travelers are caught by the thick, sticky mud; every step costs them an effort.

Andrey Ptakha is a trifle provoked. He is scrutinizing the vagrant and trying to understand how a live, sober man could forget his name.

"You belong to the Orthodox Church, don't you?" he asks.

"I do," answers the tramp briefly.

"H'm—have you been christened?"

"Of course I have; I'm not a Turk! I go to church and observe the fasts and don't eat meat when it's forbidden to do so——"

"Well, then, what name shall I call you by?"

"Call me what you please, lad."

Ptakha shrugs his shoulders and slaps his thigh in extreme perplexity. The other soldier, Nikander, preserves a sedate silence. He is not so simple as Ptakha, and evidently knows very well reasons which might induce a member of the Orthodox Church to conceal his identity. His expressive face is stern and cold. He walks apart and disdains idle gossip with his companions. He seems to be endeavoring to show to everyone and everything, even to the mist, how grave and sensible he is.

"The Lord only knows what to think about you!" pursues Ptakha. "Are you a peasant or not? Are you a gentleman or not? Or are you something between the two? I was rinsing out a sieve in a pond one day and caught a little monster as long as my finger here, with gills and a tail. Thinks I—it's a fish! Then I take another look at it—and

I'll be blessed if it didn't have feet! It wasn't a fish and it wasn't a reptile—the devil only knows what it was! That's just what you are. What class do you belong to?"

"I am a peasant by birth," sighs the tramp. "My mother was a house serf. In looks I'm not a peasant, and that is because fate has willed it so, good man. My mother was a nurse in a gentleman's house and had every pleasure the heart could desire, and I, as her flesh and blood, belonged, in her lifetime, to the household. They petted me and spoiled me and beat me till they beat me from common to well-bred. I slept in a bed, had a real dinner every day, and wore trousers and low shoes like any little noble. Whatever my mother had to eat, I had. They gave her dresses and dressed me, too. Oh, we lived well! The candy and cake I ate in my childhood would buy a good horse now if I could sell them! My mother taught me to read and write, and from the time I was a baby instilled the fear of God into me and trained me so well that to this day I couldn't use an impolite, peasant word. I don't drink vodka, lad, and I dress cleanly and can make a respectable appearance in good society. God give her health if she is still alive; if she is dead, take her soul, O Lord, to rest in thy heavenly kingdom where the blessed find peace!"

The tramp uncovers his head, with its sparse bristles, casts his eyes upward, and makes the sign of the cross twice.

"Give her peace, O Lord, in green places!" he says in a drawling voice, more like an old woman's than a man's. "Keep thy slave Ksenya in all thy ways, O Lord! If it had not been for my good mother I should have been a simple peasant now, not knowing a thing. As it is, lad, ask me what you please; I know everything: the Holy Scriptures, all godly things, all the prayers, and the Catechisms. I live according to the Scriptures; I do wrong to no one; I keep my body pure; I observe the fasts and eat as it is ordered. Some men find pleasure only in vodka and brawling, but when I have time I sit in a corner and read a book, and as I read I cry and cry——"

"Why do you cry?"

"Because the things they tell of are so pitiful. Sometimes you pay only five kopeks for a book and weep and wail over it to despair——"

"Is your father dead?" asks Ptakha.

"I don't know, lad. It's no use hiding a sin; I don't know who my father was. What I think is that I was an illegitimate son of my mother's. My mother lived all her life with the gentry and never would marry a common peasant."

"So she flew higher, up to his master!" laughs Ptakha.

"That is so. My mother was pious and godly, and of course it is a sin, a great sin, to say so, but, nevertheless, maybe I have noble blood in my veins. Maybe I am a peasant in station only and am really a high-born gentleman."

The "high-born gentleman" utters all this in a soft, sickly sweet voice, wrinkling his narrow brows and emitting squeaky noises from his cold, red, little nose.

Ptakha listens to him, eyes him with astonishment, and still shrugs his shoulders.

After going four miles the soldiers and the tramp sit down on a little knoll to rest.

"Even a dog can remember his name," mutters Ptakha. "I am called Andrey and he is called Nikander; every man has his God-given name and no one could possibly forget it—not possibly!"

"Whose business is it of anyone's to know who I am?" sighs the tramp, leaning his cheek on his hand. "And what good would it do me if they knew? If I were allowed to go wherever I liked I should be worse off than I am now. I know the law, my Christian friends—now I am a vagrant who does not remember his name, and the worst they could do to me would be to send me to eastern Siberia with thirty or forty lashes, but if I should tell them my real name and station I should be sent to hard labour again—I know!"

"You mean to say you have been a convict?"

"I have, my good friend. My head was shaved and I wore chains for four years."

"What for?"

"For murder, good man. When I was still a boy, about eighteen years old, my mother put arsenic into our master's glass by mistake instead of soda. There were a great many different little boxes in the store-room and it was not hard to mistake them."

The tramp sighs, shakes his head, and continues:

"She was a godly woman, but who can say? The soul of another is a dark forest. Maybe she did it by mistake. Maybe it was because her master had attached another servant to himself and her heart could not forgive the insult. Perhaps she did put it in on purpose—God only knows! I was young then and couldn't understand everything. I remember now that our master did, in fact, take another mistress at that time and that my mother was deeply hurt. Our trial went on for two years after that. My mother was condemned to twenty years' penal servitude and I to seven on account of my youth."

"And what charge were you convicted on?"

"For being an accomplice. I handed our master the glass. It was always that way: my mother would prepare the soda and I would hand him the glass. But I am confessing all this before you, brothers, as before God. You won't tell anyone——"

"No one will ever ask us," says Ptakha. "So that means you ran away from prison, does it?"

"Yes, I ran away, good friend. Fourteen of us escaped. God be with them! They ran away and took me along, too. Now judge for yourself, lad, and tell me honestly whether I have any reason for telling my name? I should be condemned to penal servitude again; and what sort of a convict am I? I am delicate and sickly; I like cleanliness in my food and in the places where I sleep. When I pray to God I like to have a little shrine-lamp or a candle burning, and I don't like to have noises going on round me when I'm praying. When I prostrate myself I don't like to have the floor all filthy and spat over, and I prostrate myself forty times morning and night for my mother's salvation."

The tramp takes off his cap and crosses himself.

"But let them send me to eastern Siberia if they want to!" he cries. "I'm not afraid of that."

"What? Is that better?"

"It is an entirely different affair. At hard labor you are no better off than a crab in a basket. You are crowded and pushed and hustled; there's not a quiet corner to take breath; it's a hell on earth—the Mother of God forbid it! A ruffian you are, and a ruffian's treatment you receive—worse than any dog's. You get nothing to eat; there is nowhere to sleep and nowhere to say your prayers. In exile it's different. You first enroll yourself in the company, as everyone else does. The government is compelled by law to give you your share of land. Yes, indeed! Land, they say, is cheap there, as cheap as snow. You can take all you want! They would give me land for farming, lad, and land for a garden, and land for a house. Then I would plough and sow, as other men do, raise cattle and bees and sheep and dogs—I'd get myself a Siberian cat to keep the rats and mice from eating my property, I'd build me a house, brothers, and buy icons; and, God willing, I'd marry and have children——"

The tramp is murmuring to himself now and has ceased looking at his listeners; he is gazing off somewhere to one side. Artless as his reveries are, he speaks with such sincerity and such heartfelt earnestness that it is hard not to believe what he says. The little mouth of the vagrant is twisted by a smile, and his whole face, his eyes, and his nose are numbed and paralyzed by the foretaste of far-off happiness. The soldiers listen and regard him earnestly, not without compassion. They also believe what he says.

"I am not afraid of Siberia," the tramp murmurs on. "Siberia and Russia are the same thing. They have the same God there as here, and the same Tsar, and they speak the language of Orthodox Christians, as I am speaking with you; only there is greater plenty, and the people are richer. Everything is better there. Take, for example, the rivers. They are a thousand times finer than ours. And fish! The fishing in them is simply beyond words! Fishing, brothers, is the greatest joy of my life. I don't ask for bread; only let me sit and hold a fishing-line! Indeed, that is true! I catch fish on a hook and line and in pots and with bow nets, and when the ice comes I use cast nets. I am not strong enough to fish with a cast net myself; so I have to hire a peasant for five kopeks to do that for me. Heavens, what fun it is! It's like seeing your own brother again to catch an eel or a mudfish! And you have to treat every fish differently, I can tell you. You use a minnow for one, and a worm for another, and a frog or a grasshopper for a third; you've got to know all that. Take, for example, the eel. The eel isn't a dainty fish; it will take even a newt. Pikes like earthworms—garfish, butterflies. There is no greater joy on earth than fishing for chubs in swift water. You bait your hook with a butterfly or a beetle, so that it will float on the surface; and you let your line run out some twenty or thirty yards without a sinker; then you stand in the water without your trousers and let the bait float down with the current till—tug! and there's a chub on the hook! Then you have to watch ever so closely for just the right moment to hook it or the confounded thing will go off with your bait. The moment it twitches the line you've got to pull; there isn't a second to lose! The number of fish I have caught in my life is a caution! When we were escaping and the other convicts were asleep in the forest, I couldn't sleep and would go off in search of a river. The rivers there are so wide and swift and steep-banked —it's a caution. And all along their shores lie dense forests. The trees are so high that it makes your head swim to look up to the top of them. According to prices here every one of those pine-trees is worth ten rubles——"

Under the confused stress of his imagination, the dream pictures of the past, and the sweet foretaste of happiness, the piteous little man stops speaking and only moves his lips as if whispering to himself. The feeble, beatific smile does not leave his face. The soldiers say nothing. Their heads have sunk forward onto their breasts, and they are lost in meditation. In the autumn silence, when a chill, harsh fog from the earth settles on the soul and rises like a prison wall before one to testify to the narrow limits of man's freedom, ah! then it is sweet to dream of wide, swift rivers with bold, fertile banks, of dense forests, of boundless plains! Idly, peacefully, the fancy pictures to itself a man, a tiny speck, appearing on the steep, uninhabited bank of a river in the early morning, before the flush of dawn has faded from the sky. The summits of the everlasting pines rise piled high in terraces on either side of the stream and, muttering darkly, look sternly at that free man. Roots, great rocks, and thorny bushes obstruct his path, but he is strong of body and valiant of heart and fears neither the pines nor the rocks nor the solitude nor the rolling echoes that reiterate every footfall.

The imagination of the soldiers is painting for them pictures of a free life which they have never lived. Is it that they darkly recall images of things heard long ago? Or have these visions of a life of liberty come down to them with their flesh and blood as an inheritance from their remote, wild ancestors? God only knows!

The first to break the silence is Nikander, who until now has not let fall a word. Perhaps he is jealous of the vagrant's visionary happiness; perhaps he feels in his heart that dreams of bliss are incongruous amidst surroundings of gray mist and brown-black mud—at any rate, he looks sternly at the tramp and says:

"That is all very well, brother; that is all very fine, but you'll never reach that land of plenty! How could you? You would go thirty miles and then give up the ghost—a little half-dead creature like you! You've only walked four miles today, and yet look at you! You can't seem to get rested at all!"

The tramp turns slowly to Nikander and the blissful smile fades from his face. He looks with dismay at the grave countenance of the soldier as if he had been caught doing wrong and seems to have recollected something, for he nods his head. Silence falls once more. All three are busy with their own thoughts. The soldiers are trying to force their minds to grasp what perhaps God alone can conceive of: the terrible expanse that lies between them and that land of freedom. Images more clear, precise, and terrifying are crowding into the vagrant's head—courts of justice, dungeons for exiles and for convicts, prison barracks, weary halts along the road, the cold of winter, illness, the death of his companions—all rise vividly before him.

The tramp blinks, and little drops stand out upon his brow. He wipes his forehead with his sleeve, draws a deep breath as if he had just jumped out of a hot oven, wipes his forehead with the other sleeve, and glances fearfully behind him.

"It is quite true that you could never get there," Ptakha assents. "You're not a walker! Look at yourself—all skin and bone! It would kill you, brother."

"Of course it would kill him; he couldn't possibly do it," declares Nikander. "He'll be sent straight to the hospital, anyway, as it is. That's a fact!"

The nameless wanderer looks with terror at the stern, impassive faces of his evil-boding fellow travellers; then, lowering his eyes, he rapidly crosses himself without taking off his cap. He is trembling all over, his head is shaking, and he is beginning to writhe like a caterpillar that some one has stepped on.

"Come on! Time to go!" cries Nikander, rising. "We have rested long enough!"

Another minute and the travellers are plodding along the muddy road. The tramp is stooping more than before and has thrust his hands still deeper into the sleeves of his coat. Ptakha is silent.

1886

Vanka

Nine-year-old Vanka Zhukov, who had been apprenticed three months ago to Alyakhin the shoemaker, did not go to bed on Christmas eve. He waited till his master and mistress and the senior apprentices had gone to church, and then took from the cupboard a bottle of ink and a pen with a rusty nib, spread out a crumpled sheet of paper, and was all ready to write. Before tracing the first letter he glanced several times anxiously at the door and window, peered at the dark icon, with shelves holding cobbler's lasts stretching on either side of it, and gave a quivering sigh. The paper lay on the bench, and Vanka knelt on the floor at the bench.

"Dear Grandad Konstantin Makarich," he wrote. "I am writing a letter to you. I send you Christmas greetings and hope God will send you his blessings. I have no Father and no Mummie and you are all I have left."

Vanka raised his eyes to the dark window-pane, in which the reflection of the candle flickered, and in his imagination distinctly saw his grandfather, Konstantin Makarich, who was night watchman on the estate of some gentlefolk called Zhivarev. He was a small, lean old man about sixty-five, but remarkably lively and agile, with a smiling face and eyes bleary with drink. In the daytime he either slept in the back kitchen, or sat joking with the cook and the kitchen-maids, and in the night, wrapped in a great sheepskin coat, he walked round and round the estate, sounding his rattle. After him, with drooping heads, went old Kashtanka and another dog, called Eel, on account of his black coat and long, weasel-like body. Eel was wonderfully respectful and insinuating, and turned the same appealing glance on friends and strangers alike, but he inspired confidence in no one. His deferential manner and docility were a cloak for the most Jesuitical spite and malice. He was an adept at stealing up, to snap at a foot, creeping into the ice-house, or snatching a peasant's chicken. His hind-legs had been slashed again and again, twice he had been strung up, he was beaten within an inch of his life every week, but he survived it all.

Grandad was probably standing at the gate at this moment, screwing up his eyes to look at the bright red light coming from the church windows, or stumping about in his felt boots, fooling with the servants. His rattle would be fastened to his belt. He would be throwing out his arms and hugging himself against the cold, or, with his old man's titter, pinching a maid, or one of the cooks.

"Have a nip," he would say, holding out his snuffbox to the women.

The women would take a pinch and sneeze. Grandfather would be overcome with delight, breaking out into jolly laughter, and shouting:

"Good for frozen noses!"

Even the dogs would be given snuff. Kashtanka would sneeze, shake her head and walk away, offended. But Eel, too polite to sneeze, would wag his tail. And the weather was glorious. The air still, transparent, fresh. It was a dark night, but the whole village with its white roofs, the smoke rising from the chimneys, the trees, silver with rime, the snow-drifts, could be seen distinctly. The sky was sprinkled with gaily twinkling stars, and the Milky Way stood out as clearly as if newly scrubbed for the holiday and polished with snow. . . .

Vanka sighed, dipped his pen in the ink, and went on writing:

"And yesterday I had such a hiding. The master took me by the hair and dragged me out into the yard and beat me with the stirrup-strap because by mistake I went to sleep rocking their baby. And one day last week the mistress told me to gut a herring and I began from the tail and she picked up the herring and rubbed my face with the head. The other apprentices make fun of me, they send me to the tavern for vodka and make me steal the masters cucumbers and the master beats me with the first thing he finds. And there is nothing to eat. They give me bread in the morning and gruel for dinner and in the evening bread again but I never get tea or cabbage soup they gobble it all up themselves. And they make me sleep in the passage and when their baby cries I dont get any sleep at all I have to rock it. Dear Grandad for the dear Lords sake take me away from here take me home to the village I cant bear it any longer. Oh Grandad I beg and implore you and I will always pray for you do take me away from here or I'll die. . . ."

Vanka's lips twitched, he rubbed his eyes with a black fist and gave a sob.

"I will grind your snuff for you," he went on. "I will pray for you and you can flog me as hard as you like if I am naughty. And if you think there is nothing for me to do I will ask the steward to take pity on me and let me clean the boots or I will go as a shepherd-boy instead of Fedya. Dear Grandad I cant stand it it is killing me. I thought I would run away on foot to the village but I have no boots and I was afraid of the frost. And when I grow up to be a man I will look after you and I will not let anyone hurt you and when you die I will pray for your soul like I do for my Mummie.

"Moscow is such a big town there are so many gentlemens houses and such a lot of horses and no sheep and the dogs are not a bit fierce. The boys dont go about with the star at Christmas and they dont let you sing in church and once I saw them selling fish-hooks in the shop all together with the lines and for any fish you like very good ones and there was one would hold a sheat-fish weighing thirty pounds and I have seen shops where there are all sorts of guns just like the master has at home they must cost a hundred rubles each. And in the butchers shops there are grouse and wood-cock and hares but the people in the shop dont say where they were shot.

"Dear Grandad when they have a Christmas tree at the big house take a gilded nut for me and put it away in the green chest. Ask Miss Olga Ignatyevna tell her its for Vanka."

Vanka gave a sharp sigh and once more gazed at the window-pane. He remembered his grandfather going to get a Christmas tree for the gentry, and taking his grandson with him. Oh, what happy times those had been! Grandfather would give a chuckle, and the frost-bound wood chuckled, and Vanka, following their example, chuckled, too. Before chopping down the fir-tree, Grandfather would smoke a pipe, take a long pinch of snuff, and laugh at the shivering Vanka. . . . The young fir-trees, coated with frost, stood motionless, waiting to see which one of them was to die. And suddenly a hare would come leaping over a snow-drift, swift as an arrow. . . . Grandfather could never help shouting:

"Stop it, stop it . . . stop it! Oh, you stub-tailed devil!"

Grandfather would drag the tree to the big house, and they would start decorating it. . . . Miss Olga Ignatyevna, Vanka's favorite, was the busiest of all. While Pelageya, Vanka's mother, was alive and in service at the big house, Olga Ignatyevna used to give Vanka sweets, and amuse herself by teaching him to read, write and count to a hundred, and even to dance the quadrille. But when Pelageya died, the orphaned Vanka was sent down to the back kitchen to his grandfather, and from there to Moscow, to Alyakhin the shoe-maker. . . .

"Come to me dear Grandad," continued Vanka. "I beg you for Christs sake take me away from here. Pity me unhappy orphan they beat me all the time and I am always hungry and I am so miserable here I cant tell you I cry all the time. And one day the master hit me over the head with a last and I fell down and thought I would never get up again. I have such a miserable life worse than a dogs. And I send my love to Alyona one-eyed Yegor and the coachman and dont give my concertina to anyone. I remain your grandson Ivan Zhukov dear Grandad do come."

Vanka folded the sheet of paper in four and put it into an envelope which he had bought the day before for a kopek. . . . Then he paused to think, dipped his pen into the ink-pot, wrote: "To Grandfather in the village," scratched his head, thought again, then added:

"TO KONSTANTIN MAKARICH"

Pleased that no one had prevented him from writing, he put on his cap and ran out into the street without putting his coat on over his shirt.

The men at the butcher's told him, when he asked them the day before, that letters are put into letter-boxes, and from these boxes sent all over the world on mail coaches with three horses and drunken drivers and jingling bells. Vanka ran as far as the nearest letter-box and dropped his precious letter into the slit. . . .

An hour later, lulled by rosy hopes, he was fast asleep. . . . He dreamed of a stove. On the stove-ledge sat his grandfather, his bare feet dangling, reading the letter to the cooks. . . . Eel was walking backwards and forwards in front of the stove, wagging his tail. . . .

1886

At Home

"Somebody came from the Grigorievs' to fetch a book, but I said you were not at home. The postman has brought the newspapers and two letters. And, by the way, sir, I wish you would give your attention to Seriozha. I saw him smoking today and also day before yesterday. When I told him how wrong it was he put his fingers in his ears, as he always does, and began to sing loudly so as to drown my voice."

Evgeni Bykovski, an attorney of the circuit court, who had just come home from a session and was taking off his gloves in his study, looked at the governess who was making this statement and laughed.

"So Seriozha has been smoking!" he said with a shrug of his shoulders. "Fancy the little tyke with a cigarette in his mouth! How old is he?"

"Seven years old. It seems of small consequence to you, but at his age smoking is a bad, a harmful habit; and bad habits should be nipped in the bud."

"You are absolutely right. Where does he get the tobacco?"

"From your table."

"He does? In that case, send him to me."

When the governess had gone, Bykovski sat down in an easy chair before his writing-table and began to think. For some reason he pictured to himself his Seriozha enveloped in clouds of tobacco smoke, with a huge, yard-long cigarette in his mouth, and this caricature made him smile. At the same time the earnest, anxious face of the governess awakened in him memories of days long past and half forgotten, when smoking at school and in the nursery aroused in masters and parents a strange, almost incomprehensible horror. It really was horror. Children were unmercifully flogged, and expelled from school, and their lives were blighted, although not one of the teachers nor fathers knew exactly what constituted the harm and offense of smoking. Even very intelligent people did not hesitate to combat the vice they did not understand. Bykovski called to mind the principal of his school, a highly educated, good-natured old man, who was so shocked when he caught a scholar with a cigarette that he would turn pale and immediately summon a special meeting of the school board and sentence the offender to expulsion. No doubt that is one of the laws of society—the less an evil is understood the more bitterly and harshly is it attacked.

The attorney thought of the two or three boys who had been expelled and of their subsequent lives, and could not but reflect that punishment is, in many cases, more productive of evil than crime itself. The living organism possesses the faculty of quickly adapting itself to every condition; if it were not so man would be conscious every moment of the unreasonable foundations on which his reasonable actions rest and of how little of justice and assurance are to be found even in those activities which are fraught with so much responsibility and which are so appalling in their consequences, such as education, literature, the law——

And thoughts such as these came floating into Bykovski's head; light, evanescent thoughts such as only enter weary, resting brains. One knows not whence they are nor why they come; they stay but a short while and seem to spread across the surface of the brain without ever sinking very far into its depths. For those whose minds for hours and days together are forced to be occupied with business and to travel always along the same lines, these homelike, un-trammeled musings bring a sort of comfort and a pleasant restfulness of their own.

It was nine o'clock. On the floor overhead someone was pacing up and down, and still higher up, on the third story, four hands were playing scales on the piano. The person who was pacing the floor seemed, from his nervous strides, to be the victim of torment-ing thoughts or of the toothache; his footsteps and the monotonous scales added to the quiet of the evening something somnolent that predisposed the mind to idle reveries.

In the nursery, two rooms away, Seriozha and his governess were talking.

"Pa-pa has come!" sang the boy. "Papa has co-o-ome! Pa! Pa! Pa!"

"*Votre père vous appelle, allez vite!*"[1] cried the governess, twittering like a frightened bird.

"What shall I say to him?" thought Bykovski.

But before he had had time to think of anything to say his son Seriozha had already entered the study. This was a little person whose sex could only be divined from his clothes—he was so delicate, and fair, and frail. His body was as languid as a hot-house plant and everything about him looked wonderfully dainty and soft —his movements, his curly hair, his glance, his velvet tunic.

"Good evening, Papa," he said in a gentle voice, climbing onto his father's knee and swiftly kissing his neck. "Did you send for me?"

"Wait a bit, wait a bit, Master," answered the lawyer, putting him aside. "Before you and I kiss each other we must have a talk, a serious talk. I am angry with you, and I don't love you anymore; do you understand that, young man? I don't love you, and you are no son of mine."

Seriozha looked steadfastly at his father and then turned his regard to the table and shrugged his shoulders.

"What have I done?" he asked, perplexed, and blinked. "I didn't go into your study once today, and I haven't touched a thing."

"Miss Natalie has just been complaining to me that you have been smoking; is that so? Have you been smoking?"

"Yes, I smoked once. That is so."

"There! So now you have told a lie into the bargain!" said the lawyer, disguising his smile by a frown. "Miss Natalie saw you smoking twice. That means that you have been caught doing three naughty things: smoking, taking tobacco that doesn't belong to you off my table, and telling a lie. Three accusations!"

"Oh, ye-es!" Seriozha remembered, and his eyes smiled. "That is true, true! I did smoke twice—today and one other time."

"There, you see, so it was twice and not once. I am very, very displeased with you. You used to be a good boy, but now I see you have grown bad and naughty."

Bykovski straightened Seriozha's little collar and thought:

"What shall I say to him next?"

"Yes, it was very wrong," he went on. "I did not expect this of you. For one thing, you have no right to take tobacco that doesn't belong to you. People only have a right to use their own things; if a man takes other people's things he—he is bad. ["That isn't what I ought to say to him," thought Bykovski.] For instance, Miss Natalie has a trunk with dresses in it. That trunk belongs to her, and we—that is, you and I—must not dare to touch it, because it isn't ours. You have your little horses and your pictures. I don't take

---

1. "Your father is calling you, go at once."

them, do I? Perhaps I should like to, but they are not mine they are yours."

"You can take them if you want to," said Seriozha, raising his eyebrows. "Don't mind, papa, you may have them. The little yellow dog that is on your table is mine, but I don't care if it stays there."

"You don't understand me," said Bykovski. "You made me a present of that little dog; it belongs to me now, and I can do what I like with it; but I didn't give you the tobacco, the tobacco belongs to me. ["I'm not explaining it to him right," thought the lawyer, "not right at all."] If I want to smoke tobacco that isn't mine I must first get permission to do so——"

And so, slowly coupling sentence to sentence, and counterfeiting the speech of a child, Bykovski went on to explain to his son the meaning of possession. Seriozha's eyes rested on his father's chest, and he listened attentively (he liked to converse with his father in the evening); then he rested his elbows on the edge of the table and, half closing his near-sighted eyes, began contemplating the paper and the inkstand. His glance roamed across the table and was arrested by a bottle of glue.

"Papa, what is glue made of?" he suddenly asked, raising the bottle to his eyes.

Bykovski took the bottle away from him, put it where it belonged, and continued:

"In the next place, you have been smoking. That is very naughty indeed. If I smoke, it does not mean that smoking is good. When I smoke I know it is a stupid thing to do, and I am angry with myself and blame myself for doing it. ["Oh, what a wily teacher I am!" thought the lawyer.] Tobacco is very bad for the health, and men who smoke die sooner than they should. It is especially bad to smoke when one is as little as you are. Your chest is weak, you have not grown strong yet, and tobacco smoke gives weak people consumption and other diseases. Your Uncle Ignatius died of consumption; if he hadn't smoked he might have been living today."

Seriozha looked thoughtfully at the lamp, touched the shade with his finger, and sighed.

"Uncle Ignatius used to play the violin," he said. "The Grigorievs have his violin now."

Seriozha again leaned his elbows on the edge of the table and became lost in thought. From the expression fixed on his pale features he seemed to be listening to something, or to be intent on the unfolding of his own ideas; sadness and something akin to fear appeared in his great, unblinking eyes; he was probably thinking of death, which such a little while ago had taken away his mother and his Uncle Ignatius. Death carries mothers and uncles away to another world, and their children and violins stay behind on earth.

Dead people live in heaven, somewhere near the stars, and from there they look down upon the earth. Can they bear the separation?

"What shall I say to him?" thought Bykovski. "He isn't listening. It is obvious that he doesn't attach any importance to his offense or to my arguments. What can I say to touch him?"

The lawyer rose and walked about the study.

"In my day these questions were settled with singular simplicity," he reflected. "If a youngster was caught smoking he was thrashed. This would, indeed, make a poor-spirited, cowardly boy give up smoking, but a clever and plucky one would carry his tobacco in his boot after the whipping and smoke in an outhouse. When he was caught in the outhouse and whipped again he would go down and smoke by the river, and so on until the lad was grown up. My mother used to give me money and candy to keep me from smoking. These expedients now seem to us weak and immoral. Taking up a logical standpoint, the educator of today tries to instill the first principles of right into a child by helping him to understand them and not by rousing his fear or his desire to distinguish himself and obtain a reward."

While he was walking and meditating Seriozha had climbed up and was standing with his feet on a chair by the side of the table and had begun to draw pictures. A pile of paper cut especially for him and a blue pencil lay on the table so that he should not scribble on any business papers or touch the ink.

"Cook cut her finger today while she was chopping cabbage," he said, moving his eyebrows and drawing a house. "She screamed so that we were all frightened and ran into the kitchen. She was so silly! Miss Natalie told her to dip her finger in cold water, but she would only suck it. How could she put her dirty finger in her mouth! Papa, that wasn't nice, was it?"

Then he went on to narrate how an organ-grinder had come into the yard during dinner, with a little girl who had sung and danced to the music.

"He has his own field of thought," the lawyer reflected. "He has a little world of his own in his head, and knows what, according to him, is important and what is not. One cannot cheat him of his attention and consciousness by simply aping his language, one must also be able to think in his fashion. He would have understood me perfectly had I really regretted the tobacco, and been offended and burst into tears. That is why nothing can replace the mother in education, because she is able to feel and weep and laugh with her children. Nothing can be accomplished by logic and ethics. Well, what shall I say to him? What?"

And it seemed to Bykovski laughable and strange that an experienced student of justice like himself, who had spent half a lifetime in the study of every phase of the prevention and punishment of crime, should find himself completely at sea and unable to think of what to say to a boy.

"Listen! Give me your word of honor that you won't smoke again," he said.

"Wo-ord of honor!" sang Seriozha. "Wo-ord of ho-nor! nor! nor!"

"I wonder if he knows what word of honor means?" Bykovski asked himself. "No, I'm a bad teacher. If one of our educators or jurists could look into my head at this moment he would call me a muddle-head and very likely accuse me of too much subtlety. But the fact is, all these confounded questions are settled so much more easily at school or in court than at home. Here, at home, one has to do with people whom one unreasoningly loves, and love is exacting and complicates things. If this child were my pupil or a prisoner at the bar, instead of being my son, I would not be such a coward and my thoughts would not wander as they now do."

Bykovski sat down at the table and drew toward him one of Seriozha's drawings. The picture represented a crooked-roofed little house with smoke coming in zigzags, like lightning, out of the chimneys and rising to the edge of the paper. Near the house stood a soldier with dots for eyes and a bayonet that resembled the figure 4.

"A man cannot possibly be higher than a house," said the lawyer. "See here, your roof reaches up only to the soldier's shoulders."

Seriozha climbed onto his father's lap and wriggled there a long time trying to get himself comfortably settled.

"No, Papa," he said, contemplating his drawing. "If you made the soldier little, his eyes wouldn't show."

What need was there to have corrected him? From daily observation of his son the lawyer had become convinced that children, like savages, have their own artistic viewpoint and their own odd requirements, which are beyond the scope of an adult intelligence. Under close observation, Seriozha might appear abnormal to an adult because he found it possible and reasonable to draw a man higher than a house, giving his pencil his own perceptions as well as a subject. Thus, the sounds of an orchestra he represented by round, smoky spots; a whistle, by a twisted thread; in his mind, sound was intimately connected with form and color, so that in painting letters he invariably colored the sound L, yellow; M, red; A, black; and so forth.

Throwing aside the drawing, Seriozha wriggled again, took a convenient position, and turned his attention to his father's beard. First he smoothed it carefully and then combed it apart in the form of side-whiskers.

"Now you look like Ivan Stepanovich," he murmured, "and now in a minute you're going to look like—our porter. Papa, why do porters stand at doors? To keep robbers from coming in?"

The lawyer felt the child's breath on his face, the soft hair brushed his cheek, and warmth and tenderness crept into his heart as if his whole soul, and not his hands alone, were lying on the velvet of Seriozha's tunic.

He looked into the boy's large, dark eyes and seemed to see mother and wife and everything he had once loved gazing out of those wide pupils.

"How could one whip him?" he thought. "How could one bewilder him by punishment? No, we shouldn't pretend to know how to educate children. People used to be simpler; they thought less and so decided their problems more boldly; but we think too much; we are eaten up by logic. The more enlightened a man is the more he is given to reflection and hair-splitting; the more undecided he is, the more full of scruples, and the more timidly he approaches a task. And, seriously considered, how much bravery, how much self-reliance must a man not have to undertake teaching, or judging, or writing a big book!"

The clock struck ten.

"Come, boy, time for bed!" said the lawyer. "Say good night and then go."

"No, Papa," pouted Seriozha. "I want to stay a little longer. Tell me something; tell me a story."

"Very well; but as soon as the story is told—off we go!"

On his free evenings the lawyer was in the habit of telling Seriozha stories. Like most busy people, he did not know one piece of poetry by heart, neither could he remember a single story, so he was forced to improvise something new every time. He generally took for his keynote "Once upon a time," and then went on heaping one bit of innocent nonsense on another, not knowing, as he told the beginning, what the middle or the end would be. The scenes, the characters, and the situations he would seize at random, and the plot and the moral would trickle in of their own accord, independent of the will of the storyteller. Seriozha loved these improvisations, and the lawyer noticed that the more modest and uncomplicated the plot turned out to be the more deeply it affected the boy.

"Listen," he began, raising his eyes to the ceiling. "Once upon a time there lived an old, a very old king who had a long, gray beard and—and—whiskers as long as this. Well, this king lived in a palace of crystal that sparkled and flashed in the sunlight like a great big block of pure ice. The palace, little son, stood in a great big garden, and in this garden, you know, there grew oranges and bergamot pears and wild cherry-trees; and tulips and roses and lilies-of-the-valley blossomed there and bright-colored birds sang. Yes, and on the trees there hung little crystal bells that rang so sweetly when the wind blew that one never grew tired of listening to them. Crystal gives out a softer, sweeter tone than metal. Well, and what do you

think? In that garden there were fountains. Don't you remember—
you saw a fountain once at Aunt Sonia's summer house? Well, there
were fountains just like that in the king's garden, only they were
ever so much larger and their spray reached right up to the tip of
the highest poplar-trees——"

Bykovski reflected an instant and continued:

"The old king had only one son, who was heir to the kingdom, a
little boy, just as little as you are. He was a good boy; he was never
capricious, and he went to bed early, and never touched anything
on his father's table—and—and was as nice as he could be in every
way. He had only one failing—he smoked."

Seriozha was listening intently, looking steadily into his father's
eyes. The lawyer thought to himself: "How shall I go on?" He
ruminated for a long time and then ended thus:

"Because he smoked, the king's son fell ill of consumption and
died when he was twenty years old. The old man, decrepit and ill,
was left without anyone to take care of him, and there was no one
to govern the kingdom or to protect the palace. Foes came and
killed the old man and destroyed the palace, and now there are no
wild cherry-trees left in the garden, and no birds and no bells, and
so, Sonny——"

An ending like this seemed to Bykovski artless and absurd, but
the whole tale had made a deep impression on Seriozha. Once more
sadness and something resembling terror crept into his eyes; he
gazed for a minute at the dark window and said in a low voice:

"I won't smoke anymore——"

When he had said good-night and gone to bed, his father walked
softly back and forth across the floor and smiled.

"It will be said that beauty and artistic form were the influences
in this case," he mused. "That may be so, but it is no consolation.
After all, those are not genuine means of influence. Why is it that
morals and truth must not be presented in their raw state but always
in a mixture, sugar-coated and gilded, like pills? It is not right. That
sort of thing is falsification, trickery, deceit——"

He remembered the jurymen who invariably had to be harangued
in an "address"; the public who could only assimilate history by
means of legends and historical novels and poems.

"Medicine must be sweet, truth must be beautiful; this has been
man's folly since the days of Adam. Besides, it may all be quite
natural, and perhaps it is as it should be. Nature herself has many
tricks of expediency and many deceptions——"

He sat down to his work, but the idle, domestic thoughts long
continued to flit through his brain. The scales could no longer be
heard overhead, but the dweller on the second floor continued to
walk back and forth.

1887

The Siren's Song

After one of the sessions of the local court in the town of N. the judges gathered in the conference-room in order to take off their robes, rest a moment, and then go home to dine. The presiding judge, a very stately man with fluffy side-whiskers, did not concur with the court on one of the cases that had just been heard and hastened to set down his dissenting opinion. District justice of the peace Milkin, a young man with a languid, melancholy face who had a reputation as a philosopher dissatisfied with the social environment and seeking the aims of existence, stood at the window and moodily gazed at the courtyard. Another district judge and deputy judge had already left. Another deputy judge, a flabby fat man who breathed heavily, and the assistant prosecuting attorney, a young German with a catarrhal face, sat on a little divan and waited for the presiding judge to finish so that they might go to dine together. The clerk of the court, Zhilin, a small man with little side-whiskers around his ears and a saccharine expression on his face, stood before them. Looking at the fat man with a honeyed smile he said in a low voice:

"We all wish to eat now because we've worn ourselves out and it is already after three, but that, my dear Grigory Savvich, isn't a real appetite. A real appetite, a wolfish appetite, when you think you could eat your own father, that only comes about after physical movement, for example, after riding to the hounds, or when you have rushed over a hundred versts[1] without a stop in an ordinary carriage. Imagination, also, plays a great role, sir. If, let us suppose, you are coming home from the hunt and wish to dine with real appetite, you must never think of anything intelligent; the intelligent and the scholarly destroys the appetite. You yourselves know that so far as eating is concerned, philosophers and scholars are the very lowest, and even pigs, if you'll pardon the expression, don't eat worse than they. While going home you must try to make your head think only about the little decanter and the little appetizers. Once on the road I shut my eyes and pictured a little suckling pig with horse-radish in my mind to such an extent that I had an attack of hysterics from the appetite. Well, sir, and when you reach home and enter the courtyard, at that time there has to be some sort of a smell from the kitchen, such as, don't you know . . ."

"Roast geese are experts for smelling," said the deputy justice, breathing heavily.

"Don't say that, my dear Grigory Savvich, ducks or woodcocks are way ahead of geese. The goose bouquet lacks tenderness and delicacy. The headiest smell of all is young onion when, don't you

1. A verst is approximately thirty-five hundred feet.

know, it's beginning to fry up and, don't you see, hisses, the rascal, through the whole house. Well, sir, when you enter the house the table must already be set, and when you sit down, at once tuck the napkin behind your cravat and reach out without hurry for the little decanter with vodka. But don't pour it, the darling, into a little wine-glass, but into some sort of antediluvian silver mug heirloom or some pot-bellied little glass with an inscription "Monks Also Partake of This," and drink it not at a gulp, but first you sigh, rub your hands, look at the ceiling unconcernedly, then, still without hurrying, raise it, the vodka, that is, to the lips and at once sparks fly from your stomach throughout the whole body. . . ."

A blissful expression spread over the clerk's saccharine face.

"Sparks," he repeated, frowning. "As soon as you've drunk you must immediately have something for an appetizer."

"Look here," said the presiding judge, raising his eyes to the clerk, "Speak more quietly! That's the second sheet I've spoiled because of you."

"Ah, pardon me, Peter Nikolaich, sir! I'll be quieter," the clerk said, and continued half-whispering: "Well, sir, but to have appetizers, my dear Grigory Savvich, you also have to use skill. You have to know what to have. The very best appetizer, if you wish to know, is herring. When you've eaten a little bite of it with a little onion and with mustard sauce, immediately, my benefactor, while you still feel sparks in your stomach, have some caviar by itself, or, if you wish it, with a little touch of lemon, then a raw radish with salt, then herring once more, but best of all, benefactor, are salted pink mushrooms, if they're minced like caviar and, don't you know, with onion, with olive oil . . . delicious! But eelpout liver—that's Tragedy!"

"Mmm-yes," the deputy judge agreed, screwing up his eyes. "Good appetizers are also those . . . braised king mushrooms."

"Yes, yes, yes . . with onion, you understand, with bayleaf and all sorts of spices. You lift the pot-cover, and vapor rises from it, a mushroomy fragrance . . . it can even bring tears to your eyes at times. Well, sir, as soon as the coulibiac[2] has been brought in from the kitchen, you must immediately, without delay, drink a second glass."

"Ivan Gurich!" the presiding judge said in a tearful voice, "I've spoiled a third sheet because of you!"

"What the devil, he can only think about food!" grumbled the philosopher Milkin, grimacing contemptuously. "Are there really no other interests in life than mushrooms and coulibiacs?"

"Well, sir, to have a glass before the coulibiac," continued the clerk in a low voice; he was by now so carried away that, like a nightingale at song, he heard nothing but his own voice. "The

---

2. A pie of buckwheat groats, salmon, eggs, dill, and/or other ingredients.

coulibiac[3] has to be appetizing, shameless, completely naked, so there'll be temptation. You wink your eye at it, cut off a little piece, like, and you flit your fingers over it like this, from an overflow of feelings. You start to eat it, the butter drips from it like tears, the stuffing, fat, juicy, with eggs, with innards, with onion . . ."

The clerk rolled his eyes and his mouth spread to his very ears. The deputy judge groaned and, probably picturing the coulibiac to himself, flitted his fingers about.

"That's just impossible . . ." grumbled the district judge, moving off to another window.

"You eat two pieces, but save a third for the *shchi*,"[4] the clerk continued, inspired. "Just as soon as you've finished the coulibiac, order the *shchi* to be served immediately, not to let the appetite flag. . . . The *shchi* must be hot, scalding. But best of all, My Benefactor, is a nice little Ukrainian beet *borshch* with nice little bits of ham and nice sausages. It's served with sour cream and fresh-snipped parsley and dill. A *rassolnik* of innards and baby kidneys is also marvelous, and if you like soup, then the best of all soups is the soup strewn with root and other vegetables: carrots, asparagus, cauliflower, and every kind of similar jurisprudence."

"Yes, a marvelous thing . . . " the presiding judge sighed, lifting his eyes from the paper, but immediately caught himself and groaned: "For God's sake! At that rate I won't finish the dissenting opinion until evening! That's the fourth sheet I've ruined!"

"I won't, I won't! Forgive me, sir!" the clerk excused himself, and continued in a whisper. "Just as soon as you've finished the little *borshch* or the soup, order the fish course to be served at once, benefactor. The very best of the mute fish is crucian carp poached in sour cream, only it must be kept alive in milk for twenty-four hours to give it delicacy and eliminate the smell of slime."

"Sterlet in a little ring is also very nice," said the deputy judge, closing his eyes, but immediately, totally unexpectedly, he tore himself from his place, made a wild face, and howled in the presiding judge's direction: "Pyotr Nikolaich, are you going to be long? I can't wait any longer, I can't!"

"Let me finish!"

"Well, I'll go by myself, then! Go to the devil!"

The fat man flung up his hands, grabbed his hat, and ran out of the room without saying good-bye. The clerk sighed and, bending over to the ear of the assistant prosecutor, continued in a low voice:

"Pike-perch or carp served with tomatoes and little mushrooms is

3. The Russian word is feminine in gender.
4. The clerk mentions three Russian soups: *shchi* is a cabbage soup; *borshch* contains meat, sausage, and other things, in addition to cabbage; *rassolnik* contains kidneys and pickles.

also very good. But fish isn't filling enough for you, Stepan Frant-sych; that's an insubstantial kind of food, the main thing at dinner isn't fish or sauces but the roast. What bird do you adore most?"

The assistant prosecutor made a sour face and said with a sigh:

"Unfortunately, I can't share your feelings. I have a catarrh of the stomach."

"What are you talking about, my good sir! A catarrh of the stomach is something the doctors have thought up! That sickness has its origin mostly from free-thinking and also from pride. Don't pay any attention to it. Let us suppose you don't feel like eating or you're nauseous, don't you pay any attention and just go ahead and eat. If a little brace of snipe is served for the roast, let us suppose, and if one were to add a little partridge or a little brace of plump little quail, then you'd forget about any sort of catarrh, I give you my noble word of honor. And roast turkey? White, plump, so juicy, like a nymph, don't you know . . ."

"Yes, probably that's tasty," said the prosecutor, smiling sadly. "I might, in fact, eat turkey."

"Good Lord, and duck? If you take a young duckling which has just been touched by ice during the first frosts, and roast it in a dripping pan with potatoes, but the potatoes must be cut small, and start to color a bit, but they must soak up the duck fat, but they . . ."

The philosopher Milkin made a wild face and wanted to say something, but suddenly smacked his lips, probably imagining the roast duck, and, without saying a single word, drawn by a mysterious force, grabbed his hat and ran off.

"Yes, I might, in fact, eat some duck, too . . ." the assistant prosecutor sighed.

The presiding judge rose, walked around, and sat down again.

"After the roast, man becomes full and falls into a delightful blankness," the clerk continued. "At that point the body feels good and the soul is filled with tender emotion. For a treat you could drink two or three glasses of a nice little spiced brandy."

The presiding judge grunted and crossed out the sheet.

"That's the sixth sheet I've ruined," he said angrily. "That's wicked!"

"Keep writing, keep writing, Benefactor!" the clerk whispered. "I won't! I'll be very quiet. I'll tell you honestly, Stepan Frantsych," he continued in a barely audible whisper, "a nice little home-brewed spiced brandy is better than any champagne. After the first little glass, your whole soul is enveloped by a fragrance, such a mirage, and you imagine that you aren't sitting at home in an armchair, but somewhere in Australia, on some sort of softest possible ostrich. . . ."

"Oh, let's get going, Pyotr Nikolaich!" said the prosecutor, impatiently twitching his leg.

"Yes, sir," continued the clerk. "While sipping the brandy it's pleasant to smoke a nice little cigar and blow rings, and during that time the most remarkable thoughts come into your head, like your being a generalissimo, or you're married to the world's most beautiful woman and that beauty floats all day before your windows in such a pool with nice little goldfish. She floats there, and you call to her, 'Darling, come kiss me!' "

"Pyotr Nikolaich!" groaned the assistant prosecutor.

"Yes, sir," the clerk continued. "When you've finished smoking, you gather the skirts of your dressing-gown, and off to your little bed! You lie down on your back with your tummy up, and pick up the paper. It's pleasant to read about politics when you can't keep your eyes open and your whole body is overcome by drowsiness: there Austria has done something careless, and look, France displeased somebody, there the Roman Pope has done something in defiance—it's very pleasant to read."

The presiding judge jumped up, flung his pen aside and grabbed for his hat with both hands. The assistant prosecutor, forgetting his catarrh and nearly fainting with impatience, also jumped up.

"Let's go!" he shouted.

"But Pyotr Nikolaich, what about the dissenting opinion?" the clerk said in fright. "When will you write it, benefactor? You have to go to town at six o'clock!"

The presiding judge flung up his hands and rushed to the door. The assistant prosecutor also flung up his hands and, grabbing his briefcase, disappeared together with the presiding judge. The clerk sighed, looked after them reproachfully, and started to gather the papers.

1887

Sleepy

Night. Varka, the little nurse, a girl of thirteen, is rocking the cradle in which the baby is lying, and humming hardly audibly:

> "Hush-a-bye, my baby wee,
> While I sing a song for thee."

A little green lamp is burning before the icon; there is a string stretched from one end of the room to the other, on which baby-clothes and a pair of big black trousers are hanging. There is a big patch of green on the ceiling from the icon-lamp, and the baby-clothes and the trousers throw long shadows on the stove, on the cradle, and on Varka. . . . When the lamp begins to flicker, the green patch and the shadows come to life, and are set in motion, as though by the wind. It is stuffy. There is a smell of cabbage soup, and of the inside of a boot-shop.

The baby is crying. For a long while he has been hoarse and exhausted with crying; but he still goes on screaming, and there is no knowing when he will stop. And Varka is sleepy. Her eyes are glued together, her head droops, her neck aches. She cannot move her eyelids or her lips, and she feels as though her face is dried and wooden, as though her head has become as small as the head of a pin.

"Hush-a-bye, my baby wee," she hums, "while I cook the groats for thee. . . ."

A cricket is churring in the stove. Through the door in the next room the master and the apprentice Afanasy are snoring. . . . The cradle creaks plaintively, Varka murmurs—and it all blends into that soothing music of the night to which it is so sweet to listen, when one is lying in bed. Now that music is merely irritating and oppressive, because it goads her to sleep, and she must not sleep; if Varka—God forbid!—should fall asleep, her master and mistress would beat her.

The lamp flickers. The patch of green and the shadows are set in motion, forcing themselves on Varka's fixed, half-open eyes, and in her half slumbering brain are fashioned into misty visions. She sees dark clouds chasing one another over the sky, and screaming like the baby. But then the wind blows, the clouds are gone, and Varka sees a broad high road covered with liquid mud; along the high road stretch files of wagons, while people with wallets on their backs are trudging along and shadows flit backwards and forwards; on both sides she can see forests through the cold harsh mist. All at once the people with their wallets and their shadows fall on the ground in the liquid mud. "What is that for?" Varka asks. "To sleep, to sleep!" they answer her. And they fall sound asleep, and sleep sweetly, while crows and magpies sit on the telegraph wires, scream like the baby, and try to wake them.

"Hush-a-bye, my baby wee, and I will sing a song to thee," murmurs Varka, and now she sees herself in a dark stuffy hut.

Her dead father, Yefim Stepanov, is tossing from side to side on the floor. She does not see him, but she hears him moaning and rolling on the floor from pain. "His guts have burst," as he says; the pain is so violent that he cannot utter a single word, and can only draw in his breath and clack his teeth like the rattling of a drum:

"Boo—boo—boo—boo. . . ."

Her mother, Pelagea, has run to the master's house to say that Yefim is dying. She has been gone a long time, and ought to be back. Varka lies awake on the stove, and hears her father's "boo—boo—boo." And then she hears someone has driven up to the hut.

It is a young doctor from the town, who has been sent from the big house where he is staying on a visit. The doctor comes into the hut; he cannot be seen in the darkness, but he can be heard coughing and rattling the door.

"Light a candle," he says.

"Boo—boo—boo," answers Yefim.

Pelagea rushes to the stove and begins looking for the broken pot with the matches. A minute passes in silence. The doctor, feeling in his pocket, lights a match.

"In a minute, sir, in a minute," says Pelagea. She rushes out of the hut, and soon afterwards comes back with a bit of candle.

Yefim's cheeks are rosy and his eyes are shining, and there is a peculiar keenness in his glance, as though he were seeing right through the hut and the doctor.

"Come, what is it? What are you thinking about?" says the doctor, bending down to him. "Aha! have you had this long?"

"What? Dying, your honor, my hour has come. . . . I am not to stay among the living. . . ."

"Don't talk nonsense! We will cure you!"

"That's as you please, your honor, we humbly thank you, only we understand. . . . Since death has come, there it is."

The doctor spends a quarter of an hour over Yefim, then he gets up and says:

"I can do nothing. You must go into the hospital, there they will operate on you. Go at once. . . . You must go! It's rather late, they will all be asleep in the hospital, but that doesn't matter, I will give you a note. Do you hear?"

"Kind sir, but what can he go in?" says Pelagea. "We have no horse."

"Never mind. I'll ask your master, he'll let you have a horse."

The doctor goes away, the candle goes out, and again there is the sound of "boo—boo—boo." Half an hour later someone drives up to the hut. A cart has been sent to take Yefim to the hospital. He gets ready and goes. . . .

But now it is a clear bright morning. Pelagea is not at home; she has gone to the hospital to find what is being done to Yefim. Somewhere there is a baby crying, and Varka hears someone singing with her own voice:

"Hush-a-bye, my baby wee, I will sing a song to thee."

Pelagea comes back; she crosses herself and whispers:

"They put him to rights in the night, but towards morning he gave up his soul to God. . . . The Kingdom of Heaven be his and peace everlasting. . . . They say he was taken too late. . . . He ought to have gone sooner. . . ."

Varka goes out into the road and cries there, but all at once someone hits her on the back of her head so hard that her forehead knocks against a birch tree. She raises her eyes and sees, facing her, her master, the shoemaker.

"What are you about, you scabby slut?" he says. "The child is crying, and you are asleep!"

He gives her a sharp slap behind the ear, and she shakes her head, rocks the cradle, and murmurs her song. The green patch and the shadows from the trousers and the baby-clothes move up and down, nod to her, and soon take possession of her brain again. Again she sees the high road covered with liquid mud. The people with wallets on their backs and the shadows have lain down and are fast asleep. Looking at them, Varka has a passionate longing for sleep; she would lie down with enjoyment, but her mother Pelagea is walking beside her, hurrying her on. They are hastening together to the town to find jobs.

"Give alms, for Christ's sake!" her mother begs of the people they meet. "Show us the divine mercy, kindhearted gentlefolk!"

"Give the baby here!" a familiar voice answers. "Give the baby here!" the same voice repeats, this time harshly and angrily. "Are you asleep, you wretched girl?"

Varka jumps up, and looking round grasps what is the matter: there is no high road, no Pelagea, no people meeting them, there is only her mistress, who has come to feed the baby, and is standing in the middle of the room. While the stout, broad-shouldered woman nurses the child and soothes it, Varka stands looking at her and waiting till she has done. And outside the windows the air is already turning blue, the shadows and the green patch on the ceiling are visibly growing pale, it will soon be morning.

"Take him," says her mistress, buttoning up her chemise over her bosom; "he is crying. He must be bewitched."

Varka takes the baby, puts him in the cradle, and begins rocking it again. The green patch and the shadows gradually disappear, and now there is nothing to force itself on her eyes and cloud her brain. But she is as sleepy as before, fearfully sleepy! Varka lays her head on the edge of the cradle, and rocks her whole body to overcome her sleepiness, but yet her eyes are glued together, and her head is heavy.

"Varka, heat the stove!" she hears the master's voice through the door.

So it is time to get up and set to work. Varka leaves the cradle, and runs to the shed for firewood. She is glad. When one moves and runs about, one is not so sleepy as when one is sitting down. She brings the wood, heats the stove, and feels that her wooden face is getting supple again, and that her thoughts are growing clearer.

"Varka, set the samovar!" shouts her mistress.

Varka splits a piece of wood, but has scarcely time to light the splinters and put them in the samovar, when she hears a fresh order:

"Varka, clean the master's galoshes!"

She sits down on the floor, cleans the galoshes, and thinks how nice it would be to put her head into a big deep galosh, and have a little nap in it. . . . And all at once the galosh grows, swells, fills up the whole room. Varka drops the brush, but at once shakes her head, opens her eyes wide, and tries to look at things so that they may not grow big and move before her eyes.

"Varka, wash the steps outside; I am ashamed for the customers to see them!"

Varka washes the steps, sweeps and dusts the rooms, then heats another stove and runs to the shop. There is a great deal of work: she hasn't one minute free.

But nothing is so hard as standing in the same place at the kitchen table peeling potatoes. Her head droops over the table, the potatoes dance before her eyes, the knife tumbles out of her hand while her fat, angry mistress is moving about near her with her sleeves tucked up, talking so loud that it makes a ringing in Varka's ears. It is agonising, too, to wait at dinner, to wash, to sew, there are minutes when she longs to flop on to the floor regardless of everything, and to sleep.

The day passes. Seeing the windows getting dark, Varka presses her temples that feel as though they were made of wood, and smiles, though she does not know why. The dusk of evening caresses her eyes that will hardly keep open, and promises her sound sleep soon. In the evening visitors come.

"Varka, set the samovar!" shouts her mistress.

The samovar is a little one, and before the visitors have drunk all the tea they want, she has to heat it five times. After tea Varka stands for a whole hour on the same spot, looking at the visitors, and waiting for orders.

"Varka, run and buy three bottles of beer!"

She starts off, and tries to run as quickly as she can, to drive away sleep.

"Varka, fetch some vodka! Varka, where's the corkscrew? Varka, clean a herring!"

But now, at last, the visitors have gone; the lights are put out, the master and mistress go to bed.

"Varka, rock the baby!" she hears the last order.

The cricket churrs in the stove; the green patch on the ceiling and the shadows from the trousers and the baby-clothes force themselves on Varka's half-opened eyes again, wink at her and cloud her mind.

"Hush-a-bye, my baby wee," she murmurs, "and I will sing a song to thee."

And the baby screams, and is worn out with screaming. Again Varka sees the muddy high road, the people with wallets, her mother Pelageya, her father Yefim. She understands everything, she recognizes everyone, but through her half sleep she cannot understand the force which binds her, hand and foot, weighs upon her, and prevents her from living. She looks round, searches for that force that she may escape from it, but she cannot find it. At last, tired to death, she does her very utmost, strains her eyes, looks up at the flickering green patch, and listening to the screaming, finds the foe who will not let her live.

That foe is the baby.

She laughs. It seems strange to her that she has failed to grasp such a simple thing before. The green patch, the shadows, and the cricket seem to laugh and wonder too.

The hallucination takes possession of Varka. She gets up from her stool, and with a broad smile on her face and wide unblinking eyes, she walks up and down the room. She feels pleased and tickled at the thought that she will be rid directly of the baby that binds her hand and foot. . . . Kill the baby and then sleep, sleep, sleep. . . .

Laughing and winking and shaking her fingers at the green patch, Varka steals up to the cradle and bends over the baby. When she has strangled him, she quickly lies down on the floor, laughs with delight that she can sleep, and in a minute is sleeping as soundly as the dead.

1888

The Grasshopper

I

All of Olga Ivanovna's friends and acquaintances went to her wedding.

"Look at him—there *is* something about him, isn't there?" she said to her friends, nodding towards her husband—apparently anxious to explain how it was that she had agreed to marry a commonplace, in no way remarkable man.

Osip Stepanovich Dymov, her husband, was a doctor with the rank of titular counselor.[1] He worked in two hospitals, in one as non-resident physician, and in the other as prosector. From nine till noon he received outpatients and visited his ward, and in the afternoon took the horse-tram to another hospital, where he performed post-mortems on patients who had died there. His private practice amounted to very little, about five hundred rubles a year. And that

---

1. A low grade in the hierarchy, with a very low salary.

is all. There is nothing more to say about him. Whereas Olga Ivanovna and her friends and acquaintances were by no means ordinary people. Each of them was distinguished in some way or other, and not altogether unknown, having already made a name and gained a certain celebrity, or, if not exactly celebrated yet, all gave promise of a brilliant future. One was an actor, whose genuine dramatic talents had already found recognition; he was elegant, clever and discreet, recited beautifully, and gave Olga Ivanovna lessons in elocution; another was an opera singer, fat and good-humored, who assured Olga Ivanovna with a sigh that she was ruining herself—if she were not so lazy, if she would only take herself in hand, she would make a fine singer; besides these there were several artists, chief among them Ryabovsky, who went in for painting problem pictures, animals, and landscapes, and was an extremely handsome fair young man of about twenty-five, whose pictures made a hit at exhibitions—his latest had fetched five hundred rubles. He used to finish off Olga Ivanovna's sketches for her, and always said that something might come of her painting. Then there was a cellist who could make his cello "weep," and who declared openly that of all the women whom he knew, the only one capable of accompanying him was Olga Ivanovna. And a writer, young, but already well known, who had produced short novels, plays and stories. Who else? Oh, yes, there was Vasili Vasilievich, a genteel landowner, amateur book-illustrator and creator of vignettes; he had a true feeling for the old Russian style, and for the legendary epic. He could produce veritable miracles on paper, on china, and on smoked plates. Amidst this artistic, liberal society, these favorites of fortune, who, while perfectly urbane and well-bred, remembered the existence of doctors only when they were ill, and in whose ears the name of Dymov was equivalent to such common names as Sidorov or Tarasov, Dymov seemed like a stranger, superfluous, small, though he was actually very tall and broad-shouldered. His frock-coat seemed to have been made for someone else, and he had a beard like a tradesman's. Of course, if he had been a writer or an artist everyone would have said that his beard made him look like Zola.

The actor told Olga Ivanovna that with her flaxen hair and in her wedding attire she was exactly like a slender cherry-tree, when covered in the spring with delicate white blossom.

"No, but listen!" Olga Ivanovna said, seizing him by the hand. "How could it have happened? Listen to me, listen. . . . My father and Dymov worked in the same hospital, you know. When poor father fell ill Dymov watched by his bedside day and night. Such a self-sacrifice! Listen, Ryabovsky! And you listen, writer, you'll find it very interesting. Come nearer. Such self-sacrifice, such sincere sympathy. I didn't sleep at night, either, I sat by my father, and all of a sudden—I won the heart of the lusty youth—just like that! My Dymov was head-over-heels in love. How queer fate can be! Well, after my father died Dymov came to see me sometimes, and we sometimes met out-of-doors, and one fine day—lo and behold—a proposal, like a bolt from the blue! I cried all night, I fell madly in love, too. And here I am a married woman. There *is* something strong, something powerful, bearish, about him, isn't there, now? He's three-quarter face to us now, the light's all wrong, but when he turns full face just have a look at his forehead. What have you to say to such a forehead, Ryabovsky? Dymov, we're talking about you!" she shouted to her husband. "Come here! Give Ryabovsky your honest hand. . . . That's right. You must be friends."

Dymov held his hand out to Ryabovsky with a naïve, good-humored smile.

"Delighted," he said. "There was a Ryabovsky with me at college. He's no relation of yours, I suppose?"

II

Olga Ivanovna was twenty-two, Dymov, thirty-one. They had a wonderful life after their marriage. Olga Ivanovna covered the walls of her drawing-room with sketches, framed and unframed, by herself and her friends, and surrounded the grand piano and the furniture with an artistic jumble of Chinese parasols, easels, many-colored drapes, daggers, small busts, photographs. . . . In the dining-room she hung cheap colored prints, bast shoes, and scythes on the wall, and grouped a scythe and a rake in the corner, thus achieving a dining-room *à la russe*. She draped the ceiling and walls of the bedroom with dark cloth, to make it look like a cave, hung a Venetian lantern over the beds, and placed a figure holding a halberd at the door. And everyone said that the young couple had made themselves a very cosy nest.

Olga Ivanovna got up at eleven every day, played the piano, or, if there was sunshine, painted in oils. A little after twelve she went to her dressmaker. She and Dymov had very little money, only just enough for their needs, and if she was to appear constantly in new dresses, and look effective, the dressmaker and she had to resort to all sorts of cunning. Again and again sheer miracles were achieved, and a thing of utter enchantment, not a dress, but a dream, was created from an old, dyed frock and some odd bits of tulle and lace. From the dressmaker Olga Ivanovna usually went on to an actress friend, and while she was about it, tried to wangle tickets for some first night, or somebody's "benefit." From the actress she had to visit an artist's studio, or go to a picture-show, and then on to some celebrity to invite him to her house, to return a call, or simply to chatter. And everywhere she was greeted with gaiety and cordiality and assured that she was good, sweet, unusual. . . . Those whom she called celebrated and great received her as one of them, on an equal footing, and declared unanimously that with her gifts, taste, and mind she would come to something big, if only she would stop wasting her talents in so many directions. She sang, played the piano, painted in oils, modelled in clay, acted in amateur theatricals, and all this not just anyhow, but displaying real talent. Whatever she did, whether it was making lanterns for illuminations, dressing up, or simply tying somebody's tie, turned out artistic, graceful, charming. But in nothing did her talents display themselves so vividly as in her ability to strike up lightning friendships and get on intimate terms with celebrated folk. The moment anyone distinguished himself in the very slightest degree, or got himself talked about, she scraped up an acquaintance with him, made friends instantly, and invited him to her house. Every time she made a new acquaintance was a veritable red-letter day for her. She worshipped the famous, she was proud of them, she dreamed of them every night. She thirsted for celebrities and could never slake this thirst. Old friends disappeared and were forgotten, new ones came to take their place, but she soon grew tired of these, too, or they disappointed her, and she began eagerly seeking new friends, new celebrities, and, when she had found them, looking for others. And why?

Between four and five she had dinner at home with her husband. His simplicity, common sense and good humor reduced her to a state of admiration and ecstasy. She was continually jumping up, flinging her arms round his neck, and showering kisses on him.

"You are a wise, high-minded man, Dymov," she told her. "But you have one very grave defect. You take no interest whatever in art. You quite ignore music and painting."

"I don't understand them," he said humbly. "I have worked at natural science and medicine my whole life, and I never had any time to go in for art."

"But that's awful, Dymov!"

"Why? Your friends know nothing about natural science or medicine, and you don't hold it against them. Everyone to his own. I don't understand landscapes or operas, but I look at it this way: since some clever people devote their whole lives to them, and other clever people pay enormous sums for them, they must be necessary. I don't understand, but that doesn't mean that I ignore them."

"Let me press your honest hand!"

After dinner Olga Ivanovna paid calls, then she went to the theatre or a concert, and did not get home till after midnight. And this went on every day.

On Wednesday evenings she was at home to visitors. There was no card-playing or dancing on these Wednesday evenings, and the company entertained themselves with the arts. The well-known actor recited, the singer sang, the artists made drawings in Olga's innumerable albums, the cellist played, and the hostess herself drew, modeled, sang and played accompaniments. In the intervals between reciting, playing and singing, they talked and argued about literature, the theatre, art. There were no ladies present, for Olga Ivanovna considered all women, except actresses and her dressmaker, trivial and boring. There was not a single Wednesday evening when the hostess did not start at every ring at the doorbell, saying with a triumphant countenance: "It's him!" by which pronoun she indicated some newly invited celebrity. Dymov was never in the drawing-room, and nobody so much as remembered his existence. But precisely at half-past eleven, the door into the dining-room opened and Dymov appeared in the doorway, with his good-natured, gentle smile, rubbing the palms of his hands together, and saying:

"Come to supper, gentlemen!"

Everyone filed into the dining-room, and every time their eyes were greeted by the same objects: a dish of oysters, a round of ham or veal, sardines, cheese, caviar, pickled mushrooms, vodka, and two decanters of wine.

"My darling *maître d'hôtel*," Olga Ivanovna would say, clasping her hands in ecstasy. "You're simply charming! Do look at his forehead, everyone! Dymov, turn your profile to us! Look, everyone— the face of a Bengal tiger, and an expression as sweet and kind as a doe's! You pet!"

The guests ate, glancing at Dymov, and thinking: "He really is a nice chap"; but they soon forgot about him and went on talking about the theatre, music, art.

The young couple were happy, and their life went smoothly on. True, the third week of their honeymoon did not pass quite happily, indeed it was sad. Dymov caught erysipelas at the hospital, and had to stay in bed six days and have his beautiful black hair cropped to the roots. Olga Ivanovna sat at his bedside weeping bitterly, but when he got a little better she tied a white kerchief over his cropped head and began painting him as a Bedouin. And they both thought it great fun. Three days after he had quite recovered and begun going to the hospital again, a fresh misfortune overtook him.

"I have no luck, Mama," he said to her one day at dinner. "I had four post-mortems today, and I got two of my fingers cut at once. And I only noticed after I got home."

Olga Ivanovna was alarmed. He smiled and said it was a trifle and that he often cut his hands during post-mortems.

"I get carried away, Mama, and then I'm absent-minded."

Olga Ivanovna nervously awaited the onset of blood poisoning, and prayed every night that it might be averted; it all passed off harmlessly. And the old happy, tranquil life, untouched by grief or anxiety, was resumed. The present was splendid, and soon spring would be coming, smiling at them from afar, and promising a hundred joys. Happiness would go on forever. For April, May and June there would be the country cottage a long way from Moscow, walks, sketches, fishing, nightingales, and then, from July right up to the autumn, the artists' excursion on the Volga, an excursion in which Olga Ivanovna, as a permanent member of their circle, would take part. She had already had herself made two traveling costumes of coarse linen, and had bought paints, brushes, canvas and a new palette for the journey. Ryabovsky visited her almost every day to see how her painting was getting on. When she showed him her work he would thrust his hands deep into his pockets, compress his lips firmly, sniff and say:

"Well, well. . . . That cloud screams: that's not an evening light. The foreground is a bit messy, and there's something, you know what I mean—lacking. . . . Your hut looks as if it had been squashed and was whining piteously. . . . Make that corner darker. But on the whole it's not so dusty. . . . I'm pleased."

And the more obscure his way of speaking, the more easily Olga Ivanovna understood what he meant.

III

On Whitmonday Dymov went out in the afternoon and bought some snacks and sweets to take to his wife in the country. He had not seen her for a fortnight, and missed her sorely. In the railway carriage, and afterwards, while trying to find his cottage in a thick copse, he felt the pangs of hunger, and indulged in dreams of sitting down to a leisurely supper with his wife, and afterwards tumbling into bed. It cheered him up to look at his parcel, which contained caviar, cheese, and smoked fish.

By the time he had found and recognized the cottage the sun had gone down. The elderly servant told him that the mistress was not at home, but that she would probably soon be back. The cottage, a highly unattractive structure, with low ceilings, writing-paper on the walls, and uneven floors, full of gaps, contained only three rooms. In one was a bed, in the next canvases, paintbrushes, a piece of dirty paper, men's coats and hats on chairs and windowsills; and in the third Dymov came upon three strange men. Two were dark and bearded, and the third was clean-shaven and stout, an actor apparently. A samovar was steaming on the table.

"What do you want?" asked the actor in a bass voice, casting an unfriendly glance at Dymov. "To see Olga Ivanovna? Wait a minute. She'll be here soon."

Dymov sat down and waited. One of the dark men, looking at him with drowsy languor, poured out some tea, and asked:

"Have some tea?"

Dymov was both hungry and thirsty, but he refused the tea so as not to take the edge off his appetite. Soon steps were heard and a familiar laugh. A door banged and Olga Ivanovna burst into the room, in a broad-brimmed hat, carrying a box; after her, holding a big parasol and a folding stool, came Ryabovsky, red-cheeked and in high spirits.

"Dymov!" screamed Olga Ivanovna, flushing up with delight. "Dymov!" she repeated, laying her head and both her hands on his chest. "It's you! Why haven't you been for such a long time? Why? Why?"

"When could I, Mama? I'm always busy, and when I have any free time it always happens there's no suitable train."

"Oh, how glad I am to see you! I dreamed of you all night, all night, I was afraid you were ill or something. Oh, if only you knew what a darling you are, and how lucky it is you came! You are my deliverer! You're the only one who can save me! There's going to be the most original wedding here tomorrow," she went on, laughing and re-tying her husband's tie. "The telegraph-operator at the station is going to be married, Chikeldeyev his name is. Good-looking boy, and no fool, there's something strong, bearish about his face, you know. . . . He could sit for the portrait of a youthful Varangian.[2] All we summer visitors take an interest in him and have given our word of honor to be at his wedding. . . . He's hard up, lonely, shy, it would be a sin to refuse him our sympathy. Fancy, the wedding will be just after the service, and everyone is going straight from the church to the home of the bride. . . . The grove, the singing of birds, spots of sun on the grass, you know, and all of us colored spots against a bright green background—ever so original, just like the French expressionists. But, Dymov, what am I to wear at church?" said Olga Ivanovna, making a dolorous face. "I have nothing here, literally nothing. No dress, no flowers, no gloves. . . . You simply must save me! Your coming just now means fate intended you to save me. Take my keys, darling, go home, and get me my pink dress out of the wardrobe. You know it, it's hanging right in front. . . . And on the floor of the box-room you'll see two cardboard boxes. When you open the top one you'll see nothing but tulle, tulle, tulle and all sorts of scraps, and underneath them, flowers. Take out all the flowers very carefully, try not to crumple them, my pet, I'll choose something from them afterwards. And buy me a pair of gloves."

"Very well," said Dymov. "I'll go back tomorrow and send them."

"Tomorrow?" repeated Olga Ivanovna, gazing at him in conster-

2. Scandinavians or Norsemen who founded a dynasty in Russia in the ninth century.

nation. "You couldn't possibly be in time tomorrow! The first train leaves at nine tomorrow, and the wedding's at eleven. No, love, you'll have to go today, you'll simply have to! If you can't come tomorrow yourself, send everything with a messenger. Go on, now. . . . The train will be here soon. Don't be late, my pet."

"All right."

"How I hate to let you go!" said Olga Ivanovna, and tears welled up in her eyes. "What a fool I was to promise the telegraph-operator!"

Dymov, gulping down a glass of tea and picking up a biscuit smiled meekly and went to the station. The caviar, cheese and smoked fish were eaten by the two dark men and the fat actor.

IV

On a still moonlit night in July, Olga Ivanovna stood on the deck of a Volga steamer, looking in turns at the water and the exquisite riverbank. Beside her stood Ryabovsky, telling her that the black shadows on the surface of the water were not shadows but a dream, that it would be good to forget everything, to die, to become a memory, surrounded by this magical, gleaming water, this infinite sky, these mournful, pensive banks, all speaking to us of the vanity of our lives, and of the existence of something higher, something eternal, blissful. The past was trivial and devoid of interest, the future was blank, and even this divine, never-to-be-repeated night would soon end, would become part of eternity—why, then, live?

And Olga Ivanovna listened in turn to Ryabovsky's voice and to the silence of the night, and told herself that she was immortal, that she would never die. The opalescent water, which was like nothing she had ever before seen, the sky, the banks, the black shadows, and the unaccountable joy filling her soul, all told her that she would one day be a great artist, and that somewhere, beyond the distance, beyond the moonlit night, in infinite space, there awaited her success, glory, the love of the people. . . . When she gazed long and unblinkingly into the distance she seemed to see crowds, lights, the sounds of solemn music, cries of enthusiasm, herself in a white dress, and flowers raining upon her from all sides. She told herself, too, that beside her, leaning on the rail, stood a truly great man, a genius, one of God's elect. . . . Everything he had done up to now was wonderful, fresh, unusual, and the work he would do in time, when his extraordinary talent had matured with the years, would be striking, immeasurably lofty, and all this could be seen in his face, in his way of expressing himself, and in his attitude to nature. He had his own special language for describing the shadows, the hues of evening, the brilliance of the moonlight, and the charm of his power over nature was almost irresistible. He was good-looking, too, and original, and his life, independent, free, without earthly ties, was like the life of a bird.

"It's getting chilly," said Olga Ivanovna, and she shivered.

Ryabovsky wrapped his coat round her, saying mournfully:

"I feel I am in your power. I am a slave. What makes you so fascinating today?"

He gazed at her all the time, never looking away, and there was something terrible in his eyes, she was afraid to look at him.

"I am madly in love with you . . ." he whispered, breathing on her cheek. "Only say the word and I will stop living, give up art . . ." he murmured, profoundly stirred. "Love me, love me. . . ."

"Don't talk like that," said Olga Ivanovna, closing her eyes. "It's awful. And what about Dymov?"

"What does Dymov matter? Why Dymov? What have I to do with Dymov? The Volga, the moon, beauty, my love, my ecstasy, but no Dymov. . . . Oh, I know nothing. . . . I don't need the past, give me only one moment . . . One little moment!"

Olga Ivanovna's heart beat violently. She tried to think of her husband, but the entire past, her wedding, Dymov, her Wednesday evenings, now seemed to her small, insignificant, dull, useless, and far, far away. . . . And after all—what did Dymov matter? Why Dymov? What had she to do with Dymov? Was there really such a person, wasn't he just a dream?

"The happiness he has had is quite enough for an ordinary man like him," she told herself, covering her face with her hands. "Let them judge *there*, let them curse me, I will go to my ruin, yes, to my ruin, just to spite them. . . . One should try everything once. Oh, God, how terrifying, and how lovely!"

"Well? Well?" murmured the artist, putting his arms round her and eagerly kissing the hands with which she was feebly trying to push him away. "Do you love me? Do you? Oh, what a night! What a divine night!"

"Yes, what a night!" she whispered, looking into his eyes, which were shining with tears, and then, looking away quickly, she put her arms round him and kissed him firmly on the lips.

"We'll be at Kineshma[3] in a minute," said someone from the other side of the deck. Heavy steps were heard. It was the man from the refreshment-room passing.

"Listen," called Olga Ivanovna to him, laughing and crying from joy. "Bring us some wine."

The artist, pale with agitation, sat down on a bench, looking at Olga Ivanovna with adoring, grateful eyes, and then shut his own, and said with a weary smile:

---

3. A minor stop on the Volga route, about 150 miles northeast of Moscow. Chekhov may be using the name for its prosaic implications and coarse sound.

"I'm tired."

And he laid his head on the rail.

V

The second of September was a warm, still day, but misty. A light fog had hovered over the Volga in the early morning, and after nine o'clock it began to drizzle. And there was not the slightest hope of its clearing up. At breakfast Ryabovsky had told Olga Ivanovna that painting was the most ungrateful and tedious of the arts, that he was no artist, that no one but fools believed in his talent, and suddenly, without the faintest warning, he seized a knife and slashed at his most successful sketch. After breakfast he sat moodily at the window and looked out at the river. And the Volga, no longer shining, was dimmed, dull, cold-looking. Everything spoke of the approach of the sad, bleak autumn. It seemed as if the lush green carpets on the banks, the diamond-like reflections of the sun's rays, the transparent, blue distance, and all the elegant show of nature had been taken from the Volga and laid away in a chest till next spring, and the crows flew over the river, teasing it: "Bare! Bare!" Ryabovsky listened to their cawing and told himself that he had painted himself out and lost his talent, that everything in the world was conventional, relative, idiotic, and that he should never have got mixed up with this woman. . . . In a word, he was dejected and depressed. . . .

Olga Ivanovna sat on the bed on the other side of the partition, passing her fingers through her beautiful flaxen hair, seeing herself in imagination in her drawing-room, in the bedroom, in her husband's study. Her imagination bore her to the theatre, to the dressmaker, to her celebrated friends. What were they doing at this moment? Did they ever think of her? The season had begun and it was time to think of her Wednesday evenings. And Dymov? Dear Dymov! How meekly and with what childish plaintiveness he kept begging her in his letters to come home. Every month he sent her seventy-five rubles, and when she wrote him that she had borrowed a hundred rubles from the artists he sent her another hundred. What a good, generous man! The journey had tired Olga Ivanovna, she was bored, she was longing to get away from these peasants, from the smell of damp rising from the river, to shake off the feeling of physical uncleanliness which never left her, while living in peasant huts and migrating from village to village. If Ryabovsky had not given the artists his word of honor that he would stay with them till the twentieth of September they could have gone away this very day. And wouldn't that have been nice!

"My God," groaned Ryabovsky. "Whenever will the sun come

out? I can't go on with a sunlit landscape when there isn't any sun."

"You have a sketch with a cloudy sky,", said Olga Ivanovna, coming out from behind the partition. "Don't you remember—with a wood in the right foreground and a herd of cows and geese on the left. You might finish it now."

"For God's sake!" The artist made a grimace of distaste. "Finish! Do you really consider me too much of a fool to know what I ought to do?"

"How you have changed toward me," sighed Olga Ivanovna.

"And a good thing, too!"

Olga Ivanovna's features twitched, she crossed over to the stove, and stood there, crying.

"And now tears—if that isn't the limit! Stop it! I have a thousand reasons for crying, but I don't cry."

"Reasons!" sobbed Olga Ivanovna. "The chief reason of all is that you are sick of me. Yes, you are!" And her sobs increased. "The whole truth is that you are ashamed of our love. You are afraid of the artists noticing, though there's no concealing it, and they've known about it for ages."

"Olga, I ask you only one thing," said the artist in imploring tones, placing his hand on his heart. "Only one thing—leave me alone! That's all I want from you."

"But swear that you still love me!"

"This is torture!" the artist hissed through clenched teeth, and he leaped to his feet. "It'll end in my throwing myself into the Volga or going mad! Leave me alone!"

"Kill me, then, go on, kill me!" cried Olga Ivanovna. "Kill me!"

She burst out sobbing and went behind the partition again. The rain rustled on the straw thatch. Ryabòvsky clutched at his head and paced up and down the room for a time, and then, an expression of determination on his face, as if he were clinching an argument with someone, he put on his cap, threw his gun over his shoulder, and went out of the hut.

After he had gone, Olga Ivanovna lay on her bed for a long time, crying. At first she thought how nice it would be to take poison, and for Ryabovsky to find her dead when he came back, but very soon her thoughts flew back to her drawing-room, to her husband's study, and she saw herself sitting quite still beside Dymov, enjoying the physical sensations of peace and cleanliness, and then seated in the theater listening to Mazzini. And the yearning for civilization, for the noises of the city, for celebrated men, struck a pang to her heart. A country-woman came into the hut and began heating the stove with leisurely movements, in preparation for cooking dinner. There was a smell of smoldering wood, and the air turned blue with smoke. The artists came in in their muddy high boots, their faces wet with rain, looked at one another's sketches, and consoled themselves with the reflection that the Volga had its charms even in bad weather. And the pendulum of the cheap clock on the wall went tick-tick-tick. Chilly flies clustered in the corner next to the icons, buzzing faintly, and cockroaches crawled about in the bulging files under the benches.

Ryabovsky returned to the hut at sunset. He flung his cap on the table, sank on to the bench, pale, exhausted, still in his muddy boots, and closed his eyes.

"I'm tired," he said, his eyebrows twitching in the effort to lift his eyelids.

Olga Ivanovna, in her anxiety to ingratiate herself, and show him that she was not really angry, went over to him, kissed him in silence, and passed a comb through his fair hair. She felt a sudden desire to comb his hair.

"What's this?" he said, starting as if something clammy had touched him, and opening his eyes. "What's this? Leave me in peace, I beg you!"

He pushed her from him and moved away and she caught an expression of disgust and annoyance on his face. Just then the woman came up to him, holding a plate of cabbage soup carefully in both hands, and Olga Ivanovna noticed that her thick thumbs were wet with the soup. And the dirty woman with her skirt drawn tight over her stomach, the cabbage soup, which Ryabovsky fell upon eagerly, the hut, this life which had at first seemed so delightful in its simplicity and artistic disorder, now struck her as appalling. Suddenly affronted, she said coldly:

"We shall have to part for a time, or we shall quarrel outright, from sheer boredom. I'm sick of all this! I shall leave today."

"How? Riding a hobby-horse?"

"Today's Thursday, so the steamer will arrive at nine-thirty."

"Will it? Oh, yes. . . . Very well, go then," said Ryabovsky softly, wiping his lips with a towel, for want of a napkin. "It's dull for you here, and I'm not such an egoist as to try and detain you. Go, we'll meet again after the twentieth."

Olga Ivanovna started packing with a light heart, her cheeks flaming with satisfaction. "Could it really be," she asked herself, "that she would soon be sitting in her drawing-room, painting, sleeping in a bedroom, and dining with a cloth on the table?" A load seemed to fall from her shoulders, and she was no longer angry with the artist.

"I'll leave you my paints and brushes, Ryabusha," she called out. "If there are any left over you can bring them back. . . . Now mind you don't get lazy when I'm not here, don't indulge in the blues—work! You're swell, Ryabusha!"

At nine o'clock Ryabovsky kissed her good-bye, so as not to have to kiss her on the deck in front of the artists, she was sure, and saw her to the landing-stage. The steamer soon hove in sight and bore her away.

She was home in two and a half days. Without removing her hat and raincoat, breathing heavily in her agitation, she went into the drawing-room and from there to the dining-room. Dymov was seated at the table in his shirt sleeves, his waistcoat unbuttoned, sharpening a knife on the prongs of a fork; on a plate before him was a roasted grouse. Olga Ivanovna had entered the flat with the conviction that she must conceal everything from her husband, and that she had the ability and strength to do this, but at the sight of his broad, meek, joyful smile and the happiness shining in his eyes she felt that it would be as base and detestable, as impossible for her to deceive such a man as it would be to slander, to steal, or to murder, and she then and there decided to tell him all that had occurred. Allowing him to kiss and embrace her, she sank down on her knees before him and covered her face with her hands.

"What is it? What is it, Mama?" he asked her tenderly. "Did you miss me so?"

She lifted her face, red with shame, and cast a guilty look, full of entreaty, at him, but shame and fear prevented her from telling him the truth.

"It's nothing. . . ." she said. "I'm just . . ."

"Let's sit down," he said, raising her, and seating her at the table. "That's the way. . . . Have some grouse. You're hungry, poor darling."

She inhaled the familiar atmosphere eagerly, and ate some grouse, while he gazed at her affectionately, laughing with delight.

VI

It was apparently sometime in the middle of the winter that Dymov began to suspect that he was being deceived. He could no longer look his wife in the eyes, as if it were he whose conscience was not clear, no longer smiled joyfully when he met her, and in order to be as little alone with her as possible often brought home to dinner his friend Korostelev, a crop-headed little man with puckered features, who started buttoning and unbuttoning his coat from sheer embarrassment whenever Olga Ivanovna addressed him, and then fell to tweaking the left side of his moustache with his right hand. During dinner the doctors remarked that when the diaphragm was too high up, palpitations sometimes occurred, or that there had been a great deal of nervous disease lately, or that Dymov, the evening before, performing a post-mortem on a patient said to have died of pernicious anemia, had discovered cancer of the pancreas. And they seemed to carry on this medical conversation just to give Olga Ivanovna an excuse not to talk, that is, not to lie. After dinner Korostelev would sit down at the piano, and Dymov would sigh and call out:

"Come on, old boy! What are you waiting for? Give us something nice and sad."

His shoulders raised and his fingers outspread, Korostelev would strike a few chords and begin singing in a tenor voice: "Show me, show me the place in our country, where the Russian peasant does not groan!" and Dymov would give another sigh, prop his head on his fist and plunge into thought.

Olga Ivanovna had now begun to behave extremely incautiously. She woke up every morning in the worst possible spirits, to the thought that she no longer loved Ryabovsky, and that it was all over between them, thank God. But after she had had a cup of coffee she would remind herself that Ryabovsky had robbed her of her husband and that she was now left without a husband, and without Ryabovsky. Then she would remember that her friends were speaking of some marvelous picture Ryabovsky was finishing for a show, a kind of mixture of landscape and problem picture, in the style of Polenov, and that everyone who visited his studio was in ecstasies about it. But he had created this picture under her influence, she told herself, he had improved enormously, thanks to her influence. Her influence had been so beneficial, so real, that if she were to leave him he might go all to pieces. She remembered, moreover, that the last time he had come to see her he had worn a gray coat with silvery threads in it and a new tie, and had asked her in languishing tones: "Do I look nice?" And he had certainly looked very nice, in his smart coat, with his long curls and blue eyes (or at least she had thought so), and he had been very affectionate with her.

Remembering all this and more, and forming her own conclusions, Olga Ivanovna would dress and go in a state of great excitement to Ryabovsky's studio. She usually found him in excellent spirits and full of admiration for his picture, which really was very good. When he was in a playful mood, he would fool about and parry serious questions with a joke. Olga Ivanovna was jealous of the picture and detested it, but always stood in front of it in polite silence for five minutes, and then would say, sighing as people sigh in a shrine:

"Yes, you never painted anything like it before. You know, it quite frightens me."

Then she would implore him to love her, not to throw her over, to pity her, poor, unhappy thing. She would weep, kiss his hands, try to drag an assurance of love out of him, pointing out that without her good influence he would stray from the path and be lost. Then, having thoroughly upset him and humiliated herself, she would go to the dressmaker or to an actress friend about a theatre-ticket.

On the days when she did not find him in his studio she left him a note threatening to take poison if he did not come to see her that very day. Alarmed, he would go to her and stay to dinner. Unabashed by the presence of her husband, he would make insulting remarks to her, she repaying him in his own coin. They both felt that they were in each other's way, that they were tyrants and enemies, and this infuriated them, and in their fury they did not notice how indecent their behavior was and that even the crop-headed Korostelev could not fail to understand everything. After dinner Ryabovsky would bid them a hasty farewell and go.

"Where are you going?" Olga Ivanovna would ask him in the hall, looking at him with hatred.

Frowning and narrowing his eyes he would name some lady whom they both knew, and it was obvious that he was making fun of her jealousy and wanted to annoy her. She would go to her bedroom and lie down. In her jealousy, rage, humiliation and shame she would bite the pillow and sob loudly. Then Dymov would leave Korostelev in the drawing-room and step into the bedroom, looking shy and embarrassed, and say in a low voice:

"Don't cry so, Mama! What's the good? You ought to keep quiet about it. You mustn't let people see. . . . What's done can't be undone, you know."

Unable to control her jealousy, which made her very temples throb, and telling herself that it was not too late to put things right, she would get up and wash, powder her tear-stained face, and rush off to the lady he had mentioned. Not finding Ryabovsky there, she would drive to another, and another. . . . At first she felt shame in these journeys, but she soon got used to them, and sometimes visited all the women she knew in a single evening, in her search for Ryabovsky, and they all understood her motive.

Once she said to Ryabovsky of her husband:

"That man oppresses me with his magnanimity."

This phrase pleased her so much that whenever she met any of the artists who were in the secret of her affair with Ryabovsky, she would mention her husband, saying, with a powerful gesture:

"That man oppresses me with his magnanimity."

Their routine of life went on just the same as the preceding year. On Wednesday evenings there were the at-homes. The actor recited, the artists drew, the cellist played, the singer sang, and invariably at half-past eleven the door into the dining-room opened and Dymov said, smiling: "Come to supper, gentlemen."

As before, Olga Ivanovna sought out great men, found them, and, still not satisfied, went to look for others. As before, she came home late every night, but Dymov was never asleep when she returned, as he had been the year before, but sat working at something in his study. He went to bed at three and got up at eight.

One evening when she was taking a last look at herself in the glass before going to the theatre, Dymov came into the bedroom in a frock-coat and white tie. He smiled meekly and looked straight into her eyes, as he used to formerly. His face was radiant.

"I've just presented my thesis," he said, sitting down and smoothing the knees of his trousers.

"Was it a success?" asked Olga Ivanovna.

"Wasn't it just!" he laughed, craning his neck to catch sight of his wife's face in the mirror, for she still stood with her back towards him putting the finishing touches to her hair. "Wasn't it just!" he repeated. "And it's highly probable, you know, that they'll make me assistant professor in general pathology. It looks very like it."

It was obvious from his blissful, radiant expression that if Olga Ivanovna had shared his joy and triumph he would have forgiven her all, both present and future, and would have forgotten all, but she understood neither what an assistant professor was nor what general pathology meant, besides she was afraid of being late for the theatre, and so she said nothing.

He sat on for a few minutes, and then, smiling apologetically, went away.

VII

It had been a most restless day.

Dymov had a violent headache. He had no breakfast and did not go to the hospital, but lay all day on the couch in his study. Olga Ivanovna went off as usual to Ryabovsky soon after twelve, to show him a sketch for a still life that she had made, and asked him why he had not been to see her the day before. She knew her sketch was poor, and had only painted it so as to have an excuse to go and see the artist.

She went in without ringing and while she was taking off her galoshes in the hall she thought she heard soft steps in the studio, accompanied by the rustle of a woman's dress, and when she glanced hastily in she was just in time to catch a glimpse of a brown skirt, which flashed by one moment and disappeared the next behind a large canvas over which a sheet of black calico was draped, covering the easel and reaching to the floor. There could be no doubt that a woman was hiding there. How often had Olga Ivanovna found herself a hiding-place behind this canvas! Ryabovsky, obviously profoundly embarrassed, stretched out both his hands towards her, as if astonished to see her, and said with a strained smile:

"A-a-ah! Glad to see you! What's your news?"

Olga Ivanovna's eyes filled with tears. She felt ashamed and wretched, and would not for anything in the world have spoken in front of that other woman, her rival, that liar, who was now standing behind the canvas and no doubt laughing up her sleeve.

"I just wanted to show you my sketch," she said, in a high, timid voice, and her lips quivered. "It's a *nature-morte*."[4]

"A-a-a-h, a sketch. . . ."

The artist took the sketch in his hands, and, his eyes fixed on it, strolled as it were absent-mindedly into the next room.

Olga Ivanovna followed him submissively.

"*Nature-morte*, of the very best sort," he muttered, mechanically seeking rhymes, "kur-ort,[5] sport, port, short. . . ."

The sound of hasty steps and the rustling of skirts came from the studio. This meant *she* had gone. Olga Ivanovna felt an impulse to cry out, to hit the artist over the head with something heavy, and run away, but she was blinded with tears, crushed with shame, and felt she was no longer Olga Ivanovna, the artist, but some wretched little insect.

"I'm tired," said the artist in languishing tones, looking at the sketch and trying to shake off his fatigue with a toss of his head. "It's quite nice, of course, but it's a sketch today, and a sketch last year and in a month's time another sketch. . . . Aren't you sick of them? In your place I would give up art and go in for music or something seriously. You're not an artist, you know, you're a musician. But if you only knew how tired I am! I'll tell them to bring us some tea, shall I?"

He went out of the room and Olga Ivanovna could hear him saying something to his manservant. To avoid a leave-taking and a scene, above all to prevent herself from bursting out crying, she ran out into the hall before Ryabovsky had time to get back, put on her galoshes, and went out. Once in the street she breathed more freely, feeling that she had shaken off Ryabovsky, art, and the unendurable sense of humiliation she had undergone in the studio, for good and all. This was the end.

She went to her dressmaker, then to Barnai, who had only just come back, from Barnai to a music-shop, thinking all the time of the cold, ruthless and dignified letter she would write to Ryabovsky, and of how she would go to the Crimea with Dymov in the spring or summer, there to shake off the past forever, and begin a new life.

She got home quite late, but instead of going to her room to

4. French for "still-life."
5. Health resort, spa (the Russian word is the same as the German).

undress she went straight to the drawing-room to compose her letter. Ryabovsky had told her she was not an artist, and in revenge she would now tell him that he painted the same picture year after year, that he said the same things day after day, that he had gone off, that he would never achieve any more than he had already achieved. She intended to add that he was greatly indebted to her good influence and that if he was now behaving badly it was because her influence had been stultified by all sorts of disreputable creatures, like the one who had hidden behind the picture today.

"Mama," called Dymov from his study, without opening the door. "Mama."

"What d'you want?"

"Don't come near me, Mama, but just come to the door. That's right. I caught diphtheria a day or two ago in the hospital and . . . I feel very bad. Send for Korostelev."

Olga Ivanovna always called her husband by his surname, as she did all her men friends. His name was Osip, and she did not like it, for it reminded her of Gogol's Osip and a silly pun on the names Osip and Arkhip.[6] But now she exclaimed:

"Oh, Osip, it can't be true!"

"Send for him. I feel bad. . . ." said Dymov from inside the room, and she could hear him walk over to the sofa and lie down. "Send for him." His voice sounded hollow.

"Can it really be?" thought Olga Ivanovna, cold with horror. "Why, it's dangerous!"

Without knowing why she lit a candle and took it to her bedroom, and while trying to decide what she ought to do, she caught sight of herself in the looking-glass. With her pale, frightened face, in her jacket with the high, puffy sleeves, and yellow flounces in front, and the eccentric diagonal stripes on her skirt, she saw herself as an awful fright, a revolting creature. An infinite pity for Dymov surged up within her, for his boundless love for her, his young life and even his lonely bed, in which he had not slept for so long and she remembered his invariable, meek, submissive smile. She wept bitterly and wrote an imploring note to Korostelev. It was two o'clock in the morning.

VIII

When Olga Ivanovna, her head heavy from lack of sleep, her hair not done, a guilty expression on her face, and looking quite plain, came out of her bedroom soon after seven the next morning, a gentleman with a black beard, a doctor apparently, passed her in the hall. There was a smell of medicaments. Korostelev was standing at

6. The pun in *Dead Souls* is *"Ósip osíp"*   *okhrip* ("Arkhip lost his voice").
("Joseph became hoarse") and *Arkhip*

the door in the study, tweaking the left side of his moustache with his right hand.

"Sorry, but I can't let you go to him," he said morosely to Olga Ivanovna. "You might catch it. And besides, there's no point in your going to him. He's delirious."

"Has he really got diphtheria?" whispered Olga Ivanovna.

"I would have everyone who courts danger needlessly sent to prison," muttered Korostelev, not answering her question. "D'you know how he got infected? He sucked up pus from the throat of a little boy with diphtheria. And what for? Sheer folly, imbecility!"

"Is it very dangerous?" asked Olga Ivanovna.

"Yes, they say it's a very bad case. What we ought to do is to send for Shreck."

A red-haired little man with a long nose and a Jewish accent came, and after him a tall, stooping, shaggy man, rather like an archdeacon, and then a younger man, stout and red-faced, wearing spectacles. They were all doctors who came to take turns at the bedside of their comrade. Korostelev, who did not go home when his watch was over, wandered about the rooms like a ghost. The maid made tea for the doctors and was always running to the chemist's, so there was no one to do the rooms. It was very quiet, very dreary.

Olga Ivanovna sat in her bedroom telling herself that God was punishing her for deceiving her husband. The silent, unmurmuring, enigmatic being, his individuality sapped by good nature, yielding, weakened by excess of kindness, now lay on the couch, suffering in silence. If he had complained, if he had even raved in delirium, the doctors keeping watch over him would have discovered that it was not only diphtheria that was to blame. They might have asked Korostelev, he knew all, and it was not for nothing that he regarded his friend's wife with eyes which seemed to say that it was she who was the evil genius, and that the diphtheria was merely her ally. She forgot the moonlit night on the Volga, the assurances of love, the poetic life in the peasant hut, and remembered only that she had plunged head and shoulders into something foul and sticky, from which she would never be able to wash herself clean—and all out of sheer caprice, for the sake of trivial amusement.

"What a liar I have been!" she said to herself, remembering the restless love which had existed between Ryabovsky and herself. "A curse on it all!"

At four o'clock she had dinner with Korostelev. He ate nothing, only drinking some red wine and frowning. She, too, ate nothing. She prayed silently, promising God that if Dymov recovered she would love him again and be a faithful wife. And then, forgetting her troubles for a moment, she would look at Korostelev and wonder: "Surely it must be a bore to be such an insignificant, obscure person, with such a puckered-up face and such bad manners!" And again it seemed to her that God might strike her down this very moment for, in her fear of infection, never once having been in her husband's study. Her prevailing mood was a feeling of dull misery and the conviction that her life was ruined and spoiled beyond repair. . . .

After dinner the dusk soon fell. When Olga Ivanovna went into the drawing-room she found Korostelev asleep on the sofa, his head on a silk cushion embroidered in gilt thread. "Hup-wah," he snored. "Hup-wah."

The doctors, coming and going on their visits to the bedside, were quite unaware of all this irregularity. The strange man snoring in the drawing-room, the pictures on the walls, the eccentric furniture, the mistress of the house going about with her hair not done and her dress in disarray, all this was now incapable of arousing the slightest interest. One of the doctors happened to laugh at something, and the laugh sounded strangely timid, making everyone feel uneasy.

When Olga Ivanovna next went into the drawing-room Korostelev was awake sitting up on the sofa, smoking.

"The diphtheria has settled in the nasal cavities," he said in an undertone. "His heart is already beginning to show the strain. Things look bad, bad."

"Why don't you send for Shreck?" asked Olga Ivanovna.

"He's been. It was he who noticed that the diphtheria had gone into the nose. And who's Shreck, anyhow? Shreck is nothing special, really. He's Shreck and I'm Korostelev, and that's all."

Time passed with agonizing slowness. Olga Ivanovna, fully dressed, lay dozing on her bed, unmade since the morning. The whole flat seemed to be filled from floor to ceiling by a huge block of iron, and she felt that if only this block could be removed, everyone would cheer up. Waking with a start, she realized that it was not a block of iron but Dymov's illness.

"*Nature-morte*, port," she said to herself, again falling into a doze, "sport, kur-ort. . . . And who's Shreck? Shreck, treck . . . wreck . . . kreck. And where are all my friends? Do they know we are in trouble? Oh, God, save us, have mercy. . . . Shreck, treck. . . ."

And again the block of iron. . . . Time dragged on endlessly, though the clock on the floor below seemed to be always striking the hour. And every now and then there came rings at the bell; the doctors coming to Dymov. . . . The maid came into the room holding a tray with an empty glass on it.

"Shall I do your bed, Ma'am?" she asked.

Getting no reply she went out again. The clock downstairs struck the hour, Olga Ivanovna dreamed it was raining on the Volga, and again someone came into her room, a stranger apparently. But the next moment she recognized Korostelev, and sat up in bed.

"What's the time?" she asked.

"About three."

"How is he?"

"How is he? I came to tell you he's dying."

He swallowed a sob, and sat down on the bed beside her, wiping away his tears with his cuff. She did not take it in at first, but went suddenly cold and crossed herself slowly.

"Dying," he repeated in a high voice and again sobbed. "Dying, because he sacrificed himself. What a loss to science!" he said with bitter emphasis. "In comparison with all the rest of us he was a great man, a remarkable man. What a gift! What hopes he inspired in us all!" went on Korostelev, wringing his hands. "My God, my God, he would have been such a scientist, such a rare scientist! Osip Dymov, Osip Dymov, what have you done? Oh. God!"

In his despair Korostelev covered his face with both hands.

"And what moral force!" he continued, getting more and more angry with someone. "Kind, pure, affectionate soul—crystal-clear! He served science and he died in the cause of science. Worked like a horse, day and night, nobody spared him, and he, young, learned, a future professor, had to look for private practice, sit up at night doing translations, to pay for those—miserable rags!"

Korostelev looked at Olga Ivanovna with loathing, seized the sheet in both his hands and tore angrily at it, as if it were to blame.

"He did not spare himself and nobody spared him. But what's the good of talking?"

"Yes, he was a remarkable man," came in deep tones from the drawing-room.

Olga Ivanovna went back in memory over her whole life with him, from beginning to end, in the utmost detail, and suddenly realized that he really had been a remarkable man, an unusual man, a great man, in comparison with all the others she had known. And remembering the attitude to him of her late father, and of all his colleagues, she realized that they had all seen in him a future celebrity. The walls, the ceiling, the lamp and the carpet on the floor winked mockingly at her, as if trying to say: "You've missed your chance!" She rushed weeping out of the bedroom, almost running into a strange man in the drawing-room, and burst into the study to her husband. He lay motionless on the couch, a blanket covering him up to the waist. His face was terrible drawn and thin and had that grayish-yellow tinge never seen on the living. Only his forehead, his black eyebrows, and his familiar smile showed that it was Dymov. Olga Ivanovna touched his breast, his brow and his hands with rapid movements. The breast was still warm, but the brow and hands were unpleasantly cold. And the half-shut eyes gazed, not at Olga Ivanovna, but at the blanket.

"Dymov!" she called out loud. "Dymov!"

She wanted to explain to him that it had all been a mistake, that everything was not yet lost, that life might yet be beautiful and happy, that he was an unusual, a remarkable, a great man, and that she would worship him all her life, would kneel before him, would feel a sacred awe of him. . . .

"Dymov!" she called, shaking him by the shoulder, unable to believe that he would never again wake up. "Dymov, Dymov, I say!"

And in the drawing-room Korostelev was saying to the maid:

"What is there to ask about? Go round to the church and ask where the almswomen live. They'll wash the body and put everything in order—they'll do all that is necessary."

1892

In Exile

Old Semyon, nicknamed Preacher, and a young Tatar, whom no one knew by name, were sitting on the riverbank by the campfire; the other three ferry-men were in the hut. Semyon, an old man of sixty, lean and toothless, but broad-shouldered and still healthy-looking, was drunk; he would have gone in to sleep long before, but he had a bottle in his pocket and he was afraid that the fellows in the hut would ask him for vodka. The Tatar was ill and weary, and wrapping himself up in his rags was describing how nice it was in the Simbirsk province, and what a beautiful and clever wife he had left behind at home. He was not more than twenty-five, and now, by the light of the campfire, with his pale and sick, mournful face, he looked like a boy.

"To be sure, it is not paradise here," said Preacher. "You can see for yourself, the water, the bare banks, clay, and nothing else. . . . Easter has long passed and yet there is ice on the river, and this morning there was snow. . . ."

"It's bad! it's bad!" said the Tatar, and looked round him in terror.

The dark, cold river was flowing ten paces away; it grumbled, lapped against the hollow clay banks and raced on swiftly towards the faraway sea. Close to the bank there was the dark blur of a big barge, which the ferrymen called a "karbas."[1] Far away on the further bank, lights, dying down and flickering up again, zigzagged

---

1. A kind of rowboat with four to ten oars.

like little snakes; they were burning last year's grass. And beyond
the little snakes there was darkness again. There little icicles could
be heard knocking against the barge. It was damp and cold. . . .

The Tatar glanced at the sky. There were as many stars as at
home, and the same blackness all round, but something was lacking.
At home in Simbirsk province the stars were quite different, and so
was the sky.

"It's bad! it's bad!" he repeated.

"You will get used to it," said Semyon, and he laughed. "Now
you are young and foolish, the milk is hardly dry on your lips, and
it seems to you in your foolishness that you are more wretched than
anyone; but the time will come when you will say to yourself: 'I
wish no one a better life than mine.' You look at me. Within a week
the floods will be over and we shall set up the ferry; you will all go
wandering off about Siberia while I shall stay and shall begin going
from bank to bank. I've been going like that for twenty-two years,
day and night. The pike and the salmon are under the water while I
am on the water. And thank God for it, I want nothing; God give
everyone such a life."

The Tatar threw some dry twigs on the campfire, lay down closer
to the blaze, and said:

"My father is a sick man. When he dies my mother and wife will
come here. They have promised."

"And what do you want your wife and mother for?" asked
Preacher. "That's mere foolishness, my lad. It's the Devil confound-
ing you, damn his soul! Don't you listen to him, the cursed one.
Don't let him have his way. He is at you about the women, but you
spite him; say, 'I don't want them!' He is on at you about freedom,
but you stand up to him and say: 'I don't want it!' I want nothing,
neither father nor mother, nor wife, nor freedom, nor post, nor
paddock; I want nothing, damn their souls!"

Semyon took a pull at the bottle and went on:

"I am not a simple peasant, not of the working class, but the son
of a deacon, and when I was free I lived at Kursk; I used to wear a
frock-coat, and now I have brought myself to such a pass that I can
sleep naked on the ground and eat grass. And I wish no one a better
life. I want nothing and I am afraid of nobody, and the way I look
at it is that there is nobody richer and freer than I am. When they
sent me here from Russia from the first day I stuck it out; I want
nothing! The Devil was at me about my wife and about my home
and about freedom, but I told him: 'I want nothing.' I stuck to it,
and here you see I live well, and I don't complain, and if anyone
gives way to the Devil and listens to him, if but once, he is lost,
there is no salvation for him: he is sunk in the bog to the crown of
his head and will never get out.

"It is not only a foolish peasant like you, but even gentlemen, well-educated people, are lost. Fifteen years ago they sent a gentleman here from Russia. He hadn't shared something with his brothers and had forged something in a will. They did say he was a prince or a baron, but maybe he was simply an official—who knows? Well, the gentleman arrived here, and first thing he bought himself a house and land in Mukhortinskoe. 'I want to live by my own work,' says he, 'in the sweat of my brow, for I am not a gentleman now,' says he, 'but a settler.' 'Well,' says I, 'God help you, that's the right thing.' He was a young man then, busy and careful; he used to mow himself and catch fish and ride sixty miles on horseback. Only this is what happened: from the very first year he took to riding to Gyrino for the post; he used to stand on my ferry and sigh: 'Ech, Semyon, how long it is since they sent me any money from home!' 'You don't want money, Vassily Sergeyich,' says I. 'What use is it to you? You cast away the past, and forget it as though it had never been at all, as though it had been a dream, and begin to live anew. Don't listen to the Devil,' says I; 'he will bring you to no good, he'll draw you into a snare. Now you want money,' says I, 'but in a very little while you'll be wanting something else, and then more and more. If you want to be happy,' says I, 'the chief thing is not to want anything. Yes. . . . If,' says I, 'if Fate has wronged you and me cruelly, it's no good asking for her favor and bowing down to her, but you despise her and laugh at her, or else she will laugh at you.' That's what I said to him. . . .

"Two years later I ferried him across to this side, and he was rubbing his hands and laughing. 'I am going to Gyrino to meet my wife,' says he. 'She was sorry for me,' says he; 'she has come. She is good and kind.' And he was breathless with joy. So a day later he came with his wife. A beautiful young lady in a hat; in her arms was a baby girl. And lots of luggage of all sorts. And my Vassily Sergeyich was fussing round her; he couldn't take his eyes off her and couldn't say enough in praise of her. 'Yes, brother Semyon, even in Siberia people can live!' 'Oh, all right,' thinks I, 'it will be a different tale presently.' And from that time forward he went almost every week to inquire whether money had not come from Russia. He wanted a lot of money. 'She is losing her youth and beauty here in Siberia for my sake,' says he, 'and sharing my bitter lot with me, and so I ought,' says he, 'to provide her with every comfort. . . .'

"To make it livelier for the lady he made acquaintance with the officials and all sorts of riffraff. And of course he had to give food and drink to all that crew, and there had to be a piano and a shaggy lapdog on the sofa—plague take it! . . . Luxury, in fact, self-indulgence. The lady did not stay with him long. How could she? The clay, the water, the cold, no vegetables for you, no fruit. All around you ignorant and drunken people and no sort of manners, and she was a spoiled lady from Petersburg or Moscow. . . . To be sure she moped. Besides, her husband, say what you like, was not a gentleman now, but a settler—not the same rank.

"Three years later, I remember, on the eve of the Assumption, there was shouting from the further bank. I went over with the ferry, and what do I see but the lady, all wrapped up, and with her a young gentleman, an official. A sleigh with three horses. . . . I ferried them across here, they got in and away like the wind. They were soon lost to sight. And towards morning Vassily Sergeyich galloped down to the ferry. 'Didn't my wife come this way with a gentleman in spectacles, Semyon?' 'She did,' said I; 'you may look for the wind in the fields!' He galloped in pursuit of them. For five days and nights he was riding after them. When I ferried him over to the other side afterwards, he flung himself on the ferry and beat his head on the boards of the ferry and howled. 'So that's how it is,' says I. I laughed, and reminded him 'people can live even in Siberia!' And he beat his head harder than ever. . . .

"Then he began longing for freedom. His wife had slipped off to Russia, and of course he was drawn there to see her and to get her away from her lover. And he took, my lad, to galloping almost every day, either to the post or the town to see the commanding officer; he kept sending in petitions for them to have mercy on him and let him go back home; and he used to say that he had spent some two hundred rubles on telegrams alone. He sold his land and mortgaged his house to the Jews. He grew gray and bent, and yellow in the face, as though he was in consumption. If he talked to you he would go, khee—khee—khee, . . . and there were tears in his eyes. He kept rushing about like this with petitions for eight years, but now he has grown brighter and more cheerful again: he has found another whim to give way to. You see, his daughter has grown up. He looks at her, and she is the apple of his eye. And to tell the truth she is all right, good-looking, with black eyebrows and a lively disposition. Every Sunday he used to ride with her to church in Gyrino. They used to stand on the ferry, side by side, she would laugh and he could not take his eyes off her. 'Yes, Semyon,' says he, 'people can live even in Siberia. Even in Siberia there is happiness. Look,' says he, 'what a daughter I have got! I warrant you wouldn't find another like her for a thousand versts round.' 'Your daughter is all right,' says I, 'that's true, certainly.' But to myself I thought: 'Wait a bit, the wench is young, her blood is dancing, she wants to live, and there is no life here.' And she did begin to pine, my lad. . . . She faded and faded, and now she can hardly crawl about. Consumption.

"So you see what Siberian happiness is, damn its soul! You see how people can live in Siberia. . . . He has taken to going from one doctor to another and taking them home with him. As soon as he hears that two or three hundred miles away there is a doctor or a sorcerer, he will drive to fetch him. A terrible lot of money he spent on doctors, and to my thinking he had better have spent the money on drink. . . . She'll die just the same. She is certain to die, and then it will be all over with him. He'll hang himself from grief or run away to Russia—that's a sure thing. He'll run away and they'll catch him, then he will be tried, sent to prison, he will have a taste of the lash. . . ."

"Good! Good!" said the Tatar, shivering with cold.

"What is good?" asked Preacher.

"His wife, his daughter. . . . What of prison and what of sorrow! —anyway, he did see his wife and his daughter. . . . You say, want nothing. But 'nothing' is bad! His wife lived with him three years— that was a gift from God. 'Nothing' is bad, but three years is good. How not understand?"

Shivering and hesitating, with effort picking out the Russian words of which he knew but few, the Tatar said that God forbid one should fall sick and die in a strange land, and be buried in the cold and dark earth; that if his wife came to him for one day, even for one hour, that for such happiness he would be ready to bear any suffering and to thank God. Better one day of happiness than nothing.

Then he described again what a beautiful and clever wife he had left at home. Then, clutching his head in both hands, he began crying and assuring Semyon that he was not guilty, and was suffering for nothing. His two brothers and an uncle had carried off a peasant's horses, and had beaten the old man till he was half dead, and the peasant commune had not judged fairly, but had contrived a sentence by which all the three brothers were sent to Siberia, while the uncle, a rich man, was left at home.

"You will get used to it!" said Semyon.

The Tatar was silent, and stared with tear-stained eyes at the fire; his face expressed bewilderment and fear, as though he still did not understand why he was here in the darkness and the wet, beside strangers, and not in the Simbirsk province.

Preacher lay near the fire, chuckled at something, and began humming a song in an undertone.

"What joy has she with her father?" he said a little later. "He loves her and he rejoices in her, that's true; but, mate, you must mind your p's and q's with him, he is a strict old man, a harsh old man. And young wenches don't want strictness. They want petting and ha-ha-ha! and ho-ho-ho! and scent and pomade. Yes. . . . Ech! life, life," sighed Semyon, and he got up heavily. "The vodka is all gone, so it is time to sleep. Eh? I am going, my lad. . . ."

Left alone, the Tatar put on more twigs, lay down and stared at the fire; he began thinking of his own village and of his wife. If his wife could only come for a month, for a day; and then if she liked she might go back again. Better a month or even a day than nothing. But if his wife kept her promise and came, what would he have to feed her on? Where could she live here?

"If there were not something to eat, how could she live?" the Tatar asked aloud.

He was paid only ten kopeks for working all day and all night at the oar; it is true that travelers gave him tips for tea and for vodka, but the men shared all they received among themselves, and gave nothing to the Tatar, but only laughed at him. And from poverty he was hungry, cold, and frightened. . . . Now, when his whole body was aching and shivering, he ought to go into the hut and lie down to sleep; but he had nothing to cover him there, and it was colder than on the riverbank; here he had nothing to cover him either, but at least he could make up the fire. . . .

In another week, when the floods were quite over and they set the ferry going, none of the ferrymen but Semyon would be wanted, and the Tatar would begin going from village to village begging for alms and for work. His wife was only seventeen; she was beautiful, spoiled, and shy; could she possibly go from village to village begging alms with her face unveiled? No, it was terrible even to think of that. . . .

It was already getting light; the barge, the bushes of willow on the water, and the waves could be clearly discerned, and if one looked round there was the steep clay slope; at the bottom of it the hut thatched with dingy brown straw, and the huts of the village lay clustered higher up. The cocks were already crowing in the village.

The rusty red clay slope, the barge, the river, the strange, unkind people, hunger, cold, illness, perhaps all that was not real. Most likely it was all a dream, thought the Tatar. He felt that he was asleep and heard his own snoring. . . . Of course he was at home in Simbirsk province, and he had only to call his wife by name for her to answer; and in the next room was his mother. . . . What terrible dreams there are, though! What are they for? The Tatar smiled and opened his eyes. What river was this, the Volga?

Snow was falling.

"Boat!" was shouted on the further side. "Boat!"

The Tatar woke up, and went to wake his mates and row over to the other side. The ferrymen came on to the riverbank, putting on their torn sheepskins as they walked, swearing with voices husky from sleepiness and shivering from the cold. On waking from their sleep, the river, from which came a breath of piercing cold, seemed to strike them as revolting and horrible. They jumped into the barge without hurrying themselves. . . . The Tatar and the three ferrymen took the long, broad-bladed oars, which in the darkness looked like the claws of crabs; Semyon leaned his stomach against the tiller. The shout on the other side still continued, and the two shots were fired from a revolver, probably with the idea that the ferrymen were asleep or had gone to the tavern in the village.

"All right, you have plenty of time," said Semyon in the tone of a man convinced that there was no necessity in this world to hurry—that it would lead to nothing, anyway.

The heavy, clumsy barge moved away from the bank and floated between the willow-bushes, and only the willows slowly moving back showed that the barge was not standing still but moving. The ferrymen swung the oars evenly in time; Semyon lay with his stomach on the tiller and, describing a semicircle in the air, flew from one side to the other. In the darkness it looked as though the men were sitting on some antediluvian animal with long paws, and were moving on it through a cold, desolate land, the land of which one sometimes dreams in nightmares.

They passed beyond the willows and floated out into the open. The creak and regular splash of the oars was heard on the further shore, and a shout came: "Make haste! make haste!"

Another ten minutes passed, and the barge banged heavily against the landing-stage.

"And it keeps sprinkling and sprinkling," muttered Semyon, wiping the snow from his face; "and where it all comes from God only knows."

On the bank stood a thin man of medium height, in a jacket lined with fox-fur and in a white lambskin cap. He was standing at a little distance from his horses and not moving; he had a gloomy, concentrated expression, as though he were trying to remember something and was angry with his untrustworthy memory. When Semyon went up to him and took off his cap, smiling, he said:

"I am hastening to Anastasyevka. My daughter's worse again, and they say that there is a new doctor at Anastasyevka."

They dragged the carriage on to the barge and floated back. The man whom Semyon addressed as Vassily Sergeyich stood all the time motionless, tightly compressing his thick lips and staring off into space; when his coachman asked permission to smoke in his presence he made no answer, as though he had not heard. Semyon, lying with his stomach on the tiller, looked mockingly at him and said:

"Even in Siberia people can live—can li-ive!"

There was a triumphant expression on Preacher's face, as though he had proved something and was delighted that things had happened as he had foretold. The unhappy helplessness of the man in the foxskin coat evidently afforded him great pleasure.

"It's muddy driving now, Vassily Sergeyich," he said when the horses were harnessed again on the bank. "You should have put off going for another fortnight, when it will be drier. Or else not have gone at all. . . . If any good would come of your going—but as you know yourself, people have been driving about for years and years, day and night, and it's always been no use. That's the truth."

Vassily Sergeyich tipped him without a word, got into his carriage and drove off.

"There, he has galloped off for a doctor!" said Semyon, shrinking from the cold. "But looking for a good doctor is like chasing the wind in the fields or catching the Devil by the tail, plague take your soul! What a queer chap, Lord forgive me a sinner!"

The Tatar went up to Preacher, and, looking at him with hatred and repulsion, shivering, and mixing Tatar words with his broken Russian, said: "He is good . . . good; but you are bad! You are bad! The gentleman is a good soul, excellent, and you are a beast, bad! The gentleman is alive, but you are a dead carcass. . . . God created man to be alive, and to have joy and grief and sorrow; but you want nothing, so you are not alive, you are stone, clay! A stone wants nothing and you want nothing. You are a stone, and God does not love you, but He loves the gentleman!"

Everyone laughed; the Tatar frowned contemptuously, and with a wave of his hand wrapped himself in his rags and went to the campfire. The ferrymen and Semyon sauntered to the hut.

"It's cold," said one ferryman huskily as he stretched himself on the straw with which the damp clay floor was covered.

"Yes, it's not warm," another assented. "It's a dog's life. . . ."

They all lay down. The door was thrown open by the wind and the snow drifted into the hut; nobody felt inclined to get up and shut the door: they were cold, and it was too much trouble.

"I am all right," said Semyon as he began to doze. "I wouldn't wish anyone a better life."

"You are a tough one, we all know. Even the devils won't take you!"

Sounds like a dog's howling came from outside.

"What's that? Who's there?"

"It's the Tatar crying."

"I say. . . . He's a queer one!"

"He'll get u-used to it!" said Semyon, and at once fell asleep.

The others were soon asleep too. The door remained unclosed.

1892

Rothschild's Fiddle

It was a tiny town, worse than a village, inhabited chiefly by old people who so seldom died that it was really vexatious. Very few coffins were needed for the hospital and the jail; in a word, business was bad. If Yakov Ivanov had been a maker of coffins in the county town, he would probably have owned a house of his own by now, and would have been called Mr. Ivanov, but here in this little place he was simply called Yakov, and for some reason his nickname was Bronze. He lived as poorly as any common peasant in a little old hut of one room, in which he and Martha, and the stove, and a double bed, and the coffins, and his joiner's bench, and all the necessities of housekeeping were stowed away.

The coffins made by Yakov were serviceable and strong. For the peasants and townsfolk he made them to fit himself and never went wrong, for, although he was seventy years old, there was no man, not even in the prison, any taller or stouter than he was. For the gentry and for women he made them to measure, using an iron yardstick for the purpose. He was always very reluctant to take orders for children's coffins, and made them contemptuously without taking any measurements at all, always saying when he was paid for them:

"The fact is, I don't like to be bothered with trifles."

Beside what he received for his work as a joiner, he added a little to his income by playing the violin. There was a Jewish orchestra in the town that played for weddings, led by the tinsmith Moses Shakess, who took more than half of its earnings for himself. As Yakov played the fiddle extremely well, especially Russian songs, Shakess used sometimes to invite him to play in his orchestra for the sum of fifty kopeks a day, not including the presents he might receive from the guests. Whenever Bronze took his seat in the orchestra, the first thing that happened to him was that his face grew red, and the perspiration streamed from it, for the air was always hot, and reeking of garlic to the point of suffocation. Then his fiddle would begin to moan, and a double bass would croak hoarsely into his right ear, and a flute would weep into his left. This flute was played by a gaunt, red-bearded Jew with a network of red and blue veins on his face, who bore the name of a famous rich man, Rothschild. This confounded Jew always contrived to play even the merriest tunes sadly. For no obvious reason Yakov little by little began to conceive a feeling of hatred and contempt for all Jews, and especially for Rothschild. He quarreled with him and abused him in ugly language, and once even tried to beat him, but Rothschild took offense at this, and cried with a fierce look:

"If I had not always respected you for your music, I should have thrown you out of the window long ago!"

Then he burst into tears. So after that Bronze was not often invited to play in the orchestra, and was only called upon in cases of dire necessity, when one of the Jews was missing.

Yakov was never in a good humor, because he always had to endure the most terrible losses. For instance, it was a sin to work on a Sunday or a holiday, and Monday was always a bad day, so in that way there were about two hundred days a year in which he was compelled to sit with his hands folded in his lap. That was a great loss to him. If any one in town had a wedding without music, or if Shakess did not ask him to play, there was another loss. The police inspector had lain ill with consumption for two years while Yakov impatiently waited for him to die, and then had gone to take a cure in the city and had died there, which of course had meant another loss of at least ten rubles, as the coffin would have been an expensive one lined with brocade.

The thought of his losses worried Yakov at night more than at any other time, so he used to lay his fiddle at his side on the bed, and when those worries came trooping into his brain he would touch the strings, and the fiddle would give out a sound in the darkness, and Yakov's heart would feel lighter.

Last year on the sixth of May, Martha suddenly fell ill. The old woman breathed with difficulty, staggered in her walk, and felt terribly thirsty. Nevertheless, she got up that morning, lit the stove, and even went for the water. When evening came she went to bed. Yakov played his fiddle all day. When it grew quite dark, because he had nothing better to do, he took the book in which he kept an account of his losses, and began adding up the total for the year. They amounted to more than a thousand rubles. He was so shaken by this discovery that he threw the counting board on the floor and trampled in under foot. Then he picked it up again and rattled it once more for a long time, heaving as he did so sighs both deep and long. His face grew purple, and perspiration dripped from his brow. He was thinking that if those thousand rubles he had lost had been in the bank then, he would have had at least forty rubles interest by the end of the year. So those forty rubles were still another loss! In a word, wherever he turned he found losses and nothing but losses.

"Yakov!" cried Martha unexpectedly, "I am dying!"

He looked round at his wife. Her face was flushed with fever and looked unusually joyful and bright. Bronze was troubled, for he had been accustomed to seeing her pale and timid and unhappy. It seemed to him that she was actually dead, and glad to have left this hut, and the coffins, and Yakov at last. She was staring at the ceiling, with her lips moving as if she saw her deliverer Death approaching and were whispering with him.

The dawn was just breaking and the eastern sky was glowing with a faint radiance. As he stared at the old woman it somehow seemed to Yakov that he had never once spoken a tender word to her or pitied her; that he had never thought of buying her a kerchief or of bringing her back some sweets from a wedding. On the contrary, he had shouted at her and abused her for his losses, and had shaken his fist at her. It was true he had never beaten her, but he had frightened her no less, and she had been paralyzed with fear every time he had scolded her. Yes, and he had not allowed her to drink tea because his losses were heavy enough as it was, so she had had to be content with hot water. Now he understood why her face looked so strangely happy, and horror overwhelmed him.

As soon as it was light he borrowed a horse from a neighbor and took Martha to the hospital. As there were not many patients, he had not to wait very long—only about three hours. To his great satisfaction it was not the doctor who was receiving the sick that day, but his assistant, Maxim Nikolaich, an old man of whom it was said that although he quarreled and drank, he knew more than the doctor did.

"Good morning, Your Honor," said Yakov leading his old woman into the office. "Excuse us for intruding upon you with our trifling affairs. As you see, this subject has fallen ill. My life's friend, if you will allow me to use the expression——"

Knitting his gray eyebrows and stroking his whiskers, the doctor's assistant fixed his eyes on the old woman. She was sitting all in a heap on a low stool, and with her thin, long-nosed face and her open mouth, she looked like a thirsty bird.

"Well, well—yes—" said the doctor slowly, heaving a sigh. "This is a case of influenza and possibly fever; there is typhoid in town. What's to be done? The old woman has lived her span of years, thank God. How old is she?"

"She lacks one year of being seventy, Your Honor."

"Well, well, she has lived long. There must come an end to everything."

"You are certainly right, Your Honor," said Yakov, smiling out of politeness. "And we thank you sincerely for your kindness, but allow me to suggest to you that even an insect dislikes to die!"

"Never mind if it does!" answered the doctor, as if the life or death of the old woman lay in his hands. "I'll tell you what you must do, my good man. Put a cold bandage around her head, and give her two of these powders a day. Now then, good-bye! *Bonjour!*"

Yakov saw by the expression on the doctor's face that it was too late now for powders. He realized clearly that Martha must die very soon, if not today, then tomorrow. He touched the doctor's elbow gently, blinked, and whispered:

"She ought to be cupped, doctor!"

"I haven't time, I haven't time, my good man. Take your old woman and go, in God's name. Good-bye."

"Please, please, cup her, doctor!" begged Yakov. "You know yourself that if she had a pain in her stomach, powders and drops would do her good, but she has a cold! The first thing to do when one catches cold is to let some blood, doctor!"

But the doctor had already sent for the next patient, and a woman leading a little boy came into the room.

"Go along, go along!" he cried to Yakov, frowning. "It's no use making a fuss!"

"Then at least put some leeches on her! Let me pray to God for you for the rest of my life!"

The doctor's temper flared up and he shouted:

"Don't say another word to me, blockhead!"

Yakov lost his temper, too, and flushed hotly, but he said nothing and, silently taking Martha's arm, led her out of the office. Only when they were once more seated in their wagon did he look fiercely and mockingly at the hospital and say:

"They're a pretty lot in there, they are! That doctor would have cupped a rich man, but he even begrudged a poor one a leech. The pig!"

When they returned to the hut, Martha stood for nearly ten minutes supporting herself by the stove. She felt that if she lay down Yakov would begin to talk to her about his losses, and would scold her for lying down and not wanting to work. Yakov contemplated her sadly, thinking that tomorrow was St. John the Baptist's day, and day after tomorrow was St. Nicholas the Wonder-Worker's day, and that the following day would be Sunday, and the day after that would be Monday, a bad day for work. So he would not be able to work for four days, and as Martha would probably die on one of these days, the coffin would have to be made at once. He took his iron yardstick in hand, went up to the old woman, and measured her. Then she lay down, and he crossed himself and went to work on the coffin.

When the task was completed Bronze put on his spectacles and wrote in his book:

"For 1 coffin for Martha Ivanov—2 rubles, 40 kopeks."

He sighed. All day the old woman lay silent with closed eyes, but toward evening, when the daylight began to fade, she suddenly called the old man to her side.

"Do you remember, Yakov?" she asked. "Do you remember how fifty years ago God gave us a little baby with curly golden hair? Do you remember how you and I used to sit on the bank of the river and sing songs under the willow tree?" Then with a bitter smile she added: "The baby died."

Yakov racked his brains, but for the life of him he could not recall the child or the willow tree.

"You are dreaming," he said.

The priest came and administered the Sacrament and Extreme Unction. Then Martha began muttering unintelligibly, and toward morning she died.

The neighboring old women washed her and dressed her, and laid her in her coffin. To avoid paying the deacon, Yakov read the psalms over her himself, and her grave cost him nothing as the watchman of the cemetery was his cousin. Four peasants carried the coffin to the grave, not for money but for love. The old women, the beggars, and two village idiots followed the body, and the people whom they passed on the way crossed themselves devoutly. Yakov was very glad that everything had passed off so nicely and decently and cheaply, without giving offense to any one. As he said farewell to Martha for the last time he touched the coffin with his hand and thought:

"That's a fine job!"

But walking homeward from the cemetery he was seized with great distress. He felt ill, his breath was burning hot, his legs grew weak, and he longed for a drink. Beside this, a thousand thoughts came crowding into his head. He remembered again that he had never once pitied Martha or said a tender word to her. The fifty years of their life together lay stretched far, far behind him, and somehow, during all that time, he had never once thought about her at all or noticed her more than if she had been a dog or a cat. And yet she had lit the stove every day, and had cooked and baked and fetched water and chopped wood, and when he had come home drunk from a wedding she had hung his fiddle reverently on a nail each time, and had silently put him to bed with a timid, anxious look on her face.

But here came Rothschild toward him, bowing and scraping and smiling.

"I have been looking for you, uncle!" he said. "Moses Shakess presents his compliments and wants you to go to him at once."

Yakov did not feel in a mood to do anything. He wanted to cry.

"Leave me alone!" he exclaimed, and walked on.

"Oh, how can you say that?" cried Rothschild, running beside him in alarm. "Moses will be very angry. He wants you to come at once!"

Yakov was disgusted by the panting of the Jew, by his blinking eyes, and by the quantities of reddish freckles on his face. He looked with aversion at his long green coat and at the whole of his frail, delicate figure.

"What do you mean by pestering me, garlic?" he shouted. "Get away!"

The Jew grew angry and shouted back:

"Don't yell at me like that or I'll send you flying over that fence!"

"Get out of my sight!" bellowed Yakov, shaking his fist at him. "There's no living in the same town with mangy curs like you!"

Rothschild was petrified with terror. He sank to the ground and waved his hands over his head as if to protect himself from falling blows; then he jumped up and ran away as fast as his legs could carry him. As he ran he leaped and waved his arms, and his long, gaunt back could be seen quivering. The little boys were delighted at what had happened, and ran after him screaming: "Jew, Jew!" The dogs also joined barking in the chase. Somebody laughed and then whistled, at which the dogs barked louder and more vigorously than ever.

Then one of them must have bitten Rothschild, for a piteous, despairing scream rent the air.

Yakov walked across the common to the edge of the town without knowing where he was going, and the little boys shouted after him. "There goes old man Bronze! There goes old man Bronze!" He found himself by the river where the snipe were darting about with shrill cries, and the ducks were quacking and swimming to and fro. The sun was shining fiercely and the water was sparkling so brightly that it was painful to look at. Yakov struck into a path that led along the riverbank. He came to a stout, red-cheeked woman just leaving a bath-house. "Aha, you otter, you!" he thought. Not far from the bath-house some little boys were fishing for crabs with pieces of meat. When they saw Yakov they shouted mischievously: "Old man Bronze! Old man Bronze!" But there before him stood an ancient, spreading willow tree with a massive trunk, and a crow's nest among its branches. Suddenly there flashed across Yakov's memory with all the vividness of life a little child with golden curls, and the willow of which Martha had spoken. Yes, this was the same tree, so green and peaceful and sad. How old it had grown, poor thing!

He sat down at its foot and thought of the past. On the opposite shore, where that meadow now was, there had stood in those days a wood of tall birch-trees, and that bare hill on the horizon yonder had been covered with the blue bloom of an ancient pine forest. And sailboats had plied the river then, but now all lay smooth and still, and only one little birch-tree was left on the opposite bank, a graceful young thing, like a girl, while on the river there swam only ducks and geese. It was hard to believe that boats had once sailed there. It even seemed to him that there were fewer geese now than there had been. Yakov shut his eyes, and one by one white geese came flying toward him, an endless flock.

He was puzzled to know why he had never once been down to the river during the last forty or fifty years of his life, or, if he had been there, why he had never paid any attention to it. The stream was fine and large; he might have fished in it and sold the fish to the merchants and the government officials and the restaurant-keeper at the station, and put the money in the bank. He might have rowed in a boat from farm to farm and played on his fiddle. People of every rank would have paid him money to hear him. He might have tried to run a boat on the river, that would have been better than making coffins. Finally, he might have raised geese, and killed them, and sent them to Moscow in the winter. Why, the down alone would have brought him ten rubles a year! But he had missed all these chances and had done nothing. What losses were here! Ah, what terrible losses! And, oh, if he had only done all these things at the same time! If he had only fished, and played the fiddle, and sailed a boat, and raised geese, what capital he would have had by now! But he had not even dreamed of doing all this; his life had gone by without profit or pleasure. It had been lost for nothing, not even a trifle. Nothing was left ahead; behind lay only losses, and such terrible losses that he shuddered to think of them. But why shouldn't men live so as to avoid all this waste and these losses? Why, oh why, should those birch and pine forests have been felled? Why should those meadows be lying so deserted? Why did people always do exactly what they ought not to do? Why had Yakov scolded and growled and clenched his fists and hurt his wife's feelings all his life? Why, oh why, had he frightened and insulted that Jew just now? Why did people in general always interfere with one another? What losses resulted from this! What terrible losses! If it were not for envy and anger they would get great profit from one another.

All that evening and night Yakov dreamed of the child, of the willow tree, of the fish and the geese, of Martha with her profile like a thirsty bird, and of Rothschild's pale, piteous mien. Queer faces seemed to be moving toward him from all sides, muttering to him about his losses. He tossed from side to side, and got up five times during the night to play his fiddle.

He rose with difficulty next morning, and walked to the hospital. The same doctor's assistant ordered him to put cold bandages on his head, and gave him little powders to take; by his expression and the tone of his voice Yakov knew that the state of affairs was bad, and that no powders could save him now. As he walked home he reflected that one good thing would result from his death: he would no longer have to eat and drink and pay taxes, neither would he offend people anymore, and, as a man lies in his grave for hundreds of thousands of years, the sum of his profits would be immense. So, life to a man was a loss—death, a gain. Of course this reasoning was correct, but it was also distressingly sad. Why should the world be so strangely arranged that a man's life, which was only given to him once, must pass without profit?

He was not sorry then that he was going to die, but when he reached home, and saw his fiddle, his heart ached, and he regretted it deeply. He would not be able to take his fiddle with him into the grave, and now it would be left an orphan, and its fate would be that of the birch grove and the pine forest. Everything in the world had been lost, and would always be lost for ever. Yakov went out and sat on the threshold of his hut, clasping his fiddle to his breast. And as he thought of his life so full of waste and losses he began playing without knowing how piteous and touching his music was, and the tears streamed down his cheeks. And the more he thought the more sorrowfully sang his violin.

The latch clicked and Rothschild came in through the garden gate, and walked boldly halfway across the garden. Then he suddenly stopped, crouched down, and, probably from fear, began making signs with his hands as if he were trying to show on his fingers what time it was.

"Come on, don't be afraid!" said Yakov gently, beckoning him to advance. "Come on!"

With many mistrustful and fearful glances Rothschild went slowly up to Yakov, and stopped about two yards away.

"Please don't beat me!" he said with a ducking bow. "Moses Shakess has sent me to you again. 'Don't be afraid,' he said, 'go to Yakov,' says he, 'and say that we can't possibly manage without him.' There is a wedding next Thursday. Ye-es sir. Mr. Shapovalov is marrying his daughter to a very fine man. It will be an expensive wedding, ai, ai!" added the Jew with a wink.

"I can't go" said Yakov breathing hard. "I'm ill, brother."

And he began to play again, and the tears gushed out of his eyes over his fiddle. Rothschild listened intently with his head turned away and his arms folded on his breast. The startled, irresolute look on his face gradually gave way to one of suffering and grief. He cast up his eyes as if in an ecstasy of agony and murmured: "Okh—okh!" And the tears began to trickle slowly down his cheeks, and to drip over his green coat.

All day Yakov lay and suffered. When the priest came in the evening to administer the Sacrament he asked him if he could not think of any particular sin.

Struggling with his fading memories, Yakov recalled once more Martha's sad face, and the despairing cry of the Jew when the dog had bitten him. He murmured almost inaudibly:

"Give my fiddle to Rothschild."

"It shall be done," answered the priest.

So it happened that everyone in the little town began asking:

"Where did Rothschild get that good fiddle? Did he buy it or steal it or get it out of a pawnshop?"

Rothschild has long since abandoned his flute, and now only plays on the violin. The same mournful notes flow from under his bow that used to come from his flute, and when he tries to repeat what Yakov played as he sat on the threshold of his hut, the result is an air so plaintive and sad that everyone who hears him weeps, and he himself at last raises his eyes and murmurs: "Okh—okh!"

And this new song has so delighted the town that the merchants and government officials vie with each other in getting Rothschild to come to their houses, and sometimes make him play it ten times in succession.

1894

The Student

At first the weather was fine and still. The thrushes were calling, and in the swamps close by something alive droned pitifully with a sound like blowing into an empty bottle. A snipe flew by, and the shot aimed at it rang out with a gay, resounding note in the spring air. But when it began to get dark in the forest a cold, penetrating wind blew inappropriately from the east, and everything sank into silence. Needles of ice stretched across the pools, and it felt cheerless, remote, and lonely in the forest. There was a whiff of winter.

Ivan Velikopolsky, the son of a sacristan, and a student of the clerical academy, returning home from shooting, kept walking on the path by the water-logged meadows. His fingers were numb and his face was burning with the wind. It seemed to him that the cold that had suddenly come on had destroyed the order and harmony of things, that nature itself felt ill at ease, and that was why the evening darkness was falling more rapidly than usual. All around it was deserted and peculiarly gloomy. The only light was one gleaming in the widows' gardens near the river; the village, over three miles away, and everything in the distance all round was plunged in the cold evening mist. The student remembered that, as he had left the house, his mother was sitting barefoot on the floor in the entryway, cleaning the samovar, while his father lay on the stove coughing; as it was Good Friday nothing had been cooked, and the student was terribly hungry. And now, shrinking from the cold, he thought that just such a wind had blown in the days of Rurik[1] and in the time of Ivan the Terrible and Peter, and in their time there had been just the same desperate poverty and hunger, the same thatched roofs with holes in them, ignorance, misery, the same desolation around, the same darkness, the same feeling of oppression—all these had existed, did exist, and would exist, and the lapse of a thousand years would make life no better. And he did not want to go home.

The gardens were called the widows' because they were kept by two widows, mother and daughter. A campfire was burning brightly with a crackling sound, throwing out light far around on the ploughed earth. The widow Vasilisa, a tall, fat old woman in a man's coat, was standing by and looking thoughtfully into the fire;

1. The first ruler of Russia, 862–879.

her daughter Lukerya, a little pockmarked woman with a stupid-looking face, was sitting on the ground, washing a cauldron and spoons. Apparently they had just had supper. There was a sound of men's voices; it was the laborers watering their horses at the river.

"Here you have winter back again," said the student, going up to the campfire. "Good evening."

Vasilisa started, but at once recognized him and smiled cordially.

"I did not know you; God bless you," she said. "You'll be rich."

They talked. Vasilisa, a woman of experience who had been in service with the gentry, first as a wet-nurse, afterwards as a children's nurse expressed herself with refinement, and a soft, sedate smile never left her face; her daughter Lukerya, a village peasant woman who had been beaten by her husband, simply screwed up her eyes at the student and said nothing, and she had a strange expression like that of a deaf-mute.

"At just such a fire the Apostle Peter warmed himself," said the student, stretching out his hands to the fire, "so it must have been cold then, too. Ah, what a terrible night it must have been, granny! An utterly dismal long night!"

He looked round at the darkness, shook his head abruptly and asked:

"No doubt you have heard the reading of the Twelve Apostles?"

"Yes, I have," answered Vasilisa.

"If you remember, at the Last Supper Peter said to Jesus, 'I am ready to go with Thee into darkness and unto death.' And our Lord answered him thus: 'I say unto thee, Peter, before the cock croweth thou wilt have denied Me thrice.' After the supper Jesus went through the agony of death in the garden and prayed, and poor Peter was weary in spirit and faint, his eyelids were heavy and he could not struggle against sleep. He fell asleep. Then you heard how Judas the same night kissed Jesus and betrayed Him to His tormentors. They took Him bound to the high priest and beat Him, while Peter, exhausted, worn out with misery and alarm, hardly awake, you know, feeling that something awful was just going to happen on earth, followed behind. . . . He loved Jesus passionately, intensely, and now he saw from far off how He was beaten. . . ."

Lukerya left the spoons and fixed an immovable stare upon the student.

"They came to the high priest's," he went on; "they began to question Jesus, and meantime the laborers made a fire in the yard as it was cold, and warmed themselves. Peter, too, stood with them near the fire and warmed himself as I am doing. A woman, seeing him, said: 'He was with Jesus, too'—that is as much as to say that he, too, should be taken to be questioned. And all the laborers that were standing near the fire must have looked sourly and suspiciously at him, because he was confused and said: 'I don't know Him.' A little while after again someone recognized him as one of

Jesus' disciples and said: 'Thou, too, art one of them,' but again he denied it. And for the third time someone turned to him: 'Why, did I not see thee with Him in the garden today?' For the third time he denied it. And immediately after that time the cock crowed, and Peter, looking from afar off at Jesus, remembered the words He had said to him in the evening. . . . He remembered, he came to himself, went out of the yard and wept bitterly—bitterly. In the Gospel it is written: 'He went out and wept bitterly.' I imagine it: the still, still, dark, dark garden, and in the stillness, faintly audible, smothered sobbing. . . ."

The student sighed and sank into thought. Still smiling, Vasilisa suddenly gave a gulp, big tears flowed freely down her cheeks, and she screened her face from the fire with her sleeve as though ashamed of her tears, and Lukerya, staring immovably at the student, flushed crimson, and her expression became strained and heavy like that of someone enduring intense pain.

The laborers came back from the river, and one of them riding a horse was quite near, and the light from the fire quivered upon him. The student said good-night to the widows and went on. And again the darkness was about him and his fingers began to be numb. A cruel wind was blowing, winter really had come back and it did not feel as though Easter would be the day after tomorrow.

Now the student was thinking about Vasilisa: since she had shed tears all that had happened to Peter the night before the Crucifixion must have some relation to her. . . .

He looked round. The solitary light was still gleaming in the darkness and no figures could be seen near it now. The student thought again that if Vasilisa had shed tears, and her daughter had been troubled, it was evident that what he had just been telling them about, which had happened nineteen centuries ago, had a relation to the present—to both women, to the desolate village, to himself, to all people. The old woman had wept, not because he could tell the story touchingly, but because Peter was near to her, because her whole being was interested in what was passing in Peter's soul.

And joy suddenly stirred in his soul, and he even stopped for a minute to take breath. "The past," he thought, "is linked with the present by an unbroken chain of events flowing one out of another." And it seemed to him that he had just seen both ends of that chain; that when he touched one end the other quivered.

When he crossed the river by the ferryboat and afterwards, mounting the hill, looked at his village and towards the west where the cold crimson sunset lay a narrow streak of light, he thought that truth and beauty which had guided human life there in the garden and in the yard of the high priest had continued without interruption to this day, and had evidently always been the chief thing in human life and in all earthly life, indeed; and the feeling of youth, health, vigor—he was only twenty-two—and the inexpressible sweet expectation of happiness, of unknown mysterious happiness, took possession of him little by little, and life seemed to him enchanting, marvellous, and full of lofty meaning.

1894

The Teacher of Literature[1]

I

There was the thud of horses' hoofs on the wooden floor; they brought out of the stable the black horse, Count Nulin;[2] then the white, Giant; then his sister Maika. They were all magnificent, expensive horses. Old Shelestov saddled Giant and said, addressing his daughter Masha:

"Well, Maria Godefroy,[3] come, get on! Hopla!"

Masha Shelestov was the youngest of the family; she was eighteen, but her family could not get used to thinking that she was not a little girl, and so they still called her Manya and Manyusa; and after there had been a circus in the town which she had eagerly visited, everyone began to call her Maria Godefroy.

"Hop-la!" she cried, mounting Giant. Her sister Varya got on Maika, Nikitin on Count Nulin, the officers on their horses, and the long picturesque cavalcade, with the officers in white tunics and the ladies in their riding habits, moved at a walking pace out of the yard.

Nikitin noticed that when they were mounting the horses and afterwards riding out into the street, Masha for some reason paid attention to no one but himself. She looked anxiously at him and at Count Nulin and said:

"You must hold him on the curb all the time, Sergey Vassilich. Don't let him shy. He's pretending."

And either because her Giant was very friendly with Count Nulin, or perhaps by chance, she rode all the time beside Nikitin, as she had done the day before, and the day before that. And he looked at her graceful little figure sitting on the proud white beast, at her delicate profile, at the chimney-pot hat, which did not suit her at all and made her look older than her age—looked at her with joy, with tenderness, with rapture; listened to her, taking in little of what she said, and thought:

1. The first chapter appeared as a story entitled *The Philistines* (*Obyvateli*) in 1889. The second was published in 1894. (See Chekhov's letter to Suvorin, November 12, 1889.)
2. "Count Zero"—after Pushkin's jocular satirical poem of 1825.
3. A famous bareback rider of the time.

"I promise on my honor, I swear to God, I won't be afraid and I'll speak to her today."

It was seven o'clock in the evening—the time when the scent of white acacia and lilac is so strong that the air and the very trees seem heavy with the fragrance. The band was already playing in the town gardens. The horses made a resounding thud on the pavement, on all sides there were sounds of laughter, talk, and the banging of gates. The soldiers they met saluted the officers, the schoolboys bowed to Nikitin, and all the people who were hurrying to the gardens to hear the band were pleased at the sight of the party. And how warm it was! How soft-looking were the clouds scattered carelessly about the sky, how kindly and comforting the shadows of the poplars and the acacias, which stretched across the street and reached as far as the balconies and second stories of the houses on the other side.

They rode on out of town and set off at a trot along the highroad. Here there was no scent of lilac and acacia, no music of the band, but there was the fragrance of the fields, there was the green of young rye and wheat, the marmots were squeaking, the rooks were cawing. Wherever one looked it was green, with only here and there black patches of bare ground, and far away to the left in the cemetery a white streak of faded apple-blossom.

They passed the slaughterhouses, then the brewery, and overtook a military band hastening to the suburban gardens.

"Polyansky has a very fine horse, I don't deny that," Masha said to Nikitin, with a glance towards the officer who was riding beside Varya. "But it has blemishes. That white patch on its left leg ought not to be there, and, look, it tosses its head. You can't train it not to now; it will toss its head till the end of its days."

Masha was as passionate a lover of horses as her father. She felt a pang when she saw other people with fine horses, and was pleased when she saw defects in them. Nikitin knew nothing about horses; it made absolutely no difference to him whether he held his horse on the bridle or on the curb, whether he trotted or galloped; he only felt that his position was strained and unnatural, and that consequently the officers who knew how to sit in their saddles must please Masha more than he could. And he was jealous of the officers.

As they rode by the suburban gardens someone suggested their going in and getting some seltzer-water. They went in. There were no trees but oaks in the gardens; they had only just come into leaf, so that through the young foliage the whole garden could still be seen with its platform, little tables, and swings, and the crows' nests were visible, looking like big hats. The party dismounted near a table and asked for seltzer-water. People they knew, walking about the garden, came up to them. Among them were the army doctor, in high boots, and the conductor of the band, waiting for the musicians. The doctor must have taken Nikitin for a student, for he asked:

"Have you come for the summer holidays?"

"No, I am here permanently," asked Nikitin. "I am a teacher at the school."

"You don't say so?" said the doctor, with surprise. "So young and already a teacher?"

"Young, indeed! My goodness, I'm twenty-six!"

"You have a beard and moustache, but yet one would never guess you were more than twenty-two or twenty-three. How young-looking you are!"

"What a beast!" thought Nikitin. "He, too, takes me for a whippersnapper!"

He disliked it extremely when people referred to his youth, especially in the presence of women or the schoolboys. Ever since he had come to the town as a master in the school he had detested his own youthful appearance. The schoolboys were not afraid of him, old people called him "young man," ladies preferred dancing with him to listening to his long arguments, and he would have given a great deal to be ten years older.

From the garden they went on to the Shelestovs' farm. There they stopped at the gate and asked the bailiff's wife, Praskovya, to bring some fresh milk. Nobody drank the milk; they all looked at one another, laughed, and galloped back. As they rode back the band was playing in the suburban garden; the sun was setting behind the cemetery, and half the sky was crimson from the sunset.

Masha again rode beside Nikitin. He wanted to tell her how passionately he loved her, but he was afraid he would be overheard by the officers and Varya, and he was silent. Masha was silent, too, and he felt why she was silent and why she was riding beside him, and was so happy that the earth, the sky, the lights of the town, the black outline of the brewery—all blended for him into something very pleasant and comforting, and it seemed to him as though Count Nulin were stepping on air and would climb up into the crimson sky.

They arrived home. The samovar was already boiling on the table, old Shelestov was sitting with his friends, officials in the Circuit Court, and as usual he was criticizing something.

"It's loutishness!" he said. "Loutishness and nothing more. Yes!"

Since Nikitin had been in love with Masha, everything at the Shelestovs' pleased him: the house, the garden, and the evening tea, and the wickerwork chairs, and the old nurse, and even the word "loutishness," which the old man was fond of using. The only thing he did not like was the number of cats and dogs and the Egyptian pigeons, who moaned disconsolately in a big cage in the veranda. There were so many house-dogs and yard-dogs that he had learned to recognize only two of them in the course of his acquaintance with the Shelestovs: Mushka and Som. Mushka was a little mangy dog with a shaggy face, spiteful and spoiled. She hated Nikitin: when she saw him she put her head on one side, showed her teeth, and began to growl: "Rrr . . . ga-nga-nga . . . rrr . . . !" Then she would get under his chair, and when he would try to drive her away she would go off into piercing yaps, and the family would say: "Don't be frightened. She doesn't bite. She is a good dog."

Som was a tall black dog with long legs and a tail as hard as a stick. At dinner and tea he usually moved about under the table, and thumped on people's boots and on the legs of the table with his tail. He was a good-natured, stupid dog, but Nikitin could not endure him because he had the habit of putting his head on people's knees at dinner and messing their trousers with saliva. Nikitin had more than once tried to hit him on his head with a knife-handle, to flip him on the nose; he had abused him, had complained of him, but nothing saved his trousers.

After their ride the tea, jam, rusks, and butter seemed very nice. They all drank their first glass in silence and with great relish; over the second they began an argument. It was always Varya who started the arguments at tea; she was good-looking, handsomer than Masha, and was considered the cleverest and most cultured person in the house, and she behaved with dignity and severity, as an eldest daughter should who has taken the place of her dead mother in the house. As the mistress of the house, she felt herself entitled to wear a dressing-gown in the presence of her guests, and to call the officers by their surnames; she looked on Masha as a little girl, and talked to her as though she were a schoolmistress. She used to speak of herself as an old maid—so she was certain she would marry.

Every conversation, even about the weather, she invariably turned into an argument. She had a passion for catching at words, pouncing on contradictions, quibbling over phrases. You would begin talking to her, and she would stare at you and suddenly interrupt: "Excuse me, excuse me, Petrov, the other day you said the very opposite!"

Or she would smile ironically and say: "I notice, though, you begin to advocate the principles of the secret police. I congratulate you."

If you jested or made a pun, you would hear her voice at once: "That's stale," "That's pointless." If an officer ventured on a joke, she would make a contemptuous grimace and say, "An army joke!"

And she rolled the *r* so impressively that Mushka invariably answered from under a chair, "Rrr . . . nga-nga-nga . . . !"

On this occasion at tea the argument began with Nikitin's mentioning the school examinations.

"Excuse me, Sergey Vassilich," Varya interrupted him. "You say it's difficult for the boys. And whose fault is that, let me ask you? For instance, you set the boys in the eighth class an essay on 'Pushkin as a Psychologist.' To begin with, you shouldn't set such a difficult subject; and, secondly, Pushkin was not a psychologist. Shchedrin[4] now, or Dostoevsky let us say, is a different matter, but Pushkin is a great poet and nothing more."

"Shchedrin is one thing, and Pushkin is another," Nikitin answered sulkily.

"I know you don't think much of Shchedrin at the high school, but that's not the point. Tell me, in what sense is Pushkin a psychologist?"

"Why, do you mean to say he was not a psychologist? If you like, I'll give you examples."

And Nikitin recited several passages from *Onegin* and then from *Boris Godunov*.[5]

"I see no psychology in that." Varya sighed. "The psychologist is the man who describes the recesses of the human soul, and that's fine poetry and nothing more."

"I know the sort of psychology you want," said Nikitin, offended. "You want someone to saw my finger with a blunt saw while I howl at the top of my voice—that's what you mean by psychology."

"That's poor! But still you haven't shown me in what sense Pushkin is a psychologist."

When Nikitin had to argue against anything that seemed to him narrow, conventional, or something of that kind, he usually leaped up from his seat, clutched at his head with both hands, and began, with a moan, running from one end of the room to another. And it was the same now: he jumped up, clutched his head in his hands, and with a moan walked round the table; then he sat down a little way off.

The officers took his part. Captain Polyansky began assuring Varya that Pushkin really was a psychologist, and to prove it quoted two lines from Lermontov;[6] Lieutenant Gernet said that if Pushkin had not been a psychologist they would not have erected a monument to him in Moscow.

"That's loutishness!" was heard from the other end of the table. "I said as much to the governor: 'It's loutishness, Your Excellency,' I said."

"I won't argue anymore," cried Nikitin. "It's unending. . . . Enough! Ach, get away, you nasty dog!" he cried to Som, who laid his head and paw on his knee.

"Rrr . . . nga-nga-nga!" came from under the table.

4. Aleksandr Pushkin (1799–1837), Russia's greatest poet; M. E. Saltykov-Shchedrin (1826–1889), satirist and novelist.
5. Works by Pushkin: *Evgeny Onegin*, a "novel in verse"; *Boris Godunov*, a historical drama.
6. Mikhail Lermontov (1814–41), poet and novelist.

"Admit that you are wrong!" cried Varya. "Own up!"

But some young ladies came in, and the argument dropped of itself. They all went into the drawing-room. Varya sat down at the piano and began playing dances. They danced first a waltz, then a polka, then a quadrille with a grand chain which Captain Polyansky led through all the rooms, then a waltz again.

During the dancing the old men sat in the drawing-room, smoking and looking at the young people. Among them was Shebaldin, the director of the municipal bank, who was famed for his love of literature and dramatic art. He had founded the local Musical and Dramatic Society, and took part in the performances himself, confining himself, for some reason, to playing comic footmen or to reading in a sing-song voice *The Woman Sinner*.[7] His nickname in the town was "the Mummy," as he was tall, very lean and scraggy, and always had a solemn air and a fixed, lustreless eye. He was so devoted to the dramatic art that he even shaved his moustache and beard, and this made him still more like a mummy.

After the grand chain, he shuffled up to Nikitin sideways, coughed, and said:

"I had the pleasure of being present during the argument at tea. I fully share your opinion. We are of one mind, and it would be a great pleasure to me to talk to you. Have you read Lessing's *Hamburg Dramaturgy?*"[8]

"No, I haven't."

Shebaldin was horrified, and, waving his hands as though he had burned his fingers, and saying nothing more, he staggered back from Nikitin. Shebaldin's appearance, his question, and his surprise, struck Nikitin as funny, but he thought nonetheless:

"It really is awkward. I am a teacher of literature, and to this day I've not read Lessing. I must read him."

Before supper the whole company, old and young, sat down to play "fate." They took two packs of cards: one pack was dealt round to the company, the other was laid on the table face downwards.

"The one who has his card in his hand," old Shelestov began solemnly, lifting the top card of the second pack, "is fated to go into the nursery and kiss nurse."

The pleasure of kissing the nurse fell to the lot of Shebaldin. They all crowded around him, took him to the nursery, and laughing and clapping their hands, made him kiss the nurse. There was a great uproar and shouting.

"Not so ardently!" cried Shelestov with tears of laughter. "Not so ardently!"

7. *Greshnitsa*, a poem by Count A. K. Tolstoy (1858).
8. Gotthold Lessing's *Hamburgische*   *Dramaturgie* (1767–69) is a central text in dramatic theory and in modern theater.

It was Nikitin's "fate" to hear the confessions of all. He sat on a chair in the middle of the drawing-room. A shawl was brought and put over his head. The first who came to confess to him was Varya.

"I know your sins," Nikitin began, looking in the darkness at her stern profile. "Tell me, madam, how do you explain your walking with Polyansky every day? Oh, it's not for nothing she walks with an hussar!"[9]

"That's poor," said Varya, and walked away.

Then under the shawl he saw the shine of big motionless eyes, caught the lines of a dear profile in the dark, together with a familiar, precious fragrance which reminded Nikitin of Masha's room.

"Maria Godefroy," he said, and did not know his own voice, it was so soft and tender, "what are your sins?"

Masha screwed up her eyes and put out the tip of her tongue at him, then she laughed and went away. And a minute later she was standing in the middle of the room, clapping her hands and crying:

"Supper, supper, supper!"

And they all streamed into the dining-room. At supper Varya had another argument, and this time with her father. Polyansky ate stolidly, drank red wine, and described to Nikitin how once in a winter campaign he had stood all night up to his knees in a bog; the enemy was so near that they were not allowed to speak or smoke, the night was cold and dark, a piercing wind was blowing. Nikitin listened and stole side-glances at Masha. She was gazing at him immovably, without blinking, as though she was pondering something or was lost in a reverie. . . . It was pleasure and agony to him both at once.

"Why does she look at me like that?" was the question that fretted him. "It's awkward. People may notice it. Oh, how young, how naïve she is!"

The party broke up at midnight. When Nikitin went out at the gate, a window opened on the first floor, and Masha showed herself at it.

"Sergey Vassilich!" she called.

"What is it?"

"I tell you what . . ." said Masha, evidently thinking of something to say. "I tell you what. . . . Polyansky said he would come in a day or two with his camera and take us all. We must meet here."

"Very well."

Masha vanished, the window was slammed, and someone immediately began playing the piano in the house.

"Well, it is a house!" thought Nikitin while he crossed the street. "A house in which there is no moaning except from Egyptian

---

9. An inexact quotation of an epigram by Lermontov (1831).

pigeons, and they only do it because they have no other means of expressing their joy!"

But the Shelestovs were not the only festive household. Nikitin had not gone two hundred paces before he heard the strains of a piano from another house. A little further he met a peasant playing the balalaika at the gate. In the gardens the band struck up a potpourri of Russian songs.

Nikitin lived nearly half a mile from the Shelestovs' in a flat of eight rooms at the rent of three hundred rubles a year, which he shared with his colleague Ippolit Ippolitich, a teacher of geography and history. When Nikitin went in, this Ippolit Ippolitich, a snub-nosed, middle-aged man with a reddish beard and a coarse, good-natured, un-intellectual face like a workman's, was sitting at the table correcting his pupils' maps. He considered that the most important and necessary part of the study of geography was the drawing of maps, and of the study of history the learning of dates: he would sit for nights together correcting in blue pencil the maps drawn by the boys and girls he taught, or making chronological tables.

"What a lovely day it has been!" said Nikitin, going in to him. "I wonder at you—how can you sit indoors?"

Ippolit Ippolitich was not a talkative person; he either remained silent or talked of things which everybody knew already. Now what he answered was:

"Yes, very fine weather. It's May now; we soon shall have real summer. And summer's a very different thing from winter. In the winter you have to heat the stoves, but in summer you can keep warm without. In summer you have your window open at night and still are warm, and in winter you are cold even with the double frames in."

Nikitin had not sat at the table for more than one minute before he was bored.

"Good-night!" he said, getting up and yawning. "I wanted to tell you something romantic concerning myself, but you are—geography! If one talks to you of love, you will ask one at once, 'What was the date of the Battle of Kalka?'[1] Confound you, with your battles and your capes in Siberia!"

"What are you cross about?"

"Why, it is vexatious!"

And vexed that he had not spoken to Masha, and that he had no one to talk to of his love, he went to his study and lay down upon the sofa. It was dark and still in the study. Lying gazing into the darkness, Nikitin for some reason began thinking how in two or three years he would go to Petersburg, how Masha would see him

1. This battle occurred in 1228.

off at the station and would cry; in Petersburg he would get a long letter from her in which she would entreat him to come home as quickly as possible. And he would write to her. . . . He would begin his letter like that: "My dear little rat!"

"Yes, my dear little rat!" he said, and he laughed.

He was lying in an uncomfortable position. He put his arms under his lead and put his left leg over the back of the sofa. He felt more comfortable. Meanwhile a pale light was more and more perceptible at the windows, sleepy cocks crowed in the yard. Nikitin went on thinking how he would come back from Petersburg, how Masha would meet him at the station, and with a shriek of delight would fling herself on his neck; or, better still, he would surprise her and come home by stealth late at night: the cook would open the door, then he would go on tiptoe to the bedroom, undress noiselessly, and jump into bed! And she would wake up and be overjoyed.

It was beginning to get quite light. By now there were no windows, no study. On the steps of the brewery by which they had ridden that day Masha was sitting, saying something. Then she took Nikitin by the arm and went with him to the suburban garden. There he saw the oaks and the crows' nests like hats. One of the nests rocked; out of it peeped Shebaldin, shouting loudly: "You have not read Lessing!"

Nikitin shuddered all over and opened his eyes. Ippolit Ippolitich was standing before the sofa and, throwing back his head, was putting on his cravat.

"Get up; it's time for school," he said. "You shouldn't sleep in your clothes; it spoils your clothes. You should sleep in your bed, undressed."

And as usual he began slowly and emphatically saying what everybody knew.

Nikitin's first lesson was on Russian language in the second class. When at nine o'clock punctually he went into the classroom, he saw written on the blackboard two large letters—M. S. That, no doubt, meant Masha Shelestov.

"They've scented it out already, the rascals . . ." thought Nikitin. "How is it they know everything?"

The second lesson was in the fifth class. And there two letters, M. S., were written on the blackboard; and when he went out of the classroom at the end of the lesson, he heard the shout behind him as though from a theatre gallery:

"Hurrah for Masha Shelestov!"

His head was heavy from sleeping in his clothes, his limbs were weighted down with inertia. The boys, who were expecting every day to break up before the examinations, did nothing, were restless, and so bored that they got into mischief. Nikitin, too, was restless, did not notice their pranks, and was continually going to the window. He could see the street brilliantly lighted up with the sun; above the houses the blue limpid sky, the birds, and far, far away, beyond the gardens and the houses, vast indefinite distance, the forests in the blue haze, the smoke from a passing train. . . .

Here two officers in white tunics, playing with their whips, passed in the street in the shade of the acacias. Here a lot of Jews, with gray beards, and caps on, drove past in a wagonette. . . . The governess walked by with the director's granddaughter. Som ran by in the company of two other dogs. . . . And then Varya, wearing a simple gray dress and red stockings, carrying the *European Herald*[2] in her hand, passed by. She must have been to the town library. . . .

And it would be a long time before lessons were over at three o'clock! And after school he could not go home nor to the Shelestovs', but must go to give a lesson at Wolf's. This Wolf, a wealthy Jew who had turned Lutheran, did not send his children to the high school, but had them taught at home by the high-school masters, and paid five rubles a lesson.

He was bored, bored, bored.

At three o'clock he went to Wolf's and spent there, as it seemed to him, an eternity. He left there at five o'clock, and before seven he had to be at the high school again to a meeting of the masters—to draw up the plan for the oral examination of the fourth and sixth classes.

When late in the evening he left the high school and went to the Shelestovs', his heart was beating and his face was flushed. A month before, even a week before, he had, every time that he made up his mind to speak to her, prepared a whole speech, with an introduction and a conclusion. Now he had not one word ready; everything was in a muddle in his head, and all he knew was that today he would *certainly* declare himself, and that it was utterly impossible to wait any longer.

"I will ask her to come to the garden," he thought; "we'll walk about a little and I'll speak."

There was not a soul in the hall; he went into the dining-room and then into the drawing-room. . . . There was no one there either. He could hear Varya arguing with someone upstairs and the clink of the dressmaker's scissors in the nursery.

There was a little room in the house which had three names: the little room, the passage room, and the dark room. There was a big cupboard in it where they kept medicines, gunpowder, and their hunting gear. Leading from this room to the first floor was a narrow wooden staircase where cats were always asleep. There were two doors in it—one leading to the nursery, one to the drawing-room. When Nikitin went into this room to go upstairs, the door from the

2. A liberal monthly periodical.

nursery opened and shut with such a bang that it made the stairs and the cupboard tremble; Masha, in a dark dress, ran in with a piece of blue material in her hand, and, not noticing Nikitin, darted towards the stairs.

"Stay . . ." said Nikitin, stopping her. 'Good-evening, Godefroy. . . . Allow me. . . ."

He gasped, he did not know what to say; with one hand he held her hand and with the other the blue material. And she was half frightened, half surprised, and looked at him with big eyes.

"Allow me . . ." Nikitin went on, afraid she would go away. "There's something I must say to you. . . . Only . . . it's inconvenient here. I cannot, I am incapable. . . . Understand, Godefroy, I can't— that's all. . . ."

The blue material slipped onto the floor, and Nikitin took Masha by the other hand. She turned pale, moved her lips, then stepped back from Nikitin and found herself in the corner between the wall and the cupboard.

"On my honor, I assure you . . ." he said softly. "Masha, on my honor. . . ."

She threw back her head and he kissed her lips, and that the kiss might last longer he put his fingers to her cheeks; and it somehow happened that he found himself in the corner between the cupboard and the wall, and she put her arms round his neck and pressed her head against his chin.

Then they both ran into the garden. The Shelestovs had a garden of nine acres. There were a score of old maples and lime-trees in it; there was one fir-tree, and all the rest were fruit-trees: cherries, apples, pears, chestnuts, silvery olive-trees. . . . There were masses of flowers, too.

Nikitin and Masha ran along the avenues in silence, laughed, asked each other from time to time disconnected questions which they did not answer. A crescent moon was shining over the garden, and drowsy tulips and irises were stretching up from the dark grass in its faint light, as though begging for words of love for themselves, too.

When Nikitin and Masha went back to the house, the officers and the young ladies were already assembled and dancing the mazurka. Again Polyansky led the grand chain through all the rooms, again after dancing they played "fate." Before supper, when the visitors had gone into the dining-room, Masha, left alone with Nikitin, pressed close to him and said:

"You must speak to Papa and Varya yourself; I am embarrassed."

After supper he talked to the old father. After listening to him, Shelestov thought a little and said:

"I am very grateful for the honor you do me and my daughter, but let me speak to you as a friend. I will speak to you, not as a father, but as one gentleman to another. Tell me, why do you want to be married so young? Only peasants are married so young, and that, of course, is loutishness. But why should you? Where's the satisfaction of putting on the fetters at your age?"

"I am not young!" said Nikitin, offended. "I am in my twenty-seventh year."

"Papa, the farrier has come!" cried Varya from the other room.

And the conversation broke off. Varya, Masha, and Polyansky saw Nikitin home. When they reached his gate, Varya said:

"Why is it your mysterious Metropolit Metropolitich never shows himself anywhere? He might come and see us."

The mysterious Ippolit Ippolitich was sitting on his bed, taking off his trousers, when Nikitin went in to him.

"Don't go to bed, my dear fellow," said Nikitin breathlessly. "Stop a minute; don't go to bed!"

Ippolit Ippolitich put on his trousers hurriedly and asked in a flutter:

"What is it?"

"I am going to be married."

Nikitin sat down beside his companion and looking at him wonderingly, as though surprised at himself, said:

"Only fancy, I am going to be married! To Masha Shelestov! I made an offer today."

"Well? She seems a good sort of girl. Only she is very young."

"Yes, she is young," sighed Nikitin, and shrugged his shoulders with a careworn air. "Very, very young!"

"She was my pupil at the high school. I know her. She wasn't bad at geography, but she was no good at history. And she was inattentive in class, too."

Nikitin for some reason felt suddenly sorry for his companion, and longed to say something kind and comforting to him.

"My dear fellow, why don't you get married?" he asked. "Why don't you marry Varya, for instance? She is a splendid, first-rate girl! It's true she is very fond of arguing, but a heart . . . what a heart! She was just asking about you. Marry her, my dear boy! Eh?"

He knew perfectly well that Varya would not marry this dull, snub-nosed man, but still he urged him to marry her—why?

"Marriage is a serious step," said Ippolit Ippolitich after a moment's thought. "One has to look at it all round and weigh things thoroughly; it's not to be done rashly. Prudence is always a good thing, and especially in marriage, when a man, ceasing to be a bachelor, begins a new life."

And he talked of what everyone has known for ages. Nikitin did not stay to listen, said good-night, and went to his own room. He undressed quickly and quickly got into bed, in order to be able to think the sooner of his happiness, of Masha, of the future; he smiled, then suddenly recalled that he had not read Lessing.

"I must read him," he thought. "Though, after all, why should I? "To hell with him!"

And exhausted by his happiness, he fell asleep at once and went on smiling till the morning.

He dreamed of the thud of horses' hoofs on a wooden floor; he dreamed of the black horse Count Nulin, then of the white Giant and its sister Maika, being led out of the stable.

II

"It was very crowded and noisy in the church, and once someone cried out, and the head priest, who was marrying Masha and me, looked through his spectacles at the crowd, and said severely: 'Don't move about the church, and don't make a noise, but stand quietly and pray. You should have the fear of God in your hearts.'

"My best men were two of my colleagues, and Masha's best men were Captain Polyansky and Lieutenant Gernet. The bishop's choir sang superbly. The sputtering of the candles, the brilliant light, the gorgeous dresses, the officers, the numbers of gay, happy faces, and a special ethereal look in Masha, everything together—the surroundings and the words of the wedding prayers—moved me to tears and filled me with triumph. I thought how my life had blossomed, how poetically it was shaping itself! Two years ago I was still a student, I was living in cheap furnished rooms, without money, without relations, and, as I fancied then, with nothing to look forward to. Now I am a teacher in the high school in one of the best provincial towns, with a secure income, loved, spoiled. It is for my sake, I thought, this crowd is collected, for my sake three candelabra have been lighted, the deacon is booming, the choir is doing its best; and it's for my sake that this young creature, whom I soon shall call my wife, is so young, so elegant, and so joyful. I recalled our first meetings, our rides into the country, my declaration of love and the weather, which, as though expressly, was so exquisitely fine all the summer; and the happiness which at one time in my old rooms seemed to me possible only in novels and stories, I was now experiencing in reality—I was now, as it were, holding it in my hands.

"After the ceremony they all crowded in disorder round Masha and me, expressed their genuine pleasure, congratulated us and wished us joy. The brigadier-general, an old man of seventy, confined himself to congratulating Masha, and said to her in a squeaky, aged voice, so loud that it could be heard all over the church:

" 'I hope that even after you are married you may remain the rose you are now, my dear.'

"The officers, the director, and all the teachers smiled from politeness, and I was conscious of an agreeable artificial smile on my face, too. Dear Ippolit Ippolitich, the teacher of history and geography, who always says what everyone has heard before, pressed my hand warmly and said with feeling:

" 'Hitherto you have been unmarried and have lived alone, and now you are married and no longer single.'

"From the church we went to a two-story house which I am receiving as part of the dowry. Besides that house Masha is bringing me twenty thousand rubles, as well as a piece of wasteland with a shanty on it, where I am told there are numbers of hens and ducks which are not looked after and are turning wild. When I got home from the church, I stretched myself at full length on the low sofa in my new study and began to smoke; I felt snug, cosy, and comfortable, as I never had in my life before. And meanwhile the wedding party were shouting 'Hurrah!' while a wretched band in the hall played flourishes and all sorts of trash. Varya, Masha's sister, ran into the study with a wineglass in her hand, and with a queer, strained expression, as though her mouth were full of water; apparently she had meant to go on further, but she suddenly burst out laughing and sobbing, and the wineglass crashed on the floor. We took her by the arms and led her away.

" 'Nobody can understand!' she muttered afterwards, lying on the old nurse's bed in a back room. 'Nobody, nobody! My God, nobody can understand!'

"But everyone understood very well that she was four years older than her sister Masha, and still unmarried, and that she was crying, not from envy, but from the melancholy consciousness that her time was passing, and perhaps had passed. When they danced the quadrille, she was back in the drawing-room with a tear-stained and heavily powdered face, and I saw Captain Polyansky holding a plate of ice before her while she ate it with a spoon.

"It is past five o'clock in the morning. I took up my diary to describe my complete and perfect happiness, and thought I would write a good six pages, and read it tomorrow to Masha; but, strange to say, everything is muddled in my head and as misty as a dream, and I can remember vividly nothing but that episode with Varya, and I want to write, 'Poor Varya!' I could go on sitting here and writing 'Poor Varya!' By the way, the trees have begun rustling; it will rain. The crows are cawing, and my Masha, who has just gone to sleep, has for some reason a sorrowful face."

For a long while afterwards Nikitin did not write his diary. At the beginning of August he had school examinations, and after the fifteenth classes began. As a rule he set off for school before nine in the morning, and before ten o'clock he was looking at his watch and pining for his Masha and his new house. In the lower forms he would set some boy to dictate, and while the boys were writing, would sit in the window with his eyes shut, dreaming; whether he dreamed of the future or recalled the past, everything seemed to him equally delightful, like a fairy tale. In the senior classes they were reading aloud Gogol[3] or Pushkin's prose works, and that made him sleepy; people, trees, fields, horses, rose before his imagination, and he would say with a sigh, as though fascinated by the author:

"How lovely!"

At the midday recess Masha used to send him lunch in a snow-white napkin, and he would eat it slowly, with pauses, to prolong the enjoyment of it; and Ippolit Ippolitich, whose lunch as a rule consisted of nothing but bread, looked at him with respect and envy, and gave expression to some familiar fact, such as:

"Men cannot live without food."

After school Nikitin went straight to give his private lessons, and when at last by six o'clock he got home, he felt excited and anxious, as though he had been away for a year. He would run upstairs breathless, find Masha, throw his arms round her, and kiss her and swear that he loved her, that he could not live without her, declare that he had missed her fearfully, and ask her in trepidation how she was and why she looked so depressed. Then they would dine together. After dinner he would lie on the sofa in his study and smoke, while she sat beside him and talked in a low voice.

His happiest days now were Sundays and holidays, when he was at home from morning till evening. On those days he took part in the naïve but extraordinarily pleasant life which reminded him of a pastoral idyll. He was never weary of watching how his sensible and practical Masha was arranging her nest, and anxious to show that he was of some use in the house, he would do something useless— for instance, bring the chaise out of the stable and look at it from every side. Masha had installed a regular dairy with three cows, and in her cellar she had many jugs of milk and pots of sour cream, and she kept it all for butter. Sometimes, by way of a joke, Nikitin would ask her for a glass of milk, and she would be quite upset because it was against her rules; but he would laugh and throw his arms round her, saying:

"There, there; I was joking, my darling! I was joking!"

Or he would laugh at her strictness when, finding in the cupboard some stale bit of cheese or sausage as hard as a stone, she would say seriously:

"They will eat that in the kitchen."

He would observe that such a scrap was fit only for a mousetrap, and she would reply warmly that men knew nothing about house-keeping, and that it was just the same to the servants if you were to send down a hundredweight of savories to the kitchen. He would agree, and embrace her enthusiastically. Everything that was just in what she said seemed to him extraordinary and amazing; and what did not fit in with his convictions seemed to him naïve and touching.

Sometimes he was in a philosophical mood, and he would begin to discuss some abstract subject while she listened and looked at his face with curiosity.

"I am immensely happy with you, my joy," he used to say, playing with her fingers or plaiting and unplaiting her hair. "But I don't look upon this happiness of mine as something that has come to me by chance, as though it had dropped from heaven. This happiness is a perfectly natural, consistent, logical consequence. I believe that man is the creator of his own happiness, and now I am enjoying just what I have myself created. Yes, I speak without false modesty: I have created this happiness myself and I have a right to it. You know my past. My unhappy childhood, without father or mother; my depressing youth, poverty—all this was a struggle, all this was the path by which I made my way to happiness. . . ."

In October the school sustained a heavy loss: Ippolit Ippolitich was taken ill with erysipelas on the head and died. For two days before his death he was unconscious and delirious, but even in his delirium he said nothing that was not perfectly well known to everyone.

"The Volga flows into the Caspian Sea. . . . Horses eat oats and hay. . . ."

There were no lessons at the high school on the day of his funeral. His colleagues and pupils were the coffin-bearers, and the school choir sang all the way to the grave the anthem "Holy God." Three priests, two deacons, all his pupils and the staff of the boys' high school, and the bishop's choir in their best caftans, took part in the procession. And passers-by who met the solemn procession crossed themselves and said:

"God grant us all such a death."

Returning home from the cemetery much moved, Nikitin got out his diary from the table and wrote:

"We have just consigned to the tomb Ippolit Ippolitich Ryzhitsky. Peace to your ashes, modest worker! Masha, Varya, and all the women at the funeral wept from genuine feeling, perhaps because they knew this uninteresting, humble man had never been loved by a woman. I wanted to say a warm word at my colleague's grave, but I was warned that this might displease the director, as he did not like our poor friend. I believe that this is the first day since my marriage that my heart has been heavy."

There was no other event of note in the scholastic year.

The winter was mild, with wet snow and no frost; on Epiphany Eve, for instance, the wind howled all night as though it were autumn, and water trickled off the roofs; and in the morning, at the ceremony of the blessing of the water, the police allowed no one to go on the river, because they said the ice was swelling up and looked dark. But in spite of bad weather Nikitin's life was as happy as in summer. And, indeed, he acquired another source of pleasure; he learned to play vint.[4] Only one thing troubled him, moved him to anger, and seemed to prevent him from being perfectly happy: the cats and dogs which formed part of his wife's dowry. The rooms, especially in the morning, always smelt like a menagerie, and nothing could destroy the odor; the cats frequently fought with the dogs. The spiteful beast Mushka was fed a dozen times a day; she still refused to recognize Nikitin and growled at him: "Rrr . . . nga-nga-nga!"

One night in Lent he was returning home from the club where he had been playing cards. It was dark, raining, and muddy. Nikitin had an unpleasant feeling at the bottom of his heart and could not account for it. He did not know whether it was because he had lost twelve rubles at cards, or whether because one of the players, when they were settling up, had said that of course Nikitin had pots of money, with obvious reference to his wife's dowry. He did not regret the twelve rubles, and there was nothing offensive in what had been said; but, still, there was the unpleasant feeling. He did not even feel a desire to go home.

"Foo, how horrid!" he said, standing still at a lamp-post.

It occurred to him that he did not regret the twelve rubles because he got them for nothing. If he had been a working man he would have known the value of every penny, and would not have been so careless whether he lost or won. And his good-fortune had all, he reflected, come to him by chance, for nothing, and really was as superfluous for him as medicine for the healthy. If, like the vast majority of people, he had been harassed by anxiety for his daily bread, had been struggling for existence, if his back and chest had ached from work, then supper, a warm snug home, and domestic happiness, would have been the necessity, the compensation, the crown of his life; as it was, all this had a strange, indefinite significance for him.

"Foo, how horrid!" he repeated, knowing perfectly well that these reflections were in themselves a bad sign.

When he got home Masha was in bed: she was breathing evenly and smiling, and was evidently sleeping with great enjoyment. Near her the white cat lay curled up, purring. While Nikitin lit the candle and lighted his cigarette, Masha woke up and greedily drank a glass of water.

---

4. A card game resembling auction bridge, with a scoring system that can make for enormous gains and losses.

"I ate too many sweets," she said, and laughed. "Have you been to our house?" she asked after a pause.

"No."

Nikitin knew already that Captain Polyansky, on whom Varya had been building great hopes of late, was being transferred to one of the western provinces, and was already making his farewell visits in the town, and so it was depressing at his father-in-law's.

"Varya looked in this evening," said Masha, sitting up. "She did not say anything, but one could see from her face how wretched she is, poor darling! I can't bear Polyansky. He is fat and bloated, and when he walks or dances his cheeks shake. . . . He is not a man I would choose. But, still, I did think he was a decent person."

"I think he is a decent person now," said Nikitin.

"Then why has he treated Varya so badly?"

"Why badly?" asked Nikitin, beginning to feel irritation against the white cat, who was stretching and arching its back. "As far as I know, he has made no proposal and has given her no promises."

"Then why was he so often at the house? If he didn't mean to marry her, he oughtn't to have come."

Nikitin put out the candle and got into bed. But he felt disinclined to lie down and to sleep. He felt as though his head were immense and empty as a barn, and that new, peculiar thoughts were wandering about in it like tall shadows. He thought that, apart from the soft light of the icon-lamp, that beamed upon their quiet domestic happiness, that apart from this little world in which he and this cat lived so peacefully and happily, there was another world. . . . And he had a passionate, poignant longing to be in that other world, to work himself at some factory or big workshop, to address big audiences, to write, to publish, to raise a stir, to exhaust himself, to suffer. . . . He wanted something that would engross him till he forgot himself, ceased to care for the personal happiness which yielded him only sensations so monotonous. And suddenly there rose vividly before his imagination the figure of Shebaldin with his clean-shaven face, saying to him with horror: "You haven't even read Lessing! You are quite behind the times! How you have gone to seed!"

Masha woke up and again drank some water. He glanced at her neck, at her plump shoulders and throat, and remembered the word the brigadier-general had used in church—"rose."

"Rose," he muttered, and laughed.

His laugh was answered by a sleepy growl from Mushka under the bed: "Rrr . . . nga-nga-nga . . . !"

A heavy anger sank like a cold weight on his heart, and he felt tempted to say something rude to Masha, and even to jump up and hit her; his heart began throbbing.

"So then," he asked, restraining himself, "since I went to your house, I was obligated to marry you?"

"Of course. You know that very well."

"That's nice." And a minute later he repeated: "That's nice."

To relieve the throbbing of his heart, and to avoid saying too much, Nikitin went to his study and lay down on the sofa, without a pillow; then he lay on the floor on the carpet.

"What nonsense it is!" he said to reassure himself. "You are a teacher, you are working in the noblest of callings. . . . What need have you of any other world? What rubbish!"

But almost immediately he told himself with conviction that he was not a real teacher, but simply a government employee, as commonplace and mediocre as the Czech who taught Greek. He had never had a vocation for teaching, he knew nothing of the theory of teaching, and never had been interested in the subject; he did not know how to treat children; he did not understand the significance of what he taught, and perhaps did not teach the right things. Poor Ippolit Ippolitich had been frankly stupid, and all the boys, as well as his colleagues, knew what he was and what to expect from him; but he, Nikitin, like the Czech, knew how to conceal his stupidity and cleverly deceived everyone by pretending that, thank God, his teaching was a success. These new ideas frightened Nikitin; he rejected them, called them stupid, and believed that all this was due to his nerves, that he would laugh at himself.

And he did, in fact, by the morning laugh at himself and call himself an old woman; but it was clear to him that his peace of mind was lost, perhaps, forever, and that in that little two-story house happiness was henceforth impossible for him. He realized that the illusion had evaporated, and that a new life of unrest and clear sight was beginning which was incompatible with peace and personal happiness.

Next day, which was Sunday, he was at the school chapel, and there met his colleagues and the director. It seemed to him that they were entirely preoccupied with concealing their ignorance and discontent with life, and he, too, to conceal his uneasiness, smiled affably and talked of trivialities. Then he went to the station and saw the mail train come in and go out, and it was agreeable to him to be alone and not to have to talk to anyone.

At home he found Varya and his father-in-law, who had come to dinner. Varya's eyes were red with crying, and she complained of a headache, while Shelestov ate a great deal, saying that young men nowadays were unreliable, and that there was very little gentlemanly feeling among them.

"It's loutishness!" he said. "I shall tell him so to his face: 'It's loutishness, sir,' I shall say."

Nikitin smiled affably and helped Masha to look after their guests, but after dinner he went to his study and shut the door.

The March sun was shining brightly in at the windows and shedding its warm rays on the table. It was only the twentieth of the month, but already the cabmen were driving with wheels,[5] and the starlings were noisy in the garden. It was just the weather in which Masha would come in, put one arm round his neck, tell him the horses were saddled or the chaise was at the door, and ask him what she should put on to keep warm. Spring was beginning as exquisitely as last spring, and it promised the same joys. . . . But Nikitin was thinking that it would be nice to take a holiday and go to Moscow, and stay at his old lodgings there. In the next room they were drinking coffee and talking of Captain Polyansky, while he tried not to listen and wrote in his diary: "Where am I, my God? I am surrounded by vulgarity and vulgarity. Wearisome, insignificant people, pots of sour cream, jugs of milk, cockroaches, stupid women. . . . There is nothing more terrible, mortifying, and distressing than vulgarity. I must escape from here, I must escape today, or I shall go out of my mind!"

1889–94

Whitebrow

A hungry she-wolf got up to go hunting. Her cubs, all three of them, were sound asleep, huddled in a heap and keeping each other warm. She licked them and went off.

It was already March, a month of spring, but at night the trees snapped with the cold, as they do in December, and one could hardly put one's tongue out without its being nipped. The wolf-mother was in delicate health and nervous; she started at the slightest sound, and kept hoping that no one would hurt the little ones at home while she was away. The smell of the tracks of men and horses, logs, piles of sticks, and the dark road with horse-dung on it frightened her; it seemed to her that men were standing behind the trees in the darkness, and that dogs were howling somewhere beyond the forest.

She was no longer young and her scent had grown feebler, so that it sometimes happened that she took the track of a fox for that of a dog, and even at times lost her way, a thing that had never been in her youth. Owing to the weakness of her health she no longer hunted calves and big sheep as she had in old days, and kept her distance now from mares with colts; she fed on nothing but carrion;

---

5. In winter, sleigh-runners were used.

fresh meat she tasted very rarely, only in the spring when she would come upon a hare and take away her young, or make her way into a peasant's stall where there were lambs.

Some three miles from her lair there stood a winter hut on the posting road. There lived the keeper Ignat, an old man of seventy, who was always coughing and talking to himself; at night he was usually asleep, and by day he wandered about the forest with a single-barreled gun, whistling to the hares. He must have worked among machinery in early days, for before he stood still he always shouted to himself: "Stop the machine!" and before going on: "Full speed!" He had a huge black dog of indeterminate breed, called Arapka. When it ran too far ahead he used to shout to it: "Reverse action!" Sometimes he used to sing, and as he did so staggered violently, and often fell down (the wolf thought the wind blew him over), and shouted: "Run off the rails!"

The wolf remembered that, in the summer and autumn, a ram and two ewes were pasturing near the winter hut, and when she had run by not so long ago she fancied that she had heard bleating in the stall. And now, as she got near the place, she reflected that it was already March, and, by that time, there would certainly be lambs in the stall. She was tormented by hunger, she thought with what greediness she would eat a lamb, and these thoughts made her teeth snap, and her eyes glitter in the darkness like two sparks of light.

Ignat's hut, his barn, cattle-stall, and well were surrounded by high snowdrifts. All was still. Arapka was, most likely, asleep in the barn.

The wolf clambered over a snowdrift onto the stall, and began scratching away the thatched roof with her paws and her nose. The straw was rotten and decaying, so that the wolf almost fell through; all at once a smell of warm steam, of manure, and of sheep's milk floated straight to her nostrils. Down below, a lamb, feeling the cold, bleated softly. Leaping through the hole, the wolf fell with her four paws and chest on something soft and warm, probably a sheep, and at the same moment, something in the stall suddenly began whining, barking, and going off into a shrill little yap; the sheep huddled against the wall, and the wolf, frightened, snatched the first thing her teeth fastened on, and dashed away. . . .

She ran at her utmost speed, while Arapka, who by now had scented the wolf, howled furiously, the frightened hens cackled, and Ignat, coming out into the porch, shouted: "Full speed! Blow the whistle!"

And he whistled like a steam-engine, and then shouted: "Ho-ho-ho-ho!" and all this noise was repeated by the forest echo. When, little by little, it all died away, the wolf somewhat recovered herself, and began to notice that the prey she held in her teeth and dragged along the snow was heavier and, as it were, harder than lambs usually were at that season; and it smelt somehow different, and uttered strange sounds. . . . The wolf stopped and laid her burden on the snow, to rest and begin eating it, then all at once she leapt back in disgust. It was not a lamb, but a black puppy, with a big head and long legs, of a large breed, with a white patch on his brow, like Arapka's. Judging from his manners he was a simple, ignorant, yard-dog. He licked his crushed and wounded back, and, as though nothing was the matter, wagged his tail and barked at the wolf. She growled like a dog, and ran away from him. He ran after her. She looked round and snapped her teeth. He stopped in perplexity, and, probably deciding that she was playing with him, craned his head in the direction he had come from, and went off into a shrill, gleeful bark, as though inviting his mother Arapka to play with him and the wolf.

It was already getting light, and when the wolf reached her home in the thick aspen wood, each aspen tree could be seen distinctly, and the woodcocks were already awake, and the beautiful male birds often flew up, disturbed by the incautious gambols and barking of the puppy.

"Why does he run after me?" thought the wolf with annoyance. "I suppose he wants me to eat him."

She lived with her cubs in a shallow hole; three years before, a tall old pine tree had been torn up by the roots in a violent storm, and the hole had been formed by it. Now there were dead leaves and moss at the bottom, and around it lay bones and bullocks' horns, with which the little ones played. They were by now awake, and all three of them, very much alike, were standing in a row at the edge of their hole, looking at their returning mother, and wagging their tails. Seeing them, the puppy stopped a little way off, and stared at them for a very long time; seeing that they, too, were looking very attentively at him, he began barking angrily, as at strangers.

By now it was daylight and the sun had risen, the snow sparkled all around, but still the puppy stood a little way off and barked. The cubs sucked their mother, pressing her thin belly with their paws, while she gnawed a horse's bone, dry and white; she was tormented by hunger, her head ached from the dog's barking, and she felt inclined to fall on the uninvited guest and tear him to pieces.

At last the puppy was hoarse and exhausted; seeing they were not afraid of him, and not even attending to him, he began somewhat timidly approaching the cubs, alternately squatting down and bounding a few steps forward. Now, by daylight, it was easy to have a good look at him. . . . His white forehead was big, and on it was a hump such as is only seen on very stupid dogs; he had little, blue, dingy-looking eyes, and the expression of his whole face was extremely stupid. When he reached the cubs he stretched out his broad paws, laid his head upon them, and began:

"Mnya, myna . . . nga—nga—nga . . . !"

The cubs did not understand what he meant, but they wagged their tails. Then the puppy gave one of the cubs a smack on its big head with his paw. The cub, too, gave him a smack on the head. The puppy stood sideways to him, and looked at him askance, wagging his tail, then dashed off, and ran round several times on the frozen snow. The cubs ran after him, he fell on his back and kicked up his legs, and all three of them fell upon him, squealing with delight, and began biting him, not to hurt but in play. The crows sat on the high pine tree, and looked down on their struggle, and were much troubled by it. They grew noisy and merry. The sun was hot, as though it were spring; and the woodcocks, continually flitting through the pine tree that had been blown down by the storm, looked as though made of emerald in the brilliant sunshine.

As a rule, wolf-mothers train their children to hunt by giving them prey to play with; and now watching the cubs chasing the puppy over the frozen snow and struggling with him, the mother thought:

"Let them learn."

When they had played long enough, the cubs went into the hole and lay down to sleep. The puppy howled a little from hunger, then he, too, stretched out in the sunshine. And when they woke up they began playing again.

All day long, and in the evening, the wolf-mother was thinking how the lamb had bleated in the cattle-shed the night before, and how it had smelt of sheep's milk, and she kept snapping her teeth from hunger, and never left off greedily gnawing the old bone, pretending to herself that it was the lamb. The cubs sucked their mother, and the puppy, who was hungry, ran round them and sniffed at the snow.

"I'll eat him . . ." the mother-wolf decided.

She went up to him, and he licked her nose and yapped at her, thinking that she wanted to play with him. In the past she had eaten dogs, but the dog smelt very doggy, and in the delicate state of her health she could not endure the smell; she felt disgusted and walked away. . . .

Towards night it grew cold. The puppy felt depressed and went home.

When the wolf-cubs were fast asleep, their mother went out hunting again. As on the previous night she was alarmed at every sound, and she was frightened by the stumps, the logs, the dark juniper bushes, which stood out singly, and in the distance were like human beings. She ran on the ice-covered snow, keeping away from the road. . . . All at once she caught a glimpse of something dark, far away on the road. She strained her eyes and ears: yes, something really was walking on in front, she could even hear the regular thud of footsteps. Surely not a badger? Cautiously holding her breath, and keeping always to one side, she overtook the dark patch, looked round, and recognized it. It was the puppy with the white brow, going with a slow, lingering step homewards.

"If only he doesn't hinder me again," thought the wolf, and ran quickly on ahead.

But the homestead was by now near. Again she clambered on to the cattle-shed by the snowdrift. The gap she had made yesterday had been already mended with straw, and two new rafters stretched across the roof. The wolf began rapidly working with her legs and nose, looking round to see whether the puppy were coming, but the smell of the warm steam and manure had hardly reached her nose before she heard a gleeful burst of barking behind her. It was the puppy. He leapt up to the wolf on the roof, then into the hole, and, feeling himself at home in the warmth, recognizing his sheep, he barked louder than ever. . . . Arapka woke up in the barn, and, scenting a wolf, howled, the hens began cackling, and by the time Ignat appeared in the porch with his single-barreled gun the frightened wolf was already far away.

"Fuite!" whistled Ignat. "Fuite! Full steam ahead!"

He pulled the trigger—the gun missed fire; he pulled the trigger again—again it missed fire; he tried a third time—and a great blaze of flame flew out of the barrel and there was a deafening boom, boom. It kicked him violently on the shoulder, and, taking his gun in one hand and his axe in the other, he went to see what the noise was about.

A little later he went back to the hut.

"What was it?" a pilgrim, who was staying the night at the hut and had been awakened by the noise, asked in a husky voice.

"It's all right," answered Ignat. "Nothing of consequence. Our Whitebrow has taken to sleeping with the sheep in the warm. Only he hasn't the sense to go in at the door, but always tries to wriggle in by the roof. The other night he tore a hole in the roof and went off on the spree, the rascal, and now he has come back and scratched away the roof again."

"Stupid dog."

"Yes, there is a spring snapped in his brain. I do detest fools," sighed Ignat, clambering on to the stove. "Come, man of God, it's early yet to get up. Let us sleep full steam! . . ."

In the morning he called Whitebrow, smacked him hard about the ears, and then, showing him a stick, kept repeating to him:

"Go in at the door! Go in at the door! Go in at the door!"

1895

Anna on the Neck

I

After the wedding they did not even have light refreshments; the happy pair simply drank a glass of champagne, changed into their travelling things, and drove to the station. Instead of a gay wedding ball and supper, instead of music and dancing, they went on a journey to pray at a shrine a hundred and fifty miles away. Many people commended this, saying that Modest Alekseich was a man high up in the service and no longer young, and that a noisy wedding might not have seemed quite suitable; and music is apt to sound dreary when a government official of fifty-two marries a girl who is only just eighteen. People said, too, that Modest Alekseich, being a man of principle, had arranged this visit to the monastery expressly in order to make his young bride realize that even in marriage he put religion and morality above everything.

The happy pair were seen off at the station. The crowd of relations and colleagues in the service stood, with glasses in their hands, waiting for the train to start to shout "Hurrah!" and the bride's father, Pyotr Leontich, wearing a top-hat and the uniform of a teacher, already drunk and very pale, kept craning towards the window, glass in hand and saying in an imploring voice:

"Anyuta! Anya, Anya! one word!"

Anna bent out of the window to him, and he whispered something to her, enveloping her in a stale smell of alcohol, blew into her ear—she could make out nothing—and made the sign of the cross over her face, her bosom, and her hands; meanwhile he was breathing in gasps and tears were shining in his eyes. And the schoolboys, Anna's brothers, Petya and Andrusha, pulled at his coat from behind, whispering in confusion:

"Father, hush! . . . Father, that's enough. . . ."

When the train started, Anna saw her father run a little way after the train, staggering and spilling his wine, and what a kind, guilty, pitiful face he had:

"Hurra—ah!" he shouted.

The happy pair were left alone. Modest Alekseich looked about the compartment, arranged their things on the shelves, and sat down, smiling, opposite his young wife. He was an official of medium height, rather stout and puffy, who looked exceedingly well nourished, with long whiskers and no moustache. His clean-shaven, round, sharply defined chin looked like the heel of a foot. The most characteristic point in his face was the absence of moustache, the bare, freshly shaven place, which gradually passed into the fat cheeks, quivering like jelly. His deportment was dignified, his movements were deliberate, his manner was soft.

"I cannot help remembering now one circumstance," he said, smiling. "When, five years ago, Kosorotov received the order of St. Anna of the second grade, and went to thank His Excellency, His Excellency expressed himself as follows: "So now you have three Annas: one in your buttonhole and two on your neck.'[1] And it must be explained that at that time Kosorotov's wife, a quarrelsome and frivolous person, had just returned to him, and that her name was Anna. I trust that when I receive the Anna of the second grade His Excellency will not have occasion to say the same thing to me."

He smiled with his little eyes. And she, too, smiled, troubled at the thought that at any moment this man might kiss her with his thick damp lips, and that she had no right to prevent his doing so. The soft movements of his fat person frightened her; she felt both fear and disgust. He got up, without haste took the order off his neck, took off his coat and waistcoat, and put on his dressing-gown.

"That's better," he said, sitting down beside Anna.

Anna remembered what agony the wedding had been, when it had seemed to her that the priest, and the guests, and everyone in church had been looking at her sorrowfully and asking why, why was she, such a sweet, nice girl, marrying such an elderly, uninteresting gentleman. Only that morning she was delighted that everything had been satisfactorily arranged, but at the time of the wedding, and now in the railway carriage, she felt cheated, guilty, and ridiculous. Here she had married a rich man and yet she had no money, her wedding-dress had been bought on credit, and when her father and brothers had been saying good-bye, she could see from their faces that they had not a penny. Would they have any supper that day? And tomorrow? And for some reason it seemed to her that her father and the boys were sitting tonight hungry without her, and feeling the same misery as they had the day after their mother's funeral.

"Oh, how unhappy I am!" she thought. "Why am I so unhappy?"

With the awkwardness of a man with settled habits, unaccustomed to dealing with women, Modest Alekseich touched her on the waist and patted her on the shoulder, while she went on thinking about money, about her mother and her mother's death. When her mother died, her father, Pyotr Leontich, a teacher of drawing and writing at the high school, had taken to drink; impoverishment had followed, the boys had not had boots or galoshes, their father had

---

1. Russian decorations came in different grades. The first would usually be pinned somewhere on the chest; the second hung around the neck; lower grades might be buttonhole rosettes.

been hauled up before the magistrate, the warrant officer had come and made an inventory of the furniture. . . . What a disgrace! Anna had had to look after her drunken father, darn her brothers' stockings, go to market, and when she was complimented on her youth, her beauty, and her elegant manners, it seemed to her that everyone was looking at her cheap hat and the holes in her boots that were inked over. And at night there had been tears and a haunting dread that her father would soon, very soon, be dismissed from the school for his weakness, and that he would not survive it, but would die, too, like their mother. But ladies of their acquaintance had taken the matter in hand and looked about for a good match for Anna. This Modest Alekseich, who was neither young nor good-looking but had money, was soon found. He had a hundred thousand in the bank and the family estate, which he had rented out. He was a man of principle and stood well with His Excellency; it would be nothing to him, so they told Anna, to get a note from His Excellency to the directors of the high school, or even to the Education Commissioner, to prevent Pyotr Leontich from being dismissed.

While she was recalling these details, she suddenly heard strains of music which floated in at the window, together with the sound of voices. The train was stopping at a station. In the crowd beyond the platform an accordion and a cheap squeaky fiddle were being briskly played, and the sound of a military band came from beyond the villas and the tall birches and poplars that lay bathed in the moonlight; there must have been a dance in the place. Summer visitors and townspeople, who used to come out here by train in fine weather for a breath of fresh air, were parading up and down on the platform. Among them was the wealthy owner of all the summer villas—a tall, stout, dark man called Artynov. He had prominent eyes and looked like an Armenian. He wore a strange costume; his shirt was unbuttoned, showing his chest; he wore high boots with spurs, and a black cloak hung from his shoulders and dragged on the ground like a train. Two boar-hounds followed him with their sharp noses to the ground.

Tears were still shining in Anna's eyes, but she was not thinking now of her mother, nor of money, nor of her marriage; but shaking hands with schoolboys and officers she knew, she laughed gaily and said quickly:

"How do you do? How are you?"

She went out on to the platform between the carriages into the moonlight, and stood so that they could all see her in her new splendid dress and hat.

"Why are we stopping here?" she asked.

"This is a junction. They are waiting for the mail train to pass."

Seeing that Artynov was looking at her, she screwed up her eyes coquettishly and began talking aloud in French; and because her voice sounded so pleasant, and because she heard music and the moon was reflected in the pond, and because Artynov, the notorious Don Juan and spoiled child of fortune, was looking at her eagerly and with curiosity, and because everyone was in good spirits—she suddenly felt joyful, and when the train started and the officers of her acquaintance saluted her, she was humming the polka the strains of which reached her from the military band playing beyond the trees; and she returned to her compartment feeling as though it had been proved to her at the station that she would certainly be happy in spite of everything.

The happy pair spent two days at the monastery, then went back to town. They lived in a rent-free apartment. When Modest Alekseich had gone to the office, Anna played the piano, or shed tears of depression, or lay down on a couch and read novels or looked through fashion papers. At dinner Modest Alekseich ate a great deal and talked about politics, about appointments, transfers, and promotions in the service, about the necessity of hard work, and said that, family life not being a pleasure but a duty, if you took care of the kopeks the rubles would take care of themselves, and that he put religion and morality before everything else in the world. And holding his knife in his fist as though it were a sword, he would say:

"Everyone ought to have his duties!"

And Anna listened to him, was frightened, and could not eat, and she usually got up from the table hungry. After dinner her husband lay down for a nap and snored loudly, while Anna went to see her own family. Her father and the boys looked at her in a peculiar way, as though just before she came in they had been blaming her for having married for money a tedious, wearisome man she did not love; her rustling skirts, her bracelets, and her general air of a married lady offended them and made them uncomfortable. In her presence they felt a little embarrassed and did not know what to talk to her about; but yet they still loved her as before, and were not used to having dinner without her. She sat down with them to cabbage soup, porridge, and fried potatoes, smelling of mutton dripping. Pyotr Leontich filled his glass from the decanter with a trembling hand and drank it off hurriedly, greedily, with repulsion, then poured out a second glass and then a third. Petya and Andrusha, thin, pale boys with big eyes, would take the decanter and say desperately:

"You mustn't, father. . . . Enough, father. . . ."

And Anna, too, was troubled and entreated him to drink no more; and he would suddenly fly into a rage and beat the table with his fists:

"I won't allow anyone to dictate to me!" he would shout. "Wretched boys! wretched girl! I'll turn you all out!"

But there was a note of weakness, of good-nature in his voice, and no one was afraid of him. After dinner he usually dressed in his best. Pale, with a cut on his chin from shaving, craning his thin neck, he would stand for half an hour before the glass, prinking, combing his hair, twisting his black moustache, sprinkling himself with scent, tying his cravat in a bow; then he would put on his gloves and his top-hat, and go off to give his private lessons. Or if it was a holiday he would stay at home and paint, or play the harmonium, which wheezed and growled; he would try to wrest from it pure, harmonious sounds and would sing to it; or would storm at the boys:

"Wretches! Good-for-nothing boys! You have spoiled the instrument!"

In the evening Anna's husband played cards with his colleagues, who lived under the same roof in the government quarters. The wives of these gentlemen would come in—ugly, tastelessly dressed women, as coarse as cooks—and in the apartment gossip would begin, as tasteless and unattractive as the ladies themselves. Sometimes Modest Alekseich would take Anna to the theater. In the intermissions he would never let her stir a step from his side, but walked about arm in arm with her through the corridors and the foyer. When he bowed to someone, he immediately whispered to Anna: "A civil councilor . . . visits at His Excellency's," or "A man of means . . . has a house of his own." When they passed the buffet Anna had a great longing for something sweet; she was fond of chocolate and apple cakes, but she had no money, and she did not like to ask her husband. He would take a pear, pinch it with his fingers, and ask uncertainly:

"How much?"

"Twenty-five kopeks!"

"I say!" he would reply, and put it down; but as it was awkward to leave the buffet without buying anything, he would order some seltzer-water and drink the whole bottle himself, and tears would come into his eyes. And Anna hated him at such times.

And, suddenly flushing crimson, he would say to her rapidly:

"Bow to that old lady!"

"But I don't know her."

"No matter. That's the wife of the director of the local treasury! Bow, I tell you," he would grumble insistently. "Your head won't drop off."

Anna bowed, and her head certainly did not drop off, but it was agonizing. She did everything her husband wanted her to, and was furious with herself for having let him deceive her like the merest idiot. She had married him only for his money, and yet she had less money now than before her marriage. In the old days her father would sometimes give her twenty kopeks, but now she had not a farthing. To take money by stealth or ask for it, she could not; she was afraid of her husband, she trembled before him. She felt as though she had been afraid of him for years. In her childhood the director of the high school had always seemed the most impressive and terrifying force in the world, sweeping down like a thunderstorm or a steam-engine ready to crush her; another similar force of which the whole family talked, and of which they were for some reason afraid, was His Excellency; then there were a dozen others, less formidable, and among them the teachers at the high school, with shaven upper lips, stern, implacable; and now finally, there was Modest Alekseich, a man of principle, who even resembled the director in the face. And in Anna's imagination all these forces blended together into one, and, in the form of a terrible, huge white bear, menaced the weak and erring such as her father. And she was afraid to say anything in opposition to her husband, and gave a forced smile, and tried to make a show of pleasure when she was coarsely caressed and defiled by embraces that terrified her.

Only once Pyotr Leontich had the temerity to ask for a loan of fifty rubles in order to pay some very irksome debt, but what an agony it had been!

"Very good; I'll give it to you," said Modest Alekseich after a moment's thought; "but I warn you I won't help you again till you give up drinking. Such a failing is disgraceful in a man in the government service! I must remind you of the well-known fact that many capable people have been ruined by that passion, though they might possibly, with temperance, have risen in time to a very high position."

And long-winded phrases followed: "inasmuch as . . . ," "following upon which proposition . . . ," "in view of the aforesaid contention . . ."; and Pyotr Leontich was in agonies of humiliation and felt an intense craving for alcohol.

And when the boys came to visit Anna, generally in broken boots and threadbare trousers, they, too, had to listen to sermons.

"Every man ought to have his duties!" Modest Alekseich would say to them.

And he did not give them money. But he did give Anna bracelets, rings, and brooches, saying that these things would come in useful for a rainy day. And he often unlocked her drawer and made an inspection to see whether they were all safe.

II

Meanwhile winter came on. Long before Christmas there was an announcement in the local papers that the usual winter ball would take place on the twenty-ninth of December in the Hall of Nobility. Every evening after cards Modest Alekseich was excitedly whispering with his colleagues' wives and glancing at Anna, and then paced up and down the room for a long while, thinking. At last, late one evening, he stood still, facing Anna, and said:

"You ought to get yourself a ball dress. Do you understand? Only please consult Marya Grigoryevna and Natalya Kuzminishna."

And he gave her a hundred rubles. She took the money, but she did not consult anyone when she ordered the ball dress; she spoke to no one but her father, and tried to imagine how her mother would have dressed for a ball. Her mother had always dressed in the latest fashion and had always taken trouble over Anna, dressing her elegantly like a doll, and had taught her to speak French and dance the mazurka superbly (she had been a governess for five years before her marriage). Like her mother, Anna could make a new dress out of an old one, clean gloves with benzine, rent jewels; and, like her mother, she knew how to screw up her eyes, lisp, assume graceful attitudes, fly into raptures when necessary, and throw a mournful and enigmatic look into her eyes. And from her father she had inherited the dark color of her hair and eyes, her highly-strung nerves, and the habit of always making herself look her best.

When, half an hour before setting off for the ball, Modest Alekseich went into her room without his coat on, to put his order round his neck before her mirror, dazzled by her beauty and the splendor of her fresh, ethereal dress, he combed his whiskers complacently and said:

"So that's what my wife can look like . . . so that's what you can look like! Anyuta!" he went on, dropping into a tone of solemnity, "I have made your fortune, and now I beg you to do something for mine. I beg you to get introduced to the wife of His Excellency! For God's sake, do! Through her I may get the post of senior reporting clerk!"

They went to the ball. They reached the Hall of Nobility, the entrance with the hall porter. They came to the vestibule with the hat-stands, the fur coats; footmen scurrying about, and ladies with low necklines putting up their fans to screen themselves from the drafts. There was a smell of gas and of soldiers. When Anna, walking upstairs on her husband's arm, heard the music and saw herself full length in the looking-glass in the full glow of the lights, there was a rush of joy in her heart, and she felt the same presentiment of happiness as in the moonlight at the station. She walked in proudly, confidently, for the first time feeling herself not a girl but a lady, and unconsciously imitating her mother in her walk and in her manner. And for the first time in her life she felt rich and free. Even her husband's presence did not oppress her, for as she crossed the threshold of the hall she had guessed instinctively that the proximity of an old husband did not detract from her in the least, but, on the contrary, gave her that shade of piquant mystery that is so attractive to men. The orchestra was already playing and the dances had begun. After their flat Anna was overwhelmed by the lights, the bright colors, the music, the noise, and looking round the room, thought, "Oh, how lovely!" She at once distinguished in the crowd all her acquaintances, everyone she had met before at parties or on picnics—all the officers, the teachers, the lawyers, the officials, the landowners, His Excellency, Artynov, and the ladies of the highest standing, dressed up and very *décolletées*, handsome and ugly, who had already taken up their positions in the stalls and pavilions of the charity bazaar, to begin selling things for the benefit of the poor. A huge officer in epaulettes—she had been introduced to him in Staro-Kievsky Street when she was a schoolgirl, but now she could not remember his name—seemed to spring from out of the ground, begging her for a waltz, and she flew away from her husband, feeling as though she were floating away in a sailing-boat in a violent storm, while her husband was left far away on the shore. She danced passionately, with fervor, a waltz, then a polka and a quadrille, being snatched by one partner as soon as she was left by another, dizzy with music and the noise, mixing Russian with French, lisping, laughing, and with no thought of her husband or anything else. She excited great admiration among the men—that was evident, and indeed it could not have been otherwise; she was breathless with excitement, felt thirsty, and convulsively clutched her fan. Pyotr Leontich, her father, in a crumpled dress-coat that smelled of benzine, came up to her, offering her a plate of pink ices.

"You are enchanting this evening," he said, looking at her rapturously, "and I have never so much regretted that you were in such a hurry to get married. . . . What was it for? I know you did it for our sake, but . . ." With a shaking hand he drew out a roll of notes and said: "I got the money for my lessons today, and can pay your husband what I owe him."

She put the plate back into his hand, and was pounced upon by someone and borne off to a distance. She caught a glimpse over her partner's shoulder of her father gliding over the floor, putting his arm round a lady and whirling down the ballroom with her.

"How sweet he is when he is sober!" she thought.

She danced the mazurka with the same huge officer; he moved gravely, as heavily as a dead carcass in a uniform, twitched his shoulders and his chest, stamped his feet very languidly—he felt fearfully disinclined to dance. She fluttered round him, provoking him by her beauty, her bare neck; her eyes glowed defiantly, her movements were passionate, while he became more and more indifferent, and held out his hands to her as graciously as a king.

"Bravo, bravo!" said people watching them.

But little by little the huge officer, too, broke out; he grew lively, excited, and, overcome by her fascination, was carried away and danced lightly, youthfully, while she merely moved her shoulders and looked slyly at him as though she were now the queen and he were her slave; and at that moment it seemed to her that the whole room was looking at them, and that everybody was thrilled and envied them. The huge officer had hardly had time to thank her for the dance, when the crowd suddenly parted and the men drew themselves up in a strange way, with their hands at their sides. His Excellency, with two stars on his dress-coat, was walking up to her. Yes, His Excellency was walking straight towards her, for he was staring directly at her with a sugary smile, while he licked his lips as he always did when he saw a pretty woman.

"Delighted, delighted . . ." he began. "I shall order your husband to be clapped in a lock-up for keeping such a treasure hidden from us till now. I've come to you with a message from my wife," he went on, offering her his arm. "You must help us. . . . M-m-yes. . . . We ought to give you the prize for beauty as they do in America. . . . M-m-yes. . . . The Americans. . . . My wife is expecting you impatiently."

He led her to a stall and presented her to a middle-aged lady, the lower part of whose face was disproportionately large, so that she looked as though she were holding a big stone in her mouth.

"You must help us," she said through her nose in a singsong voice. "All the pretty women are working for our charity bazaar, and you are the only one enjoying yourself. Why won't you help us?"

She went away, and Anna took her place by the cups and the silver samovar. She was soon doing a lively trade. Anna asked no less than a ruble for a cup of tea, and made the huge officer drink three cups. Artynov, the rich man with prominent eyes, who suffered from asthma, came up, too; he was not dressed in the strange costume in which Anna had seen him in the summer at the station, but wore a dress-coat like everyone else. Keeping his eyes fixed on Anna, he drank a glass of champagne and paid a hundred rubles for it, then drank some tea and gave another hundred—all this without saying a word, as he was short of breath because of asthma. . . . Anna invited purchasers and got money out of them, firmly convinced by now that her smiles and glances could not fail to afford these people great pleasure. She realized now that she was created exclusively for this noisy, brilliant, laughing life, with its music, its dancers, its adorers, and her old terror of a force that was sweeping down upon her and menacing to crush her seemed to her ridiculous: she was afraid of no one now, and regretted only that her mother could not be there to rejoice at her success.

Pyotr Leontich, pale by now but still steady on his legs, came up to the stall and asked for a glass of brandy. Anna turned crimson, expecting him to say something inappropriate (she was already ashamed of having such a poor and ordinary father); but he emptied his glass, took ten rubles out of his roll of notes, flung it down, and walked away with dignity without uttering a word. A little later she saw him dancing in the grand chain, and by now he was staggering and kept shouting something, to the great confusion of his partner; and Anna remembered how at the ball three years before he had staggered and shouted in the same way, and it had ended in the police-sergeant's taking him home to bed, and next day the director had threatened to dismiss him from his post. How inappropriate that memory was!

When the samovars were put out in the stalls and the exhausted ladies handed over their takings to the middle-aged lady with the stone in her mouth, Artynov took Anna on his arm to the hall where supper was served to all who had assisted at the bazaar. There were some twenty people at supper, not more, but it was very noisy. His Excellency proposed a toast:

"In this magnificent dining-room it will be appropriate to drink to the success of the cheap dining-rooms, which are the object of today's bazaar."

The brigadier-general proposed the toast: "To the power by which even the artillery is vanquished," and all the company clinked glasses with the ladies. It was very, very gay.

When Anna was escorted home it was daylight and the cooks were going to market. Joyful, intoxicated, full of new sensations, exhausted, she undressed, dropped into bed, and at once fell asleep. . . .

It was past one in the afternoon when the servant waked her and announced that M. Artynov had called. She dressed quickly and went down into the drawing-room. Soon after Artynov, His Excellency called to thank her for her assistance in the bazaar. With a sugary smile, chewing his lips, he kissed her hand, and asking her permission to come again, took his leave, while she remained standing in the middle of the drawing-room, amazed, enchanted, unable to believe that this change in her life, this marvelous change, had taken place so quickly; and at that moment Modest Alekseich walked in . . . and he, too, stood before her now with the same ingratiating, sugary, cringingly respectful expression which she was accustomed to see on his face in the presence of the great and powerful; and with rapture, with indignation, with contempt, convinced that no harm would come to her from it, she said, articulating distinctly each word:

"Be off, you blockhead!"

From this time forward Anna never had one day free, as she was always taking part in picnics, expeditions, performances. She returned home every day after midnight, and went to bed on the floor in the drawing-room, and afterwards used to tell everyone, touchingly, how she slept under flowers. She needed a very great deal of money, but she was no longer afraid of Modest Alekseich, and spent his money as though it were her own; and she did not ask, did not demand it, simply sent him in the bills: "Give bearer two hundred rubles," or "Pay one hundred rubles at once."

At Easter Modest Alekseich received the Anna of the second grade. When he went to offer his thanks, His Excellency put aside the paper he was reading and settled himself more comfortably in his chair.

"So now you have three Annas," he said, scrutinizing his white hands and pink nails—"one on your buttonhole and two on your neck."

Modest Alekseich put two fingers to his lips as a precaution against laughing too loud and said:

"Now I have only to look forward to the arrival of a little Vladimir. I make bold to beg Your Excellency to stand godfather."

He was alluding to Vladimir of the fourth grade, and was already imagining how he would tell everywhere the story of this pun, so apt in its readiness and audacity, and he wanted to say something equally apt, but His Excellency was buried again in his newspaper. and merely gave him a nod.

And Anna went on driving about with three horses, going out hunting with Artynov, playing in one-act dramas, going out to supper, and was more and more rarely with her own family; they dined now alone. Pyotr Leontich was drinking more heavily than ever; there was no money, and the harmonium had been sold long ago for debt. The boys did not let him go out alone in the street now, but looked after him for fear he might fall down; and whenever they met Anna driving in Staro-Kievsky Street with a pair of horses and Artynov on the box instead of a coachman, Pyotr Leontich took off his top-hat, and was about to shout to her, but Petya and Andrusha took him by the arm, and said imploringly:

"You mustn't, father. Hush, father!"

1895

The House with the Mansard
(AN ARTIST'S STORY)

I

All this happened six or seven years ago when I was living in the province of T., on the estate of a landed proprietor called Belokurov, a young man who rose very early, went about in a full-skirted peasant coat, drank beer of an evening, and was always complaining that he never met with sympathy anywhere. He lived in an annex in the garden, and I took up my quarters in the old mansion, in a huge pillared ballroom, with no furniture but a wide sofa on which I slept, and a table at which I played patience. All the time, even in still weather, the ancient stoves hummed, and during thunderstorms the whole house shook as if it were on the point of falling to pieces; this was rather alarming, especially on stormy nights, when the ten great windows were lit up by lightning.

Doomed as I was to a life of idleness, I did nothing whatever. For hours at a time I looked out of the window at the sky, the birds, the garden walks, read whatever the post brought me, and slept. Sometimes I left the house and roamed about till late at night.

On my way home from one of these rambles, I happened upon an estate I had never seen before. The sun was setting and the shades of evening lay over the flowering rye. Two rows of ancient, towering fir-trees, planted close together so that they formed almost solid walls, enclosed a walk of somber beauty. I climbed easily over some railings and made my way along this walk, my feet slipping on the carpet of pine-needles which lay an inch thick on the ground. It was still and dark but for the brilliant gold of the sunlight shimmering rainbow-like in the spiders' webs. The fragrance spread by the fir-trees was almost overpowering. I soon turned into a long avenue of lime-trees. Here, too, everything spoke of neglect and age. Last year's leaves rustled mournfully underfoot, and shadows lurked in the twilight between the trunks of the trees. On my right, in an ancient orchard, an oriole warbled feebly and listlessly—the bird, like everything else here, was probably old. And then the lime-trees came to an end in front of an old house with a verandah and a mansard, and suddenly I had a view of the courtyard, a big pond with a bathing-place on the bank, a huddle of green willows, and, in the midst of a village on the other side of the pond, a high, narrow belfry, the cross on its top lit up in the last rays of the departing sun.

For a moment I was under the spell of something familiar, something I had known long ago, as if I had seen this panorama before, at some time during my childhood.

A sturdy white stone gateway, adorned with lions, led from the courtyard into the open fields, and in this gateway stood two girls. The older of the two, slender, pale, very pretty, with a great knot of auburn hair on the top of her head and a small, obstinate mouth, looked very severe, and scarcely took any notice of me; the other, who looked extremely young, hardly more than seventeen or eighteen, was pale and slender, too, but her mouth was large and she looked shy, gazing at me from great wondering eyes and dropping out a word or two in English as I passed by; and it seemed to me that I had known these charming faces, too, at some distant time. I returned home, feeling as if I had had a delightful dream.

At noon, a few days later, Belokurov and I were walking about in front of the house, when the tall grass rustled beneath the wheels of a light carriage suddenly turning into the yard. In it sat one of the girls I had seen, the older one. She had brought a subscription list for aid to the victims of a fire. Not looking at us, she told us gravely, and in much detail the number of houses burned in the village of Siyanovo, the number of men, women and children rendered homeless, and the temproary measures proposed by the committee, of which she was a member, for rendering aid to the victims. After giving us the list to sign, she put it away and prepared to take her leave immediately.

"You've quite forgotten us, Pyotr Petrovich," she said to Belokurov, putting out her hand to him. "Come and see us, and if Monsieur N. [she named me] would like to make the acquaintance of some of his admirers, my mother and I would be very glad to see him."

I bowed.

When she had gone Pyotr Petrovich began telling me about her. He said she came from a good family, and was called Lidia Volchaninova, and both the estate on which she lived with her mother and sister, and the village on the other side of the pond, were called Shelkovka. Her father had occupied a prominent post in Moscow, and had died with the rank of privy councilor. Though quite well off, the Volchaninovs lived in the country all the year round, and Lidia taught in the *zemstvo*[1] school in her home village of Shelkovka, receiving a monthly salary of twenty-five rubles. She made this money suffice for her personal expenditure, and was proud to earn her own living.

"A very interesting family," said Belokurov. "We must pay them a visit. They would be very pleased if you went."

One day after dinner—it was some saint's day—we remembered the Volchaninovs, and set off to Shelkovka. We found the mother and both daughters at home. The mother, Yekaterina Pavlovna, must once have been good-looking, but had grown stouter than her age warranted, and was short-winded, melancholy and absent-minded. She tried to entertain me with talk about art. Having learned from her daughter that I might visit Shelkovka, she had hastily recalled two or three landscapes of mine which she had seen at exhibitions in Moscow, and now asked me what I had intended to express by them. Lidia, or, as she was called at home, Lida, spoke more to Belokurov than to me. Her face grave and unsmiling, she

1. In pre-revolutionary Russia, a district council whose members were elected locally.

asked him why he did not work in the *zemstvo*, and why he had never been at a single one of its meetings.

"It's not right, Pyotr Petrovich," she said reproachfully. "Really it isn't—you ought to be ashamed of yourself."

"Quite true, Lida, quite true," agreed her mother. "It's not right."

"Our whole district is in the hands of Balagin," continued Lida, turning to me. "He is the chairman of the local board and has put his nephews and sons-in-law into all the district posts, and does whatever he likes. We must resist. We young people ought to make up a strong party, but you see what our young people are like. It's too bad, Pyotr Petrovich!"

Zhenya, the younger sister, said nothing while the *zemstvo* was being discussed. She took no part in serious conversation, not being considered as a grown-up person by the family, among whom she went under the childish pet name of Missuse,[1] because that was what she had called her governess, when she was a little girl. She kept looking at me with curiosity, telling me all about the originals of the family album I was looking through. "That's my uncle . . . that's my godfather," she said, touching the portraits with her finger, her shoulder brushing artlessly against mine, giving me a clear view of her slight undeveloped breasts, her slender shoulders, her plait, and her whole thin figure, tightly drawn in at the waist by her belt.

We played croquet and tennis, walked about the garden, drank tea, and afterwards sat a long time over supper. After the huge, empty, pillared ballroom I felt quite at ease in the comfortable little house in which there were no oleograph pictures on the walls, and they said "you" and not the familiar "thou" to the servants. Lida and Missuse made the atmosphere seem pure and youthful, and everything breathed integrity. At supper Lida again talked to Belokurov about the *zemstvo*, Balagin, and school libraries. She was lively, sincere, strong in her convictions. She was an interesting talker, though she spoke a great deal, and very loud—perhaps because she was accustomed to addressing classes. My friend Pyotr Petrovich, on the other hand, still clung to the habit of his student days—the habit of turning every conversation into an argument. He held forth listlessly, tediously, and at length, with an obvious desire to show off his intelligence and his progressive views. He gesticulated and knocked a sauce-boat over with his cuff, and a large pool formed on the tablecloth, but no one but myself seemed to notice it.

When we set off for home it was dark and still.

"Good breeding does not consist in not upsetting sauce on the table, but in not noticing if someone else does," sighed Belokurov.

---

1. Apparently a mispronunciation of "Miss Hughes."

"Yes, they're a delightful, cultured family. I've lost touch with nice people—I've deteriorated. There's so much to do, so much!"

He spoke of the work to be done if you wanted to be a model landlord. And I thought what a lazy, unmanageable fellow he was. When he spoke of serious things he interspersed his speech with painfully emphatic "er-er's" and he did everything in the same way as he spoke—slowly, always getting behind, never finishing anything in time. I did not believe he was a bit practical, if only because when I gave him letters to post he kept them in his pocket for weeks.

"And the worst of it is," he muttered, as he walked by my side, "you work and work, and meet with no sympathy from anyone. No sympathy whatever."

II

I got into the habit of visiting the Volchaninovs. My usual place there was on the lowest of the steps leading to the verandah. I was devoured by remorse, deploring my life which was passing so rapidly and trivially, and continually telling myself that it would be a good thing if I could tear out my heart, which was such a heavy burden to me. And all the time there was talk going on on the verandah, the sound of skirts rustling, and pages being turned. I soon grew accustomed to the knowledge that Lida received patients, gave out books and went often to the village with a parasol over her uncovered head in the daytime, and in the evening talked in a loud voice about the *zemstvo* and schools. Whenever this girl, slender, good-looking, invariably severe, with her small, daintily curved mouth, began talking about practical things, she would preface her remarks by saying to me coldly:

"This won't interest you."

Me she disliked. She disliked me for being a landscape painter and not trying to show the needs of the people in my pictures, and also because she felt I was indifferent to all in which she believed so firmly. I remember riding along the shores of Lake Baikal,[2] and meeting a Buryat girl in a shirt and blue denim trousers, riding astride. I asked her to sell me her pipe, but she only glanced contemptuously at my European features and hat, and, too bored to spend more than a minute talking to me, galloped past with a wild whoop. And Lida, too, felt there was something alien in me. She gave no outward signs of her dislike, but I could feel it, and, seated on the lowest step of the verandah, gave way to my irritation and said that to treat the peasants without being oneself a doctor was to

2. Lake Baikal, located in southeastern Siberia, is the largest freshwater lake in Eurasia. The Buryats are a Mongol people living in the region which includes Lake Baikal.

deceive them, and that when one had any amount of broad acres, it was easy to be charitable.

But her sister Missuse had not a care in the world, and, like myself, passed the time in complete idleness. The moment she got up of a morning she began reading, seated in a deep armchair on the verandah, her feet scarcely reaching the floor, or secluded herself with her book in the lime-tree walk, or passed through the gate into the fields. She read all day, scanning the pages avidly, and only an occasional weary and listless glance and the extreme pallor of her face showed that this reading was a mental strain. When I arrived and she caught sight of me, she would blush faintly, eagerly relinquish her book, and, fixing her great eyes on my face, begin to tell me what had happened since she last saw me—that the chimney had been on fire in the servants' quarters, that one of the workmen had caught a big fish in the pond, and so on. On weekdays she usually wore a colored blouse and a dark-blue skirt. She and I used to stroll about, pick cherries for jam, or go rowing, and when she jumped up to reach a cherry, or bent over to the oars, her thin, delicate arms showed through her wide sleeves. Or I would sketch, and she would stand by, watching admiringly.

One Sunday in the end of July, I set off for the Volchaninovs at about nine o'clock in the morning. I walked about the park, keeping as far from the house as possible, looking for mushrooms, which were very plentiful that summer, and marking the places where I found them with sticks, so as later to gather them with Zhenya. A warm wind was blowing. I could see Zhenya and her mother, both in light-colored Sunday dresses, coming home from church, Zhenya holding her hat on against the wind. Then I heard sounds which meant they were having tea on the verandah.

For a carefree individual like myself, always seeking an excuse to be idle, these summer Sunday mornings on our country estates hold a special charm. When the garden, green and sparkling with dew, lies radiant and happy in the rays of the sun, when the oleanders and the mignonette in the flowerbeds near the house spread their perfume, and the young folk, just returned from church, are having tea in the garden, and everyone is so cheerful and so charmingly dressed; when I remind myself that all these healthy, well-nourished, good-looking people will do nothing at all the livelong day, I long for life to be always like this. This particular morning I was thinking these same thoughts and walking about the garden, ready to stroll about aimlessly, with nothing to do, the whole day, the whole summer.

Zhenya appeared with a basket over her arm. Her expression showed that she had known, or at any rate felt, that she would find me in the garden. We gathered mushrooms and talked, and when she put a question to me she went in front, so as to see my face.

"There was a miracle in the village yesterday," she said. "Lame Pelagea has been ill a whole year, no doctors or medicine were any use, and yesterday a wise woman whispered over her, and she isn't ill anymore."

"That's nothing," I said. "We ought not to look for miracles only when people are ill or old. Isn't health a miracle in itself? And life? Everything we don't understand is a miracle."

"And aren't you frightened by things you can't understand?"

"No. I approach phenomena I don't understand boldly, I don't give in to them. I am above them. A human being should rate himself higher than lions, tigers and stars, higher than the whole of nature, even higher than things which we cannot understand and regard as miraculous, otherwise he is not a man, but a mouse, afraid of everything."

Zhenya supposed that, being an artist, I knew a great deal, and could divine accurately what I did not know. She wanted me to waft her to some exquisite eternal sphere, to that higher world where, she believed, I was quite at home, and she spoke to me of God, of life everlasting, of miracles. And I, unwilling to admit that myself and my imagination would perish altogether after death, would reply: "Yes, human beings are immortal," "Yes, life everlasting awaits us." And she would listen, believing me without demanding proofs.

As we were going back to the house she suddenly came to a halt and said:

"Isn't Lida splendid? I adore her and would sacrifice my life for her at a moment's notice. But why—" Zhenya put a finger on my coat-sleeve, "why do you always argue with her? Why are you so irritable?"

"Because she's wrong."

Zhenya shook her head disapprovingly, and tears came into her eyes.

"How hard that is to understand," she said.

At that moment Lida, who had just returned from somewhere or other, stood by the porch with a riding-crop in her hand—slender, pretty, lit up by the rays of the sun—giving orders to a workman. She treated two or three sick people, in great haste, talking loudly, and then went from room to room looking extremely businesslike and preoccupied, opening one wardrobe after another, and going to the mansard. They looked for her to call her to dinner for a long time, and by the time she came we had finished our soup. Somehow I recall all these trivial details affectionately, and I have the liveliest remembrance of this day, though nothing particular happened on it. After dinner Zhenya read, reclining in a deep armchair, and I sat on the lowest step of the verandah. Nobody spoke. The sky was enveloped in clouds, and there was a light drizzle. It was warm, the wind had long fallen, and it seemed as if this day would go on forever. Yekaterina Pavlovna, who was still heavy with sleep, came on to the verandah, holding a fan.

"Oh, Mamma," said Zhenya, kissing her hand. "It's bad for you to sleep in the daytime!"

They adored each other. When one of them went into the garden, the other was sure to appear on the verandah, and call out, her glance traveling among the trunks of the trees: "Cooee, Zhenya!" or "Mamma, where are you?" They always said their prayers together, and they were equally devout, understanding each other perfectly, even when they said nothing. And their opinions of other people were the same. Yekaterina Pavlovna very soon got fond of me, too, and when I did not come for two or three days she would send to know if I was well. She, too, inspected my sketches admiringly, and told me everything that happened as freely and frankly as Missuse, not infrequently confiding her domestic secrets in me.

She went in awe of her eldest daughter. Lida had no caressing ways, and talked only about serious things. She lived her own special life and was for her mother and her sister the sacred, somewhat enigmatic figure that the admiral, sequestered in his cabin, is for sailors.

"Our Lida is a fine person, isn't she?" the mother often said.

And now, while the rain fell gently, we talked about Lida.

"She's marvelous," said the mother, adding in conspiratorial undertones, glancing timidly around, "there are very few like her, but, you know, I begin to be rather alarmed. Schools, dispensaries, books—are all very well, but why go to extremes? She's nearly twenty-four, it's time for her to be thinking seriously about her future. All those books and dispensaries make one blind to the passage of time. . . . It's time for her to get married."

Zhenya, pale from her reading, her hair rumpled, raised her head and said, as if to herself, but looking at her mother:

"We are all in the hands of God, Mummie."

And plunged into her book again.

Belokurov appeared in his peasant jacket and embroidered shirt. We played croquet and tennis, and, when it got dark, sat long round the supper-table, Lida again talking about schools and about Balagin, who had gotten the whole district into his hands. When I left the Volchaninovs that evening I carried away an impression of a long, long, idle day, and told myself mournfully that everything comes to an end in this world, however long it is. Zhenya saw us to the gate, and, perhaps because I had spent the whole day with her from morn till eve, I began to feel I should be lonely without her, to realize how dear this whole charming family was to me. And for the first time that summer the desire to paint a picture rose in me.

"Why should *your* life be so dull and colorless?" I asked Belokurov, as we walked home together. "*My* life is dull, boring, monotonous, because I'm an artist, a crank, I have been eaten up with envy, remorse, and disbelief in my own work from my youth up. I shall always be poor, I am a tramp, but you—you are a healthy, normal man, a landowner, a gentleman—why is your life so dreary, why do you get so little out of it? What is there to prevent you from falling in love with Lida or Zhenya, for instance?"

"You forget I love another woman," replied Belokurov.

I knew he meant Lyubov Ivanovna, the woman who lived with him in the annex. Every day I saw this lady, stout, chubby-faced, pompous, rather like a Michaelmas goose, walking about the garden, wearing Russian national costume and bead necklaces, always carrying an open parasol, and always being called by the servant to have a meal, or take tea. Three years before she had rented one of the annexes for the summer, and had remained there with Belokurov, apparently for the rest of her life. She was about ten years older than Belokurov, and kept him well in hand, so that before going anywhere he had to ask her permission. She often sobbed, in hoarse, masculine tones, and I had to send and tell her that if she did not stop I would give up my room; and then she would stop sobbing.

When we got home Belokurov sat on my sofa, thinking, his brows knitted, while I paced up and down the room, a prey to soft agitation, for all the world as if I were in love. I felt a desire to talk about the Volchaninovs.

"Lida is capable of loving only some member of the *zemstvo*, somebody as keen on hospitals and schools as herself," I said. "But for a girl like that a man should be willing to walk about in iron boots, like the lover in the fairy-tale, not to speak of becoming a member of the *zemstvo*. And Missuse? What a darling that Missuse is!"

With many an "er," Belokurov embarked upon protracted reflections on pessimism—the disease of our times. He spoke confidently, and by his tone it might have been thought that I was arguing with him. An endless, monotonous, sun-bleached steppe is not more dreary than a single individual who sits in one's room talking and talking, as if he never meant to stop.

"It's not a matter of pessimism or optimism," I said irately. "The point is that ninety per cent of people have no brains."

Belokurov took this remark as a personal affront, and went away offended.

III

"The Prince is staying at Malozemovo, and sends you greetings," said Lida to her mother. She had just come back from some visit and was taking off her gloves. "He was very interesting. He promised to raise the question of a medical post at Malozemovo at the next meeting of the council, but he says there's not much hope. Excuse me," she said, turning to me. "I keep forgetting this sort of thing can't be very interesting to you."

I felt a surge of irritation.

"Why not?" I asked, shrugging my shoulders. "You don't care to know my opinion, but I assure you this question interests me intensely."

"Does it?"

"Yes, it does. In my opinion a medical post is not required in Malozemovo."

My irritation communicated itself to her. Looking at me from narrowed eyes, she said:

"What is required then—landscape paintings?"

"Landscapes are not required, either. Nothing is required."

She had drawn off her gloves and was opening the newspaper which had just been brought from the post-office. A minute after she said quietly, obviously trying to keep her feelings under control:

"Last week Anna died in childbirth; if there had been a medical-aid post in the neighborhood she would be alive now. I can't help thinking that even landscape-painters should deign to have some convictions in this respect."

"I have extremely definite convictions in this respect, I assure you," I replied, but she hid from me behind the newspaper, as if not wishing to hear me. "In my opinion medical-aid posts, schools, libraries, dispensaries only serve the cause of enslavement under existing circumstances. The people are fettered by heavy chains, and you do nothing to break them asunder, only add new links—there you have my convictions."

She raised her eyes to my face and smiled scornfully, but I went on, endeavoring to pin down my basic idea.

"What matters is not that Anna died in childbirth, but that Anna, Martha, and Pelagea must stoop over their work from morning to night, fall sick from onerous toil, spend their whole lives worrying over their hungry, sickly children, in fear of death and disease, dose themselves all their lives, fade early, age early, and die in filth and stench. As soon as their children grow up, they follow the example of their mothers, and hundreds of years pass like this, millions of people living in worse conditions than animals, merely to gain a crust of bread, to live in perpetual fear. And the true horror of their situation is that they never have time to think of their souls, of themselves as images of God. Hunger, cold, physical terror, perpetual toil are like snowdrifts cutting off all paths to spiritual activities, to everything distinguishing human beings from animals and making life worth living. You go to their aid with hospitals and schools, but this does not deliver them from their chains, on the contrary, it enslaves them still more, since, by introducing fresh superstitions into their lives, you increase their demands, not to mention the fact that they have to pay the *zemstvo* for their leeches and their books, and, consequently, to work still harder."

"I shall not argue with you," said Lida, lowering the newspaper. "I have heard all this before. I will only say one thing—one can't just sit and do nothing. True, we are not saving humanity and perhaps we make mistakes, but we do what we can, and—we are right. The loftiest and most sacred task of a cultured person is to serve his neighbors, and we endeavor to do so to the best of our abilities. You don't like what we do, but one can't please everyone, after all."

"True, Lida, true," said her mother.

She was always timid in Lida's presence, glancing nervously at her when she spoke, afraid of saying something foolish or inappropriate. And she never contradicted her, always agreeing with her: "True, Lida, true."

"Peasant literacy, books full of wretched moralizings and popular maxims, and medical-aid posts can no more lessen their ignorance or their mortality rate than the light from your windows can light up this huge garden," I said. "You give them nothing, merely by your interference in the lives of these people creating fresh demands, fresh motives for working."

"But goodness me, something must be done!" said Lida irately, and the tone in which she spoke showed that she considered my arguments trifling and contemptible.

"People must be freed from heavy physical labor," I said. "Their burden must be lightened, they must be given a breathing-space, so that they do not have to spend their whole lives at the stove and the wash-tub, or working in the fields, but have time to think of their souls, too, and of God, and get a chance to display their spiritual abilities. Every individual has a spiritual vocation—the continual search for the truth and significance of life. Free them from coarse, physical toil, let them feel that they have liberty, then you will see the mockery that these books and dispensaries really are. When a person feels his true vocation, the only things that can satisfy him are religion, science, art—and not such trifles."

"Free them from toil!" mocked Lida. "As if that were possible!"

"Yes. Undertake some of their work yourself. If we all, town and country dwellers, all without exception, agreed to take our part in the labor on which the mass of humanity spend their time for the satisfaction of physical requirements, perhaps each one of us would not have to work more than two or three hours a day. Think how it would be if we all, rich and poor alike, worked only three hours a day, and had the rest of the time to ourselves! And think what it would mean if, in order to depend still less on our bodies and work still less, we were to invent machinery to substitute toil, and try to reduce the number of our requirements to a minimum! We would harden ourselves and our children, so that they need not fear hunger and cold, and we need not worry constantly over their health, as Anna, Martha, and Pelagea do. Just think, if we did not take medicine and maintain dispensaries, tobacco factories, and distilleries—what a lot of spare time we should have as a result! We could devote this time to united work on science and art. Just as the peasants sometimes repair the roads in a body, we could, all together, by general consent, search for the truth and meaning of life, and—of this I am sure—the truth would very soon be discovered, humanity would be freed from the perpetual, agonizing, oppressive fear of death—and even from death itself."

"But you contradict yourself," said Lida. "You preach science, and reject the idea of literacy."

"The literacy which enables a person to do no more than spell out tavern-signs, and every now and then read books he cannot understand, has existed in our country since the time of Rurik; Gogol's Petrushka[3] has long been able to read, and yet the countryside is just as it was in Rurik's time. It is not literacy that we need, but leisure for the full display of our spiritual abilities. It is not schools, but universities that we need."

"You deny medicine."

"Yes. It would be required only for the study of disease as a natural phenomenon, and not for its cure. If treatment is required, let it be, not of disease, but of its causes. Remove the main cause—physical labor, and there will be no more diseases. I do not recognize that science which aspires to heal," I continued excitedly. "True science and art aim not at temporary, partial measures, but at what is eternal and general. They seek for the truth and meaning of life, they seek God, the soul, and when they are fastened down to the needs of the moment, to dispensaries and libraries, they can only complicate and burden life. We have plenty of doctors, chemists and lawyers, and there are plenty of literate persons now, but no biologists, mathematicians, philosophers, poets. Our brains, our spiritual energy, are wasted on the satisfaction of temporary, passing needs. . . . Scientists, writers and painters work with a will; thanks to them the comforts of life increase daily, our physical demands multiply, and yet we are far from the truth, and man still remains the most predatory, the uncleanest of animals, and everything tends towards the degeneracy of humanity as a whole and the irreparable loss of vitality. In such conditions the life of the artist is meaningless, and the more talented he is, the worse and the more

3. The servant in *Dead Souls* (1842) who sounds out letters and is gratified that they form words.

incomprehensible his function, since superficially it would appear that he works for the entertainment of a predatory, unclean animal, by supporting the existing order of things. And I don't want to work, and I won't. . . . Nothing is wanted, let the whole world go to pot. . . ."

"Go away, Missuse," said Lida to her sister, apparently considering my words unsuited to the hearing of so young a girl.

Zhenya glanced mournfully from her sister to her mother, and went away.

"People usually say nice things like that when they wish to justify their own indifference," said Lida. "It's much easier to deny the usefulness of hospitals and schools than to cure and to teach. . . ."

"True, Lida, true," said her mother.

"You say you will throw up painting," continued Lida. "Apparently you rate your work very high. Let's stop arguing, we shall never agree, for I rate the most imperfect of those libraries and dispensaries, you have just referred to so contemptuously, higher than all the landscape paintings in the world." And she turned abruptly to her mother, and began speaking in quite a different voice. "The Prince has gotten very thin and has changed greatly since he was last here. They're sending him to Vichy."

She talked to her mother about the Prince, to avoid talking to me. Her face was flushed, and to conceal her agitation, she bent low over the table as if she were shortsighted, and pretended to be reading the paper. My presence was evidently disagreeable to her. I took my leave and went home.

IV

It was very still in the courtyard. The village on the other side of the pond was already asleep, not a light was to be seen, but for the pale reflections of the stars shimmering almost imperceptibly on the surface of the pond. At the gates with the lions Zhenya stood motionless, waiting to see me out. "They're all asleep in the village," I said, trying to make out her features in the darkness, but only seeing a pair of dark, mournful eyes fixed on my face. "The innkeeper and the horsethieves are peacefully asleep, but we, respectable folk, irritate one another and argue."

It was a melancholy August night, melancholy, because there was a hint of autumn in the air. The moon was rising from behind a crimson cloud, but it scarcely lit up the road, on either side of which extended the autumn fields. Shooting stars darted continually about the sky. Zhenya walked beside me along the road and tried not to look up, so as not to see the shooting stars, which for some reason or other frightened her.

"I think you are right," she said, shivering in the evening dampness. "If all of us, all together, were to devote ourselves to spiritual activities, we would soon discover everything."

"Of course. We are higher beings, and if we really appreciated the power of human genius and lived only for higher aims, we should at last become like gods. But that will never be—humanity is degenerating, and soon there will not be a trace of genius left."

When we were out of sight of the gates, Zhenya stood still and hastily pressed my hand.

"Good-night," she said, shivering. She had nothing but a thin blouse over her shoulders, and cringed with cold. "Come tomorrow."

The thought of being alone, in this irritated state of dissatisfaction with myself and others, terrified me. I, too, began trying not to look at the shooting stars.

"Stay with me a little longer," I said. "Do!"

I was in love with Zhenya. Perhaps I had fallen in love with her for her way of meeting me and seeing me off, for the tender, admiring glances she cast at me. Her pale face, thin neck and arms, her delicacy, her idleness, her books, held a wistful appeal for me. And her mind? I suspected her of having an unusual brain. I admired her broad-mindedness, perhaps because she thought differently from the severe, beauteous Lida, who did not like me. Zhenya liked me as an artist, I had conquered her heart by my talent, and I desired passionately to paint for her alone, dreaming of her as my little queen, who would, together with me, hold sway over these villages, fields, this mist, and evening glow, this countryside, so delightful, so exquisite, amidst which I had till now felt so hopelessly lonely and superfluous.

"Wait a little longer," I pleaded. "Only a few minutes."

I took off my coat and put it over her chilly shoulders. Afraid of looking funny and ugly in a man's coat, she laughed and threw it off, and I put my arms round her and began showering kisses on her face, shoulders and hands.

"Till tomorrow," she whispered, embracing me cautiously, as if afraid to disturb the stillness of the night. "We have no secrets from one another, I shall have to tell my mother and sister everything, immediately. . . . Oh, dear, I'm so frightened! Mamma's all right, Mamma is fond of you—but Lida!"

She ran back towards the gate.

"Good-bye!" she cried.

I stood listening to her retreating footsteps for a minute or two. I did not want to go home, and there was no reason for going there. I stood deep in thought for a short time, and then sauntered slowly back, to have another look at the house in which she lived, the dear innocent old house, with its mansard windows looking down at me as if they were eyes, as if they understood everything. I passed the verandah, sat on a bench near the tennis court, in the darkness beneath an ancient willow, and looked at the house from there. In the windows of the mansard, where Missuse's room was, a light shone brilliantly, and then turned a sober green—someone had put a shade on the lamp. Shadows moved. . . . My heart was filled with tenderness, calm and content—delighted to discover that I was capable of falling in love—and yet at the same time I was worried by the thought that at this moment, a few paces away, Lida lived in one of the rooms of this house, Lida, who disliked, perhaps detested, me. I sat there waiting for Zhenya to appear, straining my ears, and it seemed to me I could hear talking in the mansard.

About an hour passed. The green light went out and the shadows could no longer be seen. The moon now rode high over the house and lit up the sleeping garden and deserted walks. The dahlias and roses in the bed in front of the house stood out distinctly, but they all looked the same color. It grew really cold. I went out of the garden, picked up my coat from the road, and wandered slowly homewards.

When I went to the Volchaninovs the next afternoon, the glass door into the garden was wide open. I sat down on the verandah, hoping Zhenya would suddenly appear on the tennis court, or on one of the paths, listening for the sound of her voice from the house. Then I went into the drawing-room and after that the dining-room. Not a soul was in sight. From the dining-room I made my way through the long passage into the hall, and back again. There were several doors opening into the passage, and from one of the rooms could be heard Lida's voice:

"The crow had somewhere found a bit of—"[1] she was saying loudly, in a singsong voice—dictating probably. ". . a bit of cheese. . . . The crow— Who's there?" she cried suddenly, hearing my steps.

"It's me."

"Oh. Excuse me, I can't come to you just now, I'm giving Dasha her lesson."

"Is Yekaterina Pavlovna in the garden?"

"No. She and my sister left this morning on a visit to my aunt in Penza province. And in the winter they'll probably go abroad," she added, after a short pause.

"A crow had . . . somewhere . . . found . . . a bit of cheese. . . . Written that down?"

I went into the hall and stood there, staring vacantly at the pond and the distant village, my ears still assailed by the words: ". . . a bit of cheese. . . . The crow had somewhere found a bit of cheese. . . ."

I went off the estate by the road I had approached it from the first time, but in reverse—from the courtyard to the garden, past the house, till I got to the lime-tree avenue . . . . Here a small boy ran

---

1. The beginning of the fable "The Crow and the Fox" by I. A. Krylov. Like Aesop's fable it shows how flattery may lead to less—the reverse of the situation in the story.

after me and gave me a note. "I told my sister everything and she insists that we part," I read. "I had not the heart to grieve her by disobedience. May God send you happiness—forgive me! If you only knew how bitterly Mamma and I are crying."

Then came the fir walk, the broken railings. . . . In the field where the rye had been in bloom and the quail had given its cries, there now wandered cows and hobbled horses. Here and there on hillocks the winter crops showed green. A prosaic everyday mood enveloped me and I was ashamed of all I had said at the Volchaninovs', and once more life became a tedious affair. When I got home I packed up my things, and I left for Petersburg that evening.

I never saw the Volchaninovs again. Not so long ago I met Belokurov in the train on my way to the Crimea. He was still wearing his peasant coat and embroidered shirt, and when I asked him how he was, he replied: "Quite well, thanks to your prayers!" We had a talk. He had sold his estate and bought another, a smaller one, in the name of Lyubov Ivanovna. He could not tell me much about the Volchaninovs. Lida still lived at Shelkovka and taught in the village school. She had gradually contrived to gather round her a circle of people in sympathy with her ideas, and these composed a powerful party, and at the last *zemstvo* meetings they had black-balled Balagin, who till then had kept the whole distirict in his hands. All he could tell me of Zhenya was that she did not live at home, and he did not know where she was.

I have begun to forget the house with the mansard, but every once in a while, painting or reading, I recall for no apparent reason the green light in the window, the sound of my own steps echoing in the nocturnal fields, that night I returned home, in love, chafing my cold hands. Still less frequently, in moments of loneliness and melancholy, I yield to vague memories, till I gradually being to feel that I, too, am remembered, that I am being waited for, and that we shall meet. . . .

Missuse . . . where are you?

1896

The Pecheneg[1]

One hot summer's day Ivan Zhmukhin was returning from town to his farm in southern Russia. Zhmukhin was an old, retired Cossack officer who had served in the Caucasus, and had once been lusty and strong, but he was an old man now, shriveled and bent, with bushy eyebrows and a long, greenish-gray moustache. He had been fasting in town, and had made his will, for it was only two

1. A member of a marauding Turkic tribe that attacked ancient Rus during the ninth, tenth, and eleventh centuries. The implication is "savage."

weeks since he had had a paralytic stroke, and now, sitting in the train, he was full of deep, gloomy thoughts of his approaching death, of the vanity of life, and of the transient quality of all earthly things. At Provalye, one of the stations on the Don railway, a fair-haired, middle-aged man, carrying a worn portfolio under his arm, entered the compartment and sat down opposite the old Cossack. They began talking together.

"No," said Zhmukhin gazing pensively out of the window. "It is never too late to marry. I myself was forty-eight when I married, and everyone said it was too late, but it has turned out to be neither too late nor too early. Still, it is better never to marry at all. Everyone soon gets tired of a wife, though not everyone will tell you the truth, because, you know, people are ashamed of their family troubles, and try to conceal them. It is often 'Manya, dear Manya,' with a man when, if he had his way, he would put that Manya of his into a sack, and throw her into the river. A wife is a nuisance and a bore, and children are no better, I can assure you. I have two scoundrels myself. There is nowhere they can go to school on the steppe, and I can't afford to send them to Novocherkask, so they are growing up here like young wolf cubs. At any moment they may murder someone on the highway."

The fair-haired man listened attentively, and answered all questions addressed to him briefly, in a low voice. He was evidently gentle and unassuming. He told his companion that he was an attorney, on his way to the village of Duevka on business.

"Why, for heaven's sake, that's only nine miles from where I live!" cried Zhmukhin, as if someone had been disputing it. "You won't be able to get any horses at the station this evening. In my opinion the best thing for you to do is to come home with me, you know, and spend the night at my house, you know, and let me send you on tomorrow with my horses."

After a moment's reflection the attorney accepted the invitation.

The sun was hanging low over the steppe when they arrived at the station. The two men remained silent as they drove from the railway to the farm, for the jolting that the road gave them forbade conversation. The *tarantass*[2] boundéd and whined and seemed to be sobbing, as if its leaps caused it the keenest pain, and the attorney, who found his seat very uncomfortable, gazed with anguish before him, hoping to descry the farm in the distance. After they had driven eight miles a low house surrounded by a dark wattle fence came into view. The roof was painted green, the stucco on the walls was peeling off, and the little windows looked like puckered eyes. The farmhouse stood completely exposed to the sun; neither trees nor water were visible anywhere near it. The neighboring land-

2. A type of carriage used in southern Russia.

owners and peasants called it "Pecheneg Grange." Many years ago a passing surveyor who was spending the night at the farm had talked with Zhmukhin all night, and had gone away in the morning much displeased, saying sternly as he left: "Sir, you are nothing but a Pecheneg!" So the name "Pecheneg Grange" had been given to the farm, and had stuck to it all the more closely as Zhmukhin boys began to grow up, and to perpetrate raids on the neighboring gardens and melon fields. Zhmukhin himself was known as "old man you know," because he talked so much and used the words "you know" so often.

Zhmukhin's two sons were standing in the courtyard, near the stables, as the *tarantass* drove up. One was about nineteen, the other was a hobbledehoy a few years younger; both were barefoot and hatless. As the carriage went by the younger boy threw a hen high up over his head. It described an arc in the air, and fluttered cackling down till the elder fired a shot from his gun, and the dead bird fell to earth with a thud.

"Those are my boys learning to shoot birds on the wing," Zhmukhin said.

The travelers were met in the entryway by a woman, a thin, pale-faced little creature, still pretty and young, who, from her dress, might have been taken for a servant.

"This," said Zhmukhin, "is the mother of those sons of guns of mine. Come on, Lyubov!" he cried to his wife. "Hustle, now, mother, and help entertain our guest. Bring us some supper! Quick!"

The house consisted of two wings. On one side were the "drawing-room" and, adjoining it, the old man's bedchamber; close, stuffy apartments both, with low ceilings, infested by thousands of flies. On the other side was the kitchen, where the cooking and washing were done and the workmen were fed. Here, under benches, geese and turkeys were sitting on their nests, and here stood the beds of Lyubov and her two sons. The furniture in the drawing-room was unpainted and had evidently been made by a country joiner. On the walls hung guns, game bags, and whips, all of which old trash was rusty and gray with dust. Not a picture was on the walls; only a dark, painted board that had once been an icon hung in one corner of the room.

A young peasant woman set the table and brought in ham and borshch. Zhmukhin's guest declined vodka, and confined himself to eating cucumbers and bread.

"And what about the ham?" Zhmukhin asked.

"No, thank you, I don't eat ham," answered his guest. "I don't eat meat of any kind."

"Why not?"

"I'm a vegetarian. It's against my principles to kill animals."

Zhmukhin was silent for a moment, and then said slowly, with a sigh:

"I see—yes. I saw a man in town who didn't eat meat either. It is a new religion people have. And why shouldn't they have it? It's a good thing. One can't always be killing and shooting; one must take a rest sometimes and let the animals have a little peace. Of course it's a sin to kill, there's no doubt about that. Sometimes, when you shoot a hare, and hit him in the leg he will scream like a baby. So it hurts him!"

"Of course it hurts him! Animals suffer pain just as much as we do."

"That's a fact!" Zhmukhin agreed. "I see that perfectly," he added pensively. "Only there is one thing that I must say I can't quite understand. Suppose, for instance, you know, everyone were to stop eating meat, what would become of all our barnyard fowls, like chickens and geese?"

"Chickens and geese would go free just like all other birds."

"Ah! Now I understand. Of course. Crows and magpies get on without us all right. Yes. And chickens and geese and rabbits and sheep would all be free and happy, you know, and would praise God, and not be afraid of us anymore. So peace and quiet would reign upon earth. Only one thing I can't understand, you know," Zhmukhin continued, with a glance at the ham. "Where would all the pigs go to? What would become of them?"

"The same thing that would become of all the other animals, they would go free."

"I see—yes. But, listen, if they were not killed, they would multiply, you know, and then it would be good-bye to our meadows and vegetable gardens! Why, if a pig is turned loose and not watched, it will ruin everything for you in a day! A pig is a pig, and hasn't been called one for nothing!"

They finished their supper. Zhmukhin rose from the table, and walked up and down the room for a long time, talking interminably. He loved to think of and discuss deep and serious subjects, and was longing to discover some theory that would sustain him in his old age, so that he might find peace of mind, and not think it so terrible to die. He desired for himself the same gentleness and self-confidence and peace of mind which he saw in this guest of his, who had just eaten his fill of cucumbers and bread, and was a better man for it, sitting there on a bench so healthy and fat, patiently bored, looking like a huge heathen idol that nothing could move from his seat.

"If a man can only find some idea to hold to in life, he will be happy," Zhmukhin thought.

The old Cossack went out on the front steps, and the attorney could hear him sighing and repeating to himself:

"Yes—I see——"

Night was falling, and the stars were shining out one by one. The lamps in the house had not been lit. Someone came creeping toward the drawing-room as silently as a shadow, and stopped in the doorway. It was Lyubov, Zhmukhin's wife.

"Have you come from the city?" she asked timidly, without looking at her guest.

"Yes, I live in the city."

"Maybe you know about schools, master, and can tell us what to do if you will be so kind. We need advice."

"What do you want?"

"We have two sons, kind master, and they should have been sent to school long ago, but nobody ever comes here and we have no one to tell us anything. I myself know nothing. If they don't go to school, they will be taken into the army as common Cossacks. That is hard, master. They can't read or write, they are worse off than peasants, and their father himself despises them, and won't let them come into the house. Is it their fault? If only the younger one, at least, could be sent to school! It's a pity to see them so!" she wailed, and her voice trembled. It seemed incredible that a woman so little and young could already have grown-up children. "Ah, it is such a pity!" she said again.

"You know nothing about it, mother, and it's none of your business," said Zhmukhin, appearing in the doorway. "Don't pester our guest with your wild talk. Go away, mother!"

Lyubov went out, repeating once more in a high little voice as she reached the hall:

"Ah, it is such a pity!"

A bed was made up for the attorney on a sofa in the drawing-room, and Zhmukhin lit the little shrine lamp, so that he might not be left in the dark. Then he lay down in his own bedroom. Lying there he thought of many things: his soul, his old age, and his recent stroke which had given him such a fright and had so sharply reminded him of his approaching death. He liked to philosophize when he was alone in the dark, and at these times he imagined himself to be a very deep and serious person indeed, whose attention only questions of importance could engage. He now kept thinking that he would like to get hold of some one idea unlike any other idea he had ever had, something significant that would be the lodestar of his life. He wanted to think of some law for himself, that would make his life as serious and deep as he himself personally was. And here was an idea! He could go without meat now, and deprive himself of everything that was superfluous to his existence! The time would surely come when people would no longer kill animals or one another, it could not but come, and he pictured his future in his mind's eye, and distinctly saw himself living at peace with all the animal world. Then he remembered the pigs again, and his brain began to reel.

"What a muddle it all is!" he muttered, heaving a deep sigh.

"Are you asleep?" he asked.

"No."

Zhmukhin rose from his bed, and stood on the threshold of the door in his nightshirt, exposing to his guest's view his thin, sinewy legs, as straight as posts.

"Just look, now," he began. "Here is all this telegraph and telephone business, in a word, all these marvels, you know, and yet people are no more virtuous than they used to be. It is said that when I was young, thirty or forty years ago, people were rougher and crueler than they are now, but aren't they just the same today? Of course, they were less ceremonious when I was a youngster. I remember how once, when we had been stationed on the bank of a river in the Caucasus for four months without anything to do, quite a little romance took place. On the very bank of the river, you know, where our regiment was encamped, we had buried a prince whom we had killed not long before. So at night, you know, his princess used to come down to the grave and cry. She screamed and screamed, and groaned and groaned until we got into such a state that we couldn't sleep a wink. We didn't sleep for nights. We grew tired of it. And honestly, why should we be kept awake by that devil of a voice? Excuse the expression! So we took that princess and gave her a good thrashing, and she stopped coming to the grave. There you are! Nowadays, of course, men of that category don't exist anymore. People don't thrash one another, and they live more cleanly and learn more lessons than they used to, but their hearts haven't changed one bit, you know. Listen to this, for instance. There is a landlord near here who owns a coal mine, you know. He has all sorts of vagabonds and men without passports working for him, men who have nowhere else to go. When Saturday comes round the workmen have to be paid, and their employer never wants to do that, he is too fond of his money. So he has picked out a foreman, a vagabond, too, though he wears a hat, and he says to him: 'Don't pay them a thing,' says our gentleman, 'not even a penny. They will beat you, but you must stand it. If you do, I'll give you ten rubles every Saturday.' So every week, regularly, when Saturday evening comes round, the workmen come for their wages, and the foreman says: 'There aren't any wages!' Well, words follow, and then come abuse and a drubbing. They beat him and kick him, for the men are wild with hunger, you know; they beat him until he is unconscious, and then go off to the four winds of heaven. The owner of the mine orders cold water to be thrown over his foreman, and pitches him ten rubles. The man takes the money, and is thankful, for the fact is, he would agree to wear a noose round his neck for a penny! Yes, and on Monday a new gang of workmen arrives. They come because they have nowhere else to go. On Saturday there is the same old story over again."

The attorney rolled over, with his face toward the back of the sofa, and mumbled something incoherent.

"Take another example, for instance," Zhmukhin went on. "When we had the Siberian cattle plague here, you know, the cattle died like flies, I can tell you. The veterinary surgeons came, and strictly ordered all infected stock that died to be buried as far away from the farm as possible, and to be covered with lime and so on, according to the laws of science. Well, one of my horses died. I buried it with the greatest care, and shoveled at least 400 pounds of lime on top of it, but what do you think? That pair of young jackanapeses of mine dug up the horse one night, and sold the skin for three rubles! There now, what do you think of that?"

Flashes of lightning were gleaming through the cracks of the shutters on one side of the room. The air was sultry before the approaching storm, and the mosquitoes had begun to bite. Zhmukhin groaned and sighed, as he lay meditating in his bed, and kept repeating to himself:

"Yes—I see——"

Sleep was impossible. Somewhere in the distance thunder was growling.

"Are you awake?"

"Yes," answered his guest.

Zhmukhin rose and walked with shuffling slippers through the drawing-room, and hall, and into the kitchen to get a drink of water.

"The worst thing in the world is stupidity," he said, as he returned a few minutes later with a dipper in his hand. "That Lyubov of mine gets down on her knees and prays to God every night. She flops down on the floor and prays that the boys may be sent to school, you know. She is afraid they will be drafted into the army as common Cossacks, and have their backs tickled with sabers. But it would take money to send them to school, and where can I get it? What you haven't got you haven't got, and it's no use crying for the moon! Another reason she prays is because, like all women, you know, she thinks she is the most unhappy creature in the world. I am an outspoken man, and I won't hide anything from you. She comes of a poor priest's family—of church-bell stock, one might say—and I married her when she was seventeen. They gave her to me chiefly because times were hard, and her family were in want and had nothing to eat, and when all is said and done I do own some land, as you see, and I am an officer of sorts. She felt flattered at the idea of being my wife, you know. But she began to cry on the day of our wedding, and has cried every day since for twenty years; her eyes must be made of water! She does nothing but sit and think. What does she think about, I ask you? What can a woman think about? Nothing! The fact is, I don't consider women human beings."

The attorney jumped up impetuously, and sat up in bed.

"Excuse me, I feel a little faint," he said. "I am going outdoors."

Zhmukhin, still talking about women, drew back the bolts of the hall door, and both men went out together. A full moon was floating over the grange. The house and stables looked whiter than they had by day, and shimmering white bands of light lay among the shadows on the lawn. To the right lay the steppe, with the stars glowing softly over it; as one gazed into its depths, it looked mysterious and infinitely distant, like some bottomless abyss. To the left, heavy thunderclouds lay piled one upon another. Their margins were lit by the rays of the moon, and they resembled dark forests, seas, and mountains with snowy summits. Flashes of lightning were playing about their peaks, and soft thunder was growling in their depths; a battle seemed to be raging among them.

Quite near the house a little screech owl was crying monotonously:

"Whew! Whew!"

"What time is it?" asked the attorney.

"Nearly two o'clock."

"What a long time yet until dawn!"

They re-entered the house and lay down. It was time to go to sleep, and sleep is usually so sound before a storm, but the old man was pining for grave, weighty meditations, and he not only wanted to think, he wanted to talk as well, So he babbled on of what a fine thing it would be if, for the sake of his soul, a man could shake off this idleness that was imperceptibly and uselessly devouring his days and years one after another. He said he would like to think of some feat of strength to perform, such as making a long journey on foot or giving up meat, as this young man had done. And once more he pictured the future when men would no longer kill animals; he pictured it as clearly and precisely as if he himself had lived at that time, but suddenly his thoughts grew confused, and again he understood nothing.

The thunderstorm rolled by, but one corner of the cloud passed over the grange, and the rain began to drum on the roof. Zhmukhin got up, sighing with age and stretching his limbs, and peered into the drawing-room. Seeing that his guest was still awake, he said:

"When we were in the Caucasus, you know, we had a colonel who was a vegetarian as you are. He never ate meat and never hunted or allowed his men to fish. I can understand that, of course.

Every animal has a right to enjoy its life and its freedom. But I can't understand how pigs could be allowed to roam wherever they pleased without being watched——"

His guest sat up in bed; his pale, haggard face was stamped with vexation and fatigue. It was plain that he was suffering agonies, and that only a kind and considerate heart forbade him to put his irritation into words.

"It is already light," he said briefly. "Please let me have a horse now."

"What do you mean? Wait until the rain stops!"

"No, please!" begged the guest in a panic. "I really must be going at once!"

And he began to dress quickly.

The sun was already rising when a horse and carriage were brought to the door. The rain had stopped, the clouds were skimming across the sky, and the rifts of blue were growing wider and wider between them. The first rays of the sun were timidly lighting up the meadows below. The attorney passed through the entryway with his portfolio under his arm, while Zhmukhin's wife, with red eyes, and a face even paler than it had been the evening before, stood gazing fixedly at him with the innocent look of a little girl. Her sorrowful face showed how much she envied her guest his liberty. Ah, with what joy she, too, would have left this place! Her eyes spoke of something she longed to say to him, perhaps some advice she wanted to ask him about her boys. How pitiful she was! She was not a wife, she was not the mistress of the house, she was not even a servant, but a miserable dependent, a poor relation, a nonentity wanted by no one. Her husband bustled about near his guest, not ceasing his talk for an instant, and at last ran ahead to see him into the carriage, while she stood shrinking timidly and guiltily against the wall, still waiting for the moment to come that would give her an opportunity to speak.

"Come again! Come again!" the old man repeated over and over again. "Everything we have is at your service, you know!"

His guest hastily climbed into the *tarantass*, obviously with infinite pleasure, looking as if he were afraid every second of being detained. The *tarantass* bounded and whined as it had done the day before, and a bucket tied on behind clattered madly. The attorney looked round at Zhmukhin with a peculiar expression in his eyes. He seemed to be wanting to call him a Pecheneg, or something of the sort, as the surveyor had done, but his kindness triumphed. He controlled himself, and the words remained unsaid. As he reached the gate, however, he suddenly felt that he could no longer contain himself; he rose in his seat and cried out in a loud, angry voice:

"You bore me to death!"

And with these words he vanished through the gate. Zhmukhin's two sons were standing in front of the stable. The older was holding a gun, the younger had in his arms a gray cock with a bright red comb. The younger tossed the cock into the air with all his might; the bird shot up higher than the roof of the house, and turned over in the air. The elder boy shot, and it fell to the ground like a stone.

The old man stood nonplussed, unable to comprehend his guest's unexpected exclamation. At last he turned and slowly went into the house. Sitting down to his breakfast, he fell into a long reverie about the present tendency of thought, about the universal wickedness of the present generation, about the telegraph and the telephone and bicycles, and about how unnecessary it all was. But he grew calmer little by little as he slowly ate his meal. He drank five glasses of tea, and lay down to take a nap.

1897

A Journey by Cart

They left the city at half past eight.

The highway was dry and a splendid April sun was beating fiercely down, but the snow still lay in the woods and wayside ditches. The long, dark, cruel winter was only just over, spring had come in a breath, but for Marya Vasilyevna, driving along the road in a cart, there was nothing either new or attractive in the warmth, or in the listless, misty woods flushed with the first heat of spring, or in the flocks of crows flying far away across the wide, flooded meadows, or in the marvellous, unfathomable sky into which one felt one could sail away with such infinite pleasure. Marya Vasilyevna had been a schoolteacher for thirty years, and it would have been impossible for her to count the number of times she had driven to town for her salary, and returned home as she was doing now. It mattered not to her whether the season were spring, as now, or winter, or autumn with darkness and rain; she invariably longed for one thing and one thing only: a speedy end to her journey.

She felt as if she had lived in this part of the world for a long, long time, even a hundred years or more, and it seemed to her that she knew every stone and every tree along the roadside between her school and the city. Here lay her past and her present as well, and she could not conceive of a future beyond her school and the road and the city, and then the road and her school again, and then once more the road and the city.

Of her past before she had been a schoolteacher she had long since ceased to think—she had almost forgotten it. She had had a father and mother once, and had lived with them in a large apartment near the Red Gate in Moscow, but her recollection of that life was as vague and shadowy as a dream. Her father had died when she was ten years old, and her mother had soon followed him. She had had a brother, an officer, with whom she had corresponded at first, but he had lost the habit of writing to her after a while, and had stopped answering her letters. Of her former belongings her mother's photograph was now her only possession, and this had been so faded by the dampness of the school that her mother's features had all disappeared except the eyebrows and hair.

When they had gone three miles on their way old Daddy Semyon, who was driving the cart, turned round and said:

"They have caught one of the town officials and have shipped him away. They say he killed the mayor of Moscow with the help of some Germans."

"Who told you that?"

"Ivan Ionov read it in the paper at the inn."

For a long time neither spoke. Marya Vasilyevna was thinking of her school, and the coming examinations for which she was preparing four boys and one girl. And just as her mind was full of these examinations, a landowner named Khanov drove up with a four-in-hand harnessed to an open carriage. It was he who had held the examination in her school the year before. As he drove up alongside her cart he recognized her, bowed, and exclaimed:

"Good morning! Are you on your way home, may I ask?"

Khanov was a man of forty or thereabouts. His expression was listless and blasé, and he had already begun to age perceptibly, but he was handsome still and admired by women. He lived alone on a large estate; he had no business anywhere, and it was said of him that he never did anything at home but walk about and whistle, or else play chess with his old manservant. It was also rumored that he was a hard drinker. Marya Vasilyevna remembered that, as a matter of fact, at the last examination even the papers that he had brought with him had smelled of scent and wine. Everything he had had on that day had been new, and Marya Vasilyevna had liked him very much, and had even felt shy sitting there beside him. She was used to receiving the visits of cold, critical examiners, but this one did not remember a single prayer, and did not know what questions he ought to ask. He had been extremely considerate and polite, and had given all the children full marks for everything.

"I am on my way to visit Bakvist," he now continued to Marya Vasilyevna. "Is it true that he is away from home?"

They turned from the highway into a lane, Khanov in the lead, Semyon following him. The four horses proceeded at a foot-pace, straining to drag the heavy carriage through the mud. Semyon tacked hither and thither across the road, first driving round a bump, then round a puddle, and jumping down from his seat every minute or so to give his horse a helpful push. Marya Vasilyevna continued to think about the school, and whether the questions at the examinations would be difficult or easy. She felt annoyed with the board of the *zemstvo*,[1] for she had been there yesterday, and had found no one in. How badly it was managed! Here it was two years since she had been asking to have the school watchman discharged for loafing and being rude to her and beating her pupils, and yet no one had paid any heed to her request. The president of the board was hardly ever in his office, and when he was, would vow with tears in his eyes that he hadn't time to attend to her now. The school inspector came only three times a year, and knew nothing about his business anyway, as he had formerly been an exciseman, and had obtained the office of inspector through pull. The school board seldom met, and no one ever knew where their meetings were held. The warden was an illiterate peasant who owned a tannery, a rough and stupid man and a close friend of the watchman's. In fact, the Lord only knew whom one could turn to to have complaints remedied and wrongs put right!

"He really is handsome!" thought the schoolteacher, glancing at Khanov.

The road grew worse and worse. They entered a wood. There was no possibility of turning out of the track here, the ruts were deep and full of gurgling, running water. Prickly twigs beat against their faces.

"What a road, eh?" cried Khanov laughing.

The schoolteacher looked at him and marveled that this queer fellow should be living here.

"What good do his wealth, his handsome face, and his fine culture do him in this godforsaken mud and solitude?" she thought. "He has abandoned any advantage that fate may have given him, and is enduring the same hardships as Semyon, tramping with him along this impossible road. Why does anyone live here who could live in St. Petersburg or abroad?"

And it seemed to her that it would be worth this rich man's while to make a good road out of this bad one, so that he might not have to struggle with the mud, and be forced to see the despair written on the faces of Semyon and his coachman. But he only laughed, and was obviously absolutely indifferent to it all, asking for no better life than this.

"He is kind and gentle and unsophisticated," Marya Vasilyevna thought again. "He does not understand the hardships of life any more than he knew the suitable prayers to say at the examination.

1. District administration.

He gives globes to the school and sincerely thinks himself a useful man and a conspicuous benefactor of popular education. Much they need his globes in this wilderness!"

"Sit tight, Vasilyevna!" shouted Semyon.

The cart tipped violently to one side and seemed to be falling over. Something heavy rolled down on Marya Vasilyevna's feet; it proved to the the purchases she had made in the city. They were crawling up a steep, clayey hill now. Torrents of water were rushing noisily down on either side of the track, and seemed to have eaten away the road bed. Surely it would be impossible to get by! The horses began to snort. Khanov jumped out of his carriage and walked along the edge of the road in his long overcoat. He felt hot.

"What a road!" he laughed again. "My carriage will soon be smashed to bits at this rate!"

"And who asked you to go driving in weather like this?" asked Semyon sternly. "Why don't you stay at home?"

"It is tiresome staying at home, Daddy. I don't like it."

He looked gallant and tall walking beside old Semyon, but in spite of his grace there was an almost imperceptible something about his walk that betrayed a being already rotten at the core, weak, and nearing his downfall. And the air in the woods suddenly seemed to carry an odor of wine. Marya Vasilyevna shuddered, and began to feel sorry for this man who for some unknown reason was going to his ruin. She thought that if she were his wife or his sister she would gladly give up her whole life to rescuing him from disaster. His wife? Alas! He lived alone on his great estate, and she lived alone in a forlorn little village, and yet the very idea that they might one day become intimate and equal seemed to her impossible and absurd. Life was like that! And, at bottom, all human relationships and all life were so incomprehensible that if you thought about them at all dread would overwhelm you and your heart would stop beating.

"And how incomprehensible it is, too," she thought, "that God should give such beauty and charm and such kind, melancholy eyes to weak, unhappy, useless people, and make everyone like them so!"

"I turn off to the right here," Khanov said, getting into his carriage. "Farewell! A pleasant journey to you!"

And once more Marya Vasilyevna's thoughts turned to her scholars, and the coming examinations, and the watchman, and the school board, until a gust of wind from the right bringing her the rumbling of the departing carriage, other reveries mingled with these thoughts, and she longed to dream of handsome eyes and love and the happiness that would never be hers.

She, a wife! Alas, how cold her little room was early in the morning! No one ever lit her stove, because the watchman was always away somewhere. Her pupils came at daybreak, with a great noise, bringing in with them mud and snow, and everything was so bleak and so uncomfortable in her little quarters of one small bedroom which also served as a kitchen! Her head ached every day when school was over. She was obliged to collect money from her pupils to buy wood and pay the watchman, and then to give it to that fat, insolent peasant, the warden, and beg him for mercy's sake to send her a load of wood. And at night she would dream of examinations and peasants and snowdrifts. This life had aged and hardened her, and she had grown plain and angular and awkward, as if lead had been emptied into her veins. She was afraid of everything, and never dared to sit down in the presence of the warden or a member of the school board. If she mentioned any one of them in his absence, she always spoke of him respectfully as "His Honor." No one found her attractive; her life was spent without love, without friendship, without acquaintances who interested her. What a terrible calamity it would be were she, in her situation, to fall in love!

"Sit tight, Vasilyevna!"

Once more they were crawling up a steep hill.

She had felt no call to be a teacher; want had forced her to be one. She never thought about her mission in life or the value of education; the most important things to her were, not her pupils nor their instruction, but the examinations. And how could she think of a mission, and of the value of education? Schoolteachers, and poor doctors, and apothecaries, struggling with their heavy labors, have not even the consolation of thinking that they are advancing an ideal, and helping mankind. Their heads are too full of thoughts of their daily crust of bread, their wood, the bad roads, and their sicknesses for that. Their life is tedious and hard. Only those stand it for any length of time who are silent beasts of burden, like Marya Vasilyevna. Those who are sensitive and impetuous and nervous, and who talk of their mission in life and of advancing a great ideal, soon become exhausted and give up the fight.

To find a dryer, shorter road, Semyon sometimes struck across a meadow or drove through a back yard, but in some places the peasants would not let him pass, in others the land belonged to a priest; here the road was blocked, there Ivan Ionov had bought a piece of land from his master and surrounded it with a ditch. In such cases they had to turn back.

They arrived at Nizhni Gorodishe. In the snowy, grimy yard around the tavern stood rows of wagons laden with huge flasks of sulphuric acid. A great crowd of carriers had assembled in the tavern, and the air reeked of vodka, tobacco, and sheepskin coats. Loud talk filled the room, and the door with its weight and pulley banged incessantly. In the tap-room behind a partition some one was playing on the concertina without a moment's pause. Marya Vasilyevna sat down to her tea, while at a nearby table a group of peasants saturated with tea and the heat of the room were drinking vodka and beer.

A confused babel filled the room.

"Did you hear that, Kuzma? Ha! Ha! What's that? By God! Ivan Dementich, you'll catch it for that! Look, brother!"

A small, black-bearded, pockmarked peasant, who had been drunk for a long time, gave an exclamation of surprise and swore an ugly oath.

"What do you mean by swearing, you!" shouted Semyon angrily from where he sat, far away at the other end of the room. "Can't you see there's a lady here?"

"A lady!" mocked someone from another corner.

"You pig, you!"

"I didn't mean to do it—" faltered the little peasant with embarrassment. "Excuse me! My money is as good here as hers. How do you do?"

"How do you do?" answered the schoolteacher.

"Very well, thank you kindly."

Marya Vasilyevna enjoyed her tea, and grew as flushed as the peasants. Her thoughts were once more running on the watchman and the wood.

"Look there, brother!" she heard a voice at the next table cry. "There's the schoolmarm from Vyasovya! I know her! She's a nice lady."

"Yes, she's a nice lady."

The door banged, men came and went. Marya Vasilyevna sat absorbed in the same thoughts that had occupied her before, and the concertina behind the partition never ceased making music for an instant. Patches of sunlight that had lain on the floor when she had come in had moved up to the counter, then to the walls, and now had finally disappeared. So it was afternoon. The carriers at the table next to hers rose and prepared to leave. The little peasant went up to Marya Vasilyevna swaying slightly, and held out his hand. The others followed him; all shook hands with the schoolteacher, and went out one by one. The door banged and whined nine times.

"Get ready, Vasilyevna!" Semyon cried.

They started again, still at a walk.

"A little school was built here in Nizhni Gorodishe, not long ago," said Semyon, looking back. "Some of the people sinned greatly."

"In what way?"

"It seems the president of the school board grabbed one thousand rubles, and the warden another thousand, and the teacher five hundred."

"A school always costs several thousand rubles. It is very wrong to repeat scandal, Daddy. What you have just told me is nonsense."

"I don't know anything about it. I only tell you what people say."

It was clear, however, that Semyon did not believe the school-teacher. None of the peasants believed her. They all thought that her salary was too large (she got twenty rubles a month, and they thought that five would have been plenty), and they also believed that most of the money which she collected from the children for wood she pocketed herself. The warden thought as all the other peasants did, and made a little out of the wood himself, besides receiving secret pay from the peasants unknown to the authorities.

But now, thank goodness, they had finally passed through the last of the woods, and from here on their road would lie through flat fields all the way to Vyasovya. Onle a few miles more to go, and then they would cross the river, and then the railway track, and then they would be at home.

"Where are you going, Semyon?" asked Marya Vasilyevna. "Take the right-hand road across the bridge!"

"What's that? We can cross here. It isn't very deep."

"Don't let the horse drown!"

"What's that?"

"There is Khanov crossing the bridge!" cried Marya Vasilyevna, catching sight of a carriage and four in the distance at their right. "Isn't that he?"

"That's him all right. He must have found Bakvist away. My goodness, what a donkey to drive all the way round when this road is two miles shorter!"

They plunged into the river. In summertime it was a tiny stream, in late spring it dwindled rapidly to a fordable river after the fresh-ets, and by August it was generally dry, but during flood time it was a torrent of swift, cold, turbid water some fifty feet wide. Fresh wheel tracks were visible now on the bank leading down to the water's edge; someone, then, must have crossed here.

"Get up!" cried Semyon, madly jerking the reins and flapping his arms like a pair of wings. "Get up!"

The horse waded into the stream up to his belly, stopped, and then plunged on again, throwing his whole weight into the collar. Marya Vasilyevna felt a sharp wave of cold water lap her feet.

"Go on!" she cried, rising in her seat. "Go on!"

They drove out on the opposite bank.

"Well, of all things! My goodness!" muttered Semyon. "What a worthless lot those *zemstvo* people are——"

Marya Vasilyevna's galoshes and shoes were full of water, and the bottom of her dress and coat and one of her sleeves were soaked and dripping. Her sugar and flour were wet through, and this was harder to bear than all the rest. In her despair she could only wave her arms, and cry:

"Oh, Semyon, Semyon! How stupid you are, really——"

The gate was down when they reached the railway crossing, an express train was leaving the station. They stood and waited for the train to go by, and Marya Vasilyevna shivered with cold from head to foot.

Vyasovya was already in sight; there was the school with its green roof, and there stood the church with its blazing crosses reflecting the rays of the setting sun. The windows of the station were flashing, too, and a cloud of rosy steam was rising from the engine. Everything seemed to the schoolteacher to be shivering with cold.

At last the train appeared. Its windows were blazing like the crosses on the church, and their brilliance was dazzling. A lady was standing on the platform of one of the first-class carriages. One glance at her as she slipped past, and Marya Vasilyevna thought: "My mother!" What a resemblance there was! There was her mother's thick and luxuriant hair; there were her forehead and the poise of her head. For the first time in all these thirty years Marya Vasilyevna saw in imagination her mother, her father, and her brother in their apartment in Moscow, saw everything down to the least detail, even to the globe of goldfish in the sitting-room. She heard the strains of a piano, and the sound of her father's voice, and saw herself young and pretty and gaily dressed, in a warm, brightly lighted room with her family about her. Great joy and happiness suddenly welled up in her heart, and she pressed her hands to her temples in rapture, crying softly with a note of deep entreaty in her voice:

"Mother!"

Then she wept, she could not have said why. At that moment Khanov drove up with his four-in-hand, and when she saw him she smiled and nodded to him as if he and she were near and dear to each other, for she was conjuring up in her fancy a felicity that could never be hers. The sky, the trees, and the windows of the houses seemed to be reflecting her happiness and rejoicing with her. No! Her mother and father had not died; she had never been a schoolteacher; all that had been a long, strange, painful dream, and now she was awake.

"Vasilyevna! Sit down!"

And in a breath everything vanished. The gate slowly rose. Shivering and numb with cold Marya Vasilyevna sat down in the cart again. The four-in-hand crossed the track and Semyon followed. The watchman at the crossing took off his cap as they drove by.

"Here is Vyasovya! The journey is over!"

1897

The Man in a Case

The sportsmen, overtaken by darkness on the outskirts of the village of Mironositskoye, decided to spend the night in a shed belonging to Prokofy, the village elder. There were two of them, Ivan Ivanich, the veterinary surgeon, and Burkin, the high-school teacher. Ivan Ivanich bore a strange, hyphenated name: Chimsha-Himalaisky; the name did not seem to suit him, and everyone called him simply by his name and patronymic—Ivan Ivanich; he lived at a stud-farm not far from the town, and was now hunting for the sake of an outing in the fresh air. The high-school teacher Burkin spent every summer on the estate of Count P. and was regarded by the inhabitants of those parts as quite one of themselves.

Neither of them slept. Ivan Ivanich, a tall, lean old man with a long moustache, sat outside the door, in the moonlight, smoking his pipe. Burkin lay inside, on the hay, concealed by the darkness.

They whiled away the time by telling each other stories. They spoke of Mavra, the wife of the village elder, a perfectly healthy and by no means unintelligent woman, who had never been out of her native village in her life. She had never seen a town or a railway, and had spent the last ten years sitting by her stove, venturing out only at night.

"Is it so very strange, though?" said Burkin. "There are plenty of people in this world who are recluses by nature and strive, like the hermit-crab or the snail, to retreat within their shells. Perhaps this is just a manifestation of atavism, a return to the times when our forebears had not yet become social animals, and inhabited solitary caves. Or perhaps such people are one of the varieties of the human species, who knows? I am no naturalist, and it is not for me to attempt to solve such problems; all I want to say is that people like Mavra are by no means rare phenomena. Why, only a month or two ago there died in our town a colleague of mine, Belikov, a teacher of Greek. You must have heard of him. He was famous for never stirring out of his house, even in the best weather, without an umbrella, galoshes and a padded coat. His umbrella he kept in a case, he had a case of grey suede for his watch, and when he took out his pen-knife to sharpen a pencil, he had to draw it out of a case, too; even his face seemed to have a case of its own, since it was always hidden in his turned-up coat-collar. He wore dark glasses, and a thick jersey, and stopped up his ears with cotton wool, and when he engaged a carriage, he made the driver put up the hood. In fact, he betrayed a perpetual, irrepressible urge to create a covering for himself, as it were a case, to isolate him and protect him against external influences. Reality irritated and alarmed him and kept him in constant terror, and, perhaps to justify his timidity, the disgust which the present aroused in him, he always praised the past, and things which had never had any existence. Even the dead languages he taught were merely galoshes and umbrellas between himself and real life.

" 'How beautiful, how sonorous is the Greek language!' he would say with a beatific expression; and by way of proof he would half-close his eyes, raise a finger and murmur: 'An-thro-pos!'[1]

"Belikov tried to keep his thoughts in a case, too. Only those circulars and newspaper articles in which something was prohibited were comprehensible to him. When instructions were circulated forbidding schoolboys to be in the streets after 9 p.m., or an article was published in which indulgence in carnal love was condemned, everything was clear and definite for him—these things were prohibited once and for all. In his eyes permission and indulgence always seemed to contain some doubtful element, something left unsaid, vague. If a dramatic society or a reading-room or a café were allowed to be opened, he would shake his head and say gently:

" 'It's a very fine thing, no doubt, but . . . let's hope no evil will come of it.'

"The slightest infringement or deviation from the rules plunged him into dejection, even when it could not possibly concern him. If one of his colleagues were late for prayers, or rumors of a trick played by some schoolboys reached his ears, if a female staff-member were seen late at night in the company of an officer, he would be profoundly agitated, repeating constantly that he was afraid it would lead to no good. At the meetings of the teachers' council he fairly tormented us with his circumspection and suspicions, his apprehensions and suggestions (typical of a mind encased): the young people in both the girls' and boys' schools behave disgracefully, make a terrible noise in the classrooms—supposing the authorities get to hear of it, he hoped no evil would come of it, and wouldn't it help matters if we expelled Petrov from the second form, and Yegorov from the fourth? And what do you think? With his sighs and moans, his dark glasses on his little, white face—a ferrety sort of face, you know—he managed to depress us all to such an extent that we yielded, gave Petrov and Yegorov low marks for behavior, had them put in the lock-up, and, finally, expelled. He

---

1. The Greek word for "man."

had an old habit of visiting us in our homes. Going to the rooms of a fellow teacher, he would sit down and say nothing, with a watchful air. After an hour or so of this, he would get up and go. He called this 'keeping on friendly terms with one's colleagues,' and it was obvious that he found it an uncongenial task and came to see us only because he considered it his duty as a fellow teacher. We were all afraid of him. Even the headmaster was. Just think! Our teachers are on the whole a decent, intelligent set, brought up on Turgenev and Shchedrin,[2] and yet this mite of a man, with his eternal umbrella and overshoes, managed to keep the whole school under his thumb for fifteen years! And not only the school, but the entire town! Our ladies gave up their Saturday private theatricals for fear of his finding out about them; the clergy were afraid of eating meat or playing cards in his presence. Under the influence of men like Belikov the people in our town have begun to be afraid of everything. They are afraid to speak loudly, write letters, make friends, read books, help the poor, teach the illiterate. . . ."

Ivan Ivanich cleared his throat as if in preparation for some weighty remark, but first he relit his pipe and glanced up at the moon, and only then said, in unhurried tones:

"Quite right. A decent, intelligent set, reading Turgenev, Shchedrin and Buckle[3] and all those, and yet they submitted, they bore with him. . . . That's just it."

"Belikov and I lived in the same house," went on Burkin, "on the same floor; his door was just opposite mine, we saw quite a lot of one another, and I had a pretty good idea of what his home-life was like. It was the same story: dressing-gown, night-cap, shutters, bolts and bars, a long list of restrictions and prohibitions, and the same adage—let's hope no evil will come of it! Lenten fare did not agree with him, but he could not eat meat or people might say that Belikov did not observe Lent. So he ate pike fried in butter—it was not fasting but neither could it be called meat. He never kept female servants for fear of people getting 'notions,' but employed a male cook, Afanasy, an old man of about sixty, drunken and crazy, who knew how to cook from having served as an orderly at some time in his life. This Afanasy was usually to be seen standing outside the door with folded arms always muttering the same thing over and over again with a deep sigh:

" 'Ah, there's a sight of *them* about, nowadays!'

"Belikov's tiny bedroom was like a box, and there was a canopy over the bed. Before going to sleep he always drew the bedclothes over his head; the room was hot and stuffy, the wind rattled against the closed doors and moaned in the chimney; sighs were heard in the kitchen, ominous sighs. . . .

2. Turgenev and Shchedrin were considered to be in the forefront of liberalism and enlightened opinion in the eighteen-fifties and sixties.

3. The English historian Henry Buckle (1821–62) was much esteemed by liberals of the same period.

"And he would lie trembling under his blanket. He was afraid that some evil would come, that Afanasy would murder him, that thieves would break in, and his very dreams were haunted by these fears; and in the mornings, when we walked side by side to the school, he was always pale and languid and it was obvious that the crowded school he was approaching was the object of his terror and aversion, and that it was distasteful for him, a recluse by nature, to have to walk by my side.

" 'They make such a noise in the classrooms,' he would say, as if trying to find an explanation for his heaviness of heart. 'It's quite disgraceful.'

"And what do you think? This teacher of Greek, this hermit-crab, once nearly got married."

Ivan Ivanich turned his head sharply towards the shed.

"You don't mean it!" he said.

"Yes, he nearly got married, strange as it may sound. We were sent a new teacher for history and geography, one Kovalenko, Mikhail Savvich, a Ukrainian. He brought his sister Varya with him. He was young, tall, dark-complexioned, with enormous hands and the sort of face that goes with a deep voice; as a matter of fact he had a deep, booming voice, as if it came from a barrel. . . . His sister, who was not so young, thirty or thereabouts, was also tall; willowy, black-browed, red-cheeked, she was a peach of a girl, lively and noisy, always singing Ukrainian songs, always laughing. On the slightest provocation she would burst out into a ringing ha-ha-ha! The first time we became really acquainted with brother and sister, if I am not mistaken, was at our headmaster's name-day party. Suddenly, among the severe, conventional, dull teachers who make even going to parties a duty, a new Venus rose from the foam, one who walked about with arms akimbo, laughed, sang, danced. . . . She sang with great feeling 'The Winds Are Blowing,' following it with another song, then another, and we were all charmed, even Belikov. He sat beside her, and said, with a honeyed smile:

" 'The Ukrainian tongue in its sweetness and delightful sonority is reminiscent of the ancient Greek.'

"The lady was flattered, and began telling him with sincere feeling about her farmstead in Gadyachi District, where her Mummie lived and where there were such pears, such melons, and such taverns! Pumpkins are called taverns in the Ukraine, and taverns are called pot-houses, and they make a delicious *borshch* with blue eggplant and red tomatoes, 'ever so good, you know!'

"We sat round her, listening, and the same thought struck us all.

" 'Why shouldn't these two get married?' said the headmaster's wife to me in a low voice.

"For some reason everyone suddenly realized that our Belikov was a bachelor and we wondered how it was that we had never remarked, had completely overlooked, so important a detail in his life. What was his attitude to woman, how did he solve this vital problem for himself? We had never thought about it before; perhaps none of us could admit the idea that a man who wore overshoes all the year round and slept under a canopy was capable of loving.

" 'He's well over forty, and she's thirty . . .'" the headmaster's wife went on. 'I think she would take him.'

"The things one does out of sheer boredom in the provinces, the absurd, useless things! And all because what ought to be done never is done. Why, why did we feel we had to marry off this Belikov, whom nobody could imagine in the role of a married man? The headmaster's wife, the inspector's wife, and all the ladies who had anything to do with the school, brightened up, and actually became handsomer, as if they had at last found an object in life. The headmaster's wife took a box in the theatre, and whom do we behold in this box but Varya, fanning herself with an enormous fan, radiant, happy, and at her side Belikov, small and huddled up, as if he had been extracted from his room with pincers. I myself gave a party, to which the ladies insisted on my inviting Belikov and Varya. In a word, we started the ball rolling. The idea of marriage, it appeared, was by no means disagreeable to Varya. Her life with her brother was far from happy, they did nothing but wrangle all day long. I'll give you a typical scene in their lives: Kovalenko stalks along the street, tall and massive, wearing an embroidered shirt, his forelock tumbling over his brow from beneath the peak of his cap; a parcel of books in one hand, a gnarled walking-stick in the other. He is followed by his sister, also carrying books.

" 'But Misha, you haven't read it!" she shouts. 'You haven't, I tell you, I am absolutely certain you never read it!'

" 'And I tell you I have!' Kovalenko shouts back, knocking with his stick on the pavement.

" 'For goodness' sake, Misha! What makes you so cross? It's only a matter of principle, after all!'

" 'And I tell you I *have* read it!' shouts Kovalenko, still louder.

"And at home, whenever anyone came to see them, they would start bickering. She was probably sick of such a life, and longing for a home of her own, and then—her age: there was no time for picking and choosing, the girl would marry anyone, even a teacher of Greek. It's the same with all our girls, by the way—they'd marry anyone, simply for the sake of getting married. However that may be, Varya was beginning to show a marked liking for this Belikov of ours.

"And Belikov? He visited Kovalenko in the same way that he visited the rest of us. He would go to see him, and sit saying nothing. And there he would sit in silence, while Varya sang 'The

Winds Are Blowing,' gazing at him from her dark eyes, or suddenly breaking out into her 'ha-ha-ha!'

"In affairs of the heart, especially when matrimony is involved, suggestion is all-powerful. Everyone—his colleagues, the ladies—began assuring Belikov that he ought to marry, that there was nothing left for him in life but marriage; we all congratulated him, uttering with solemn countenances various commonplaces to the effect that marriage was a serious step, and the like; besides, Varenka was by no means plain, she might even be considered handsome, and then she was the daughter of a councillor of state, she had a farmstead of her own and, still more important, was the first woman who had ever treated him with affection. So he lost his head and persuaded himself it was his duty to marry."

"That was the moment to take his umbrella and overshoes away from him!" put in Ivan Ivanich.

"Ah, but that proved to be impossible! He placed Varenka's photograph on his desk, kept coming to me to talk about Varenka, family life, and the seriousness of marriage, went often to the Kovalenkos, but did not change his way of living in the least. On the contrary, the decision to marry seemed to have a painful effect on him, he grew thinner, paler and seemed to retreat still further into his shell.

" 'I find Varvara Savvishna an agreeable girl,' he said to me with his faint, crooked smile, 'and every man ought to get married, I know, but . . . it's all so sudden, you know. . . . One must think. . . .'

" 'What's there to think about?' I answered. 'Get married, that's all.'

" 'No, no, marriage is a serious step, one ought to weigh one's future duties and responsibilities first . . . so's to make sure no evil will come of it. . . . It worries me so, I can't sleep at night. And to tell you the truth, I am somewhat alarmed—they have such a strange way of thinking, she and her brother, their outlook, you know, is so strange, and then she is so sprightly. Supposing I marry and get mixed up in something. . . .'

"And he put off proposing to her, putting it off from day to day, much to the disappointment of the headmaster's wife and the other ladies; he kept weighing his future duties and responsibilities, walking out with Varenka almost every day, probably thinking the situation demanded it of him, and coming to me to discuss family life in all its aspects. Very likely he would have proposed in the end, contracting another of those stupid, unnecessary marriages, which are made here by the thousand, out of sheer boredom and for want of something better to do, if *ein kolossalischer Skandal*[4] had not suddenly broken out. I must tell you that Varenka's brother, Kova-

---

4. German for "a colossal scandal." (Chekhov has "Kolossalische Scandal.")

lenko, had contracted a hatred for Belikov from the very first day of their acquaintance, and could never stand him.

" 'I can't understand you,' he would say, shrugging his shoulders, 'how can you tolerate that sneak of a man, that mug? How can you live here, gentlemen? The atmosphere is stifling, poisonous. Do you call yourselves teachers, pedagogues? You're nothing but a pack of time-servers. Your school is not a temple of science but a charitable institution, there's a sickly smell about it, like in a policeman's booth. No, my friends, I shan't be long with you, I'll be going back to my farmstead, to catch crayfish and teach the Ukrainian lads. Yes, I'll go away, and you may stay with your Judas, and be damned to him!'

"Another time he would roar with laughter first in a deep bass, and then in a shrill soprano till the tears came to his eyes.

" 'Why does he sit there? What does he want—sitting and staring?'

"He gave Belikov a nickname of his own: vampire-spider.

"Naturally we avoided mentioning to him that his sister was about to marry this 'spider.' When the headmaster's wife hinted to him that it would be nice to see his sister settled down with such a solid and respected person as Belikov, he knitted his brows and said:

" 'It's none of my business. She may marry a snake for all I care. I'm not one to meddle in other people's affairs.'

"Now, hear what happened later. Some wag drew a caricature: Belikov in his overshoes, the ends of his trousers turned up, his umbrella open over his head and Varya walking arm-in-arm with him; beneath the drawing there was an inscription: 'The Anthropos in Love.' The expression of his face, you know, was very true to life. The artist must have sat up several nights over his work, for the teachers of both the schools, the girls' and the boys', and of the seminary, and all the town officials received a copy. Belikov received one, too. The caricature had the most depressing effect on him.

"One day we went out of the house together, it happened to be the first of May and a Sunday and the whole school, pupils and masters, were to meet in front of the school and walk to a wood outside the town—well, we went out, he looking very green about the gills and as black as thunder.

" 'What cruel, malicious people there are in the world,' he said, and his lips quivered.

"I could not help feeling sorry for him. We walked on, when who should we see but Kovalenko riding a bicycle, followed by Varenka, also on a bicycle, panting, red-faced, but very jolly and happy.

" 'We'll be there before all of you!' she cried. 'Isn't it a glorious day? Wonderful!'

"They were soon out of sight. My Belikov, no longer green but deathly pale, was struck dumb. He stopped and stared at me.

" 'What can the meaning of this be?' he asked. 'Or do my eyes deceive me? Is it proper for schoolteachers and women to ride bicycles?'

" 'There's nothing improper about it,' I said. 'Why shouldn't they ride bicycles?'

" 'But it is insufferable!' he cried. 'How can you talk like that?'

"The shock he had received was too great; refusing to go any further, he turned homewards.

"All the next day he kept nervously rubbing his hands together and starting, and you could see by his face that he was not well. He left school before lessons were over—a thing he had never done before. And he did not eat any dinner. Towards evening he dressed warmly, though it was a real summer day, and shuffled off to the Kovalenkos. Varenka was not in, but her brother was.

" 'Take a seat, please,' said Kovalenko coldly, knitting his brows; he had just got up from his afternoon nap, his face was still heavy with sleep, and he felt awful.

"After sitting in silence for about ten minutes, Belikov began:

" 'I have come to relieve my mind. I am very, very unhappy. A certain unknown lampoonist has made a drawing in which he ridicules me and a certain other person near to us both. I consider it my duty to assure you that it is not my fault. I have done nothing to give grounds for such ridicule, on the contrary, I have behaved like a thorough gentleman all the time.'

"Kovalenko sat silent and lowering. After a short pause Belikov went on in his low plaintive voice:

" 'And there's something else I have to say to you. I am a veteran and you are only beginning your career, and it is my duty as an older colleague of yours to warn you. You ride a bicycle and this is a highly reprehensible amusement for one who aspires to educate the young.'

" 'Why?' asked Kovalenko in his deep bass voice.

" 'Does it require explanation, Mikhail Savvich? I should have thought it was self-evident. If the master is to go about riding a bicycle, there is nothing left for the pupils but to walk on their heads. And since no circular permitting this has been issued, it is wrong. I was astounded yesterday! I nearly fainted when I saw your sister. A young lady on a bicycle—preposterous!'

" 'What exactly do you want from me?'

" 'I only want to warn you, Mikhail Savvich. You are young, you have your life before you, you must be very, very careful, and you are so reckless, so very reckless! You go about in embroidered shirts, are constantly seen carrying all sorts of books about the streets, and now this bicycle. The fact that you and your sister have been seen riding bicycles will be made known to the headmaster, it will reach the patron's ears. . . . And that's no good.'

" 'It is no man's business whether my sister and I ride bicycles or not!' said Kovalenko, flushing up. 'And if people stick their noses into my domestic and family affairs they can go to hell.'

"Belikov turned pale and rose to his feet.

" 'Since you assume such a tone with me, I cannot go on,' he said. 'And I would beg you to be careful what you say about our superiors in my presence. The authorities must be treated with deference.'

" 'And did I say anything wrong about the authorities?' asked Kovalenko, looking at him with hatred. 'Leave me alone, Sir. I am an honest man, and have nothing to say to a person like you. I abhor snakes.'

"Belikov fidgeted nervously and began hastily putting on his coat, an expression of horror on his face. Never in his life had anyone spoken so rudely to him.

" 'You may say what you like,' he said as he passed on to the landing. 'But I must warn you: somebody may have overheard us, and to prevent our conversation from being misrepresented, and the possible consequence of this, I shall have to report the purport of our conversation to the headmaster . . . its main points. It is my duty.'

" 'What? Report? Go on, then!'

"Kovalenko grasped him by the collar and gave him a push, and Belikov rolled down the stairs, his galoshes knocking against the steps. The staircase was long and steep, but he arrived at the bottom unhurt, rose to his feet and felt the bridge of his nose to see if his glasses were unbroken. But while he was rolling down the steps, Varenka, accompanied by two other ladies, entered the porch; they all three stood at the bottom of the stairs, looking at him—and for Belikov that was the worst of all his sufferings. He would a great deal sooner have broken his neck, and both legs, than appear in a ridiculous light. Now the whole town would know of it, the headmaster would be told, and probably the patron, too. And who knows what that would lead to! Someone might draw another caricature and it would end in his having to resign. . . .

"When he got up, Varya recognized him, and looking at his ridiculous face, his rumpled coat, his overshoes, without the faintest idea what had happened, but supposing that he must have slipped, she could not help bursting out with her loud 'ha-ha-ha!'

"This buoyant, resonant 'ha-ha' was the end: the end of Belikov's courting and of his earthly existence. He never again saw Varenka. The first thing he did when he got home was to remove her photograph from the top of his desk, then he lay down on his bed, never to leave it.

"Three days later Afanasy came to ask me whether he should send for the doctor, for his master was behaving very strangely. I went to see Belikov. He was lying under his canopy, covered by a blanket, mute; he answered my questions with a monosyllabic 'yes' or 'no,' and not a word more. There he lay, while Afanasy, morose and frowning, stumped round the bed, heaving deep sighs and reeking of spirits like a tavern.

"A month went by and Belikov died. Everybody, that is to say, the two schools and the seminary, went to his funeral. Now, as he lay in his coffin, the expression on his face was gentle, pleasing, even cheerful, as if he were glad at last to be put into a case which he would never have to leave. Yes, he had achieved his ideal! As if in his honor, the day was cloudy and wet, and we all wore galoshes and carried umbrellas. Varya was at the funeral, too, and shed a tear when the coffin was lowered into the grave. I have noticed with Ukrainian women that they must either laugh or weep, they do not admit of any intermediate moods.

"I must confess that it is a great pleasure to bury individuals like Belikov. But we returned from the cemetery with long, 'Lenten' faces; none of us wished to show our relief, a relief like that we felt long ago, in childhood, when the grown-ups went away and we could run about the garden for an hour or two enjoying perfect freedom. Ah, freedom! A hint of it, the faintest hope of attaining it, gives wings to our souls, doesn't it?

"We returned from the cemetery in good spirits. But hardly a week passed before everyday life, bleak, fatiguing, meaningless life, neither forbidden in one circular nor sanctioned in another, resumed its usual course; and things were no better than they had been before. After all, when you come to think of it, though we have buried Belikov, there are still plenty of men who live in a shell, and there are plenty as yet unborn."

"Yes, indeed," said Ivan Ivanich as he lit his pipe.

"And plenty as yet unborn!" repeated Burkin.

The high-school teacher came out of the shed. He was short, corpulent, quite bald, with a long black beard reaching nearly to his belt; two dogs came out with him.

"What a moon!" he said, looking up.

It was past midnight. The whole of the village was visible on the right, the long street extending for five versts or so. Everything was plunged in profound, calm sleep; not a sound, not a stir, it seemed incredible that nature could be so calm. When we gaze upon a wide village street on a moonlit night, with its dwellings and hayricks and sleeping willows, a great peace descends on our souls; in its serenity, sheltered by the shadows of the night from all toil, cares and grief, the village seems gentle, melancholy and beautiful, the very stars seem to look down upon it kindly, and there seems to be no more evil in the world, and all is well. To the left, where the village ended, stretched the fields; one could look far into them, to the very horizon, and all was silent and motionless there, too, and the vast plain was flooded with moonlight.

"Yes, indeed," repeated Ivan Ivanich. "And is not our living in towns, in our stuffy, cramped rooms, writing our useless papers, playing vint, isn't that living in an oyster-shell, too? And the fact that we spend all our life among drones, litigious boors, silly, idle women, talk nonsense and listen to nonsense, is not that our oyster-shell, too? I could tell you a highly instructive yarn, if you'd care to listen. . . ."

"I think it's time we went to sleep," said Burkin. "Keep it for tomorrow."

They went to the shed and lay down. They snuggled into the hay and began to doze when a light footstep was heard outside. Somebody was walking about not far from the shed; a few steps, then a stop, and then again the light steps. The dogs growled.

"It's Mavra having a walk," said Burkin.

The steps were heard no more.

"To have to look on and listen to people lying," said Ivan Ivanich as he turned on his side, "and then to be called a fool for tolerating all those lies; to swallow insults, humiliations, not dare to speak up and declare yourself on the side of honest, free men, to lie yourself, to smile, and all for the sake of a crust of bread and a snug corner to live in, for the sake of some miserable rank—no, no, life is intolerable!"

"That's a horse of a different color, Ivan Ivanich," said the schoolmaster. "Let's go to sleep."

In ten minutes Burkin was asleep. But Ivan Ivanich kept sighing and tossing on the hay; then he got up, went out again, and sitting down by the door, lit his pipe.

1898

Gooseberries[1]

The sky had been covered with rainclouds ever since the early morning; it was a still day, cool and dull, one of those misty days when the clouds have long been lowering overhead and you keep thinking it is just going to rain, and the rain holds off. Ivan Ivanich, the veterinary surgeon, and Burkin, the high-school teacher, had walked till they were tired, and the way over the fields seemed

1. It must be pointed out for American readers that European gooseberries are large, pink, sweet, and much appreciated.

endless to them. Far ahead they could just make out the windmill of the village of Mironositskoye, and what looked like a range of low hills at the right extending well beyond the village, and they both knew that this range was really the bank of the river, and that further on were meadows, green willow-trees, country estates; if they were on the top of these hills, they knew they would see the same boundless fields and telegraph-posts, and the train, like a crawling caterpillar in the distance, while in fine weather even the town would be visible. On this still day, when the whole of nature seemed kindly and pensive, Ivan Ivanich and Burkin felt a surge of love for this plain, and thought how vast and beautiful their country was.

"The last time we stayed in Elder Prokofy's hut," said Burkin, "you said you had a story to tell me."

"Yes. I wanted to tell you the story of my brother."

Ivan Ivanich took a deep breath and lighted his pipe as a preliminary to his narrative, but just then the rain came. Five minutes later it was coming down in torrents and nobody could say when it would stop. Ivan Ivanich and Burkin stood still, lost in thought. The dogs, already soaked, stood with drooping tails, gazing at them wistfully.

"We must try and find shelter," said Burkin. "Let's go to Alekhin's. It's quite near."

"Come on, then."

They turned aside and walked straight across the newly reaped field, veering to the right till they came to a road. Very soon poplars, an orchard, and the red roofs of barns came into sight. The surface of the river gleamed, and they had a view of an extensive reach of water, a windmill and a whitewashed bathing-shed. This was Sofyino, where Alekhin lived.

The mill was working, and the noise made by its sails drowned the sound of the rain; the whole dam trembled. Horses, soaking wet, were standing near some carts, their heads drooping, and people were moving about with sacks over their heads and shoulders. It was wet, muddy, bleak, and the water looked cold and sinister. Ivan Ivanich and Burkin were already experiencing the misery of dampness, dirt, physical discomfort, their boots were caked with mud, and when, having passed the mill-dam, they took the upward path to the landowner's barns, they fell silent, as if vexed with one another.

The sound of winnowing came from one of the barns; the door was open, and clouds of dust issued from it. Standing in the doorway was Alekhin himself, a stout man of some forty years, with longish hair, looking more like a professor or an artist than a landed proprietor. He was wearing a white shirt greatly in need of washing, belted with a piece of string, and long drawers with no trousers over them. His boots, too, were caked with mud and straw. His eyes and nose were ringed with dust. He recognized Ivan Ivanich and Burkin, and seemed glad to see them.

"Go up to the house, gentlemen," he said, smiling. "I'll be with you in a minute."

It was a large two-story house. Alekhin occupied the ground floor, two rooms with vaulted ceilings and tiny windows, where the stewards had lived formerly. They were poorly furnished, and smelled of rye-bread, cheap vodka, and harness. He hardly ever went into the upstairs rooms, excepting when he had guests. Ivan Ivanich and Burkin were met by a maidservant, a young woman of such beauty that they stood still involuntarily and exchanged glances.

"You have no idea how glad I am to see you here, dear friends," said Alekhin, overtaking them in the hall. "It's quite a surprise! Pelagea," he said, turning to the maid, "find the gentlemen a change of clothes. And I might as well change, myself. But I must have a wash first, for I don't believe I've had a bath since the spring. Wouldn't you like to go and have a bath while they get things ready here?"

The beauteous Pelagea, looking very soft and delicate, brought them towels and soap, and Alekhin and his guests set off for the bathing-house.

"Yes, it's a long time since I had a wash," he said, taking off his clothes. "As you see I have a nice bathing-place, my father had it built, but somehow I never seem to get time to wash."

He sat on the step, soaping his long locks and his neck, and all round him the water was brown.

"Yes, you certainly . . ." remarked Ivan Ivanich, with a significant glance at his host's head.

"It's a long time since I had a wash . . ." repeated Alekhin, somewhat abashed, and he soaped himself again, and now the water was dark blue, like ink.

Ivan Ivanich emerged from the shed, splashed noisily into the water, and began swimming beneath the rain, spreading his arms wide, making waves all round him, and the white water-lilies rocked on the waves he made. He swam into the very middle of the river and then dived, a moment later came up at another place and swam further, diving constantly, and trying to touch the bottom. "Ah, my God," he kept exclaiming in his enjoyment. "Ah, my God. . . ." He swam up to the mill, had a little talk with some peasants there and turned back, but when he got to the middle of the river, he floated, holding his face up to the rain. Burkin and Alekhin were dressed and ready to go, but he went on swimming and diving.

"God! God!" he kept exclaiming. "Dear God!"

"Come out!" Burkin shouted to him.

They went back to the house. And only after the lamp was lit in the great drawing-room on the upper floor, and Burkin and Ivan Ivanich, in silk dressing-gowns and warm slippers were seated in armchairs, while Alekhin, washed and combed, paced the room in his new frock-coat, enjoying the warmth, the cleanliness, his dry clothes and comfortable slippers, while the beautiful Pelageya, smiling softly, stepped noiselessly over the carpet with her tray of tea and preserves, did Ivan Ivanich embark upon his yarn, the ancient dames, young ladies and military gentlemen looking down at them severely from their gilded frames, as if they, too, were listening.

"There were two of us brothers," he began. "Ivan Ivanich (me), and my brother Nikolai Ivanich, two years younger than myself. I went in for learning and became a veterinary surgeon, but Nikolai started working in a government office when he was only nineteen. Our father, Chimsha-Himalaisky, was educated in a school for the sons of private soldiers, but was later promoted to officer's rank, and was made a hereditary nobleman and given a small estate. After his death the estate had to be sold for debts, but at least our childhood was passed in the freedom of the countryside, where we roamed the fields and the woods like peasant children, taking the horses to graze, peeling bark from the trunks of lime-trees, fishing, and all that sort of thing. And anyone who has once in his life fished for perch, or watched the thrushes fly south in the autumn, rising high over the village on clear, cool days, is spoiled for town life, and will long for the countryside for the rest of his days. My brother pined in his government office. The years passed and he sat in the same place every day, writing out the same documents and thinking all the time of the same thing—how to get back to the country. And these longings of his gradually turned into a definite desire, into a dream of purchasing a little estate somewhere on the bank of a river or the shore of a lake.

"He was a meek, good-natured chap, I was fond of him, but could feel no sympathy with the desire to lock oneself up for life in an estate of one's own. They say man only needs six feet of earth. But it is a corpse, and not man, which needs these six feet. And now people are actually saying that it is a good sign for our intellectuals to yearn for the land and try to obtain country-dwellings. And yet these estates are nothing but those same six feet of earth. To escape from the town, from the struggle, from the noise of life, to escape and hide one's head on a country-estate, is not life, but egoism, idleness, it is a sort of renunciation, but renunciation without faith. It is not six feet of earth, not a country-estate, that man needs, but the whole globe, the whole of nature, room to display his qualities and the individual characteristics of his free soul.

"My brother Nikolai sat at his office-desk, dreaming of eating soup made from his own cabbages, which would spread a delicious smell all over his own yard, of eating out of doors, on the green grass, of sleeping in the sun, sitting for hours on a bench outside his gate, and gazing at the fields and woods. Books on agriculture and all those hints printed on calendars were his delight, his favourite spiritual nourishment. He was fond of reading newspapers, too, but all he read in them was advertisements of the sale of so many acres of arable land and meadowland, with residence attached, a river, an orchard, a mill, and ponds fed by springs. His head was full of visions of garden paths, flowers, fruit, nestling-boxes, carp-ponds, and all that sort of thing. These visions differed according to the advertisements he came across, but for some reason gooseberry bushes invariably figured in them. He could not picture to himself a single estate or picturesque nook that did not have gooseberry bushes in it.

" 'Country life has its conveniences,' he would say. 'You sit on the verandah, drinking tea, with your own ducks floating on the pond, and everything smells so nice, and . . . and the gooseberries ripen on the bushes.'

"He drew up plans for his estate, and every plan showed the same features: a) the main residence, b) the servants' wing, c) the kitchen-garden, d) gooseberry bushes. He lived thriftily, never ate or drank his fill, dressed anyhow, like a beggar, and saved up all his money in the bank. He became terribly stingy. I could hardly bear to look at him, and whenever I gave him a little money, or sent him a present on some holiday, he put that away, too. Once a man gets an idea into his head, there's no doing anything with him.

"The years passed, he was sent to another province, he was over forty, and was still reading advertisements in the papers, and saving up. At last I heard he had married. All for the same purpose, to buy himself an estate with gooseberry bushes on it, he married an ugly elderly widow, for whom he had not the slightest affection, just because she had some money. After his marriage he went on living as thriftily as ever, half-starving his wife, and putting her money in his own bank account. Her first husband had been a postmaster, and she was used to pies and cordials, but with her second husband she did not even get enough black bread to eat. She began to languish on this diet and three years later yielded up her soul to God. Of course my brother did not for a moment consider himself guilty of her death. Money, like vodka, makes a man eccentric. There was a merchant in our town who asked for a plate of honey on his deathbed and ate up all his banknotes and lottery tickets with the honey, so that no one else should get them. And one day when I was examining a consignment of cattle at a railway station, a drover fell under the engine and his leg was severed from his body. We carried him all bloody into the waiting-room, a terrible sight, and he did nothing but beg us to look for his leg, worrying all the time—

there were twenty rubles in the boot, and he was afraid they would be lost."

"That's a horse of a different color," put in Burkin.

Ivan Ivanich paused for a moment, and went on: "After his wife's death my brother began to look about for an estate. You can search for five years, of course, and in the end make a mistake and buy something quite different from what you dream of. My brother Nikolai bought three hundred acres, complete with gentleman's house, servants' quarters, and a park, on a mortgage to be paid through an agent, but there were neither an orchard, gooseberry bushes, nor a pond with ducks on it. There was a river, but it was as dark as coffee, owing to the fact that there was a brick-works on one side of the estate, and bone-kilns on the other. Nothing daunted, however, my brother Nikolai Ivanich ordered two dozen gooseberry bushes and settled down as a landed proprietor.

"Last year I paid him a visit. I thought I would go and see how he was getting on there. In his letters my brother gave his address as Chumbaroklov Fallow or Himalaiskoye. I arrived at Himalaiskoye in the afternoon. It was very hot. Everywhere were ditches, fences, hedges, rows of fir-trees, and it was hard to drive into the yard and find a place to leave one's carriage. As I went a fat, ginger-colored dog, remarkably like a pig, came out to meet me. It looked as if it would have barked if it were not so lazy. The cook, who was also fat and like a pig, came out of the kitchen, barefoot, and said her master was having his after-dinner rest. I made my way to my brother's room, and found him sitting up in bed, his knees covered by a blanket. He had aged, and grown stout and flabby. His cheeks, nose and lips protruded—I almost expected him to grunt into the blanket.

"We embraced and wept—tears of joy, mingled with melancholy —because we had once been young and were now both grey-haired and approaching the grave. He put on his clothes and went out to show me over his estate.

" 'Well, how are you getting on here?' I asked.

" 'All right, thanks be, I'm enjoying myself.'

"He was no longer the poor, timid clerk, but a true proprietor, a gentleman. He had settled down, and was entering with zest into country life. He ate a lot, washed in the bathhouse, and put on flesh. He had already gotten into litigation with the village commune, the brick-works, and the bone-kilns, and took offense if the peasants failed to call him 'Your Honor.' He went in for religion in a solid, gentlemanly way, and there was nothing casual about his pretentious good works. And what were these good works? He treated all the diseases of the peasants with bicarbonate of soda and castor-oil, and had a special thanksgiving service held on his name-day, after which he provided a gallon of vodka, supposing that this was the right thing to do. Oh, those terrible gallons! Today the fat landlord hauls the peasants before the *zemstvo* representative for letting their sheep graze on his land, tomorrow, on the day of rejoicing, he treats them to a gallon of vodka, and they drink and sing and shout hurrah, prostrating themselves before him when they are drunk. Any improvement in his conditions, anything like satiety or idleness, develops the most insolent complacency in a Russian. Nikolai Ivanich, who had been afraid of having an opinion of his own when he was in the government service, was now continually coming out with axioms, in the most ministerial manner: 'Education is essential, but the people are not ready for it yet,' 'Corporal punishment is an evil, but in certain cases it is beneficial and indispensable.'

" 'I know the people and I know how to treat them,' he said. 'The people love me. I only have to lift my little finger, and the people will do whatever I want.'

"And all this, mark you, with a wise, indulgent smile. Over and over again he repeated: 'We the gentry,' or 'Speaking as a gentleman,' and seemed to have quite forgotten that our grandfather was a peasant, and our father a common soldier. Our very surname—Chimsha-Himalaisky—in reality so absurd, now seemed to him a resounding, distinguished, and euphonious name.

"But it is of myself, and not of him, that I wish to speak. I should like to describe to you the change which came over me in those few hours I spent on my brother's estate. As we were drinking tea in the evening, the cook brought us a full plate of gooseberries. These were not gooseberries bought for money, they came from his own garden, and were the first fruits of the bushes he had planted. Nikolai Ivanich broke into a laugh and gazed at the gooseberries in tearful silence for at least five minutes. Speechless with emotion, he popped a single gooseberry into his mouth, darted at me the triumphant glance of a child who has at last gained possession of a longed-for toy, and said:

" 'Delicious!'

"And he ate them greedily, repeating over and over again:

" 'Simply delicious! You try them.'

"They were hard and sour, but, as Pushkin says: 'The lie which exalts us is dearer than a thousand sober truths.'[2] I saw before me a really happy man, one whose dearest wish had come true, who had achieved his aim in life, got what he wanted, and was content with his lot and with himself. There had always been a tinge of melancholy in my conception of human happiness, and now, confronted by a happy man, I was overcome by a feeling of sadness bordering on desperation. This feeling grew strongest of all in the night. A bed was made up for me in the room next to my brother's bedroom, and

2. An inexact quotation from Pushkin's poem on Napoleon, "The Hero."

I could hear him moving about restlessly, every now and then getting up to take a gooseberry from a plate. How many happy, satisfied people there are, after all, I said to myself. What an overwhelming force! Just consider this life—the insolence and idleness of the strong, the ignorance and bestiality of the weak, all around intolerable poverty, cramped dwellings, degeneracy, drunkenness, hypocrisy, lying. . . . And yet peace and order apparently prevail in all those homes and in the streets. Of the fifty thousand inhabitants of a town, not one will be found to cry out, to proclaim his indignation aloud. We see those who go to the market to buy food, who eat in the daytime and sleep at night, who prattle away, marry, grow old, carry their dead to the cemeteries. But we neither hear nor see those who suffer, and the terrible things in life are played out behind the scenes. All is calm and quiet, only statistics, which are dumb, protest: so many have gone mad, so many barrels of drink have been consumed, so many children died of malnutrition. . . . And apparently this is as it should be. Apparently those who are happy can only enjoy themselves because the unhappy bear their burdens in silence, and but for this silence happiness would be impossible. It is a kind of universal hypnosis. There ought to be a man with a hammer behind the door of every happy man, to remind him by his constant knocks that there are unhappy people, and that happy as he himself may be, life will sooner or later show him its claws, catastrophe will overtake him—sickness, poverty, loss—and nobody will see it, just as he now neither sees nor hears the misfortunes of others. But there is no man with a hammer, the happy man goes on living and the petty vicissitudes of life touch him lightly, like the wind in an aspen-tree, and all is well.

"That night I understood that I, too, was happy and content," continued Ivan Ivanich, getting up. "I, too, while out hunting, or at the dinner table, have held forth on the right way to live, to worship, to manage the people. I, too, have declared that without knowledge there can be no light, that education is essential, but that bare literacy is sufficient for the common people. Freedom is a blessing, I have said, one can't get on without it, any more than without air, but we must wait. Yes, that is what I said, and now I ask: In the name of what must we wait?" Here Ivan Ivanich looked angrily at Burkin. "In the name of what must we wait, I ask you? What is there to be considered? Don't be in such a hurry, they tell me, every idea materializes gradually, in its own time. But who are they who say this? What is the proof that it is just? You refer to the natural order of things, to the logic of facts, but according to what order, what logic do I, a living, thinking individual, stand on the edge of a ditch and wait for it to be gradually filled up, or choked with silt, when I might leap across it or build a bridge over it? And again, in the name of what must we wait? Wait, when we have not the strength to live, though live we must and to live we desire!

"I left my brother early the next morning, and ever since I have found town life intolerable. The peace and order weigh on my spirits, and I am afraid to look into windows, because there is now no sadder spectacle for me than a happy family seated around the tea-table. I am old and unfit for the struggle, I am even incapable of feeling hatred. I can only suffer inwardly, and give way to irritation and annoyance, at night my head burns from the rush of thoughts, and I am unable to sleep. . . . Oh, if only I were young!"

Ivan Ivanich began pacing backwards and forwards, repeating:

"If only I were young still!"

Suddenly he went up to Alekhin and began pressing first one of his hands, and then the other.

"Pavel Konstantinich," he said in imploring accents. "Don't *you* fall into apathy, don't *you* let your conscience be lulled to sleep! While you are still young, strong, active, do not be weary of well-doing. There is no such thing as happiness, nor ought there to be, but if there is any sense or purpose in life, this sense and purpose are to be found not in our own happiness, but in something greater and more rational. Do good!"

Ivan Ivanich said all this with a piteous, imploring smile, as if he were asking for something for himself.

Then they all three sat in their armchairs a long way apart from one another, and said nothing. Ivan Ivanich's story satisfied neither Burkin nor Alekhin. It was not interesting to listen to the story of a poor clerk who ate gooseberries, when from the walls generals and fine ladies, who seemed to come to life in the dark, were looking down from their gilded frames. It would have been much more interesting to hear about elegant people, lovely women. And the fact that they were sitting in a drawing-room in which everything—the swathed chandeliers, the armchairs, the carpet on the floor—proved that the people now looking out of the frames had once moved about here, sat in the chairs, drunk tea, where the fair Pelagea was now going noiselessly to and fro, was better than any story.

Alekhin was desperately sleepy. He had got up early, at three o'clock in the morning, to go about his work on the estate, and could now hardly keep his eyes open. But he would not go to bed, for fear one of his guests would relate something interesting after he was gone. He could not be sure whether what Ivan Ivanich had just told them was wise or just, but his visitors talked of other things besides grain, hay, or tar, of things which had no direct bearing on his daily life, and he liked this, and wanted them to go on. . . .

"Well, time to go to bed," said Burkin, getting up. "Allow me to wish you a good night."

Alekhin said good night and went downstairs to his own room, the visitors remaining on the upper floor. They were allotted a big room for the night, in which were two ancient bedsteads of carved wood, and an ivory crucifix in one corner. There was a pleasant smell of freshly laundered sheets from the wide, cool beds which the fair Pelagea had made up for them.

Ivan Ivanich undressed in silence and lay down.

"Lord have mercy on us, sinners," he said, and covered his head with the sheet.

There was a strong smell of stale tobacco from his pipe, which he put on the table, and Burkin lay awake a long time, wondering where the stifling smell came from.

The rain tapped on the windowpanes all night.

1898

About Love

At lunch next day there were very nice pies, crayfish, and mutton cutlets; and while we were eating, Nikanor, the cook, came up to ask what the visitors would like for dinner. He was a man of medium height, with a puffy face and little eyes; he was close-shaven, and it looked as though his moustaches had not been shaved, but had been pulled out by the roots. Alekhin told us that the beautiful Pelagea was in love with this cook. As he drank and was of a violent character, she did not want to marry him, but was willing to live with him without. He was very devout, and his religious convictions would not allow him to "live in sin"; he insisted on her marrying him, and would consent to nothing else, and when he was drunk he used to abuse her and even beat her. Whenever he got drunk she used to hide upstairs and sob, and on such occasions Alekhin and the servants stayed in the house to be ready to defend her in case of necessity.

We began talking about love.

"How love is born," said Alekhin, "why Pelagea does not love somebody more like herself in her spiritual and external qualities, and why she fell in love with Nikanor, that ugly snout—we all call him 'the Snout'—how far questions of personal happiness are of consequence in love—all that is unknown; one can take what view one likes of it. So far only one incontestable truth has been uttered about love: 'This is a great mystery.' Everything else that has been written or said about love is not a conclusion, but only a statement of questions which have remained unanswered. The explanation which would seem to fit one case does not apply in a dozen others, and the very best thing, to my mind, would be to explain every case individually without attempting to generalize. We ought, as the doctors say, to individualize each case."

"Perfectly true," Burkin assented.

"We Russians of the educated class have a partiality for these questions that remain unanswered. Love is usually poeticized, decorated with roses, nightingales; we Russians decorate our loves with these momentous questions, and select the most uninteresting of them, too. In Moscow, when I was a student, I had a friend who shared my life, a charming lady, and every time I took her in my arms she was thinking what I would allow her a month for housekeeping and what was the price of beef a pound. In the same way, when we are in love we are never tired of asking ourselves questions: whether it is honorable or dishonorable, sensible or stupid, what this love is leading up to, and so on. Whether it is a good thing or not I don't know, but that it is in the way, unsatisfactory, and irritating, I do know."

It looked as though he wanted to tell some story. People who lead a solitary existence always have something in their hearts which they are eager to talk about. In town bachelors visit the baths and the restaurants in order to talk, and sometimes tell the most interesting things to bath attendants and waiters; in the country, as a rule, they unbosom themselves to their guests. Now from the window we could see a gray sky, trees drenched in the rain; in such weather we could go nowhere, and there was nothing for us to do but to tell stories and to listen.

"I have lived at Sofino and been farming for a long time," Alekhin began, "ever since I left the University. I am an idle gentleman by education, a studious person by disposition; but there was a big debt owing on the estate when I came here, and as my father was in debt partly because he had spent so much on my education, I resolved not to go away, but to work till I paid off the debt. I made up my mind to this and set to work, not, I must confess, without some repugnance. The land here does not yield much, and if one is not to farm at a loss one must employ serf labor or hired laborers, which is almost the same thing, or put it on a peasant footing—that is, work the fields oneself and with one's family. There is no middle path. But in those days I did not go into such subtleties. I did not leave a clod of earth unturned; I gathered together all the peasants, men and women, from the neighboring villages; the work went on at a tremendous pace. I myself ploughed and sowed and reaped, and was bored doing it, and frowned with disgust, like a village cat driven by hunger to eat cucumbers in the kitchen-garden. My body ached, and I slept as I walked. At first it seemed to me that I could easily reconcile this life of toil with my cultured habits; to do so, I thought, all that is necessary is to maintain a certain external order in life. I established myself upstairs here in the best rooms, and ordered them to bring me there coffee and liquor after lunch and dinner, and when I went to bed I read every night the *European Herald*.[1] But one day our priest, Father Ivan, came and drank up all my liquor at one sitting; and the *European Herald* went to the priest's daughters; as in the summer, especially at the hay-making, I did not succeed in getting to my bed at all, and slept in the sleigh in the barn, or somewhere in the forester's lodge, what chance was there of reading? Little by little I moved downstairs, began dining in the servants' kitchen, and of my former luxury nothing is left but the servants who were in my father's service, and whom it would be painful to turn away.

"In the first years I was elected here an honorary justice-of-the-peace. I used to have to go to the town and take part in the sessions of the congress and of the circuit court, and this was a pleasant change for me. When you live here for two or three months without a break, especially in the winter, you begin at last to pine for a black coat. And in the circuit court there were frock-coats, and uniforms, and dress-coats, too, all lawyers, men who have received a general education; I had someone to talk to. After sleeping in the sleigh and dining in the kitchen, to sit in an armchair in clean linen, in thin boots, with a chain on one's waistcoat, is such luxury!

"I received a warm welcome in the town. I made friends eagerly. And of all my acquaintanceships the most intimate and, to tell the truth, the most agreeable to me was my acquaintance with Lugano-vich, the vice-president of the circuit court. You both know him: a most charming personality. It all happened just after a celebrated case of incendiarism; the preliminary investigation lasted two days; we were exhausted. Luganovich looked at me and said:

" 'Look here, come round to dinner with me.'

"This was unexpected, as I knew Luganovitch very little, only officially, and I had never been to his house. I only just went to my hotel room to change and went off to dinner. And here it was my lot to meet Anna Alekseevna, Luganovich's wife. At that time she was still very young, not more than twenty-two, and her first baby had been born just six months before. It is all a thing of the past; and now I should find it difficult to define what there was so exceptional in her, what it was in her attracted me so much; at the time, at dinner, it was all perfectly clear to me. I saw a lovely, young, good, intelligent, fascinating woman, such as I had never met before; and I felt her at once some one close and already familiar, as though that face, those cordial, intelligent eyes, I had seen somewhere in my childhood, in the album which lay on my mother's chest of drawers.

"Four Jews were charged with being incendiaries, were regarded

1. A liberal monthly periodical.

as a gang of robbers, and, to my mind, quite groundlessly. At dinner I was very much excited, I was uncomfortable, and I don't know what I said, but Anna Alekseevna kept shaking her head and saying to her husband:

" 'Dmitry, how is this?'

"Luganovich is a good-natured man, one of those simple-hearted people who firmly maintain the opinion that once a man is charged before a court he is guilty, and to express doubt of the correctness of a sentence cannot be done except in legal form on paper, and not at dinner and in private conversation.

" 'You and I did not set fire to the place,' he said softly, 'and you see we are not condemned, and not in prison.'

"And both husband and wife tried to make me eat and drink as much as possible. From some trifling details, from the way they made the coffee together, for instance, and from the way they understood each other at half a word, I could gather that they lived in harmony and comfort, and that they were glad of a visitor. After dinner they played a duet on the paino; then it got dark, and I went home. That was at the beginning of spring.

"After that I spent the whole summer at Sofino without a break, and I had no time to think of the town, either, but the memory of the graceful fair-haired woman remained in my mind all those days; I did not think of her, but it was as though her light shadow were lying on my heart.

"In the late autumn there was a theatrical performance for some charitable purpose in the town. I went into the governor's box (I was invited to go there during intermission); I looked, and there was Anna Alekseevna sitting beside the governor's wife; and again the same irresistible, thrilling impression of beauty and sweet, caressing eyes, and again the same feeling of nearness. We sat side by side, then went to the foyer.

" 'You've grown thinner,' she said; 'have you been ill?'

" 'Yes, I've had rheumatism in my shoulder, and in rainy weather I can't sleep.'

" 'You look dispirited. In the spring, when you came to dinner, you were younger, more confident. You were full of eagerness, and talked a great deal then; you were very interesting, and I really must confess I was a little carried away by you. For some reason you often came back to my memory during the summer, and when I was getting ready for the theatre today I thought I should see you.'

"And she laughed.

" 'But you look dispirited today,' she repeated; 'it makes you seem older.'

"The next day I lunched at the Luganovichs'. After lunch they drove out to their summer villa, in order to make arrangements there for the winter, and I went with them. I returned with them to the town, and at midnight drank tea with them in quiet domestic surroundings, while the fire glowed, and the young mother kept going to see if her baby girl was asleep. And after that, every time I went to town I never failed to visit the Luganovichs. They grew used to me, and I grew used to them. As a rule I went in unannounced, as though I were one of the family.

" 'Who is there?' I would hear from a faraway room, in the drawling voice that seemed to me so lovely.

" 'It is Pavel Konstantinovich,' answered the maid or the nurse.

"Anna Alekseevna would come out to me with an anxious face, and would ask every time:

" 'Why is it so long since you have been? Has anything happened?'

"Her eyes, the elegant refined hand she gave me, her indoor dress, the way she did her hair, her voice, her step, always produced the same impression on me of something new and extraordinary in my life, and very important. We talked together for hours, were silent, thinking each our own thoughts, or she played for hours to me on the piano. If there were no one at home I stayed and waited, talked to the nurse, played with the child, or lay on the sofa in the study and read; and when Anna Alekseevna came back I met her in the hall, took all her parcels from her, and for some reason I carried those parcels every time with as much love, with as much solemnity, as a boy.

"There is a proverb that if a peasant woman has no troubles she will buy a pig. The Luganovichs had no troubles, so they made friends with me. If I did not come to the town I must be ill or something must have happened to me, and both of them were extremely anxious. They were worried that I, an educated man with a knowledge of languages, should, instead of devoting myself to science or literary work, live in the country, rush round like a squirrel in a cage, work hard with never a penny to show for it. They fancied that I was unhappy, and that I only talked, laughed, and ate to conceal my sufferings, and even at cheerful moments when I felt happy I was aware of their searching eyes fixed upon me. They were particularly touching when I really was depressed, when I was being worried by some creditor or had not money enough to pay interest on the proper day. The two of them, husband and wife, would whisper together at the window; then he would come to me and say with a grave face:

" 'If you really are in need of money at the moment, Pavel Konstantinovich, my wife and I beg you not to hesitate to borrow from us.'

"And he would blush to his ears with emotion. And it would

happen that, after whispering in the same way at the window, he would come up to me, with red ears, and say:

" 'My wife and I earnestly beg you to accept this present.'

"And he would give me studs, a cigar-case, or a lamp, and I would send them game, butter, and flowers from the country. They both, by the way, had considerable means of their own. In early days I often borrowed money, and was not very particular about it— borrowed wherever I could—but nothing in the world would have induced me to borrow from the Luganovichs. But why talk of it?

"I was unhappy. At home, in the fields, in the barn, I thought of her; I tried to understand the mystery of a beautiful, intelligent young woman's marrying someone so uninteresting, almost an old man (her husband was over forty), and having children by him; to understand the mystery of this uninteresting, good, simple-hearted man, who argued with such wearisome good sense, at balls and evening parties kept near the more solid people, looking listless and superfluous, with a submissive, uninterested expression, as though he had been brought there for sale, who yet believed in his right to be happy, to have children by her; and I kept trying to understand why she had met him first and not me, and why such a terrible mistake in our lives need have happened.

"And when I went to the town I saw every time from her eyes that she was expecting me, and she would confess to me herself that she had had a peculiar feeling all that day and had guessed that I should come. We talked a long time, and were silent, yet we did not confess our love to each other, but timidly and jealously concealed it. We were afraid of everything that might reveal our secret to ourselves. I loved her tenderly, deeply, but I reflected and kept asking myself what our love could lead to if we had not the strength to fight against it. It seemed to be incredible that my gentle, sad love could all at once coarsely break up the even tenor of the life of her husband, her children, and all the household in which I was so loved and trusted. Would it be honorable? She would go away with me, but where? Where could I take her? It would have been a different matter if I had had a beautiful, interesting life—if, for instance, I had been struggling for the emancipation of my country, or had been a celebrated man of science, an artist or a painter; but as it was it would mean taking her from one everyday humdrum life to another as humdrum or perhaps more so. And how long would our happiness last? What would happen to her in case I was ill, in case I died, or if we simply grew cold to one another?

"And she apparently reasoned in the same way. She thought of her husband, her children, and of her mother, who loved the husband like a son. If she abandoned herself to her feelings she would have to lie, or else to tell the truth, and in her position either would have been equally terrible and inconvenient. And she was tormented by the question whether her love would bring me happiness—would she not complicate my life, which, as it was, was hard enough and full of all sorts of trouble? She fancied she was not young enough for me, that she was not industrious nor energetic enough to begin a new life, and she often talked to her husband of the importance of my marrying a girl of intelligence and merit who would be a capable housewife and a help to me—and she would immediately add that it would be difficult to find such a girl in the whole town.

"Meanwhile the years were passing. Anna Alekseevna already had two children. When I arrived at the Luganovichs' the servants smiled cordially, the children shouted that Uncle Pavel Konstantinovich had come, and hung on my neck; every one was overjoyed. They did not understand what was happening in my soul, and thought that I, too, was happy. Everyone looked on me as a noble being. And grown-ups and children alike felt that a noble being was walking about their rooms, and that gave a peculiar charm to their manner towards me, as though in my presence their life, too, was purer and more beautiful. Anna Alekseevna and I used to go to the theatre together, always walking there; we used to sit side by side in the stalls, our shoulders touching. I would take the opera-glass from her hands without a word, and feel at that minute that she was near me, that she was mine, that we could not live without each other; but by some strange misunderstanding, when we came out of the theatre we always said good-bye and parted as though we were strangers. Goodness knows what people were saying about us in the town already, but there was not a word of truth in it all!

"In the latter years Anna Alekseevna took to going away for frequent visits to her mother or to her sister; she began to suffer from low spirits, she began to recognize that her life was spoilt and unsatisfied, and at times she did not care to see her husband nor her children. She was already being treated for neurasthenia.

"We were silent and still silent, and in the presence of outsiders she displayed a strange irritation in regard to me; whatever I talked about, she disagreed with me, and if I had an argument she sided with my opponent. If I dropped anything, she would say coldly:

" 'I congratulate you.'

"If I forgot to take the opera-glass when we were going to the theatre, she would say afterwards:

" 'I knew you would forget it.'

"Luckily or unluckily, there is nothing in our lives that does not end sooner or later. The time of parting came, as Luganovich was appointed president in one of the western provinces. They had to sell their furniture, their horses, their summer villa. When they drove out to the villa, and afterwards looked back as they were going away, to look for the last time at the garden, at the green roof, every one was sad, and I realized that I had to say good-bye not only to the villa. It was arranged that at the end of August we should see Anna Alekseevna off to the Crimea, where the doctors were sending her, and that a little later Luganovich and the children would set off for the western province.

"We were a great crowd to see Anna Alekseevna off. When she had said good-bye to her husband and her children and there was only a minute left before the third bell, I ran into her compartment to put a basket, which she had almost forgotten, on the rack, and I had to say good-bye. When our eyes met in the compartment our spiritual fortitude deserted us both; I took her in my arms, she pressed her face to my breast, and tears flowed from her eyes. Kissing her face, her shoulders, her hands wet with tears—oh, how unhappy we were!—I confessed my love for her, and with a burning pain in my heart I realized how unnecessary, how petty, and how deceptive all that had hindered us from loving was. I understood that when you love you must either, in your reasonings about that love, start from what is highest, from what is more important than happiness or unhappiness, sin or virtue in their accepted meaning, or you must not reason at all.

"I kissed her for the last time, pressed her hand, and parted for ever. The train had already started. I went into the next compartment—it was empty—and until I reached the next station I sat there crying. Then I walked home to Sofino. . . ."

While Alekhin was telling his story, the rain left off and the sun came out. Burkin and Ivan Ivanovich went out on the balcony, from which there was a beautiful view over the garden and the mill-pond, which was shining now in the sunshine like a mirror. They admired it, and at the same time they were sorry that this man with the kind, clever eyes, who had told them this story with such genuine feeling, should be rushing round and round this huge estate like a squirrel on a wheel instead of devoting himself to science or something else which would have made his life more pleasant; and they thought what a sorrowful face Anna Alekseevna must have had when he said good-bye to her in the railway-carriage and kissed her face and shoulders. Both of them had met her in the town, and Burkin knew her and thought her beautiful.

1898

A Doctor's Visit

The professor received a telegram from the Lyalikovs' factory; he was asked to come as quickly as possible. The daughter of a certain Madame Lyalikov, apparently the owner of the factory, was ill, and that was all that one could make out of the long, incoherent telegram. And the professor did not go himself, but sent instead his assistant, Korolyov.

It was two stations from Moscow, and there was a drive of three miles from the station. A carriage with three horses had been sent to the station to meet Korolyov; the coachman wore a hat with a peacock feather on it, and answered every question in a loud voice like a soldier: "No, sir!" "Certainly, sir!"

It was Saturday evening; the sun was setting, the workers were coming in crowds from the factory to the station, and they bowed to the carriage in which Korolyov was driving. And he was charmed with the evening, the farmhouses and villas on the road, and the birch-trees, and the quiet atmosphere all around, when the fields and woods and the sun seemed preparing, like the workers now on the eve of the holiday, to rest, and perhaps to pray. . . .

He had been born and had grown up in Moscow; he did not know the country, and he had never taken any interest in factories, or been inside one, but he had happened to read about factories, and had been in the houses of manufacturers and had talked to them; and whenever he saw a factory far or near, he always thought how quiet and peaceable it was outside, but within there was always sure to be impenetrable ignorance and dull egoism on the side of the owners, wearisome, unhealthy toil on the side of the workpeople, squabbling, vermin, vodka. And now when the workers timidly and respectfully made way for the carriage, in their faces, their caps, their walk, he read physical impurity, drunkenness, nervous exhaustion, bewilderment.

They drove in at the factory gates. On each side he caught glimpses of the little houses of workpeople, of the faces of women, of quilts and linen on the railings. "Look out!" shouted the coachman, not pulling up the horses. It was a wide courtyard without grass, with five immense blocks of buildings with tall chimneys a little distance one from another, warehouses and barracks, and over everything a sort of gray powder as though from dust. Here and there, like oases in the desert, there were pitiful gardens, and the green and red roofs of the houses in which the managers and clerks lived. The coachman suddenly pulled up the horses, and the carriage stopped at the house, which had been newly painted gray; here was a flower garden, with a lilac bush covered with dust, and on the yellow steps at the front door there was a strong smell of paint.

"Please come in, Doctor," said women's voices in the passage and the entry, and at the same time he heard sighs and whisperings. "Pray walk in. . . . We've been expecting you so long . . . we're in real trouble. Here, this way."

Madame Lyalikov—a stout elderly lady wearing a black silk dress with fashionable sleeves, but, judging from her face, a simple uneducated woman—looked at the doctor in a flutter, and could not bring herself to hold out her hand to him; she did not dare. Beside her stood a personage with short hair and a pince-nez; she was wearing a blouse of many colors, and was very thin and no longer young. The servants called her Christina Dmitryevna, and Korolyov guessed that this was the governess. Probably, as the person of most education in the house, she had been charged to meet and receive the doctor, for she began immediately, in great haste, stating the causes of the illness, giving trivial and tiresome details, but without saying who was ill or what was the matter.

The doctor and the governess were sitting talking while the lady of the house stood motionless at the door, waiting. From the conversation Korolyov learned that the patient was Madame Lyalikov's only daughter and heiress, a girl of twenty, called Liza; she had been ill for a long time, and had consulted various doctors, and the previous night she had suffered till morning from such violent palpitations of the heart that no one in the house had slept, and they had been afraid she might die.

"She has been, one may say, ailing from childhood," said Christina Dmitryevna in a singsong voice, continually wiping her lips with her hand. "The doctors say it is nerves; when she was a little girl she was scrofulous, and the doctors drove it inwards, so I think it may be due to that."

They went to see the invalid. Fully grown up, big and tall, but ugly like her mother, with the same little eyes and disproportionate breadth of the lower part of the face, lying with her hair in disorder, muffled up to the chin, she made upon Korolyov at the first minute the impression of a poor, destitute creature, sheltered and cared for here out of charity, and he could hardly believe that this was the heiress of the five huge buildings.

"I am the doctor come to see you," said Korolyov. "Good-evening."

He mentioned his name and pressed her hand, a large, cold, ugly hand; she sat up, and, evidently accustomed to doctors, let herself be sounded, without showing the least concern that her shoulders and chest were uncovered.

"I have palpitations of the heart," she said, "It was so awful all night. . . . I almost died of fright! Do give me something."

"I will, I will; don't worry yourself."

Korolyov examined her and shrugged his shoulders.

"The heart is all right," he said; "it's all going on satisfactorily;

everything is in good order. Your nerves must have been playing pranks a little, but that's so common. The attack is over by now, one must suppose; lie down and go to sleep."

At that moment a lamp was brought into the bedroom. The patient screwed up her eyes at the light, then suddenly put her hands to her head and broke into sobs. And the impression of a destitute, ugly creature vanished, and Korolyov no longer noticed the little eyes or the heavy development of the lower part of the face. He saw a soft, suffering expression which was intelligent and touching: she seemed to him altogether graceful, feminine, and simple; and he longed to soothe her, not with drugs, not with advice, but with simple, kindly words. Her mother put her arms round her head and hugged her. What despair, what grief was in the old woman's face! She, her mother, had reared her and brought her up, spared nothing, and devoted her whole life to having her daughter taught French, dancing, music: had engaged a dozen teachers for her; had consulted the best doctors, kept a governess. And now she could not make out the reason of these tears, why there was all this misery, she could not understand, and was bewildered; and she had a guilty, agitated, despairing expression, as though she had omitted something very important, had left something undone, had neglected to call in somebody—and whom, she did not know.

"Lizanka, you are crying again . . . again," she said, hugging her daughter to her. "My own, my darling, my child, tell me what it is! Have pity on me! Tell me."

Both wept bitterly. Korolyov sat down on the side of the bed and took Liza's hand.

"Come, stop; it's no use crying," he said kindly. "Why, there is nothing in the world that is worth those tears. Come, we won't cry; that's no good. . . ."

And inwardly he thought:

"It's high time she was married. . . ."

"Our doctor at the factory gave her Kalibromati," said the governess, "but I notice it only makes her worse. I should have thought that if she is given anything for the heart it ought to be drops. . . . I forget the name. . . . Convallaria, isn't it?"

And there followed all sorts of details. She interrupted the doctor, preventing his speaking, and there was a look of effort on her face, as though she supposed that, as the woman of most education in the house, she was obliged to keep up a conversation with the doctor, and on no other subject but medicine.

Korolyov felt bored.

"I find nothing special the matter," he said, addressing the mother as he went out of the bedroom. "If your daughter is being attended by the factory doctor, let him go on attending her. The treatment so far has been perfectly correct, and I see no reason for changing your doctor. Why change? It's such an ordinary trouble; there's nothing seriously wrong."

He spoke deliberately as he put on his gloves, while Madame Lyalikov stood without moving, and looked at him with her tearful eyes.

"I have half an hour to catch the ten o'clock train," he said. "I hope I am not too late."

"And can't you stay?" she asked, and tears trickled down her cheeks again. "I am ashamed to trouble you, but if you would be so good. . . . For God's sake," she went on in an undertone, glancing towards the door, "do stay tonight with us! She is all I have . . . my only daughter. . . . She frightened me last night; I can't get over it. . . . Don't go away, for goodness' sake! . . ."

He wanted to tell her that he had a great deal of work in Moscow, that his family were expecting him home; it was disagreeable to him to spend the evening and the whole night in a strange house quite needlessly; but he looked at her face, heaved a sigh, and began taking off his gloves without a word.

All the lamps and candles were lighted in his honor in the drawing-room and the dining-room. He sat down at the piano and began turning over the music. Then he looked at the pictures on the walls, at the portraits. The pictures, oil-paintings in gold frames, were views of the Crimea—a stormy sea with a ship, a Catholic monk with a wineglass; they were all dull, smooth daubs, with no trace of talent in them. There was not a single good-looking face among the portraits, nothing but broad cheekbones and astonished-looking eyes. Lyalikov, Liza's father, had a low forehead and a self-satisfied expression; his uniform sat like a sack on his bulky plebeian figure; on his breast was a medal and a Red Cross badge. There was little sign of culture, and the luxury was senseless and haphazard, and was as ill-fitting as that uniform. The floors irritated him with their brilliant polish, the lusters on the chandelier irritated him, and he was reminded for some reason of the story of the merchant who used to go to the baths with a medal on his neck. . . .

He heard a whispering in the entry; someone was softly snoring. And suddenly from outside came harsh, abrupt, metallic sounds, such as Korolyov had never heard before, and which he did not understand now; they roused strange, unpleasant echoes in his soul.

"I believe nothing would induce me to remain here to live . . ." he thought, and went back to the music-books again.

"Doctor, please come to supper!" the governess called him in a low voice.

He went into supper. The table was large and laid with a vast number of dishes and wines, but there were only two to supper: himself and Christina Dmitryevna. She drank Madeira, ate rapidly, and talked, looking at him through her pince-nez:

"Our workers are very contented. We have performances at the factory every winter; the workpeople act themselves. They have lectures with a magic lantern, a splendid tea-room, and everything they want. They are very much attached to us, and when they heard that Lizanka was worse they had a service sung for her. Though they have no education, they have their feelings, too."

"It looks as though you have no man in the house at all," said Korolyov.

"Not one. Pyotr Nikanorich died a year and a half ago, and left us alone. And so there are the three of us. In the summer we live here, and in winter we live in Moscow, in Polianka. I have been living with them for eleven years—as one of the family."

At supper they served sterlet, chicken croquets, and stewed fruit; the wines were expensive French wines.

"Please don't stand on ceremony, doctor," said Christina Dmitryevna, eating and wiping her mouth with her fist, and it was evident she found her life here exceedingly pleasant. "Please have some more."

After supper the doctor was shown to his room, where a bed had been made up for him, but he did not feel sleepy. The room was stuffy and it smelled of paint; he put on his coat and went out.

It was cool in the open air; there was already a glimmer of dawn, and all the five blocks of buildings, with their tall chimneys, barracks, and warehouses, were distinctly outlined against the damp air. As it was a holiday, they were not working, and the windows were dark, and in only one of the buildings was there a furnace burning; two windows were crimson, and fire mixed with smoke came from time to time from the chimney. Far away beyond the yard the frogs were croaking and the nightingales singing.

Looking at the factory buildings and the barracks, where the workers were asleep, he thought again what he always thought when he saw a factory. They may have performances for the workers, magic lanterns, factory doctors, and improvements of all sorts, but, all the same, the workers he had met that day on his way from the station did not look in any way different from those he had known long ago in his childhood, before there were factory performances and improvements. As a doctor accustomed to judging correctly of chronic complaints, the radical cause of which was incomprehensible and incurable, he looked upon factories as something baffling, the cause of which also was obscure and not removable, and all the improvements in the life of the factory workers he looked upon not as superfluous, but as comparable with the treatment of incurable illnesses.

"There is something baffling in it, of course . . ." he thought, looking at the crimson windows. "Fifteen hundred or two thousand workpeople are working without rest in unhealthy surroundings, making bad cotton goods, living on the verge of starvation, and waking from this nightmare only at rare intervals in the tavern; a hundred people act as overseers, and the whole life of that hundred is spent in imposing fines, in abuse, in injustice, and only two or three so-called owners enjoy the profits, though they don't work at all, and despise the wretched cotton. But what are the profits, and how do they enjoy them? Madame Lyalikov and her daughter are unhappy—it makes one wretched to look at them; the only one who enjoys her life is Christina Dmitryevna, a stupid, middle-aged maiden lady in pince-nez. And so it appears that all these five blocks of buildings are at work, and inferior cotton is sold in the eastern markets, simply that Christina Dmitryevna may eat sterlet and drink Madeira."

Suddenly there came a strange noise, the same sound Korolyov had heard before supper. Someone was striking on a sheet of metal near one of the buildings; he struck a note, and then at once checked the vibrations, so that short, abrupt, discordant sounds were produced, rather like "Dair . . . dair . . . dair. . . ." Then there was half a minute of stillness, and from another building there came sounds equally abrupt and unpleasant, lower bass notes: "Drin . . . drin . . . drin. . . ." Eleven times. Evidently it was the watchman striking the hour.

Near the third building he heard: "Zhuk . . . zhuk . . . zhuk. . . ." And so near all the buildings, and then behind the barracks and beyond the gates. And in the stillness of the night it seemed as though these sounds were uttered by a monster with crimson eyes— the Devil himself, who controlled the owners and the workers alike, and was deceiving both.

Korolyov went out of the yard into the open country.

"Who goes there?" some one called to him at the gates in an abrupt voice.

"It's just like being in prison," he thought, and made no answer.

Here the nightingales and the frogs could be heard more distinctly, and one could feel it was a night in May. From the station came the noise of a train; somewhere in the distance drowsy cocks were crowing; but, all the same, the night was still, the world was sleeping tranquilly. In a field not far from the factory there could be seen the framework of a house and heaps of building material: Korolyov sat down on the planks and went on thinking.

"The only person who feels happy here is the governess, and the factory hands are working for her gratification. But that's only apparent: she is only the figurehead. The real person, for whom everything is being done, is the Devil."

And he thought about the Devil, in whom he did not believe, and he looked round at the two windows where the fires were gleaming. It seemed to him that out of those crimson eyes the Devil himself was looking at him—that unknown force that had created the mutual relation of the strong and the weak, that coarse blunder which one could never correct. The strong must hinder the weak from living—such was the law of Nature; but only in a newspaper article or in a schoolbook was that intelligible and easily accepted. In the hotchpotch which was everyday life, in the tangle of trivialities out of which human relations were woven, it was no longer a law, but a logical absurdity, when the strong and the weak were both equally victims of their mutual relations, unwillingly submitting to some directing force, unknown, standing outside life, apart from man.

So thought Korolyov, sitting on the planks, and little by little he was possessed by a feeling that this unknown and mysterious force was really close by and looking at him. Meanwhile the east was growing paler, time passed rapidly; when there was not a soul anywhere near, as though everything were dead, the five buildings and their chimneys against the gray background of the dawn had a peculiar look—not the same as by day; one forgot altogether that inside there were steam motors, electricity, telephones, and kept thinking of lake-dwellings, of the Stone Age, feeling the presence of a crude, unconscious force. . . .

And again there came the sound: "Dair . . . dair . . . dair . . . dair . . ." twelve times. Then there was stillness, stillness for half a minute, and at the other end of the yard there rang out.

"Drin . . . drin . . . drin. . . ."

"Horribly disagreeable," thought Korolyov.

"Zhuk . . . zhuk . . ." there resounded from a third place, abruptly, sharply, as though with annoyance—"Zhuk . . . zhuk. . . ."

And it took four minutes to strike twelve. Then there was a hush; and again it seemed as though everything were dead.

Korolyov sat a little longer, then went to the house, but sat up for a good while longer. In the adjoining rooms there was whispering, there was a sound of shuffling slippers and bare feet.

"Is she having another attack?" thought Korolyov.

He went out to have a look at the patient. By now it was quite light in the rooms, and a faint glimmer of sunlight, piercing through the morning mist, quivered on the floor and on the wall of the drawing-room. The door of Liza's room was open, and she was sitting in a low chair beside her bed, with her hair down, wearing a dressing-gown and wrapped in a shawl. The blinds were down on the windows.

"How do you feel?" asked Korolyov.

"Well, thank you."

He touched her pulse, then straightened her hair, that had fallen over her forehead.

"You are not asleep," he said. "It's beautiful weather outside. It's spring. The nightingales are singing, and you sit in the dark and think of something."

She listened and looked into his face; her eyes were sorrowful and intelligent, and it was evident she wanted to say something to him.

"Does this happen to you often?" he said.

She moved her lips, and answered:

"Often, I feel wretched almost every night."

At that moment the watchman in the yard began striking two o'clock. They heard: "Dair . . . dair . . ." and she shuddered.

"Do those knockings worry you?" he asked.

"I don't know. Everything here worries me," she answered, and pondered. "Everything worries me. I hear sympathy in your voice; it seemed to me as soon as I saw you that I could tell you all about it."

"Tell me, I beg you."

"I want to tell you of my opinion. It seems to me that I have no illness, but that I am weary and frightened, because it is bound to be so and cannot be otherwise. Even the healthiest person can't help being uneasy if, for instance, a robber is moving about under his window. I am constantly being doctored," she went on, looking at her knees, and she gave a shy smile. "I am very grateful, of course, and I do not deny that the treatment is a benefit; but I should like to talk, not with a doctor, but with some intimate friend who would understand me and would convince me that I was right or wrong."

"Have you no friends?" asked Korolyov.

"I am lonely. I have a mother; I love her, but, all the same, I am lonely. That's how it happens to be. . . . Lonely people read a great deal, but say little and hear little. Life for them is mysterious; they are mystics and often see the Devil where he is not. Lermontov's Tamara[1] was lonely, and she saw the Devil."

"Do you read a great deal?"

"Yes. You see, my whole time is free from morning till night. I read by day, and by night my head is empty; instead of thoughts there are shadows in it."

"Do you see anything at night?" asked Korolyov.

"No, but I feel. . . ."

She smiled again, raised her eyes to the doctor, and looked at him so sorrowfully, so intelligently; and it seemed to him that she trusted him, and that she wanted to speak frankly to him, and that she thought the same as he did. But she was silent, perhaps waiting for him to speak.

And he knew what to say to her. It was clear to him that she needed as quickly as possible to give up the five buildings and the million if she had it—to leave that Devil that looked out at night; it was clear to him, too, that she thought so herself, and was only waiting for someone she trusted to confirm her.

But he did not know how to say it. How? One is shy of asking

1. The heroine of the narrative poem *The Demon* (1832–41).

men under sentence what they have been sentenced for; and in the same way it is awkward to ask very rich people what they want so much money for, why they make such a poor use of their wealth, why they don't give it up, even when they see in it their unhappiness; and if they begin a conversation about it themselves, it is usually embarrassing, awkward, and long.

"How is one to say it?" Korolyov wondered. "And is it necessary to speak?"

And he said what he meant in a roundabout way:

"You in the position of a factory owner and a wealthy heiress are dissatisfied; you don't believe in your right to it; and here now you can't sleep. That, of course, is better than if you were satisfied, slept soundly, and thought everything was satisfactory. Your sleeplessness does you credit; in any case, it is a good sign. In reality, such a conversation as this between us now would have been unthinkable for our parents. At night they did not talk, but slept sound; we, our generation, sleep badly, are restless, but talk a great deal, and are always trying to settle whether we are right or not. For our children or grandchildren that question—whether they are right or not—will have been settled. Things will be clearer for them than for us. Life will be good in fifty years' time; it's only a pity we shall not last out till then. It would be interesting to have a peep at it."

"What will our children and grandchildren do?" asked Liza.

"I don't know. . . . I suppose they will give it all up and go away."

"Go where?"

"Where? . . . Why, where they like," said Korolyov; and he laughed. "There are lots of places a good, intelligent person can go to."

He glanced at his watch.

"The sun has risen, though," he said. "It is time you were asleep. Undress and sleep soundly. Very glad to have made your acquaintance," he went on, pressing her hand. "You are a good, interesting woman. Good-night!"

He went to his room and went to bed.

In the morning when the carriage was brought round they all came out on to the steps to see him off. Liza, pale and exhausted, was in a white dress as though for a holiday, with a flower in her hair; she looked at him, as yesterday, sorrowfully and intelligently, smiled and talked, and all with an expression as though she wanted to tell him something special, important—him alone. They could hear the larks trilling and the church bells pealing. The windows in the factory buildings were sparkling gaily, and, driving across the yard and afterwards along the road to the station, Korolyov thought neither of the workers nor of lake dwellings, nor of the Devil, but thought of the time, perhaps close at hand, when life would be as bright and joyous as that still Sunday morning; and he thought how pleasant it was on such a morning in the spring to drive with three horses in a good carriage, and to bask in the sunshine.

1898

The Darling

Olenka, the daughter of the retired collegiate assessor Plemyan-niakov, was sitting on her back porch, lost in thought. It was hot, the flies were persistent and teasing, and it was pleasant to reflect that it would soon be evening. Dark rainclouds were gathering from the east, and bringing from time to time a breath of moisture in the air.

Kukin, who was the manager of an open-air theatre called the Tivoli, and who lived in the lodge, was standing in the middle of the garden looking at the sky.

"Again!" he observed despairingly. "It's going to rain again! Rain every day, as though to spite me. I might as well hang myself! It's ruin! Fearful losses every day."

He flung up his hands, and went on, addressing Olenka:

"There! that's the life we lead, Olga Semyonovna. It's enough to make one cry. One works and does one's utmost; one wears oneself out, getting no sleep at night, and racks one's brain what to do for the best. And then what happens? To begin with, one's public is ignorant, boorish. I give them the very best operetta, a dainty masque, first-rate music-hall artists. But do you suppose that's what they want? They don't understand anything of that sort. They want a clown; what they ask for is vulgarity. And then look at the weather! Almost every evening it rains. It started on the tenth of May, and it's kept it up all May and June. It's simply awful! The public doesn't come, but I've to pay the rent just the same, and pay the artists."

The next evening the clouds would gather again, and Kukin would say with an hysterical laugh:

"Well, rain away, then! Flood the garden, drown me! Damn my luck in this world and the next! Let the artists drag me into court! Send me to prison—to Siberia!—the scaffold! Ha, ha, ha!"

And the next day the same thing.

Olenka listened to Kukin with silent gravity, and sometimes tears came into her eyes. In the end his misfortunes touched her; she grew to love him. He was a small thin man, with a yellow face, and curls combed forward on his forehead. He spoke in a thin tenor; as he talked his mouth worked on one side, and there was always an expression of despair on his face; yet he aroused a deep and genuine affection in her. She was always fond of someone, and could not exist without loving. In earlier days she had loved her Papa, who now sat in a darkened room, breathing with difficulty; she had loved her aunt who used to come every other year from Bryansk; and before that, when she was at school, she had loved her French master. She was a gentle, soft-hearted, compassionate girl, with mild, tender eyes and very good health. At the sight of her full rosy cheeks, her soft white neck with a little dark mole on it, and the kind, naïve smile, which came into her face when she listened to anything pleasant, men thought, "Yes, not half bad," and smiled too, while lady visitors could not refrain from seizing her hand in the middle of a conversation, exclaiming in a gush of delight, "You darling!"

The house in which she had lived since her birth, and which was left her in her father's will, was at the extreme end of the town, not far from the Tivoli. In the evenings and at night she could hear the band playing, and the crackling and banging of fireworks, and it seemed to her that it was Kukin struggling with his destiny, storming the entrenchments of his chief foe, the indifferent public; there was a sweet thrill at her heart, she had no desire to sleep, and when he returned home at daybreak, she tapped softly at her bedroom window and, showing him only her face and one shoulder through the curtain, she gave him a friendly smile. . . .

He proposed to her, and they were married. And when he had a closer view of her neck and her plump, fine shoulders, he threw up his hands, and said:

"You darling!"

He was happy, but as it rained on the day and night of his wedding, his face still retained an expression of despair.

They got on very well together. She used to sit in his office, to look after things in the Tivoli, to put down the accounts and pay the wages. And her rosy cheeks, her sweet, naïve, radiant smile, were to be seen now at the office window, now in the refreshment bar or behind the scenes of the theatre. And already she used to say to her acquaintances that the theatre was the chief and most important thing in life, and that it was only through the drama that one could derive true enjoyment and become cultivated and humane.

"But do you suppose the public understands that?" she used to say. "What they want is a clown. Yesterday we gave *Faust Inside Out*, and almost all the boxes were empty; but if Vanichka and I had been producing some vulgar thing, I assure you the theatre would have been packed. Tomorrow Vanichka and I are doing *Orpheus in the Underworld*. Do come."

And what Kukin said about the theatre and the actors she repeated. Like him she despised the public for their ignorance and their indifference to art; she took part in the rehearsals, she corrected the actors, she kept an eye on the behavior of the musicians, and when there was an unfavorable notice in the local paper, she shed tears, and then went to the editor's office to set things right.

The actors were fond of her and used to call her "Vanichka and I," and "the darling"; she was sorry for them and used to lend them small sums of money, and if they deceived her, she used to shed a few tears in private, but did not complain to her husband.

They got on well in the winter too. They took the theatre in the town for the whole winter, and let it for short terms to a troupe from Little Russia, or to a conjurer, or to a local dramatic society. Olenka grew stouter, and was always beaming with satisfaction, while Kukin grew thinner and yellower, and continually complained of their terrible losses, although he had not done badly all the winter. He used to cough at night, and she used to give him hot raspberry tea or lime-flower water, to rub him with eau-de-Cologne and to wrap him in her warm shawls.

"You're such a sweet pet!" she used to say with perfect sincerity, stroking his hair. "You're such a pretty dear!"

Towards Lent he went to Moscow to collect a new troupe, and without him she could not sleep, but sat all night at her window, looking at the stars, and she compared herself with the hens, who are awake all night and uneasy when the cock is not in the hen-house. Kukin was detained in Moscow, and wrote that he would be back at Easter, adding some instructions about the Tivoli. But on the Sunday before Easter, late in the evening, came a sudden ominous knock at the gate; some one was hammering on the gate as though on a barrel—boom, boom, boom! The drowsy cook went flopping with her bare feet through the puddles, as she ran to open the gate.

"Please open," said some one outside in a thick bass. "There is a telegram for you."

Olenka had received telegrams from her husband before, but this time for some reason she felt numb with terror. With shaking hands she opened the telegram and read as follows:

Ivan Petrovich died suddenly to-day. Awaiting immate instructions fufuneral Tuesday.

That was how it was written in the telegram—"fufuneral," and the utterly incomprehensible word "immate." It was signed by the stage manager of the operatic company.

"My darling!" sobbed Okenka. "Vanichka, my precious, my darling! Why did I ever meet you! Why did I know you and love you! Your poor heartbroken Olenka is all alone without you!"

Kukin's funeral took place on Tuesday in Moscow, Olenka returned home on Wednesday, and as soon as she got indoors she threw herself on her bed and sobbed so loudly that it could be heard next door, and in the street.

"Poor darling!" the neighbors said, as they crossed themselves. "Olga Semyonovna, poor darling! How she does take on!"

Three months later Olenka was coming home from mass, melancholy and in deep mourning. It happened that one of her neighbors, Vassily Andreich Pustovalov, returning home from church, walked back beside her. He was the manager at Babakayev's, the timber merchant's. He wore a straw hat, a white waistcoat, and a gold watch-chain, and looked more like a country gentleman than a man in trade.

"Everything happens as it is ordained, Olga Semyonovna," he said gravely, with a sympathetic note in his voice; "and if any of our dear ones die, it must be because it is the will of God, so we ought to have fortitude and bear it submissively."

After seeing Olenka to her gate, he said good-bye and went on. All day afterwards she heard his sedately dignified voice, and whenever she shut her eyes she saw his dark beard. She liked him very much. And apparently she had made an impression on him too, for not long afterwards an elderly lady, with whom she was only slightly acquainted, came to drink coffee with her, and as soon as she was seated at table began to talk about Pustovalov, saying that he was an excellent man whom one could thoroughly depend upon, and that any girl would be glad to marry him. Three days later Pustovalov himself came. He did not stay long, only about ten minutes, and he did not say much, but when he left, Olenka loved him—loved him so much that she lay awake all night in a perfect fever, and in the morning she sent for the elderly lady. The match was quickly arranged, and then came the wedding.

Pustovalov and Olenka got on very well together when they were married.

Usually he sat in the office till dinnertime, then he went out on business, while Olenka took his place, and sat in the office till evening, making up accounts and booking orders.

"Timber gets dearer every year; the price rises twenty per cent," she would say to her customers and friends. "Only fancy we used to sell local timber, and now Vassichka always has to go for wood to the Mogilev district. And the freight!" she would add, covering her cheeks with her hands in horror. "The freight!"

It seemed to her that she had been in the timber trade for ages and ages, and that the most important and necessary thing in life was timber; and there was something intimate and touching to her in the very sound of words such as "balk," "post," "beam," "pole," "scantling," "batten," "lath," "plank," etc.

At night when she was asleep she dreamed of perfect mountains of planks and boards, and long strings of wagons, carting timber somewhere far away. She dreamed that a whole regiment of six-inch beams forty feet high, standing on end, was marching upon the timberyard; that logs, beams, and boards knocked together with the resounding crash of dry wood, kept falling and getting up again, piling themselves on each other. Olenka cried out in her sleep, and Pustovalov said to her tenderly: "Olenka, what's the matter, darling? Cross yourself!"

Her husband's ideas were hers. If he thought the room was too hot, or that business was slack, she thought the same. Her husband did not care for entertainments, and on holidays he stayed at home. She did likewise.

"You are always at home or in the office," her friends said to her. "You should go to the theatre, darling, or to the circus."

"Vassichka and I have no time to go to theatres," she would answer sedately. "We have no time for nonsense. What's the use of these theatres?"

On Saturdays Pustovalov and she used to go to the evening service; on holidays to early mass, and they walked side by side with softened faces as they came home from church. There was a pleasant fragrance about them both, and her silk dress rustled agreeably. At home they drank tea, with fancy bread and jams of various kinds, and afterwards they ate pie. Every day at twelve o'clock there was a savory smell of beet-root soup and of mutton or duck in their yard, and on fast-days of fish, and no one could pass the gate without feeling hungry. In the office the samovar was always boiling, and customers were regaled with tea and biscuits. Once a week the couple went to the baths and returned side by side, both red in the face.

"Yes, we have nothing to complain of, thank God," Olenka used to say to her acquaintances. "I wish everyone were as well off as Vassichka and I."

When Pustovalov went away to buy wood in the Mogilev district, she missed him dreadfully, lay awake, and cried. A young veterinary surgeon in the army, called Smirnin, to whom they had let their lodge, used sometimes to come in in the evening. He used to talk to her and play cards with her, and this entertained her in her husband's absence. She was particularly interested in what he told her of his home life. He was married and had a little boy, but was separated from his wife because she had been unfaithful to him, and now he hated her and sent her forty rubles a month for the maintenance of their son. And hearing of all this, Olenka sighed and shook her head. She was sorry for him.

"Well, God keep you," she used to say to him at parting, as she lighted him down the stairs with a candle. "Thank you for coming to cheer me up, and may the Mother of God give you health."

And she always expressed herself with the same sedateness and dignity, the same reasonableness, in imitation of her husband. As the veterinary surgeon was disappearing behind the door below, she would say:

"You know, Vladimir Platonich, you'd better make it up with your wife. You should forgive her for the sake of your son. You may be sure the little fellow understands."

And when Pustovalov came back, she told him in a low voice about the veterinary surgeon and his unhappy home life, and both sighed and shook their heads and talked about the boy, who, no doubt, missed his father, and by some strange connection of ideas, they went up to the holy icons, bowed to the ground before them, and prayed that God would give them children.

And so the Pustovalovs lived for six years quietly and peaceably in love and complete harmony.

But behold! one winter day after drinking hot tea in the office, Vassily Andreich went out into the yard without his cap on to see about sending off some timber, caught cold, and was taken ill. He had the best doctors, but he grew worse and died after four months' illness. And Olenka was a widow once more.

"I've nobody, now you've left me, my darling," she sobbed, after her husband's funeral. "How can I live without you, in wretchedness and misery! Pity me, good people, all alone in the world!"

She went about dressed in black with "weepers,"[1] and gave up wearing hat and gloves for good. She hardly ever went out, except to church, or to her husband's grave, and led the life of a nun. It was not till six months later that she took off the weepers and opened the shutters of the windows. She was sometimes seen in the mornings, going with her cook to market for provisions, but what went on in her house and how she lived now could only be surmised. People guessed, from seeing her drinking tea in her garden with the veterinary surgeon, who read the newspaper aloud to her, and from the fact that, meeting a lady she knew at the post-office, she said to her:

"There is no proper veterinary inspection in our town, and that's the cause of all sorts of epidemics. One is always hearing of people's getting infection from the milk supply, or catching diseases from horses and cows. The health of domestic animals ought to be as well cared for as the health of human beings."

She repeated the veterinary surgeon's words, and was of the same opinion as he about everything. It was evident that she could not live a year without some attachment, and had found new happiness in the lodge. In anyone else this would have been censured, but no one could think ill of Olenka; everything she did was so natural.

---

1. White bands worn on the cuffs of mourning clothes.

Neither she nor the veterinary surgeon said anything to other people of the change in their relations, and tried, indeed, to conceal it, but without success, for Olenka could not keep a secret. When he had visitors, men serving in his regiment, and she poured out tea or served the supper, she would begin talking of the cattle plague, of the foot and mouth disease, and of the municipal slaughterhouses. He was dreadfully embarrassed, and when the guests had gone, he would seize her by the hand and hiss angrily:

"I've asked you before not to talk about what you don't understand. When we veterinary surgeons are talking among ourselves, please don't put your word in. It's really annoying."

And she would look at him with astonishment and dismay, and ask him in alarm: "But Volodichka, what *am* I to talk about?"

And with tears in her eyes she would embrace him, begging him not to be angry, and they were both happy.

But this happiness did not last long. The veterinary surgeon departed, departed forever with his regiment, when it was transferred to a distant place—to Siberia, perhaps. And Olenka was left alone.

Now she was absolutely alone. Her father had long been dead, and his armchair lay in the attic, covered with dust and lame of one leg. She got thinner and plainer, and when people met her in the street they did not look at her as they used to, and did not smile to her; evidently her best years were over and left behind, and now a new sort of life had begun for her, which did not bear thinking about. In the evening Olenka sat in the porch, and heard the band playing and the fireworks popping in the Tivoli, but now the sound stirred no response. She looked into her yard without interest, thought of nothing, wished for nothing, and afterwards, when night came on she went to bed and dreamed of her empty yard. She ate and drank as it were unwillingly.

And what was worst of all, she had no opinions of any sort. She saw the objects about her and understood what she saw, but could not form any opinion about them, and did not know what to talk about. And how awful it is not to have any opinions! One sees a bottle, for instance, or the rain, or a peasant driving in his cart, but what the bottle is for, or the rain, or the peasant, and what is the meaning of it, one can't say, and could not even for a thousand rubles. When she had Kukin, or Pustovalov, or the veterinary surgeon, Olenka could explain everything, and give her opinion about anything you like, but now there was the same emptiness in her brain and in her heart as there was in her yard outside. And it was as harsh and as bitter as wormwood in the mouth.

Little by little the town grew in all directions. The road became a street, and where the Tivoli and the timberyard had been, there were new turnings and houses. How rapidly time passes! Olenka's house grew dingy, the roof got rusty, the shed sank on one side, and the whole yard was overgrown with docks and stinging-nettles. Olenka herself had grown plain and elderly; in summer she sat in the porch, and her soul, as before, was empty and dreary and full of bitterness. In winter she sat at her window and looked at the snow. When she caught the scent of spring, or heard the chime of the church bells, a sudden rush of memories from the past came over her, there was a tender ache in her heart, and her eyes brimmed over with tears; but this was only for a minute, and then came emptiness again and the sense of the futility of life. The black kitten, Briska, rubbed against her and purred softly, but Olenka was not touched by these feline caresses. That was not what she needed. She wanted a love that would absorb her whole being, her whole soul and reason—that would give her ideas and an object in life, and would warm her old blood. And she would shake the kitten off her skirt and say with vexation:

"Get along; I don't want you!"

And so it was, day after day and year after year, and no joy, and no opinions. Whatever Mavra, the cook, said she accepted.

One hot July day, towards evening, just as the cattle were being driven away, and the whole yard was full of dust, someone suddenly knocked at the gate. Olenka went to open it herself and was dumfounded when she looked out: she saw Smirnin, the veterinary surgeon, gray-headed, and dressed as a civilian. She suddenly remembered everything. She could not help crying and letting her head fall on his breast without uttering a word, and in the violence of her feeling she did not notice how they both walked into the house and sat down to tea.

"My dear Vladimir Platonich! What fate has brought you?" she muttered, trembling with joy.

"I want to settle here for good, Olga Semyonovna," he told her. "I have resigned my post, and have come to settle down and try my luck on my own account. Besides, it's time for my boy to go to school. He's a big boy. I am reconciled with my wife, you know."

"Where is she?" asked Olenka.

"She's at the hotel with the boy, and I'm looking for lodgings."

"Good gracious, my dear soul! Lodgings? Why not have my house? Why shouldn't that suit you? Why, my goodness, I wouldn't take any rent! cried Olenka in a flutter, beginning to cry again. "You live here, and the lodge will do nicely for me. Oh dear! how glad I am!"

Next day the roof was painted and the walls were whitewashed, and Olenka, with her arms akimbo, walked about the yard giving directions. Her face was beaming with her old smile, and she was brisk and alert as though she had waked from a long sleep. The veterinary's wife arrived—a thin, plain lady, with short hair and a peevish expression. With her was her little Sasha, a boy of ten, small for his age, blue-eyed, chubby, with dimples in his cheeks. And scarcely had the boy walked into the yard when he ran after the cat, and at once there was the sound of his gay, joyous laugh.

"Is that your puss, Auntie?" he asked Olenka. "When she has little ones, do give us a kitten. Mamma is awfully afraid of mice."

Olenka talked to him, and gave him tea. Her heart warmed and there was a sweet ache in her bosom, as though the boy had been her own child. And when he sat at the table in the evening, going over his lessons, she looked at him with deep tenderness and pity as she murmured to herself:

"You pretty pet! . . . my precious! . . . Such a fair little thing, and so clever."

" 'An island is a piece of land which is entirely surrounded by water,' " he read aloud.

"An island is a piece of land," she repeated, and this was the first opinion to which she gave utterance with positive conviction after so many years of silence and dearth of ideas.

Now she had opinions of her own, and at supper she talked to Sasha's parents, saying how difficult the lessons were at the high schools, but that yet the high school was better than a commercial one, since with a high-school education all careers were open to one, such as being a doctor or an engineer.

Sasha began going to the high school. His mother departed to Kharkov to her sister's and did not return; his father used to go off every day to inspect cattle, and would often be away from home for three days together, and it seemed to Olenka as though Sasha was entirely abandoned, that he was not wanted at home, that he was being starved, and she carried him off to her lodge and gave him a little room there.

And for six months Sasha had lived in the lodge with her. Every morning Olenka came into his bedroom and found him fast asleep, sleeping noiselessly with his hand under his cheek. She was sorry to wake him.

"Sashenka," she would say mournfully, "get up, darling. It's time for school."

He would get up, dress and say his prayers, and then sit down to breakfast, drink three glasses of tea, and eat two large biscuits and half a buttered roll. All this time he was hardly awake and a little ill-humored in consequence.

"You don't quite know your fable, Sashenka," Olenka would say, looking at him as though he were about to set off on a long journey. "What a lot of trouble I have with you! You must work and do your best, darling, and obey your teachers."

"Oh, do leave me alone!" Sasha would say.

Then he would go down the street to school, a little figure, wearing a big cap and carrying a satchel on his shoulder. Olenka would follow him noiselessly.

"Sashenka!" she would call after him, and she would pop into his hand a date or a caramel. When he reached the street where the school was, he would feel ashamed of being followed by a tall, stout woman; he would turn round and say:

"You'd better go home, Auntie. I can go the rest of the way alone."

She would stand still and look after him fixedly till he had disappeared at the school gate.

Ah, how she loved him! Of her former attachments not one had been so deep; never had her soul surrendered to any feeling so spontaneously, so disinterestedly, and so joyously as now that her maternal instincts were aroused. For this little boy with the dimple in his cheek and the big school cap, she would have given her whole life, she would have given it with joy and tears of tenderness. Why? Who can tell why?

When she had seen the last of Sasha, she returned home, contented and serene, brimming over with love; her face, which had grown younger during the last six months, smiled and beamed; people meeting her looked at her with pleasure.

"Good-morning, Olga Semyonovna, darling. How are you, darling?"

"The lessons at the high school are very difficult now," she would relate at the market. "It's too much; in the first class yesterday they gave him a fable to learn by heart, and a Latin translation and a problem. You know it's too much for a little chap."

And she would begin talking about the teachers, the lessons, and the schoolbooks, saying just what Sasha said.

At three o'clock they had dinner together: in the evening they learned their lessons together and cried. When she put him to bed, she would stay a long time making the Cross over him and murmuring a prayer; then she would go to bed and dream of that faraway misty future when Sasha would finish his studies and become a doctor or an engineer, would have a big house of his own with horses and a carriage, would get married and have children. . . . She would fall asleep still thinking of the same thing, and tears would run down her cheeks from her closed eyes, while the black cat lay purring beside her: "Mrr, mrr, mrr."

Suddenly there would come a loud knock at the gate.

Olenka would wake up breathless with alarm, her heart throbbing. Half a minute later would come another knock.

"It must be a telegram from Kharkov," she would think, beginning to tremble from head to foot. "Sasha's mother is sending for him from Kharkov. . . . Oh, mercy on us!"

She was in despair. Her head, her hands, and her feet would turn chill, and she would feel that she was the most unhappy woman in the world. But another minute would pass, voices would be heard: it would turn out to be the veterinary surgeon coming home from the club.

"Well, thank God!" she would think.

And gradually the load in her heart would pass off, and she would feel at ease. She would go back to bed thinking of Sasha, who lay sound asleep in the next room, sometimes crying out in his sleep:

"I'll give it to you! Get away! Shut up!"

1899

The Lady with the Dog

I

People were telling one another that a newcomer had been seen on the promenade—a lady with a dog. Dmitri Dmitrich Gurov had been a fortnight in Yalta,[1] and was accustomed to its ways, and he, too, had begun to take an interest in fresh arrivals. From his seat in Vernet's outdoor café, he caught sight of a young woman in a toque, passing along the promenade; she was fair and not very tall; after her trotted a white Pomeranian.

Later he encountered her in the municipal park and in the square several times a day. She was always alone, wearing the same toque, and the Pomeranian always trotted at her side. Nobody knew who she was, and people referred to her simply as "the lady with the dog."

"If she's here without her husband, and without any friends," thought Gurov, "it wouldn't be a bad idea to make her acquaintance."

He was not yet forty but had a twelve-year-old daughter and two sons in high school. He had been talked into marrying in his third year at college, and his wife now looked nearly twice as old as he did. She was a tall woman with dark eyebrows, erect, dignified, imposing, and, as she said of herself, a "thinker." She was a great reader, omitted the "hard sign"[2] at the end of words in her letters, and called her husband "Dimitry" instead of Dmitry; and though he secretly considered her shallow, narrow-minded, and dowdy, he

1. A fashionable seaside resort in the Crimea.
2. Certain progressive intellectuals omitted the hard sign after consonants in writing. They anticipated the reform in the Russian alphabet introduced later. Here used rather as emancipated affectation.

stood in awe of her, and disliked being at home. He had first begun deceiving her long ago and he was now constantly unfaithful to her, and this was no doubt why he spoke slightingly of women, to whom he referred as *the lower race*.

He considered that the ample lessons he had received from bitter experience entitled him to call them whatever he liked, but without this "lower race" he could not have existed a single day. He was bored and ill-at-ease in the company of men, with whom he was always cold and reserved, but felt quite at home among women, and knew exactly what to say to them, and how to behave; he could even be silent in their company without feeling the slightest awkwardness. There was an elusive charm in his appearance and disposition which attracted women and caught their sympathies. He knew this and was himself attracted to them by some invisible force.

Repeated and bitter experience had taught him that every fresh intimacy, while at first introducing such pleasant variety into everyday life, and offering itself as a charming, light adventure, inevitably developed, among decent people (especially in Moscow, where they are so irresolute and slow to move), into a problem of excessive complication leading to an intolerably irksome situation. But every time he encountered an attractive woman he forgot all about this experience, the desire for life surged up in him, and everything suddenly seemed simple and amusing.

One evening, then, while he was dining at the restaurant in the park, the lady in the toque came strolling up and took a seat at a neighboring table. Her expression, gait, dress, coiffure, all told him that she was from the upper classes, that she was married, that she was in Yalta for the first time, alone and bored. . . . The accounts of the laxity of morals among visitors to Yalta are greatly exaggerated, and he paid no heed to them, knowing that for the most part they were invented by people who would gladly have transgressed themselves, had they known how to set about it. But when the lady sat down at a neighboring table a few yards away from him, these stories of easy conquests, of excursions to the mountains, came back to him, and the seductive idea of a brisk transitory liaison, an affair with a woman whose very name he did not know, suddenly took possession of his mind.

He snapped his fingers at the Pomeranian and, when it trotted up to him, shook his forefinger at it. The Pomeranian growled. Gurov shook his finger again.

The lady glanced at him and instantly lowered her eyes.

"He doesn't bite," she said, and blushed.

"May I give him a bone?" he asked, and on her nod of consent added in friendly tones: "Have you been long in Yalta?"

"About five days."

"And I am dragging out my second week here."

Neither spoke for a few minutes.

"The days pass quickly, and yet one is so bored here," she said, not looking at him.

"It's the thing to say it's boring here. People never complain of boredom in godforsaken holes like Belyev or Zhizdra, but when they get here it's: 'Oh, the dullness! Oh, the dust!' You'd think they'd come from Granada to say the least."

She laughed. Then they both went on eating in silence, like complete strangers. But after dinner they left the restaurant together, and embarked upon the light, jesting talk of people free and contented, for whom it is all the same where they go, or what they talk about. They strolled along, remarking on the strange light over the sea. The water was a warm, tender purple, the moonlight lay on its surface in a golden strip. They said how close it was, after the hot day. Gurov told her he was from Moscow, had a degree in literature but worked in a bank; that he had at one time trained himself to sing in a private opera company, but had given up the idea; that he owned two houses in Moscow. . . . And from her he learned that she had grown up in Petersburg, but had gotten married in the town of S., where she had been living two years, that she would stay another month in Yalta, and that perhaps her husband, who also needed a rest, would join her. She was quite unable to explain whether her husband was a member of the province council, or on the board of the *zemstvo*,[1] and was greatly amused at herself for this. Further, Gurov learned that her name was Anna Sergeyevna.

Back in his own room he thought about her, and felt sure he would meet her the next day. It was inevitable. As he went to bed he reminded himself that only a very short time ago she had been a schoolgirl, like his own daughter, learning her lessons, he remembered how much there was of shyness and constraint in her laughter, in her way of conversing with a stranger—it was probably the first time in her life that she found herself alone, and in a situation in which men could follow her and watch her, and speak to her, all the time with a secret aim she could not fail to divine. He recalled her slender, delicate neck, her fine gray eyes.

"And yet there's something pathetic about her," he thought to himself as he fell asleep.

II

A week had passed since the beginning of their acquaintance. It was a holiday. Indoors it was stuffy, but the dust rose in clouds out of doors, and people's hats blew off. It was a parching day and Gurov

1. District administration.

kept going to the outdoor café for fruit drinks and ices to offer Anna Sergeyevna. The heat was overpowering.

In the evening, when the wind had dropped, they walked to the pier to see the steamer come in. There were a great many people strolling about the landing-place; some, bunches of flowers in their hands, were meeting friends. Two peculiarities of the smart Yalta crowd stood out distinctly—the elderly ladies all tried to dress very youthfully, and there seemed to be an inordinate number of generals about.

Owing to the roughness of the sea the steamer arrived late, after the sun had gone down, and it had to maneuver for some time before it could get alongside the pier. Anna Sergeyevna scanned the steamer and passengers through her lorgnette, as if looking for someone she knew, and when she turned to Gurov her eyes were glistening. She talked a great deal, firing off abrupt questions and forgetting immediately what it was she had wanted to know. Then she lost her lorgnette in the crush.

The smart crowd began dispersing, features could no longer be made out, the wind had quite dropped, and Gurov and Anna Sergeyevna stood there as if waiting for someone else to come off the steamer. Anna Sergeyevna had fallen silent, every now and then smelling her flowers, but not looking at Gurov.

"It's turned out a fine evening," he said. "What shall we do? We might go for a drive."

She made no reply.

He looked steadily at her and suddenly took her in his arms and kissed her lips, and the fragrance and dampness of the flowers closed round him, but the next moment he looked behind him in alarm—had anyone seen them?

"Let's go to your room," he murmured.

And they walked off together, very quickly.

Her room was stuffy and smelt of some scent she had bought in the Japanese shop. Gurov looked at her, thinking to himself: "How full of strange encounters life is!" He could remember carefree, good-natured women who were exhilarated by love-making and grateful to him for the happiness he gave them, however short-lived; and there had been others—his wife among them—whose caresses were insincere, affected, hysterical, mixed up with a great deal of quite unnecessary talk, and whose expression seemed to say that all this was not just lovemaking or passion, but something much more significant; then there had been two or three beautiful, cold women, over whose features flitted a predatory expression, betraying a determination to wring from life more than it could give, women no longer in their first youth, capricious, irrational, despotic, brainless, and when Gurov had cooled to these, their beauty aroused in him nothing but repulsion, and the lace trimming on their underclothes reminded him of fish-scales.

But here the timidity and awkwardness of youth and inexperience were still apparent; and there was a feeling of embarrassment in the atmosphere, as if someone had just knocked at the door. Anna Sergeyevna, "the lady with the dog," seemed to regard the affair as something very special, very serious, as if she had become a fallen woman, an attitude he found odd and disconcerting. Her features lengthened and drooped, and her long hair hung mournfully on either side of her face. She assumed a pose of dismal meditation, like a repentant sinner in some classical painting.

"It isn't right," she said. "You will never respect me anymore."

On the table was a watermelon. Gurov cut himself a slice from it and began slowly eating it. At least half an hour passed in silence.

Anna Sergeyevna was very touching, revealing the purity of a decent, naïve woman who had seen very little of life. The solitary candle burning on the table scarcely lit up her face, but it was obvious that her heart was heavy.

"Why should I stop respecting you?" asked Gurov. "You don't know what you're saying."

"May God forgive me!" she exclaimed, and her eyes filled with tears. "It's terrible."

"No need to seek to justify yourself."

"How can I justify myself? I'm a wicked, fallen woman, I despise myself and have not the least thought of self-justification. It isn't my husband I have deceived, it's myself. And not only now, I have been deceiving myself for ever so long. My husband is no doubt an honest, worthy man, but he's a flunky. I don't know what it is he does at his office, but I know he's a flunky. I was only twenty when I married him, and I was devoured by curiosity, I wanted something higher. I told myself that there must be a different kind of life I wanted to live, to live. . . . I was burning with curiosity . . . you'll never understand that, but I swear to God I could no longer control myself, nothing could hold me back, I told my husband I was ill, and I came here. . . . And I started going about like one possessed, like a madwoman . . . and now I have become an ordinary, worthless woman, and everyone has the right to despise me."

Gurov listened to her, bored to death. The naïve accents, the remorse, all was so unexpected, so out of place. But for the tears in her eyes, she might have been jesting or play-acting.

"I don't understand," he said gently. "What is it you want?"

She hid her face against his breast and pressed closer to him.

"Do believe me, I implore you to believe me," she said. "I love all that is honest and pure in life, vice is revolting to me, I don't know what I'm doing. The common people say they are snared by the

Devil. And now I can say that I have been snared by the Devil, too."

"Come, come," he murmured.

He gazed into her fixed, terrified eyes, kissed her, and soothed her with gentle affectionate words, and gradually she calmed down and regained her cheefulness. Soon they were laughing together again.

When, a little later, they went out, there was not a soul on the promenade, the town and its cypresses looked dead, but the sea was still roaring as it dashed against the beach. A solitary fishing-boat tossed on the waves, its lamp blinking sleepily.

They found a carriage and drove to Oreanda.

"I discovered your name in the hall, just now," said Gurov, "written up on the board. Von Diederitz. Is your husband a German?"

"No. His grandfather was, I think, but he belongs to the Orthodox Church himself."

When they got out of the carriage at Oreanda they sat down on a bench not far from the church, and looked down at the sea, without talking. Yalta could be dimly discerned through the morning mist, and white clouds rested motionless on the summits of the mountains. Not a leaf stirred, the grasshoppers chirruped, and the monotonous hollow roar of the sea came up to them, speaking of peace, of the eternal sleep lying in wait for us all. The sea had roared like this long before there was any Yalta or Oreanda, it was roaring now, and it would go on roaring, just as indifferently and hollowly, when we had passed away. And it may be that in this continuity, this utter indifference to the life and death of each of us lies hidden the pledge of our eternal salvation, of the continuous movement of life on earth, of the continuous movement toward perfection.

Side by side with a young woman, who looked so exquisite in the early light, soothed and enchanted by the sight of all this magical beauty—sea, mountains, clouds and the vast expanse of the sky—Gurov told himself that, when you came to think of it, everything in the world is beautiful really, everything but our own thoughts and actions, when we lose sight of the higher aims of life, and of our dignity as human beings.

Someone approached them—a watchman, probably—looked at them and went away. And there was something mysterious and beautiful even in this. The steamer from Feodosia could be seen coming towards the pier, lit up by the dawn, its lamps out.

"There's dew on the grass," said Anna Sergeyevna, breaking the silence.

"Yes. Time to go home."

They went back to the town.

After this they met every day at noon on the promenade, lunching and dining together, going for walks, and admiring the sea. She complained of sleeplessness, of palpitations, asked the same questions over and over again, alternately surrendering to jealousy and the fear that he did not really respect her. And often, when there was nobody in sight in the square or the park, he would draw her to him and kiss her passionately. The utter idleness, these kisses in broad daylight, accompanied by furtive glances and the fear of discovery, the heat, the smell of the sea, and the idle, smart, well-fed people continually crossing their field of vision, seemed to have given him a new lease of life. He told Anna Sergeyevna she was beautiful and seductive, made love to her with impetuous passion, and never left her side, while she was always pensive, always trying to force from him the admission that he did not respect her, that he did not love her a bit, and considered her just an ordinary woman. Almost every night they drove out of town, to Oreanda, the waterfall, or some other beauty-spot. And these excursions were invariably a success, each contributing fresh impressions of majestic beauty.

All this time they kept expecting her husband to arrive. But a letter came in which he told his wife that he was having trouble with his eyes, and implored her to come home as soon as possible. Anna Sergeyevna made hasty preparations for leaving.

"It's a good thing I'm going," she said to Gurov. "It's the intervention of fate."

She left Yalta in a carriage, and he went with her as far as the railway station. The drive took nearly a whole day. When she got into the express train, after the second bell had been rung, she said:

"Let me have one more look at you. . . . One last look. That's right."

She did not weep, but was mournful, and seemed ill, the muscles of her cheeks twitching.

"I shall think of you . . . I shall think of you all the time," she said. "God bless you! Think kindly of me. We are parting forever, it must be so, because we ought never to have met. Good-bye—God bless you."

The train steamed rapidly out of the station, its lights soon disappearing, and a minute later even the sound it made was silenced, as if everything were conspiring to bring this sweet oblivion, this madness, to an end as quickly as possible. And Gurov, standing alone on the platform and gazing into the dark distance, listened to the shrilling of the grasshoppers and the humming of the telegraph wires, with a feeling that he had only just awakened. And he told himself that this had been just one more of the many adventures in his life, and that it, too, was over, leaving nothing but a memory. . . . He was moved and sad, and felt a slight remorse. After all, this young woman whom he would never again see had not been really happy with him. He had been friendly and affectionate with her, but in his whole behaviour, in the tones of his voice, in his very caresses, there had been a shade of irony, the insulting indulgence of the fortunate male, who was, moreover, almost twice her age. She had insisted in calling him good, remarkable, high-minded. Evidently he had appeared to her different from his real self, in a word he had involuntarily deceived her. . . .

There was an autumnal feeling in the air, and the evening was chilly.

"It's time for me to be going north, too," thought Gurov, as he walked away from the platform. "High time!"

III

When he got back to Moscow it was beginning to look like winter; the stoves were heated every day, and it was still dark when the children got up to go to school and drank their tea, so that the nurse had to light the lamp for a short time. Frost had set in. When the first snow falls, and one goes for one's first sleigh-ride, it is pleasant to see the white ground, the white roofs; one breathes freely and lightly, and remembers the days of one's youth. The ancient lime-trees and birches, white with hoarfrost, have a good-natured look, they are closer to the heart than cypresses and palms, and beneath their branches one is no longer haunted by the memory of mountains and the sea.

Gurov had always lived in Moscow, and he returned to Moscow on a fine frosty day, and when he put on his fur-lined overcoat and thick gloves, and sauntered down Petrovka Street, and when, on Saturday evening, he heard the church bells ringing, his recent journey and the places he had visited lost their charm for him. He became gradually immersed in Moscow life, reading with avidity three newspapers a day, while declaring he never read Moscow newspapers on principle. Once more he was caught up in a whirl of restaurants, clubs, banquets, and celebrations, once more glowed with the flattering consciousness that well-known lawyers and actors came to his house, that he played cards in the Medical Club opposite a professor. He could once again eat a whole serving of Moscow Fish Stew served in a pan.

He had believed that in a month's time Anna Sergeyevna would be nothing but a vague memory, and that hereafter, with her wistful smile, she would only occasionally appear to him in dreams, like others before her. But the month was now well over and winter was in full swing, and all was as clear in his memory as if he had parted with Anna Sergeyevna only the day before. And his recollections grew ever more insistent. When the voices of his children at their lessons reached him in his study through the evening stillness, when he heard a song, or the sounds of a music-box in a restaurant, when the wind howled in the chimney, it all came back to him: early morning on the pier, the misty mountains, the steamer from Feodosia, the kisses. He would pace up and down his room for a long time, smiling at his memories, and then memory turned into dreaming, and what had happened mingled in his imagination with what was going to happen. Anna Sergeyevna did not come to him in his dreams, she accompanied him everywhere, like his shadow, following him everywhere he went. When he closed his eyes, she seemed to stand before him in the flesh, still lovelier, younger, tenderer than she had really been, and looking back, he saw himself, too, as better than he had been in Yalta. In the evenings she looked out at him from the bookshelves, the fireplace, the corner, he could hear her breathing, the sweet rustle of her skirts. In the streets he followed women with his eyes, to see if there were any like her. . . .

He began to feel an overwhelming desire to share his memories with someone. But he could not speak of his love at home, and outside his home who was there for him to confide in? Not the tenants living in his house, and certainly not his colleagues at the bank. And what was there to tell? Was it love that he had felt? Had there been anything exquisite, poetic, anything instructive or even amusing about his relations with Anna Sergeyevna? He had to content himself with uttering vague generalizations about love and women, and nobody guessed what he meant, though his wife's dark eyebrows twitched as she said:

"The role of a coxcomb doesn't suit you a bit, Dimitry."

One evening, leaving the Medical Club with one of his card-partners, a government official, he could not refrain from remarking:

"If you only knew what a charming woman I met in Yalta!"

The official got into his sleigh, and just before driving off, turned and called out:

"Dmitry Dmitrich!"

"Yes?"

"You were quite right, you know—the sturgeon was just a *leetle* off."

These words, in themselves so commonplace, for some reason infuriated Gurov, seemed to him humiliating, gross. What savage manners, what people! What wasted evenings, what tedious, empty days! Frantic card-playing, gluttony, drunkenness, perpetual talk always about the same thing. The greater part of one's time and energy went on business that was no use to anyone, and on discussing the same thing over and over again, and there was nothing to show for it all but a stunted wingless existence and a round of trivialities, and there was nowhere to escape to, you might as well be in a madhouse or a convict settlement.

Gurov lay awake all night, raging, and went about the whole of the next day with a headache. He slept badly on the succeeding nights, too, sitting up in bed, thinking, or pacing the floor of his room. He was sick of his children, sick of the bank, felt not the slightest desire to go anywhere or talk about anything.

When the Christmas holidays came, he packed his things, telling his wife he had to go to Petersburg in the interests of a certain young man, and set off for the town of S. To what end? He hardly knew himself. He only knew that he must see Anna Sergeyevna, must speak to her, arrange a meeting, if possible.

He arrived at S. in the morning and engaged the best suite in the hotel, which had a carpet of gray military frieze, and a dusty ink-pot on the table, surmounted by a headless rider, holding his hat in his raised hand. The hall porter told him what he wanted to know: von Diederitz had a house of his own in Staro-Goncharnaya Street. It wasn't far from the hotel, he lived on a grand scale, luxuriously, kept carriage-horses, the whole town knew him. The hall porter pronounced the name "Drideritz."

Gurov strolled over to Staro-Goncharnaya Street and discovered the house. In front of it was a long gray fence with inverted nails hammered into the tops of the palings.

"A fence like that is enough to make anyone want to run away," thought Gurov, looking at the windows of the house and the fence.

He reasoned that since it was a holiday, Anna's husband would probably be at home. In any case it would be tactless to embarrass her by calling at the house. And a note might fall into the hands of the husband, and bring about catastrophe. The best thing would be to wait about on the chance of seeing her. And he walked up and down the street, hovering in the vicinity of the fence, watching for his chance. A beggar entered the gate, only to be attacked by dogs, then, an hour later, the faint, vague sounds of a piano reached his ears. That would be Anna Sergeyevna playing. Suddenly the front door opened and an old woman came out, followed by a familiar white Pomeranian. Gurov tried to call to it, but his heart beat violently, and in his agitation he could not remember its name.

He walked on, hating the gray fence more and more, and now ready to tell himself irately that Anna Sergeyevna had forgotten him, had already, perhaps, found distraction in another—what could be more natural in a young woman who had to look at this accursed fence from morning to night? He went back to his hotel and sat on the sofa in his suite for some time, not knowing what to do, then he ordered dinner, and after dinner, had a long sleep.

"What a foolish, restless business," he thought, waking up and looking towards the dark windowpanes. It was evening by now. "Well, I've had my sleep out. And what am I to do in the night?"

He sat up in bed, covered by the cheap gray quilt, which reminded him of a hospital blanket, and in his vexation he fell to taunting himself.

"You and your lady with a dog . . . there's adventure for you! See what you get for your pains."

On his arrival at the station that morning he had noticed a poster announcing in enormous letters the first performance at the local theatre of *The Geisha*.[4] Remembering this; he got up and made for the theatre.

"It's highly probable that she goes to first nights," he told himself.

The theatre was full. It was a typical provincial theatre, with a mist collecting over the chandeliers, and the crowd in the gallery fidgeting noisily. In the first row of the stalls the local dandies stood waiting for the curtain to go up, their hands clasped behind them. There, in the front seat of the governor's box, sat the governor's daughter, wearing a boa, the governor himself hiding modestly behind the drapes, so that only his hands were visible. The curtain stirred, the orchestra took a long time tuning up their instruments. Gurov's eyes roamed eagerly over the audience as they filed in and occupied their seats.

Anna Sergeyevna came in, too. She seated herself in the third row of the stalls, and when Gurov's glance fell on her, his heart seemed to stop, and he knew in a flash that the whole world contained no one nearer or dearer to him, no one more important to his happiness. This little woman, lost in the provincial crowd, in no way remarkable, holding a silly lorgnette in her hand, now filled his whole life, was his grief, his joy, all that he desired. Lulled by the sounds coming from the wretched orchestra, with its feeble, amateurish violinists, he thought how beautiful she was . . . thought and dreamed. . . .

Anna Sergeyevna was accompanied by a tall, round-shouldered young man with small whiskers, who nodded at every step before taking the seat beside her and seemed to be continually bowing to someone. This must be her husband, whom, in a fit of bitterness, at Yalta, she had called a "flunky." And there really was something of a lackey's servility in his lanky figure, his side-whiskers, and the little bald spot on the top of his head. And he smiled sweetly, and the badge of some scientific society gleaming in his buttonhole was like the number on a footman's livery.

The husband went out to smoke in the first interval, and she was left alone in her seat. Gurov, who had taken a seat in the stalls, went up to her and said in a trembling voice, with a forced smile: "How d'you do?"

She glanced up at him and turned pale, then looked at him again in alarm, unable to believe her eyes, squeezing her fan and lorgnette

---

4. An operetta by the English composer Sidney Jones (1897).

in one hand, evidently struggling to overcome a feeling of faintness. Neither of them said a word. She sat there, and he stood beside her, disconcerted by her embarrassment, and not daring to sit down. The violins and flutes sang out as they were tuned, and there was a tense sensation in the atmosphere, as if they were being watched from all the boxes. At last she got up and moved rapidly towards one of the exits. He followed her and they wandered aimlessly along corridors, up and down stairs; figures flashed by in the uniforms of legal officials, high-school teachers and civil servants, all wearing badges; ladies, coats hanging from pegs flashed by; there was a sharp draft, bringing with it an odor of cigarette butts. And Gurov, whose heart was beating violently, thought:

"What on earth are all these people, this orchestra for? . . ."

The next minute he suddenly remembered how, after seeing Anna Sergeyevna off that evening at the station, he had told himself that all was over, and they would never meet again. And how far away the end seemed to be now!

She stopped on a dark narrow staircase over which was a notice bearing the inscription "To the upper circle."

"How you frightened me!" she said, breathing heavily, still pale and half-stunned. "Oh, how you frightened me! I'm almost dead! Why did you come? Oh, why?"

"But, Anna," he said, in low, hasty tones. "But, Anna. . . . Try to understand . . . do try. . . ."

She cast him a glance of fear, entreaty, love, and then gazed at him steadily, as if to fix his features firmly in her memory.

"I've been so unhappy," she continued, taking no notice of his words. "I could think of nothing but you the whole time, I lived on the thoughts of you. I tried to forget—why, oh, why did you come?"

On the landing above them were two schoolboys, smoking and looking down, but Gurov did not care, and, drawing Anna Sergeyevna towards him, began kissing her face, her lips, her hands.

"What are you doing, oh, what are you doing?" she said in horror, drawing back. "We have both gone mad. Go away this very night, this moment. . . . By all that is sacred, I implore you. . . . Somebody is coming."

Someone was ascending the stairs.

"You must go away," went on Anna Sergeyevna in a whisper. "D'you hear me, Dmitry Dmitrich? I'll come to you in Moscow. I have never been happy, I am unhappy now, and I shall never be happy—never! Do not make me suffer still more! I will come to you in Moscow, I swear it! And now we must part! My dear one, my kind one, my darling, we must part."

She pressed his hand and hurried down the stairs, looking back at him continually, and her eyes showed that she was in truth unhappy. Gurov stood where he was for a short time, listening, and when all was quiet, went to look for his coat, and left the theatre.

IV

And Anna Sergeyevna began going to Moscow to see him. Every two or three months she left the town of S., telling her husband that she was going to consult a specialist on female diseases, and her husband believed her and did not believe her. In Moscow she always stayed at the Slavyanski Bazaar, sending a man in a red cap to Gurov the moment she arrived. Gurov went to her, and no one in Moscow knew anything about it.

One winter morning he went to see her as usual (the messenger had been to him the evening before, but had not found him at home). His daughter was with him, for her school was on the way and he thought he might as well see her to it.

"It is forty degrees," said Gurov to his daughter, "and yet it is snowing. You see it is only above freezing close to the ground, the temperature in the upper layers of the atmosphere is quite different."

"Why doesn't it ever thunder in winter, Papa?"

He explained this, too. As he was speaking, he kept reminding himself that he was going to a rendezvous and that not a living soul knew about it, or, probably, ever would. He led a double life—one in public, in the sight of all whom it concerned, full of conventional truth and conventional deception, exactly like the lives of his friends and acquaintances, and another which flowed in secret. And, owing to some strange, possibly quite accidental chain of circumstances, everything that was important, interesting, essential, everything about which he was sincere and never deceived himself, everything that composed the kernel of his life, went on in secret, while everything that was false in him, everything that composed the husk in which he hid himself and the truth which was in him—his work at the bank, discussions at the club, his "lower race," his attendance at anniversary celebrations with his wife—was on the surface. He began to judge others by himself, no longer believing what he saw, and always assuming that the real, the only interesting life of every individual goes on as under cover of night, secretly. Every individual existence revolves around mystery, and perhaps that is the chief reason that all cultivated individuals insisted so strongly on the respect due to personal secrets.

After leaving his daughter at the door of her school Gurov set off for the Slavyanski Bazaar. Taking off his overcoat in the lobby, he went upstairs and knocked softly on the door. Anna Sergeyevna, wearing the gray dress he liked most, exhausted by her journey and by suspense, had been expecting him since the evening before. She was pale and looked at him without smiling, but was in his arms almost before he was fairly in the room. Their kiss was lingering, prolonged, as if they had not met for years.

"Well, how are you?" he asked. "Anything new?"

"Wait, I'll tell you in a minute. . . . I can't. . . ."

She could not speak, because she was crying. Turning away, she held her handkerchief to her eyes.

"I'll wait till she's had her cry out," he thought, and sank into a chair.

He rang for tea, and a little later, while he was drinking it, she was still standing there, her face to the window. She wept from emotion, from her bitter consciousness of the sadness of their life; they could only see one another in secret, hiding from people, as if they were thieves. Was not their life a broken one?

"Don't cry," he said.

It was quite obvious to him that this love of theirs would not soon come to an end, and that no one could say when this end would be. Anna Sergeyevna loved him ever more fondly, worshipped him, and there would have been no point in telling her that one day it must end. Indeed, she would not have believed him.

He moved over and took her by the shoulders, intending to caress her, to make a joke, but suddenly he caught sight of himself in the looking-glass.

His hair was already beginning to turn gray. It struck him as strange that he should have aged so much in the last few years, have lost so much of his looks. The shoulders on which his hands lay were warm and quivering. He felt a pity for this life, still so warm and exquisite, but probably soon to fade and droop like his own. Why did she love him so? Women had always believed him different from what he really was, had loved in him not himself but the man their imagination pictured him, a man they had sought for eagerly all their lives. And afterwards when they discovered their mistake, they went on loving him just the same. And not one of them had ever been happy with him. Time had passed, he had met one woman after another, become intimate with each, parted with each, but had never loved. There had been all sorts of things between them, but never love.

And only now, when he was gray-haired, had he fallen in love properly, thoroughly, for the first time in his life.

He and Anna Sergeyevna loved one another as people who are very close and intimate, as husband and wife, as dear friends love one another. It seemed to them that fate had intended them for one another, and they could not understand why she should have a husband, and he a wife. They were like two migrating birds, the male and the female, who had been caught and put into separate cages. They forgave one another all that they were ashamed of in the past and in the present, and felt that this love of theirs had changed them both.

Formerly, in moments of melancholy, he had consoled himself by the first argument that came into his head, but now arguments were nothing to him, he felt profound pity, desired to be sincere, tender.

"Stop crying, my dearest," he said. "You've had your cry, now stop. . . . Now let us have a talk, let us try and think what we are to do."

Then they discussed their situation for a long time, trying to think how they could get rid of the necessity for hiding, deception, living in different towns, being so long without meeting. How were they to shake off these intolerable fetters?

"How? How?" he repeated, clutching his head. "How?"

And it seemed to them that they were within an inch of arriving at a decision, and that then a new, beautiful life would begin. And they both realized that the end was still far, far away, and that the hardest, the most complicated part was only just beginning.

1899

The Bishop

It was on the eve of Palm Sunday; vespers were being sung in the Staro-Petrovski Convent. The hour was nearly ten when the palm leaves were distributed, and the little icon-lamps were growing dim; their wicks had burnt low, and a soft haze hung in the chapel. As the worshippers surged forward in the twilight like the waves of the sea, it seemed to His Reverence Pyotr, who had been feeling ill for three days, that the people who came to him for palm leaves all looked alike, and, men or women, old or young, all had the same expression in their eyes. He could not see the doors through the haze; the endless procession rolled toward him, and seemed as if it must go on rolling for ever. A choir of women's voices was singing and a nun was reading the canon.

How hot and close the air was, and how long the prayers! His Reverence was tired. His dry, parching breath was coming quickly and painfully, his shoulders were aching, and his legs were trembling. The occasional cries of an idiot in the gallery annoyed him. And now, as a climax, His Reverence saw, as in a delirium, his own mother whom he had not seen for nine years coming toward him in the crowd. She, or an old woman exactly like her, took a palm leaf from his hands, and moved away looking at him all the while with a glad, sweet smile, until she was lost in the crowd. And for some reason the tears began to course down his cheeks. His heart was happy and peaceful, but his eyes were fixed on a distant part of the chapel where the prayers were being read, and where no human being could be distinguished among the shadows. The tears glistened on his cheeks and beard. Then someone who was standing near him began to weep, too, and then another, and then another, until little by little the chapel was filled with a low sound of weeping. Then the convent choir began to sing, the weeping stopped, and everything went on as before.

Soon afterward the service ended. The fine, jubilant notes of the heavy chapel-bells were throbbing through the moonlit garden as the bishop stepped into his coach and drove away. The white walls, the crosses on the graves, the silvery birches, and the faraway moon hanging directly over the monastery, all seemed to be living a life of their own, incomprehensible, but very near to mankind. It was early in April, and a chilly night had succeeded a warm spring day. A light frost was falling, but the breath of spring could be felt in the soft, cool air. The road from the monastery was sandy, the horses were obliged to proceed at a walk, and, bathed in the bright, tranquil moonlight, a stream of pilgrims was crawling along on either side of the coach. All were thoughtful, no one spoke. Everything around them, the trees, the sky, and even the moon, looked so young and intimate and friendly that they were reluctant to break the spell which they hoped might last forever.

Finally the coach entered the city, and rolled down the main street. All the stores were closed but that of Erakin, the millionaire merchant. He was trying his electric lights for the first time, and they were flashing so violently that a crowd had collected in front of the store. Then came wide, dark streets in endless succession, and then the highway, and fields, and the smell of pines. Suddenly a white crenelated wall loomed before him, and beyond it rose a tall belfry flanked by five flashing golden cupolas, all bathed in moonlight. This was the Pankratievski Monastery, where His Reverence Pyotr lived. Here, too, the calm, brooding moon was floating directly above the monastery. The coach drove through the gate, its wheels crunching on the sand. Here and there the dark forms of monks started out into the moonlight and footsteps rang along the flagstone paths.

"Your mother has been here while you were away, Your Reverence," a lay brother told the bishop as he entered his room.

"My mother? When did she come?"

"Before vespers. She first found out where you were, and then drove to the convent."

"Then it was she whom I saw just now in the chapel! Oh, Father in heaven!"

And His Reverence laughed for joy.

"She told me to tell you, Your Reverence," the lay brother continued, "that she would come back tomorrow. She had a little girl with her, a grandchild, I think. She is stopping at Ovsianikov's inn."

"What time is it now?"

"It is after eleven."

"What a nuisance!"

His Reverence sat down irresolutely in his sitting-room, unwilling to believe that it was already so late. His arms and legs were racked with pain, the back of his neck was aching, and he felt uncomfortable and hot. When he had rested a few moments he went into his bedroom and there, too, he sat down, and dreamed of his mother. He heard the lay brother walking away and Father Sisoi the priest coughing in the next room. The monastery clock struck the quarter.

His Reverence undressed and began his prayers. He spoke the old, familiar words with scrupulous attention, and at the same time he thought of his mother. She had nine children, and about forty grandchildren. She had lived from the age of seventeen to the age of sixty with her husband the deacon in a little village. His Reverence remembered her from the days of his earliest childhood, and, ah, how he had loved her! Oh, that dear, precious, unforgettable childhood of his! Why did those years that had vanished forever seem so much brighter and richer and gayer than they really had been? How tender and kind his mother had been when he was ill in his childhood and youth! His prayers mingled with the memories that burned ever brighter and brighter in his heart like a flame, but they did not hinder his thoughts of his mother.

When he had prayed he lay down, and as soon as he found himself in the dark there rose before his eyes the vision of his dead father, his mother, and Lyesopolye, his native village. The creaking of wagon-wheels, the bleating of sheep, the sound of church-bells on a clear summer morning, ah, how pleasant it was to think of these things! He remembered Father Semyon, the old priest at Lyesopolye, a kind, gentle, good-natured old man. He himself had been small, and the priest's son had been a huge strapping novice with a terrible bass voice. He remembered how this young priest had scolded the cook once, and had shouted: "Ah, you she-ass of Jehovah!" And Father Semyon had said nothing, and had only been mortified because he could not for the life of him remember reading of an ass of that name in the Bible!

Father Semyon had been succeeded by Father Demyan, a hard drinker who sometimes even went so far as to see green snakes. He had actually borne the nickname of "Demian the Snake-Seer" in the village. Matvey Nikolaich had been the schoolmaster, a kind, intelligent man, but a hard drinker, too. He never thrashed his scholars, but for some reason he kept a little bundle of birch twigs hanging on his wall, under which was a tablet bearing the absolutely unintelligible inscription: "Betula Kinderbalsamica Secuta."[1] He had had a woolly black dog whom he called "Syntax."

The bishop laughed. Eight miles from Lyesopolye lay the village of Obnino, possessing a miraculous icon. A procession started from Obnino every summer bearing the wonder-working icon and making the round of all the neighboring villages. The church-bells would ring all day long first in one village, then in another, and to little Pavel (His Reverence was called little Pavel then) the air itself seemed tremulous with rapture. Barefoot, hatless, and infinitely happy, he followed the icon with a naïve smile on his lips and naïve faith in his heart.

Until the age of fifteen little Pavel had been so slow at his lessons that his parents had even thought of taking him out of the ecclesiastical school and putting him to work in the village store.

The bishop turned over so as to break the train of his thoughts, and tried to go to sleep.

"My mother has come!" he remembered, and smiled.

The moon was shining in through the window, and the floor was lit by its rays while he lay in shadow. A cricket was chirping. Father Sisoi was snoring in the next room, and there was a forlorn, friendless, even a vagrant note in the old man's cadences.

Sisoi had once been the steward of a diocesan bishop and was known as "Father Former Steward." He was seventy years old, and lived sometimes in a monastery sixteen miles away, sometimes in the city, sometimes wherever he happened to be. Three days ago he had turned up at the Pankratievski Monastery, and the bishop had kept him here in order to discuss with him at his leisure the affairs of the monastery.

The bell for matins rang at half-past one. Father Sisoi coughed, growled something, and got up.

"Father Sisoi!" called the bishop.

Sisoi came in dressed in a white cassock, carrying a candle in his hand.

"I can't go to sleep," His Reverence said. "I must be ill. I don't know what the matter is; I have fever."

"You have caught cold, your Lordship. I must rub you with tallow."

Father Sisoi stood looking at him for a while and yawned: "Ah-h —the Lord have mercy on us!"

"Erakin has electricity in his store now—I hate it!" he continued.

Father Sisoi was aged, and round-shouldered, and gaunt. He was

1. Fractured Latin and German: "Twigs children-healing flogger."

always displeased with something or other, and his eyes, which protruded like those of a crab, always wore an angry expression.

"I don't like it at all," he repeated—"I hate it."

II

Next day, on Palm Sunday, His Reverence officiated at the cathedral in the city. Then he went to the diocesan bishop's, then to see a general's wife who was very ill, and at last he drove home. At two o'clock two beloved guests were having dinner with him, his aged mother, and his little niece Katya, a child of eight. The spring sun was peeping cheerily in through the windows as they sat at their meal, and was shining merrily on the white tablecloth, and on Katya's red hair. Through the double panes they heard the rooks cawing, and the magpies chattering in the garden.

"It is nine years since I saw you last," said the old mother, "and yet when I caught sight of you in the convent chapel yesterday I thought to myself: God bless me, he has not changed a bit! Only perhaps you are a little thinner than you were, and your beard has grown longer. Oh, holy Mother, Queen of Heaven! Everybody was crying yesterday. As soon as I saw you, I began to cry myself, I don't know why. His holy will be done!"

In spite of the tenderness with which she said this, it was clear that she was not at her ease. It was as if she did not know whether to address the bishop by the familiar "thee" or the formal "you," and whether she ought to laugh or not. She seemed to feel herself more of a poor deacon's wife than a mother in his presence. Meanwhile Katya was sitting with her eyes glued to the face of her uncle the bishop as if she were trying to make out what manner of man this was. Her hair had escaped from her comb and her bow of velvet ribbon, and was standing straight up around her head like a halo. Her eyes were foxy and bright. She had broken a glass before sitting down, and now, as she talked, her grandmother kept moving first a glass, and then a wineglass, out of her reach. As the bishop sat listening to his mother, he remembered how, many, many years ago, she had sometimes taken him and his brothers and sisters to visit relatives whom they considered rich. She had been busy with her own children in those days, and now she was busy with her grandchildren, and had come to visit him with Katya here.

"Your sister Varenka has four children"—she was telling him— "Katya is the oldest. God knows why, her father fell ill and died three days before Assumption. So my Varenka has been thrown out into the cold world."

"And how is my brother Nikanor?" the bishop asked.

"He is well, thank the Lord. He is pretty well, praise be to God. But his son Nikolasha wouldn't go into the church, and is at college instead learning to be a doctor. He thinks it is best, but who knows? However, God's will be done!"

"Nikolasha cuts up dead people!" said Katya, spilling some water into her lap.

"Sit still, child!" her grandmother said, quietly taking the glass out of her hands.

"How long it is since we have seen one another!" exclaimed His Reverence, tenderly stroking his mother's shoulder and hand. "I missed you when I was abroad, I missed you dreadfully."

"Thank you very much!"

"I used to sit by my window in the evening listening to the band playing, and feeling lonely and forlorn. Sometimes I would suddenly grow so homesick that I used to think I would gladly give everything I had in the world for a glimpse of you and home."

His mother smiled and beamed, and then immediately drew a long face and said stiffly:

"Thank you very much!"

The bishop's mood changed. He looked at his mother, and could not understand where she had acquired that deferential, humble expression of face and voice, and what the meaning of it might be. He hardly recognized her, and felt sorrowful and vexed. Besides, his head was still aching, and his legs were racked with pain. The fish he was eating tasted insipid and he was very thirsty.

After dinner two wealthy lady landowners visited him, and sat for an hour and a half with faces a mile long, never uttering a word. Then an archimandrite, a gloomy, taciturn man, came on business. Then the bells rang for vespers, the sun set behind the woods, and the day was done. As soon as he got back from church the bishop said his prayers, and went to bed, drawing the covers up closely about his ears. The moonlight troubled him, and soon the sound of voices came to his ears. Father Sisoi was talking politics with his mother in the next room.

"There is a war in Japan now," he was saying. "The Japanese belong to the same race as the Montenegrins. They fell under the Turkish yoke at the same time."

And then the bishop heard his mother's voice say:

"And so, you see, when we had said our prayers, and had our tea, we went to Father Yegor——"

She kept saying over and over again that they "had tea," as if all she knew of life was tea-drinking.

The memory of his seminary and college life slowly and mistily took shape in the bishop's mind. He had been a teacher of Greek for three years, until he could no longer read without glasses, and then he had taken the vows, and had been made an inspector. When he was thirty-two he had been made the rector of a seminary, and then an archimandrite. At that time his life had been so easy and pleasant, and had seemed to stretch so far, far into the future that he could see absolutely no end to it. But his health had failed, and he had nearly lost his eyesight. His doctors had advised him to give up his work and go abroad.

"And what did you do next?" asked Father Sisoi in the adjoining room.

"And then we had tea," answered his mother.

"Why, Father, your beard is green!" exclaimed Katya suddenly. And she burst out laughing.

The bishop remembered that the color of Father Sisoi's beard really did verge on green, and he, too, laughed.

"My goodness! What a plague that child is!" cried Father Sisoi in a loud voice, for he was growing angry. "You're a spoiled baby, you are! Sit still!"

The bishop recalled the new white church in which he had offici- ated when he was abroad, and the sound of a warm sea. Eight years had slipped by while he was there; then he had been recalled to Russia, and now he was already a bishop, and the past had faded away into mist as if it had been but a dream.

Father Sisoi came into his room with a candle in his hand.

"Well, well!" he exclaimed, surprised. "Asleep already, Your Reverence?"

"Why not?"

"It's early yet, only ten o'clock! I bought a candle this evening and wanted to rub you with tallow."

"I have a fever," the bishop said, sitting up. "I suppose something ought to be done. My head feels so queer."

Sisoi began to rub the bishop's chest and back with tallow.

"There—there—" he said. "Oh, Lord God Almighty! There! I went to town to-day, and saw that—what do you call him?—that archpresbyter Sidonski. I had tea with him. I hate him! Oh, Lord God Almighty! There! I hate him!"

III

The diocesan bishop was very old and very fat, and had been ill in bed with gout for a month. So His Reverence Pyotr had been visiting him almost every day, and had received his suppliants for him. And now that he was ill he was appalled to think of the fu- tilities and trifles they asked for and wept over. He felt annoyed at their ignorance and cowardice. The very number of all those useless trivialities oppressed him, and he felt as if he could understand the diocesan bishop who had written "Lessons in Free Will" when he was young, and now seemed so absorbed in details that the memory of everything else, even of God, had forsaken him. Pyotr must have grown out of touch with Russian life while he was abroad, for it was hard for him to grow used to it now. The people seemed rough, the women stupid and tiresome, the novices and their teachers uneducated and often disorderly. And then the documents that passed through his hands by the hundreds of thousands! The provosts gave all the priests in the diocese, young and old, and their wives and children[1] marks for good behavior, and he was obliged to talk about all this, and read about it, and write serious articles on it. His Reverence never had a moment which he could call his own; all day his nerves were on edge, and he grew calm only when he found himself in church.

He could not grow accustomed to the terror which he involuntarily inspired in every breast in spite of his quiet and modest ways. Everyone in the district seemed to shrivel and quake and apologize as soon as he looked at them. Everyone trembled in his presence; even the old archpresbyters fell down at his feet, and not long ago one suppliant, the old wife of a village priest, had been prevented by terror from uttering a word, and had gone away without asking for anything. And he, who had never been able to say a harsh word in his sermons, and who never blamed people because he pitied them so, would grow exasperated with these suppliants, and hurl their petitions to the ground. Not a soul had spoken sincerely and naturally to him since he had been here; even his old mother had changed, yes, she had changed very much! Why did she talk so freely to Sisoi when all the while she was so serious and ill at ease with him, her own son? It was not like her at all! The only person who behaved naturally in his presence, and who said whatever came into his head, was old man Sisoi, who had lived with bishops all his life, and had outlasted eleven of them. And therefore His Reverence felt at ease with Sisoi, even though he was, without a doubt, a rough and quarrelsome person.

After morning prayers on Tuesday the bishop received his suppliants, and lost his temper with them. He felt ill, as usual, and longed to go to bed, but he had hardly entered his room before he was told that the young merchant Erakin, a benefactor of the monastery, had called on very important business. The bishop was obliged to receive him. Erakin stayed about an hour talking in a very loud voice, and it was hard to understand what he was trying to say.

After he had gone there came an abbess from a distant convent, and by the time she had gone the bells were tolling for vespers; it was time for the bishop to go to church.

The monks sang melodiously and rapturously that evening; a young, black-bearded priest officiated. His Reverence listened as they sang of the Bridegroom and of the chamber swept and gar-

---

1. Lower Russian Orthodox clergy are permitted to marry.

nished, and felt neither repentance nor sorrow, but only a deep peace of mind. He sat by the altar where the shadows were deepest, and was swept in imagination back into the days of his childhood and youth, when he had first heard these words sung. The tears trickled down his cheeks, and he meditated on how he had attained everything in life that it was possible for a man in his position to attain; his faith was unsullied, and yet all was not clear to him; something was lacking, and he did not want to die. It still seemed to him that he was leaving unfound the most important thing of all. Something of which he had dimly dreamed in the past, hopes that had thrilled his heart as a child, a schoolboy, and a traveler in foreign lands, troubled him still.

"How beautifully they are singing today!" he thought. "Oh, how beautifully!"

IV

On Thursday he held a service in the cathedral. It was the festival of the Washing of Feet. When the service was over, and the people had gone to their several homes, the sun was shining brightly and cheerily, and the air was warm. The gutters were streaming with bubbling water, and the tender songs of larks came floating in from the fields beyond the city, bringing peace to his heart. The trees were already awake, and over them brooded the blue, unfathomable sky.

His Reverence went to bed as soon as he reached home, and told the lay brother to close his shutters. The room grew dark. Oh, how tired he was!

As on the day before, the sound of voices and the tinkling of glasses came to him from the next room. His mother was gaily recounting some tale to Father Sisoi, with many a quaint word and saying, and the old man was listening gloomily, and answering in a gruff voice:

"Well, I never! Did they, indeed? What do you think of that!"

And once more the bishop felt annoyed, and then hurt that the old lady should be so natural and simple with strangers, and so silent and awkward with her own son. It even seemed to him that she always tried to find some pretext for standing in his presence, as if she felt uneasy sitting down. And his father? If he had been alive, he would probably not have been able to utter a word when the bishop was there.

Something in the next room fell to the floor with a crash. Katya had evidently broken a cup or a saucer, for Father Sisoi suddenly snorted, and cried angrily:

"What a terrible plague this child is! Merciful heavens! No one could keep her supplied with china!"

Then silence fell. When he opened his eyes again, the bishop saw Katya standing by his bedside staring at him, her red hair standing up around her head like a halo, as usual.

"Is that you, Katya?" he asked. "Who is that opening and shutting doors down there?"

"I don't hear anything," Katya answered and tried to listen.

"There, someone just went by."

"That's in your belly, uncle!"

He smiled and stroked her head.

"So your cousin Nikolasha cuts up dead people, does he?" he asked, after a pause.

"Yes, he is learning to."

"Is he nice?"

"Yes, very, only he drinks a lot."

"What did your father die of?"

"Papa grew weaker and weaker, and thinner and thinner, and then came his sore throat. And I was ill, too, and so was my brother Fedia. We all had sore throats. Papa died, Uncle, but we got well."

Her chin quivered, her eyes filled with tears.

"Oh, Your Reverence!" she cried in a shrill voice, beginning to weep bitterly. "Dear Uncle, Mother and all of us are so unhappy! Do give us a little money! Help us, Uncle darling!"

He also shed tears, and for a moment could not speak for emotion. He stroked her hair, and touched her shoulder, and said:

"All right, all right, little child. Wait until Easter comes, then we will talk about it. I'll help you."

His mother came quietly and timidly into the room, and said a prayer before the icon. When she saw that he was awake, she asked:

"Would you like a little soup?"

"No, thanks," he answered. "I'm not hungry."

"I don't believe you are well—I can see that you are not well. You really mustn't fall ill! You have to be on your feet all day long. My goodness, it makes one tired to see you! Never mind, Easter is no longer over the hills and far away. When Easter comes you will rest. God will give us time for a little talk then, but now I'm not going to worry you any more with my silly chatter. Come, Katya, let His Lordship have another forty winks——"

And the bishop remembered that, when he was a boy, she had used exactly the same half-playful, half-respectful tone to all high dignitaries of the church. Only by her strangely tender eyes, and by the anxious look which she gave him as she left the room could anyone have guessed that she was his mother. He shut his eyes, and seemed to be asleep, but he heard the clock strike twice, and Father Sisoi coughing next door. His mother came in again, and looked shyly at him. Suddenly there came a bang, and a door slammed; a vehicle of some kind drove up to the front steps. The lay brother came into the bishop's room, and called:

"Your Reverence!"

"What is it?"

"Here is the coach! It is time to go to our Lord's Passion——"

"What time is it?"

"Quarter to eight."

The bishop dressed, and drove to the cathedral. He had to stand motionless in the center of the church while the twelve Gospels were being read, and the first and longest and most beautiful of them all he read himself. A strong, valiant mood took hold of him. He knew this gospel, beginning "The Son of Man is risen today——," by heart, and as he repeated it, he raised his eyes, and saw a sea of little lights about him. He heard the sputtering of candles, but the people had disappeared. He felt surrounded by those whom he had known in his youth; he felt that they would always be here until—God knows when!

His father had been a deacon, his grandfather had been a priest, and his great-grandfather a deacon. He sprang from a race that had belonged to the church since Christianity first came to Russia, and his love for the ritual of the church, the clergy, and the sound of church-bells was inborn in him, deeply, inirradicably implanted in his heart. When he was in church, especially when he was taking part in the service himself, he felt active and valorous and happy. And so it was with him now. Only, after the eighth Gospel had been read, he felt that his voice was becoming so feeble that even his cough was inaudible; his head was aching, and he began to fear that he might collapse. His legs were growing numb; in a little while he ceased to have any sensation in them at all, and could not imagine what he was standing on, and why he did not fall down.

It was quarter to twelve when the service ended. The bishop went to bed as soon as he reached home, without even saying his prayers. As he pulled his blanket up over him, he suddenly wished that he were abroad; he passionately wished it. He would give his life, he thought, to cease from seeing these cheap, wooden walls and that low ceiling, to cease from smelling the stale scent of the monastery.

If there were only someone with whom he could talk, someone to whom he could unburden his heart!

He heard steps in the adjoining room, and tried to recall who it might be. At last the door opened, and Father Sisoi came in with a candle in one hand, and a teacup in the other.

"In bed already, Your Reverence?" he asked. "I have come to rub your chest with vinegar and vodka. It is a fine thing, if rubbed in good and hard. Oh, Lord God Almighty! There—there—I have just come from our monastery. I hate it. I am going away from here to-morrow, my Lord. Oh, Lord, God Almighty—there——"

Sisoi never could stay long in one place, and he now felt as if he had been in this monastery for a year. It was hard to tell from what he said where his home was, whether there was anyone or anything in the world that he loved, and whether he believed in God or not. He himself never could make out why he had become a monk, but then, he never gave it any thought, and the time when he had taken the vows had long since faded from his memory. He thought he must have been born a monk.

"Yes, I am going away tomorrow. Bother this place!"

"I want to have a talk with you—I never seem to have the time—" whispered the bishop, making a great effort to speak. "You see, I don't know anyone—or anything—here———"

"Very well then, I shall stay until Sunday, but no longer! Bother this place!"

"What sort of a bishop am I?" His Reverence went on, in a faint voice. "I ought to have been a village priest, or a deacon, or a plain monk. All this is choking me—it is choking me———"

"What's that? Oh, Lord God Almighty! There—go to sleep now, Your Reverence. What do you mean? What's all this you are saying? Good-night!"

All night long the bishop lay awake, and in the morning he grew very ill. The lay brother took fright and ran first to the archimandrite, and then for the monastery doctor who lived in the city. The doctor, a stout, elderly man, with a long, gray beard, looked intently at His Reverence, shook his head, knit his brows, and finally said:

"I'll tell you what, Your Reverence; you have typhoid."

The bishop grew very thin and pale in the next hour, his eyes grew larger, his face became covered with wrinkles, and he looked quite small and old. He felt as if he were the thinnest, weakest, puniest man in the whole world, and as if everything that had occurred before this had been left far, far behind, and would never happen again.

"How glad I am of that!" he thought. "Oh, how glad!"

His aged mother came into the room. When she saw his wrinkled face and his great eyes, she was seized with fear, and, falling down on her knees by his bedside, she began kissing his face, his shoulders, and his hands. He seemed to her to be the thinnest, weakest, puniest man in the world, and she forgot that he was a bishop, and kissed him as if he had been a little child whom she dearly, dearly loved.

"Little Pavel, my dearie!" she cried. "My little son, why do you look like this? Little Pavel, oh, answer me!"

Katya, pale and severe, stood near them, and could not understand what was the matter with her uncle, and why Granny wore such a look of suffering on her face, and spoke such heart-rending words. And he, he was speechless, and knew nothing of what was going on around him. He was dreaming that he was an ordinary man once more, striding swiftly and merrily through the open country, a staff in his hand, bathed in sunshine, with the wide sky above him, as free as a bird to go wherever his fancy led him.

"My little son! My little Pavel! Answer me!" begged his mother.

"Don't bother His Lordship," said Sisoi angrily, crossing the room. "Let him sleep. Nothing to do there . . . what for! . . .

Three doctors came, consulted together, and drove away. The day seemed long, incredibly long, and then came the long, long night. Just before dawn on Saturday morning the lay brother went to the old mother who was lying on a sofa in the sitting-room, and asked her to come into the bedroom; His Reverence had gone to eternal peace.

Next day was Easter. There were forty-two churches in the city, and two monasteries, and the deep, joyous notes of their bells pealed out over the town from morning until night. The birds were caroling, the bright sun was shining. The big marketplace was full of noise; barrel organs were droning, concertinas were squealing, and drunken voices were ringing through the air. Trotting-races were held in the main street that afternoon; in a word, all was merry and gay, as had been the year before and as, doubtless, it would be the year to come.

A month later a new bishop was appointed, and everyone forgot his Reverence Pyotr. Only the dead man's mother, who is living now in a little country town with her son the deacon, when she goes out at sunset to meet her cow, and joins the other women on the way, tells them about her children and grandchildren, and her boy who became a bishop.

And when she mentions him she looks at them shyly, for she is afraid they will not believe her.

And, as a matter of fact, not all of them do.

1902

The Betrothed

I

It was already nine o'clock in the evening, and the full moon was shining over the garden. In the Shumin house the evening service ordered by the grandmother, Marfa Mikhailovna, was only just over, and Nadya, who had slipped out into the garden for a minute, could see a cold supper being laid in the dining-room; her grandmother in her billowing silk dress hovering about the table; Father Andrey, the cathedral priest, talking to Nadya's mother, Nina Ivanovna, who looked very young seen through the window, by artificial light. Beside her stood Andrey Andreyich, Father Andrey's son, listening attentively.

It was cool and still in the garden, and dark shadows lay peacefully on the ground. From a long way off, probably outside town, came the distant croaking of frogs. There was a feeling of May, the delightful month of May, in the air. One could draw deep breaths, and imagine that somewhere, far beyond the town, beneath the sky, above the treetops, in the fields and woods, the spring was beginning its own life, that mysterious, exquisite life, rich and sacred, from which sinful mortals are shut out. It almost made one want to cry.

Nadya was now twenty-three; ever since she was sixteen years old she had been dreaming ardently of marriage, and now at last she was betrothed to Andrey Andreyich, the young man standing in the dining-room. She liked him, and the wedding was fixed for the seventh of July, but she felt no joy; she slept badly, her gaiety had deserted her. From the open windows of the basement kitchen came sounds of bustling and the clanging of knives, and the door, which closed by a pulley, banged constantly. There was a smell of roasting turkey and spiced cherries. And it seemed as if things would go on like this, without changing, for ever and ever.

Someone came out of the house and stood in the porch. It was Aleksander Timofeyich, or, as everyone called him, Sasha, who had arrived from Moscow about ten days before, on a visit. Long ago, Maria Petrovna, an impoverished widow gentlewoman, small, slight and delicate, used to visit Nadya's grandmother, to whom she was distantly related, asking for charity. She had a son called Sasha. For some reason or other people said he was a fine artist, and when his mother died, Granny, for her own soul's salvation, sent him to the Komissarov school in Moscow. A year or two later he got himself transferred to an art school, where he remained something like fifteen years, till at last he scrambled through his final examinations in the architectural department; he never worked as an architect, but found occupation in a Moscow lithographical works. He came to stay almost every summer, usually very ill, to rest and recuperate.

He was wearing a long coat buttoned up to his neck and shabby canvas trousers with frayed hems. And his shirt was unironed, and his whole appearance was dingy. He was emaciated, with huge eyes and long, bony fingers, bearded, dark-skinned, and, with it all, handsome. At the Shumins' he felt as if he were among his own people, and was quite at home in their house. And the room he occupied on his visits had long been known as Sasha's room.

He caught sight of Nadya from the porch, and went out to her.

"It's nice here," he said.

"It's ever so nice. You ought to stay till the autumn."

"Yes, I know, I shall have to, I suppose. I shall probably stay with you till September."

He laughed for no apparent reason, and sat down beside her.

"I've been standing here watching Mama," said Nadya. "She looks so young from here. Of course I know my Mama has her weaknesses," she continued after a pause, "but just the same she's a marvellous woman."

"Yes, she's very nice," agreed Sasha. "In her way your Mama is of course very good and kind, but . . . how shall I put it? I went into the kitchen this morning early and saw four servants sleeping right on the floor, no beds, only rags to lie on, a stench, bugs, cockroaches. . . . Just the same as it used to be twenty years ago, not the slighest change. Granny's not to be blamed, of course, she's old—but your mother, with her French and her amateur theatricals. . . . You'd think *she*'d understand."

When Sasha spoke he had a habit of holding up two long, bony fingers in the direction of his hearer.

"Everything here strikes me as so strange," he continued. "I'm not used to it, I suppose. Good heavens, nobody ever does anything! Your mother does nothing but stroll about like a grand-duchess, Granny does nothing at all, and nor do you. And Andrey Andreyich, your fiancé, he does nothing, either."

Nadya had heard all this last year, and, she seemed to remember, the year before, and she knew it was the only way Sasha's mind could work; there was a time when it had amused her, but now for some reason it irritated her.

"That's old stuff, I'm sick of hearing it," she said, getting up. "Can't you think of anything new?"

He laughed and got up, too, and they both went back to the house. Good-looking, tall and slender, she seemed almost offensively well-dressed and healthy, as she walked by his side. She was conscious of it herself, and felt sorry for him, and almost apologetic.

"And you talk a lot of nonsense," she said. "Look what you just said about my Andrey—you don't know him a bit, really!"

"*My* Andrey. . . . Never mind your Andrey! It's your youth I begrudge."

When they went into the dining-room everyone was just sitting down to supper. Nadya's grandmother, or, as everyone in the house called her, Granny, a corpulent, plain old woman, with heavy eyebrows and a moustache, was talking loudly, and her voice and manner of speaking showed that it was she who was the real head of the house. She owned a row of booths in the marketplace, and the old house with its pillars and garden was hers, but every morning she prayed with tears for the Lord to preserve her from ruin.

Her daughter-in-law and Nadya's mother, Nina Ivanovna, blonde, tightly corseted, who wore pince-nez and had diamond rings on all her fingers; Father Andrey, a lean, toothless old man who always looked as if he were just going to say something very funny; and Andrey Andreyich, his son and Nadya's fiancé, a stout, handsome young man with curly hair, rather like an actor or an artist, were all three talking about hypnotism.

"You'll fatten up in a week here," Granny told Sasha. "But you must eat more. Just look at yourself!" she sighed. "You look awful. A real prodigal son, that's what you are."

"He wasted his substance with riotous living," interpolated Father Andrey, bringing out the words slowly, his eyes twinkling, "and he was sent into the fields to feed swine."

"I love my old Dad," said Andrey Andreyich, patting his father on the shoulder. "Dear old man. Good old man!"

Nobody said anything. Sasha suddenly burst out laughing, and pressed his napkin to his lips.

"So you believe in hypnotism?" Father Andrey asked Nina Ivanovna.

"I can't exactly say I believe in it," replied Nina Ivanovna, assuming a grave, almost severe expression. "But I have to acknowledge that there is much that is mysterious and incomprehensible in nature."

"I quite agree with you, though I am bound to add that faith narrows the sphere of the mysterious considerably for us."

An enormous, juicy turkey was placed on the table. Father Andrey and Nina Ivanovna continued their conversation. The diamonds on Nina Ivanovna's fingers sparkled, and in her eyes sparkled tears; she was deeply moved.

"Of course I cannot venture to argue with you," she said. "But you will agree that there are many unsolved riddles in life."

"Not one, I assure you."

After supper Andrey Andreyich played the violin, Nina Ivanovna accompanying him on the piano. He had graduated from the philological department of the university ten years before, but had no employment and no fixed occupation, merely playing at occasional charity concerts. In the town he was spoken of as a musician.

Andrey Andreyich played and all listened in silence. The samovar steamed quietly on the table, and Sasha was the only one drinking tea. Just as twelve o'clock struck a fiddle-string snapped. Everyone laughed, and there was a bustle of leavetaking.

After saying good-night to her fiancé, Nadya went upstairs to the rooms she shared with her mother (the ground floor was occupied by Granny). The lights were being extinguished downstairs, in the dining-room, but Sasha still sat on, drinking tea. He always sat long over his tea, in the Moscow way, drinking six or seven glasses one after another. Long after Nadya had undressed and got into bed she could hear the servants clearing the table, and Granny scolding. At last the house was quiet but for an occasional sonorous cough from downstairs, in Sasha's room.

II

It must have been about two o'clock when Nadya awoke, for dawn was beginning to break. The night watchman could be heard striking his board in the distance. Nadya could not sleep; her bed seemed too soft to lie down in comfortably. As she had done on all the previous nights this May Nadya sat up in bed and gave herself up to her thoughts. The thoughts were just the same as those of the night before, monotonous, futile, insistent—thoughts of how Andrey Andreyich had courted her and proposed, how she had accepted him and gradually learned to appreciate this good and clever man. But somehow or other now that there was only a month left till the wedding, she began to experience fear, uneasiness, as if something vaguely sad lay in wait for her.

"Tick-tock, tick-tock," rapped out the night watchman lazily. "Tick-tock. . . ."

Through the big old-fashioned window could be seen the garden, and beyond it lilac bushes, heavy with bloom, drowsy and languid in the cold air. And a dense white mist encroached silently upon the lilacs, as if intent on enveloping them. Sleepy rooks cawed from distant trees.

"Oh, God, what makes me so sad?"

Do all girls feel like this before their weddings? Who knows? Or could it be the influence of Sasha? But Sasha had been saying the same things over and over again, as if by rote, year after year, and what he said always sounded so naïve and quaint. And why couldn't she get the thought of Sasha out of her head? Why?

The watchman had long stopped going his rounds. Birds began twittering beneath the window and in the tree tops, the mist in the garden cleared away, and now everything was gilded by the spring sunlight, everything seemed to be smiling. In a short time the whole garden, warmed by the caresses of the sun, had sprung to life, and drops of dew gleamed like diamonds on the leaves of the trees. And the old, neglected garden was young and gay for that one morning.

Granny was already awake. Sasha gave his harsh, deep cough. Downstairs the servants could be heard bringing in the samovar, moving chairs about.

The hours passed slowly. Nadya had been up and walking in the garden for a long time and the morning still dragged on.

And here came Nina Ivanovna, tearful, a glass of mineral water in her hand. She went in for spiritualism and homeopathy, read a great deal, and was fond of talking about her religious doubts, and Nadya supposed there must be some profound, mysterious significance in all this. She kissed her mother, and walked on at her side.

"What have you been crying about, Mama?" she asked.

"I read a book last night about an old man and his daughter. The old man worked at some office, and what d'you think, his chief fell in love with the old man's daughter! I haven't finished it, but I came to a place in it where I couldn't help crying," said Nina Ivanovna, and took a sip from her glass. "I remembered it this morning, and cried again."

"And I've been so depressed all these days," said Nadya after a pause. "Why can't I sleep?"

"I don't know, dearie. When I can't sleep I shut my eyes tight—like this—and imagine how Anna Karenina looked and spoke, or I try to imagine something historical, something from olden times. . . ."

Nadya felt that her mother did not understand her, that she was incapable of understanding her. She had never had this feeling before, it frightened her; she wanted to hide, and went back to her room.

At two o'clock everyone sat down to dinner. It was Wednesday, a fast-day, and Granny was served meatless *borshch*[1] and bream with buckwheat porridge.

To tease Granny, Sasha ate *borshch* as well as meat soup. He joked all through the meal, but his jokes were too elaborate and always intended to point a moral, and it was not funny at all when, before coming out with a witticism, he lifted his long, bony, dead-looking fingers; and when the thought that he was very ill and probably had not long to live crossed your mind, you felt so sorry for him you could have cried.

After dinner Granny went to her room to rest. Nina Ivanovna played the piano for a short time, and then she went out of the room, too.

"Oh, Nadya dear," Sasha said, returning to his usual after-dinner topic, "if only you would listen to me! If only you would!"

She sat curled up in an old-fashioned armchair, closing her eyes, while he paced quietly up and down the room.

"If only you would go away and study," he said. "Enlightened, saintly people are the only interesting ones, the only ones who are needed. And the more such people there are, the sooner the kingdom of heaven will be on earth. Then not one stone will be left on another, in this town of yours everything will be turned topsy-turvy,

1. See p. 62, above.

everything will change, as if by magic. And there will be huge splendid buildings, beautiful parks, marvellous fountains, fine people. . . . But that's not the chief thing. The chief thing is that then there will be no crowd anymore, as we now understand the word, that evil in its present aspect will disappear, for each individual will have faith, and know what he lives for, and nobody will seek support from the crowd. Darling, little pet, go away! Show them all that you have had enough of this stagnant, dull, corrupt life! At least show yourself that you have."

"I can't, Sasha, I'm going to get married."

"Never mind that! What does it matter?"

They went out into the garden and strolled about.

"Anyhow, my dear, you've simply got to think, you've got to understand, how abhorrent, how immoral your idle life is," continued Sasha. "Can't you see that to enable you and your Mama and your Granny to live in idleness, others have to work for you, you are devouring the life of others, is that pure, now, isn't it filthy?"

Nadya wanted to say: "Yes, you are right," wanted to tell him she understood, but tears came into her eyes and she fell silent and seemed to shrink into herself; she went to her room.

In the evening Andrey Andreyich came and played the violin a long time, as usual. He was taciturn by nature, and perhaps he loved his violin because while playing he did not have to speak. Soon after ten, when he had his coat on to go home, he took Nadya in his arms and showered passionate kisses on her face, shoulders, and hands.

"My dearest, my darling, my beautiful," he murmured. "Oh, how happy I am! I think I shall go mad with joy!"

And this, too, she seemed to have heard long, long ago, to have read it in some novel, some old, tattered volume which no one ever read anymore.

In the dining-room was Sasha, sitting at the table, drinking tea from a saucer balanced on the tips of his five long fingers. Granny was playing patience. Nina Ivanovna was reading. The flame sputtered in the icon-lamp, and everything seemed still and secure. Nadya said good-night and went up to her room, falling asleep the moment she got into bed. But, just as the night before, she waked up at the first streak of dawn. She could not sleep, something heavy and restless lay on her heart. She sat up and put her head on her knees, thinking about her fiancé, her wedding. . . . For some reason she remembered that her mother had not loved her husband, and now had nothing of her own, and was completely dependent on Granny, her mother-in-law. And try as she would, Nadya could not understand how it was that she had regarded her mother as something special, remarkable, had not seen that she was just an ordinary, unhappy woman.

Downstairs, Sasha, too, was awake—she could hear him coughing. A strange, naïve creature, thought Nadya, and there is something absurd in his dreams, in all those splendid parks, and marvellous fountains. But there was so much that was beautiful in his naivety, in his very absurdity, that the moment she began to wonder if she ought to go away and study, her whole heart, her very being, was bathed in refreshing coolness, and she was plunged in ecstasy.

"Better not think . . ." she whispered. "Better not think about it."

"Tick-tock," the distant night-watchman rapped out on the board. "Tick-tock . . . tick-tock. . . ."

III

Towards the middle of June Sasha was suddenly overcome by boredom and began to talk about going back to Moscow.

"I can't live in this town," he said morosely. "No running water, no drainage! I can hardly bear to eat my dinner—the kitchen is indescribably filthy. . . ."

"Wait a little longer, Prodigal Son," Granny whispered. "The wedding will be on the seventh."

"I simply can't!"

"You said you would stay with us till September."

"And now I don't want to. I've got to work."

The summer had turned out cold and rainy, the trees were always dripping, the garden looked somber and unfriendly, and the desire to get away and work was quite natural. Unfamiliar feminine voices could be heard in all the rooms, upstairs and downstairs, a sewing-machine whirred in Granny's room. It was all part of the bustle over the trousseau. Of winter-coats alone Nadya was to have six, and the cheapest of them, boasted Granny, had cost three hundred rubles. All this fuss irritated Sasha. He sat and sulked in his room. But they managed to persuade him to stay, and he promised not to leave before the first of July.

The time passed quickly. On St. Peter's day Andrey Andreyich took Nadya after dinner to Moscow Street to have yet another look at the house which had long been rented and furnished for the young couple. It was a two-story house, but so far only the upper floor had been furnished. In the ballroom, with its gleaming floor, painted to look like parquet, were bent-wood chairs, a grand piano, a music-stand for the violin. There was a smell of paint. On the wall was a large oil-painting in a gilt frame—a picture of a naked lady beside a purple vase with a broken handle.

"Beautiful picture," said Andrey Andreyich with an awed sigh. "It's by Shishmachevsky."[1]

Next came the drawing-room, in which were a round table, a sofa, and some armchairs upholstered in bright blue material. Over the sofa hung an enlarged photograph of Father Andrey with all his medals on, wearing a tall ceremonial hat. They passed into the dining-room with its sideboard, and from there into the bedroom. Here, in the half-light, stood two beds side by side, and it looked as if those who had furnished the bedroom had taken it for granted that life would always be happy here, that it could not be otherwise. Andrey Andreyich conducted Nadya through the rooms, never removing his arm from her waist. And she felt weak, guilty, hating all these rooms and beds and chairs, while the naked lady made her sick. She now saw quite clearly that she no longer loved Andrey Andreyich, perhaps never had loved him. But she did not know how to say this, whom to say it to, and why to say it at all, and though she thought about it day and night she came no nearer to knowing. . . . He had his arm round her waist, spoke to her so kindly, so humbly, was so happy, walking about his home. And all she saw was vulgarity, stupid, naïve, intolerable vulgarity, and his arm round her waist seemed to her cold and rigid, like an iron hoop. At any moment she was ready to run away, to burst into sobs, to jump out of the window. Andrey Andreyich led her to the bathroom, touched a tap screwed into the wall, and the water gushed out.

"What do you think of that?" he said, and laughed. "I had them put up a cistern holding three hundred gallons of water, so we shall have running water in our bathroom."

They walked about the yard for a while and then went out into the street, where they got into a carriage. The dust rose in thick clouds, and it looked as if it were just going to rain.

"Are you cold?" asked Andrey Andreyich, narrowing his eyes against the dust.

She did not answer.

"Remember Sasha reproaching me for not doing anything, yesterday?" he said, after a short pause. "Well, he was right. Infinitely right. I do nothing, and there is nothing I know how to do. Why is it, my dear one? How is it that the very thought of one day wearing a cockade in my cap and going to an office makes me feel sick? How is it that I can't stand the sight of a lawyer, or a Latin teacher, or a town councilor? Oh, Mother Russia, Mother Russia! How many idlers and useless beings you still bear on your bosom! How many beings like myself, oh, long-suffering one!"

1. No such painter is known. Chekhov probably uses the sound of the name as a further indication of speciousness and vulgarity in Andrey.

And he theorized about his own idleness, seeing it as a sign of the times.

"When we are married," he continued, "we'll go to live in the country, my dear one, we'll work. We'll buy a little plot of land with a garden and a stream, and we'll toil, observe life. . . . Oh, how lovely it will be!"

He took his hat off and his hair waved in the breeze, and she listened to him, thinking all the time: "Oh, God, I want to go home! Oh, God!" They overtook Father Andrey just before they got back to Nadya's home.

"Look, there's my father!" said Andrey Andreyich joyfully, and he waved his hat. "I love my old Dad, really I do," he said, paying off the cabby. "Dear old man! Good old man!"

Nadya went into the house feeling out-of-humor and unwell, unable to forget that all the evening there would be visitors, that she would have to entertain them, to smile, to listen to the violin, to hear all sorts of nonsense and talk about nothing but the wedding. Granny, stiff and pompous in her silk dress, was sitting beside the samovar, looking very haughty, as she always did when there were visitors. Father Andrey came into the room with his subtle smile.

"I have the pleasure and virtuous consolation of seeing you in good health," he said to Granny, and it was hard to say whether he was in earnest or joking.

IV

The wind knocked on the window-panes and on the roof. Whistling sounds could be heard, and the chimney goblin moaned his morose, plaintive song. It was one o'clock in the morning. Everyone in the house was in bed, but no one was asleep, and Nadya kept thinking she could hear the violin being played downstairs. There was a sharp report from outside; a shutter must have torn loose from its hinges. A minute later Nina Ivanovna came into the room in her chemise, holding a candle.

"What was that noise, Nadya?" she asked.

Nadya's mother, her hair in a single plait, smiling timidly, seemed on this stormy night older, plainer, and shorter than usual. Nadya remembered how, so very recently, she had considered her mother a remarkable woman and had felt pride in listening to the words she used. And now she could not for the life of her remember what those words had been—the only ones that came back to her were feeble and affected.

Bass voices seemed to be singing in the chimney, even the words "Oh, my God!" could be made out. Nadya sat up in bed, and tugged violently at her hair, sobbing.

"Mama, Mama!" she cried. "Oh, darling, if you only knew what I was going through! I beg you, I implore you—let me go away!"

"Where to?" asked Nina Ivanovna, in bewilderment, and she sat down on the side of the bed. "Where d'you want to go?"

Nadya cried and cried, unable to bring out another word.

"Let me go away from this town," she said at last. "The wedding must not, will not be, believe me. I don't love that man. . . . I can't bear to speak about him."

"No, my darling, no," said Nina Ivanovna quickly, frightened out of her wits. "Calm yourself. You're out of sorts. It'll pass. It often happens. You've probably had a quarrel with Andrey, but lovers' tiffs end in kisses."

"Go, Mama, go!" sobbed Nadya.

"Yes," said Nina Ivanovna, after a pause. "Only the other day you were a little girl, and now you're almost a bride. Nature is in a constant state of metabolism. Before you know where you are you'll be a mother yourself, and then an old woman, with a troublesome daughter like mine."

"My darling, you're kind and clever, and you're unhappy," said Nadya. "You're ever so unhappy—why do you say such commonplace things? Why, for God's sake?"

Nina Ivanovna tried to speak, but could not utter a word, only sobbed and went back to her room. Once more the bass voices moaned in the chimney, and Nadya was suddenly terrified. She jumped out of bed and ran into her mother's room. Nina Ivanovna, her eyelids swollen from crying, was lying in bed covered by a blue blanket, a book in her hands.

"Mama, listen to me," said Nadya. "Think, try to understand me, I implore you! Only think how shallow and humiliating our life is! My eyes have been opened, I see it all now. And what is your Andrey Andreyich? Why, he's not a bit clever, Mama. Oh, God, oh, God! Only think, Mama, why, he's stupid!"

Nina Ivanovna sat up with a jerk.

"You and your grandmother keep torturing me," she said, with a gasping sob. "I want to live! To live!" she repeated, smiting her chest again and again. "Can't you let me have my freedom? I'm still young, I want to live, you've made an old woman of me!"

She cried bitterly and lay down, rolling herself up in the blanket, and looking just a silly, pathetic little thing. Nadya went back to her room and dressed, then she sat at the window to wait for morning to come. All night she sat there thinking, and someone seemed to be knocking at the shutter outside and whistling.

The next morning Granny complained that the wind had beaten down all the apples and split the trunk of an old plum-tree. It was a grey, dim, joyless morning, one of those days when you feel inclined to light the lamp from the very morning. Everyone complained of the cold, and the raindrops tapped on the window-panes. After breakfast Nadya went to Sasha's room and, without a word, fell on her knees before a chair in the corner, covering her face with her hands.

"What's the matter?" asked Sasha.

"I can't go on like this, I can't!" she exclaimed. "I don't know how I could live here before, I simply can't understand it! I despise my fiancé, I despise myself, I despise this whole idle, empty life. . . ."

"Come, come . . ." Sasha interrupted her, not yet realizing what she was talking about. "Never mind . . . it's all right. . . ."

"This life is hateful to me," continued Nadya. "I won't be able to bear another day here! I shall go away tomorrow. Take me with you, for God's sake!"

Sasha gazed at her for a moment in amazement. At last the truth dawned upon him, and he rejoiced like a child, waving his arms and shuffling in his loose slippers, as if he were dancing with joy.

"Splendid!" he said, rubbing his hands. "God, how fine that is!"

She gazed at him unblinkingly, from wide-open eyes, full of love, as if fascinated, waiting for him to come out immediately with something significant, something of infinite importance. He had not told her anything yet, but she felt that something new and vast, something she had never known before, was already opening before her, and she looked at him full of expectation, ready for anything, for death itself.

"I'm leaving tomorrow," he said after a pause. "You can come to the station to see me off. I'll take your things in my trunk and buy a ticket for you. And when the third bell rings, you can get into the train, and off we go. Go with me as far as Moscow, and go to Petersburg by yourself. Have you a passport?"

"Yes."

"You will never regret it—never repent it, I'm sure!" said Sasha enthusiastically. "You will go away and study, and afterwards things will take their own course. As soon as you turn your life upside down, everything will change. The great thing is to turn your life upside down, nothing else matters. So we're off tomorrow?"

"Oh, yes! For God's sake!"

Nadya, who imagined that she was profoundly stirred and that her heart had never before been so heavy, was quite sure that now, on the eve of departure, she would suffer, be racked with anguished thoughts. But she had hardly gone upstairs to her room and lain down on the bed when she fell fast asleep, and slept soundly, with a tear-stained face and a smile on her lips, till the very evening.

V

The carriage had been sent for. Nadya, in her hat and coat, went upstairs to have one last look at her mother, at all that had been hers so long. She stood in her room beside the bed, which was still warm, and then went softly into her mother's room. Nina Ivanovna was asleep, and it was very quiet in her room. After kissing her mother and smoothing her. hair, Nadya stood for a minute or two. . . . Then she went downstairs with unhurried steps.

The rain was coming down in torrents. A carriage, dripping wet, stood in front of the porch, its hood raised.

"There's no room for you, Nadya," said Granny, when the servant began putting the luggage into the carriage. "I wonder you want to see him off in such weather! You'd better stay at home. Just look at the rain!"

Nadya tried to say something, but could not. Sasha helped her into the carriage, covering her knees with the rug. And now he was seated beside her.

"Good-bye! God bless you!" shouted Granny from the porch. "Mind you write when you get to Moscow, Sasha!"

"All right. Good-bye, Granny!"

"May the Queen of Heaven protect you!"

"What weather!" said Sasha.

It was only now that Nadya began to cry. It was only now that she realized she was really going away, a thing she had not quite believed, even when saying good-bye to Granny, or standing beside her mother. Good-bye, town! Everything came over her with a rush—Andrey, his father, the new house, the naked lady with the vase. But all this no longer frightened her or weighed upon her, it had become naïve and trivial, it was retreating farther into the past. And when they got into the railway carriage and the train started, the whole of this past, so big and important, shrank to a little lump, and a vast future, scarcely perceptible till now, opened before her. The raindrops tapped on the windows, there was nothing to be seen but the green fields, the telegraph-poles flashing by, the birds on the wires, and joy suddenly almost choked her. She remembered that she was going to be at liberty, to study, doing what used to be called in the old days "running away to the Cossacks." She laughed and cried and prayed.

"Come, come," said Sasha, smiling broadly. "Come, come!"

VI

Autumn passed, and after it winter. Nadya was now very homesick, and thought every day of her mother and Granny; she thought of Sasha, too. Letters from home were resigned and kindly, everything seemed to have been forgiven amd forgotten. After passing her May examinations, she set off, well and happy, for home, breaking her journey at Moscow to see Sasha. He was just the same as he had been the year before—bearded, shaggy, still wearing the same long old-fashioned coat and canvas trousers, his eyes as large and beautiful as ever. But he looked ill and worried, he had got older and thinner, and coughed incessantly. And to Nadya he seemed dingy and provincial.

"Why, it's Nadya!" he cried, laughing joyfully. "My darling, my pet!"

They sat together in the lithographic workshop, amidst the fumes of tobacco smoke and a stifling smell of ink and paint; then they went to his room, which reeked of smoke, too, and was littered and filthy. On the table, beside the cold samovar, was a broken plate with a bit of dark paper on it, and both floor and table were strewn with dead flies. Everything here showed that Sasha took no thought for his private life, lived in a continual mess, with utter contempt for comfort. If anyone had spoken to him about his personal happiness and private life, had asked him if there was anyone who loved him, he would have been at a loss to know what was meant, and would only have laughed.

"Everything passed off all right," said Nadya hurriedly. "Mama came to Petersburg in the autumn, to see me, she says Granny isn't angry, but keeps going into my room and making the sign of the cross on the walls."

Sasha looked cheerful, but coughed and spoke in a cracked voice, and Nadya kept looking at him, wondering if he was really seriously ill, or if it was her imagination.

"Sasha, dear Sasha," she said, "but you're ill!"

"I'm all right. A bit unwell—nothing serious. . . ."

"For goodness' sake," said Nadya, in agitated tones, "why don't you go to a doctor? Why don't you take care of your health? My dear one, Sasha, dear," she murmured, and tears sprang into her eyes, and for some reason Andrey Andreyich, and the naked lady with the vase, and the whole of her past, which now seemed as far off as her childhood, rose before her mind. And she cried because Sasha no longer seemed to her so original, clever and interesting as he had last year. "Sasha dear, you are very, very ill. I don't know what I wouldn't give for you not to be so pale and thin! I owe you so much. You can have no idea what a lot you have done for me, Sasha darling! You are now the closest, the dearest person in my life, you know."

They sat on, talking and talking. And now, after a winter in Petersburg, it seemed to her that something outmoded, old-fashioned, finished, something, perhaps, already half in the grave, could be felt in everything he said, in his smile, in the whole of him.

"I'm going for a trip down the Volga the day after tomorrow," said Sasha, "and then I'll go somewhere and take *kumiss*.[2] I want to

2. Fermented mare's milk, taken, like mineral water, as a cure for various ailments.

try *kumiss*. A friend of mine, and his wife, are going with me. The
wife is a marvelous person. I keep trying to persuade her to go and
study. I want her to turn her life topsy-turvy."

When they had talked themselves out, they went to the station.
Sasha treated her to tea and bought her some apples, and when the
train started, and he stood smiling and waving his handkerchief, she
could see by just looking at his legs how ill he was, and that he was
not likely to live long.

Nadya arrived at her native town at noon. As she drove home
from the station the streets seemed to her disproportionately wide,
the houses very small and squat. There was hardly anyone about,
and the only person she met was the German piano-tuner in his
rusty overcoat. And the houses seemed to be covered with a film of
dust. Granny, now really old, and as stout and plain as ever, put her
arms round Nadya and cried for a long time, with her face pressed
against Nadya's shoulder, as if she could not tear herself away.
Nina Ivanovna, who had aged greatly, too, had become quite plain
and seemed to have shrunk, but she was as tightly laced as ever and
the diamonds still shone from her fingers.

"My darling," she said, shaking all over. "My own darling!"

Then they sat down and wept silently. It was easy to see that both
Granny and Mama realized that the past was irrevocably lost. Gone
were their social position, their former distinction, their right to
invite guests to their house. They felt as people feel when, in the
midst of an easy, carefree life, the police break in one night and
search the house, and it is discovered that the master of the house
has committed an embezzlement or a forgery—and then farewell
forever to the easy, carefree life!

Nadya went upstairs and saw the same bed, the same window
with its demure white curtains, the same view of the garden from
the window, flooded with sunshine, gay, noisy with life. She touched
her table, sat down, fell into a reverie. She had a good dinner,
drinking tea after it, with delicious thick cream, but something was
missing, there was an emptiness in the rooms, and the ceiling struck
her as very low. When she went to bed in the evening, covering
herself with the bed-clothes, there was something ridiculous in lying
in this warm, too soft bed.

Nina Ivanovna came in for a moment, and seated herself as the
guilty do, timidly, with furtive glances.

"Well, Nadya, how is everything?" she asked. "Are you happy?
Really happy?"

"Yes, Mama."

Nina Ivanovna got up and made the sign of the cross over Nadya
and the window.

"As you see, I have turned religious," she said. "I'm studying philosophy, you know, and I keep thinking, thinking. . . . And many things are as clear as daylight to me now. It seems to me that the most important thing is to see life through a prism."

"Mama, how is Granny really?"

"She seems all right. When you went away with Sasha and Granny read your telegram, she fell down on the spot. After that she lay three days in bed without stirring. And then she began praying and crying. But she's all right now."

She got up and began pacing up and down the room.

"Tick-tock," rapped the watchman, "tick-tock."

"The great thing is for life to be seen through a prism," she said. "In other words, life must be divided up in our consciousness into its simplest elements, as if into the seven primary colors, and each element must be studied separately."

What more Nina Ivanovna said, and when she went away, Nadya did not know, for she soon fell asleep.

May passed, and June came. Nadya had got used to being at home again. Granny sat beside the samovar, pouring out tea and giving deep sighs. Nina Ivanovna talked about her philosophy in the evenings. She still lived like a dependent, and had to turn to Granny whenever she wanted a few kopeks. The house was full of flies and the ceilings seemed to be getting lower and lower. Granny and Nina Ivanovna never went out, for fear of meeting Father Andrey and Andrey Andreyich. Nadya walked about the garden and the streets, looking at the houses and the drab fences, and it seemed to her that the town had been getting old for a long time, that it had outlived its day and was now waiting, either for its end, or for the beginning of something fresh and youthful. Oh, for this new, pure life to begin, when one could go straight forward, looking one's fate boldly in the eyes, confident that one was in the right, could be gay and free! This life was bound to come sooner or later. The time would come when there would be nothing left of Granny's house, in which the only way for four servants to live was in one room, in the basement, surrounded by filth—yes, the time would come when there would not be a trace left of such a house, when everyone would have forgotten it, when there would be no one left to remember it. Nadya's only distraction was the little boys in the next house who banged on the fence when she strolled about the garden and laughed at her, shouting, "There goes the bride!"

A letter came from Saratov, from Sasha. He wrote in his reckless, staggering handwriting that the trip down the Volga had been a complete success, but that he had been taken rather ill at Saratov, and had lost his voice, and been in hospital for the last fortnight. She understood what this meant, and a foreboding amounting almost to a conviction came over her. It vexed her that this foreboding and the thought of Sasha himself no longer moved her as formerly. She felt a longing to live, to be in Petersburg, and her friendship with Sasha seemed to belong to a past, which, while dear, was now very distant. She could not sleep all night, and in the morning sat at the window, as if listening for something. And there really did come the sound of voices from below—Granny was saying something in rapid, querulous tones. Then someone cried. . . . When Nadya went downstairs Granny was standing in the corner of the room praying, and her face was tear-stained. On the table lay a telegram.

Nadya paced up and down the room for a long time, listening to Granny's crying, before picking up the telegram and reading it. It said that yesterday morning, in Saratov, Aleksander Timofeyich, Sasha for short, had died of consumption.

Granny and Nina Ivanovna went to the church to order a service for the dead, and Nadya walked about the rooms for a long time, thinking. She realized clearly that her life had been turned topsy-turvy, as Sasha had wanted it to be, that she was lonely, alien, unwanted here, and that there was nothing she wanted here, the past had been torn away and vanished, as if burned by fire, and the ashes scattered to the winds. She went into Sasha's room and stood there.

"Good-bye, dear Sasha," she thought. Life stretched before her, new, vast, spacious, and this life, though still vague and mysterious, beckoned to her, drawing her onward.

She went upstairs to pack, and the next morning said good-bye to her family, and left the town, gay and full of spirits—as she supposed, forever.

1903

Backgrounds

Selections from Chekhov's Letters†

To G. I. Rossolimo,[1] October 11, 1899

* * * Autobiography? I have a disease, "autobiographobia." It is real torture for me to read any sort of details about myself, and all the more to write them for publication. On a separate piece of paper I am sending you several dates, without embellishment, but I can't do any more. If you like, you may add that in my application for admission I wrote "Medicle School." * * *

I, A. P. Chekhov, was born January 17, 1860, in Taganrog. My education began at the Greek school of the Church of Tsar Constantine, and then continued in the Taganrog Gymnasium. In 1879 I entered the Medical School of Moscow University. I had very little notion of the various schools at that time, and I don't remember why I chose the medical school, but I did not regret my choice. In my very first year I started to publish in weekly magazines and newspapers, and these literary occupations assumed a permanent professional character by the beginning of the 1880's. In 1888 I received the Pushkin Prize. In 1890 I went to Sakhalin Island in order to write a book later on our penal colony and forced labor. Without counting court chronicles, reviews, *feuilletons*,[2] notices, everything that I wrote from day to day for newspapers and which would be difficult to locate and gather, I have written and published more than 10,000 pages of stories and tales in twenty years of literary activity. I also wrote plays.

I firmly believe that my medical studies had a vital influence on my literary activity; they significantly widened the sphere of my observation, enriched me with knowledge whose true value to me as a writer can only be appreciated by someone who is himself a doctor. They also had a guiding role and I was probably able to avoid many mistakes through my concern with medicine. Acquaintance with the natural sciences and with the scientific method always kept me on guard, and I tried where possible to keep scientific facts in mind, and where it was impossible I preferred not to write at all. I will note in passing that the conditions of artistic creativity do not always allow total agreement with scientific facts: one cannot depict death by poisoning on the stage the way it occurs

---

† The letters in this section are from A. P. Chekhov, *Palnoe sobranie sochinenii i pisem* (Moscow, 1944–51), Vol. XIV, and *Sobranie sochinenii* (Moscow, 1960–64), Vols. XI, XII. They are translated by Ralph E. Matlaw.
1. Rossolimo was a classmate of Chekhov's in medical school. At the reunion of the class of 1884 fifteen years later,

it was decided to issue a class album with pictures and autobiographies. This letter is Chekhov's response to Rossolimo's request for autobiographical information.
2. Light literature or serialized stories, usually appearing on the bottom half of a newspaper page.

in real life. But agreement with scientific facts must be felt even in those circumstances, that is, the reader and the viewer must clearly see that these are only conventions and that he is dealing with a writer who knows what is going on. I am not one of those writers who look askance at science, and I would not wish to be one of those who figure everything out with their own minds. * * *

To D. V. Grigorovich,[3] *March 28, 1886*

* * * If I do have a gift that should be respected, I confess before your pure heart that up to now I haven't respected it. I felt that I had it, but got used to considering it insignificant. There are plenty of purely external reasons to make an individual unfair, extremely suspicious, and distrustful of himself, and I reflect now that there have been plenty of such reasons in my case. All my friends and relatives were always condescending toward my writing and constantly advised me in a friendly way not to give up real work for scribbling. I have hundreds of friends in Moscow, a score of whom write, and I cannot recall a single one who read my work or considered me an artist. There is a so-called "literary circle" in Moscow: talents and mediocrities of all shapes and sizes gather once a week in a restaurant and exercise their tongues. If I were to go there and read them a mere snippet of your letter, they would laugh in my face. During the five years I have been roaming around editorial offices I managed to succumb to the general view of my literary insignificance, quickly got used to looking at my work condescendingly, and—kept plugging away! That's the first reason. The second is that I am a doctor and am up to my ears in medical work, so that the proverb about chasing two hares has cost me more sleep than anyone else.

I write all this merely to justify myself to you in the smallest way for my deep sin. Up to now I have treated my literary work extremely lightly, carelessly, haphazardly. I do not remember working more than a day on *any single* story of mine, and I wrote *The Huntsman*, which you liked, when I went swimming! I wrote my stories as reporters write their news about fires: mechanically, half-consciously, without worrying about either the reader or themselves. I wrote and constantly tried not to waste images and scenes which I valued on these stories, and I tried to save them and carefully hide them, God only knows why.

Suvorin's[4] very friendly and, so far as I can see, sincere letter,

3. D. V. Grigorovich (1822–99), an important writer in the 1840's and the later part of the century, had written to Chekhov on March 25, 1886, praising his outstanding talent and urging him to write more seriously.
4. A. S. Suvorin (1833–1911), influential publisher of the conservative paper *New Times*, became Chekhov's closest friend.

was the first thing to impel me to look at my work critically. I began to get ready to write something significant, but I still had no faith in my own literary significance. Then suddenly, completely unexpectedly, your letter came. Forgive the comparison, but it acted on me like an order "to leave town within twenty-four hours!" that is, I suddenly felt an absolute necessity to hurry, to get out of the place I was stuck in as quickly as possible. * * *

I will liberate myself from deadlines, but not at once. There is no possibility of getting out of the rut into which I have fallen. I don't mind starving as I have already done, but there are others involved too. I give my leisure to writing, two or three hours a day and a little bit of the night, that is, time that is suitable only for trifling work. This summer, when I will have more leisure and will have to earn less, I will undertake something serious. * * *

To A. P. Chekhov,[5] *May* 10, 1886

* * * *The City of the Future* is a splendid theme in both its novelty and its topicality. I think that you'll do it well if you don't get too lazy, but you're such a lazybones, damn you. *The City of the Future* will turn out to be an artistic work only under the following conditions: 1) absence of lengthy torrents of a politico-socio-economic nature; 2) total objectivity; 3) honesty in the description of characters and objects; 4) extreme brevity; 5) daring and originality; shun clichés; 6) compassion.

I think descriptions of nature should be very short and always be *à propos*. Commonplaces like "The setting sun, sinking into the waves of the darkening sea, cast its purple gold rays, etc.," "Swallows, flitting over the surface of the water, twittered gaily"—eliminate such commonplaces. You have to choose small details in describing nature, grouping them in such a way that if you close your eyes after reading it you can picture the whole thing. For example, you'll get a picture of a moonlit night if you write that on the dam of the mill a piece of broken bottle flashed like a bright star and the black shadow of a dog or a wolf rolled by like a ball, etc.[6] Nature will become animated if you don't disdain comparing its appearance with human actions, etc.

In the realm of psychology you also need details. God preserve you from commonplaces. Best of all, shun all descriptions of the characters' spiritual state. You must try to have that state emerge clearly from their actions. Don't try for too many characters. The center of gravity should reside in two: he and she.

5. Chekhov's brother Alexander (1855–1913), a minor writer.
6. Chekhov uses these lines in *The Wolf* (1886), and Treplyov mocks them as a facile literary device in *The Seagull*, Act IV.

I write all that to you as a reader with definite tastes. I am also writing so that you may not feel yourself alone while writing. It's a hard thing to be alone when creating. Bad criticism is better than nothing, isn't that right? * * *

To A. S. Suvorin, May 30, 1888

* * * You write that neither the conversation on pessimism nor Kisochka's tale[7] in any way further or solve the question of pessimism. I think that it is not for writers to solve such questions as the existence of God, pessimism, etc. The writer's function is only to describe by whom, how, and under what conditions the questions of God and pessimism were discussed. The artist must be only an impartial witness of his characters and what they said, not their judge. I heard a confused discussion by two Russians about pessimism and have to transmit that conversation in exactly the same way I heard it. Let the jurors, that is to say, the readers, evaluate it. My function is only to be talented, that is, to be able to distinguish important indications from unimportant, to know how to place them in the proper light, and to speak their language. Shcheglov-Leontiev[8] blames me for finishing the story with the sentence: "You can't figure out anything in this world!" He thinks that the artist as psychologist *must* figure things out and that that is why he is a psychologist. But I don't agree with him. It is time for writers, and particularly for artists, to admit that you can't figure out anything in this world, as Socrates once admitted and as Voltaire kept admitting. The public thinks it knows and understands everything; and the dumber it is the broader its horizons seem to be. However, if an artist whom the public believes decides to state that he understands nothing of what he sees, that in itself is of great significance in the realm of thought and is a great step forward. * * *

To A. S. Suvorin, September 11, 1888

* * * You advise me not to chase two hares at once and to give up practicing medicine. I don't see why one can't chase two hares even literally. If you have enough hounds, it's possible to do it. I probably don't have enough hounds (in the figurative sense now), but I feel more cheerful and more content with myself when I think of my having two occupations rather than merely one. Medicine is my lawful, wedded wife, and literature is my mistress. When one isn't enough for me, I spend the night with the other. That may be a little improper, but then it's less dull, and in any case, neither one loses anything by my perfidy. I would not devote all my spare time

7. In the story *Lights* (1886).   whom Chekhov corresponded.
8. A promising writer (1856–1911) with

and thoughts to literature even if I didn't have medicine. I don't have enough discipline for that. * * *

To A. N. Pleshcheev,[9] October 4, 1888

* * * Write to me after you've read my *Name-Day Party*. You won't like it, but I am not afraid of you or Anna Mikhailovna.[1] I am afraid of those who will look for tendenciousness between the lines and who are determined to see me either as a liberal or a conservative. I am neither a liberal nor a conservative, neither a gradualist nor a monk nor an indifferentist. I would like to be nothing more than a free artist, and I regret that God did not give me the gift to be one. I hate falseness and coercion in all their forms and consistorial secretaries are just as repellent to me as Notovich and Gradovsky.[2] Pharisaism, stupidity, and arbitrariness reign not merely in merchants' houses and police stations: I see them in science, in literature, among the young. That is why I have no particular passion for either policemen or butchers or scientists or writers or the young. I consider brand-names and labels a prejudice. My holy of holies is the human body, health, intelligence, talent, inspiration, love, and absolute freedom, freedom from force and falseness in whatever form they express themselves. That's the platform I'd subscribe to if I were a great artist. * * *

To A. N. Pleshcheev, October 9, 1888

* * * Is there really no "ideology" apparent in my last story [*The Name-Day Party*] either? Once you remarked to me that the element of protest is missing from my work, that there is neither sympathy nor antipathy in them. But don't I protest against falsehood from the beginning of the story to its end? Isn't that ideology? No? Well then, that means that I don't know how to bite, or that I am a flea. * * *

To A. S. Suvorin, October 27, 1888

* * * I sometimes preach heresy, but I have never yet gone so far as to deny a place in art to topical questions altogether. In conversations with the writing fraternity I always insist that the artist's function is not to solve narrowly specialized questions. It is bad for the artist to undertake something he doesn't understand. We have specialists for specialized questions; it is their function to discuss the peasant commune, the fate of capitalism, the evil of drink, shoes, women's diseases. The artist, however, must treat only what he

9. I. L. Shcheglov-Leontiev (1825–93), poet and editor of the *Northern Herald*, in which Chekhov published.
1. A. M. Efreinova, publisher of the *Northern Herald*.
2. Two supposedly unscrupulous left-wing journalists.

understands; his sphere is as limited as that of any other specialist's, I repeat that and always insist on it. Only somebody who has never written or had anything to do with images could say that there are no questions in his realm, that there is nothing but answers. The artist observes, chooses, guesses, compounds—these actions in themselves already presuppose a question at the origin; if the artist did not pose a question to himself at the beginning then there was nothing to guess or to choose. To be as brief as possible, I'll end with psychiatry: if you deny questions and intentions in creative work you must acknowledge that the artist creates unintentionally, without purpose, under the influence of a temporary aberration; therefore, if an author were to brag to me that he wrote a tale purely by inspiration, without previously having pondered his intentions, I would call him insane.

You are right in demanding that an artist approach his work consciously, but you are confusing two concepts: *the solution of a problem and the correct formulation of a problem.* Only the second is required of the artist. Not a single problem is resolved in *Anna Karenina* or *Onegin*, but they satisfy you completely only because all the problems in them are formulated correctly. The judge is required to formulate the questions correctly, but the decision is left to the jurors, each according to his own taste. * * *

You write that the main character of my *Name-Day Party* is a figure who should be developed. Good God, I am not a brute without feelings, I understand that. I understand that I cut up my characters and ruin them, that I ruin good material for nothing. Honestly speaking, I would gladly have spent half a year on the *Name-Day Party.* I like leisure and find no attraction in hasty publication. I would gladly, with pleasure, with feeling, and in detail have described *all* of my main character, his soul while his wife was in labor, his trial, his nasty feeling after the acquittal, I would have described how the midwife and the doctor drink tea at night, I would have described the rain. That would only have given me pleasure, because I like to delve into things and putter around. But what can I do? I begin a story September 10th with the knowledge that I must finish it by October 5th at the latest. If I delay it I break my promise and I remain without money. I start the beginning calmly, I don't restrain myself, but toward the middle I become uneasy and begin to fear that my story will turn out too long: I have to remember that the *Northern Herald* has little money and that I am one of their expensive collaborators. Therefore my openings always promise a great deal, as if I had started a novel; the middle is crumpled up and timid; and the ending is like fireworks, as though in a short story. When you fashion a story you necessarily concern yourself with its limits: out of a slew of main and secondary characters you choose only one—the wife or the husband—

place him against the background and describe him alone and there-fore also emphasize him, while you scatter the others in the back-ground like small change, and you get something like the night sky: a single large moon and a slew of very small stars. But the moon doesn't turn out right because you can see it only when the other stars are visible too, but the stars aren't set off. So I turn out a sort of patchwork quilt rather than literature. What can I do? I simply don't know. I will simply depend on all-healing time. * * *

To A. S. Suvorin, November 1, 1889

I am sending you a story[3] for the *feuilleton*. An insignificant trifle on the lives of provincial porpoises. Forgive my mischievous-ness. * * * Incidentally, the story has its own curious history. I had intended to finish it so that there wouldn't be a shred left of my main characters, but something made me read it to our friends; they all begged me: "Spare them! Spare them!" So I spared my main characters and that's why the story turned out so sour. I think it will fit into the *feuilleton*, and if not, I'll have to shorten it. * * *

To L. A. Avilova,[4] March 19, 1892

* * * I read your story *On the Way*. If I were the publisher of an illustrated magazine I would publish it with great pleasure. Only let me give you some advice as a reader: when you describe the mis-erable and unfortunate, and want to make the reader feel pity, try to be somewhat colder—that seems to give a kind of background to another's grief, against which it stands out more clearly. Whereas in your story the characters cry and you sigh. Yes, be more cold. * * *

To L. A. Avilova, April 29, 1892

* * * I wrote to you before that you have to be cold when you write touching stories. But you didn't understand me. You can cry over your stories and groan, and suffer together with your charac-ters, but I think it must be done in such a way that the reader never notices it. The more objective you are, the stronger will be the impression you make. That's what I wanted to say.

To A. S. Suvorin, March 27, 1894

* * * Since I have stopped smoking completely I no longer have gloomy and anxious spells. Perhaps Tolstoy's moral philosophy no

---

3. *The Philistines* (*Obyvateli*), which later became the first part of *The Teacher of Literature*.
4. Lidia Avilova (1864–1943) was a young author with whom Chekhov was reputed to have had an affair; her mem-oir *Chekhov in My Life* (1947), parts of which were first published in 1910, greatly distorts the relationship between them.

longer moves me because I don't smoke. In the depths of my heart I am antagonistic towards it and that, of course, is unfair. Peasant blood flows in my veins, and you can't astonish me with peasant virtues. I came to believe in progress and could not help doing so, as there was a fearful difference between the time I used to be beaten and the time when they stopped beating me. I have always liked intelligent people, sensitivity, courtesy, wit, and I have always been as indifferent as to whether people pick their corns or their leggings smell bad as I am to whether young ladies walk around in curlers in the morning. But Tolstoy's philosophy moved me deeply and reigned over me for six or seven years. What affected me were not his basic positions, which I had known even earlier, but Tolstoy's manner of expressing himself, his judiciousness, and, probably, a kind of hypnotism. Now something rebels within me. Prudence and fairness tell me that there is more love for humanity in electricity and steam than in chastity and abstention from meat. War is evil, and legal justice is evil, but that doesn't mean that I have to go around in bast shoes like a peasant or sleep on the stove with a worker and his wife, etc., etc. But the problem isn't there, not in "for or against," but rather that in one way or another Tolstoy has left me, he is no longer in my heart, and he went out of me saying: "Behold, your house is left unto you desolate."[5] * * *

To L. A. Avilova, October 6, 1897

* * * You complain that my characters are gloomy. Alas, it is not my fault! It turns out that way involuntarily, and while I am writing it does not seem to me that I am writing gloomily; in any case, I am always in a good mood when I work. It is noteworthy that gloomy people and melancholiacs always write merry things, while the cheerful depress people with their writings. And I am a cheerful man; at least, as the saying goes, I've enjoyed myself during the first thirty years of my life. * * *

To Maxim Gorky,[6] December 3, 1898

* * * You ask my opinion of your stories. My opinion? You unquestionably have talent, and, moreover, a genuine, major talent. For example, it expressed itself with extraordinary power in the story *In the Steppe*, and I was even envious that I had not written it. You are an artist, an intelligent man. You have a marvellous ability to feel. You are plastic, that is, when you describe an object, you can see it and feel it with your hands. That is a real art. * * * Shall I speak of your shortcomings now? * * * I will begin with what in

5. Matthew, xxiii:38.
6. Maxim Gorky (1868–1936) became the best known of all Russian writers in the early twentieth century.

my opinion is your lack of restraint. You are like a spectator in a theatre who expresses his enthusiasm so unrestrainedly that he prevents himself and others from hearing. That lack of restraint is particularly noticeable in the descriptions of nature with which you interrupt dialogues; when one reads them, these descriptions, one wishes they were more compact, shorter, say two or three lines. Frequent mention of lassitude, whispering, velvety smoothness, and so on give these descriptions a certain rhetorical quality, a monotony, and dampen the reader's ardor, almost make him weary. A lack of restraint is also noticeable in the description of women (*Malva, On the Rafts*) and in love scenes. It is a question not of a broad scope, a breadth of view, but merely of a lack of restraint. Then the frequent use of completely inappropriate words for stories of your kind: "accomplishment," "disc," "harmony"—these words interfere. You frequently write about waves. There is something strained in the description of intelligent people, something cautious, it's not because you haven't observed intelligent people enough, you know them, but you just don't know how to approach them. * * *

To Maxim Gorky, September 3, 1899

* * * Another piece of advice: when you read proof cross out as many adjectives and adverbs as you can. You have so many modifiers that the reader has trouble understanding and gets worn out. It is comprehensible when I write: "The man sat on the grass," because it is clear and does not detain one's attention. On the other hand, it is difficult to figure out and hard on the brain if I write: "The tall, narrow-chested man of medium height and with a red beard sat down on the green grass that had already been trampled down by the pedestrians, sat down silently, looking around timidly and fearfully." The brain can't grasp all that at once, and art must be grasped at once, instantaneously. And then one other thing. You are lyrical by nature, the timber of your soul is soft. If you were a composer you would avoid writing marches. It is unnatural for your talent to curse, shout, taunt, denounce with rage. Therefore, you'll understand if I advise you, in proofreading, to eliminate the "sons of bitches," "curs," and "flea-bitten mutts" that appear here and there on the pages of *Life*. * * *

To G. I. Rossolimo, January 21, 1900

* * * I think that all I have that's suitable for a children's book is two stories about dogs, which I am forwarding under separate cover. I don't think I have anything else of that sort. In general I don't know how to write for children; I write for them once in ten years and I don't like or even recognize the existence of so-called children's literature. One should give children only what is also

suitable for adults. Children read Andersen, *The Frigate Pallas*,[7] and Gogol eagerly, as do adults. One should not write for children but know how to select from what has already been written for adults, that is, from real artistic works. It is more expedient and straightforward to know what medicine to prescribe for a child, and in what doses, than to try to create some special medicine for him because he is a child. * * *

MAXIM GORKY

Anton Chekhov†

He once invited me to visit him in the village of Kuchuk-Koi, where he had a tiny plot of ground and a white, two-story house. He showed me over his "estate," talking animatedly all the time:

"If I had lots of money I would build a sanatorium here for sick village teachers. A building full of light, you know, very light, with big windows and high ceilings. I'd have a splendid library, all sorts of musical instruments, an apiary, a vegetable garden, an orchard. I'd have lectures on agronomy, meteorology, and so on—teachers ought to know everything, old man—everything!"

He broke off suddenly, coughed, cast an oblique glance at me, and smiled his sweet, gentle smile, a smile which had an irresistible charm, forcing one to follow his words with the keenest attention.

"Does it bore you to listen to my dreams? I love talking about this. If you only knew the absolute necessity for the Russian countryside of good, clever, educated teachers! In Russia we have simply got to create exceptional conditions for teachers, and that as soon as possible, since we realize that unless the people get an all-round education the state will collapse like a house built from insufficiently baked bricks. The teacher must be an actor, an artist, passionately in love with his work, and our teachers are navvies, half-educated individuals, who go to the village to teach children about as willingly as they would go to exile. They are famished, downtrodden, they live in perpetual fear of losing their livelihood. And the teacher ought to be the first man in the village, able to answer all the questions put to him by the peasants, to instill in the peasants a respect for his power worthy of attention and respect, whom no one will dare to shout at . . . to lower his dignity, as in our country everybody does—the village policeman, the rich shopkeeper, the priest, the school patron, the elder and that official who, though he is called a school inspector, busies himself, not over the improvement of conditions for education, but simply and solely over the

7. I. A. Goncharov's engrossing travelogue of his trip to the Far East (1856).
† From Maxim Gorky, *On Literature*, translated by Ivy Litvinov (Moscow, 1956), pp. 271–91.

carrying out district circulars to the letter. It's absurd to pay a niggardly pittance to one who is called upon to educate the people —to educate the people, mind! It is intolerable that such a one should go about in rags, shiver in a damp, dilapidated school, be poisoned by fumes from badly ventilated stoves, be always catching cold, and by the age of thirty be a mass of disease—laryngitis, rheumatism, tuberculosis. It's a disgrace to us! For nine or ten months in the year our teachers live the lives of hermits, without a soul to speak to, they grow stupid from loneliness, without books or amusements. And if they venture to invite friends to come and see them, people think they are disaffected—that idiotic word with which cunning folk terrify fools. . . . All this is disgusting . . . a kind of mockery of human beings doing a great and terribly important work. I tell you, when I meet a teacher I feel quite awkward in front of him—for his timidity, and for his shabbiness. I feel as if I myself were somehow to blame for the teacher's wretched state—I do, really!"

Pausing for a moment, he threw out his arm and said softly:

"What an absurd, clumsy country our Russia is!"

A shadow of profound sorrow darkened his fine eyes, and a fine network of wrinkles showed at the corners, deepening his glance. He looked around him and began making fun of himself.

"There you are—I've treated you to a full-length leading article from a liberal newspaper. Come on, I'll give you some tea as a reward for your patience. . . ."

This was often the way with him. One moment he would be talking with warmth, gravity and sincerity, and the next, he would be laughing at himself and his own words. And beneath this gentle, sorrowful laughter could be felt the subtle scepticism of a man who knew the value of words, the value of dreams. There was a shade of his attractive modesty, his intuitive delicacy in this laughter, too.

We walked back to the house in silence. It was a warm, bright day; the sound of waves sparkling in the vivid rays of the sun, could be heard. In the valley, a dog was squealing its delight about something. Chekhov took me by the arm and said slowly, his speech interrupted by coughs:

"It's disgraceful and very sad, but it is true—there are many people who envy dogs. . . ."

And then he added, laughing:

"Everything I say today sounds senile—I must be getting old."

Again and again I would hear from him:

"Listen—a teacher has just arrived . . . he's ill, he has a wife— you couldn't do anything for him, could you? I've fixed him up for the moment. . . ."

Or:

"Listen, Gorky! A teacher wants to meet you. He is bedridden, sick. Won't you go to see him?"

Or:

"There's a schoolmistress asking for books to be sent. . . ."

Sometimes I would find this "teacher" in his house—usually someone flushed with the consciousness of his own awkwardness, sitting on the edge of a chair, sweating and picking his words, trying to speak as smoothly and "educatedly" as he could, or, with the over-familiarity of a morbidly shy individual, entirely absorbed in the desire not to appear stupid in the eyes of the writer, showering Anton Pavlovich with questions that had probably only just come into his head.

Anton Pavlovich would listen attentively to the clumsy speech; and a smile would light up his mournful eyes, setting the wrinkles on his temples in play, and in his deep, gentle, hushed voice, he would begin speaking, using simple, clear words, words close to life, which immediately put his visitor at ease, so that he stopped trying to be clever and consequently became both cleverer and more interesting. . . .

I remember one of these teachers—tall, lean, with a sallow, emaciated face and a long, hooked nose drooping mournfully towards his chin—he sat opposite Anton Pavlovich, gazing steadily into his face with his dark eyes, and droning on in a morose bass:

"Impressions of this sort gathered from living conditions throughout the period of the pedagogical season accumulate in a psychic conglomerate which entirely eliminates the slightest possibility of an objective attitude to the world around. The world is, of course, nothing but our own conception of it. . . ."

Here he embarked upon philosophical ground, slipping about like a drunk man on ice.

"Tell me," asked Chekhov, quietly and kindly, "who is it that beats the children in your district?"

The teacher leaped from his chair and began waving his arms indignantly.

"What? Me? Never! *Beat* them?"

And he snorted offendedly.

"Don't get upset," continued Anton Pavlovich, smiling to pacify him. "Did I say it was you? But I remember reading in the paper that there was someone who beat the school children in your district. . . ."

The teacher sat down again, mopped his perspiring countenance, and sighed in relief, saying in his deep bass:

"Quite right. There was a case. It was Makarov. And no wonder! It's fantastic, but it is understandable. He's married, has four children, his wife is ill, he is, too, consumptive, his salary is twenty rubles . . . and the school's like a cellar, with only one room for the teacher. In such circumstances one would cuff an angel from heaven for the slightest misdemeanor, and the pupils are far from angels, believe me!"

And this man, who had the moment before been trying to impress Chekhov by his stock of grand words, suddenly, wagging his hooked nose ominously, came out with words like stones, simple and heavy, words which threw a bright light on the accursed, sinister truth of the life going on in the Russian village. . . .

When taking leave of his host the teacher pressed Chekhov's small, dry-skinned hand with its slender fingers in both of his.

"I went to see you as if I were going to see a superior," he said, "shaking in my shoes. I swelled like a turkey-cock, determined to show you that I was worth something too, and I go away as if I were leaving a good, close friend, who understands everything. What a great thing it is—to understand everything! Thank you! I'm going. I take away with me a good, precious thought: great people are simpler, they understand more, they are closer to us poor mortals than the small fry we live amidst. Good-bye, I shall never forget you."

His nose quivered, his lips relaxed in a nice smile, and he added unexpectedly:

"Bad people are unfortunate, too—damn them!"

When he had gone Anton Pavlovich, following him with his eyes, smiled, and said: "Nice chap. He won't be teaching long, though."

"Why not?"

"They'll hound him out . . . get rid of him."

After a pause he added, in low, gentle tones:

"In Russia an honest man is something like a chimney-sweep for nurses to frighten little children with. . . ."

It seems to me that in the presence of Anton Pavlovich everyone felt an unconscious desire to be simpler, more truthful, more himself, and I had many opportunities of observing how people threw off their attire of grand bookish phrases, fashionable expressions, and all the rest of the cheap trifles with which Russians, in their anxiety to appear Europeans, adorn themselves, as savages deck themselves with shells and fishes' teeth. Anton Pavlovich was not fond of fishes teeth and cocks' feathers; all that is tawdry, tinkling, alien, donned by human beings for the sake of an "imposing appearance," embarrassed him, and I noticed that whenever he met with one of these dressed-up individuals he felt an overmastering impulse to free him from his ponderous and superfluous trappings, distorting the true face and living soul of his interlocutor. All his life Anton Pavlovich lived the life of the soul, was always himself, inwardly free, and took no notice of what some expected, and others—less delicate—demanded of Anton Chekhov. He did not like conversations on "lofty" subjects—conversations which Russians, in the simplicity of their hearts, find so amusing, forgetting that it is absurd, and not in the least witty, to talk about the velvet apparel of the future, while not even possessing in the present a decent pair of trousers.

Of a beautiful simplicity himself, he loved all that was simple, real, sincere, and he had a way of his own of making others simple.

He was once visited by three extremely dressy ladies. Filling his room with the rustle of silk petticoats and the fragrance of heady perfumes, they seated themselves pompously opposite their host and, feigning an intense interest in politics, began "putting questions" to him.

"How do you think the war will end, Anton Pavlovich?"

Anton Pavlovich coughed, paused for thought and replied in his soft, grave, kindly voice:

"No doubt in peace."

"That, of course. But who will win? The Greeks or the Turks?"

"It seems to me that the stronger side will win."

"And which do you consider the stronger side?" the ladies asked in one voice.

"The side which is better fed and better educated."

"Isn't he witty?" cried one of the ladies.

"And which do you prefer—the Greeks or the Turks?" asked another.

Anton Pavlovich looked at her kindly and replied with his meek, courteous smile:

"I like fruit pastilles—do you?"

"Oh, yes!" cried the lady eagerly.

"They have such a delicious taste," corroborated the other gravely.

And all three began an animated conversation about fruit pastilles, displaying marvellous erudition and intricate knowledge of the subject. They were obviously delighted not to have to tax their brains and pretend a serious interest in Turks and Greeks, to whom till the present moment they had never given a thought.

On leaving, they promised Anton Pavlovich gaily:

"We're going to send you a box of fruit pastilles."

"You had a nice talk," I remarked, when they had gone.

Anton Pavlovich laughed softly.

"Everyone ought to speak in his own language," he said.

Another time I found a good-looking young assistant procurator in his room. Standing in front of Chekhov, tossing back his curly head, he was saying in confident tones:

"In your *Malefactor*[1] you confront me with an extremely complex problem, Anton Pavlovich. If I recognize in Denis Grigoryev the existence of a deliberate will to evil, it is my duty to commit Denis to jail unhesitatingly, since the interests of society demand it. But he is a savage, he is unconscious of the criminality of his act, I am sorry for him. If I regard him as a subject acting irrationally and yield to feelings of pity, how am I to guarantee society that Denis will not again unscrew the bolts and derail the train? That is the question. What is to be done?"

He paused, throwing himself back in his chair and fixing a searching glance on the face of Anton Pavlovich. His uniform was brand new, and the buttons down the front of it gleamed as confidently and stupidly as the eyes in the freshly-washed countenance of the youthful zealot.

"If I were the judge," said Anton Pavlovich gravely, "I would have acquitted Denis."

"On what grounds?"

"I would have said to him: 'You haven't grown into a type of the conscious criminal yet, Denis, go and do so.'"

The lawyer laughed, but immediately recovered his portentous gravity and continued:

"No, esteemed Anton Pavlovich, the problem you have raised can only be solved in the interests of society, the life and property of which I am called upon to protect. Denis is a savage, it is true, but he is a criminal, and therein lies the truth."

"Do you like listening to the gramophone?" asked Anton Pavlovich suddenly.

"Oh, yes! Very much. It's a marvellous invention," the youth hastened to reply.

"And I can't bear the gramophone," admitted Anton Pavlovich sorrowfully.

"Why not?"

"Oh well, it talks and sings, without feeling anything. All the sounds coming from it are so empty and lifeless. And do you go in for photography?"

The lawyer turned out to be a passionate admirer of photography. He began immediately to speak about it with enthusiasm, no longer taking the slightest interest in the gramophone, despite his own likeness to that "marvellous invention," which Chekhov had noticed with such subtlety and precision. Once again I saw beneath the uniform a lively and not uninteresting human being, one who was still as young in the ways of life as a puppy taken hunting.

1. A story (1885), also translated as *The Culprit*, about a man who is unable to understand why he cannot unscrew railroad bolts and use them for sinkers. [*Editor.*]

After seeing the young man out, Anton Pavlovich said morosely:

"And it's pimples like that on the backside of justice who dispose of the destinies of men."

After a pause he added: "Prosecutors are always fond of fishing. Especially for perch."

He had the art of exposing vulgarity everywhere, an art which can only be mastered by one whose own demands on life are very high, and which springs from the ardent desire to see simplicity, beauty and harmony in man. He was a severe and merciless judge of vulgarity.

Someone said in his presence that the editor of a popular magazine, a man perpetually talking about the necessity for love and sympathy for others, had insulted a railway guard without the slightest provocation, and was in the habit of treating his subordinates roughly.

"Naturally," said Anton Pavlovich, with a grim chuckle. "He's an aristocrat, a cultivated man . . . he went to a seminary. His father went about in bast shoes, but *he* wears patent-leather boots."

And the tone in which these words were spoken at once dismissed the "aristocrat" as a mediocre and ridiculous individual.

"A very gifted person," he said of a certain journalist. "His writing is always so lofty, so humane . . . saccharine. He calls his wife a fool in front of people. His servants sleep in a damp room, and they all develop rheumatism. . . ."

"Do you like So-and-So, Anton Pavlovich?"

"Oh, yes. A nice man," replies Anton Pavlovich, coughing. "He knows everything. He reads a lot. He took three books of mine and never returned them. A bit absent-minded, tells you one day that you're a fine fellow, and the next tells someone else that you stole the black silk socks with blue stripes of your mistress's husband."

Someone was heard to complain in his presence that the "serious" sections of the "heavy" magazines were dull and difficult.

"Just don't read those articles," Anton Pavlovich advised with the utmost conviction. "They're co-operative literature . . . the literature written by Messrs. Krasnov, Chernov and Belov [Red, Black and White]. One writes an article, the other criticizes it, and the third reconciles the illogicalities of the first two. It's like playing vint with a dummy. But why the reader needs all this none of them ask themselves."

He was once visited by a stout lady, healthy, good-looking, well-dressed, who immediately began to talk "the Chekhov way."

"Life is so dull, Anton Pavlovich. Everything is so dingy—people, the sky, the sea, even flowers seem dingy to me. And there's nothing to wish for—my heart aches. It's like a kind of disease. . . ."

"It is a disease," said Anton Pavlovich energetically. "That's just what it is. The Latin name for it is morbus sham-itis."

Fortunately for herself the lady did not understand Latin, or perhaps she pretended not to.

"Critics are like horse-flies which hinder the horses in their ploughing of the soil," he said, with his wise chuckle. "The muscles of the horse are as taut as fiddle-strings, and suddenly a horse-fly alights on its croup, buzzing and stinging. The horse's skin quivers, it waves its tail. What is the fly buzzing about? It probably doesn't know itself. It simply has a restless nature and wants to make itself felt—'I'm alive, too, you know!' it seems to say. 'Look, I know how to buzz, there's nothing I can't buzz about!' I've been reading reviews of my stories for twenty-five years, and can't remember a single useful point in any of them, or the slightest good advice. The only reviewer who ever made an impression on me was Skabichev-sky, who prophesied that I would die drunk in the bottom of a ditch. . . ."

A subtle mockery almost always twinkled gently in his gray mournful eyes, but occasionally these eyes would become cold, keen, harsh, and at such moments a hard note would creep into the smooth, cordial tones of his voice, and then I felt that this modest, kindly man could stand up against any hostile force, stand up firmly, without knuckling under to it.

It sometimes seemed to me that there was a shade of hopelessness in his attitude to others, something akin to a cold, still despair.

"The Russian is a strange being," he said once. "He is like a sieve, he can hold nothing for long. In his youth he crams himself eagerly with everything that comes his way, and by the time he is thirty nothing is left of it all but a heap of colorless rubbish. If one wants to lead a good life, a human life, one must work. Work with love and with faith. And we don't know how to do that in our country. An architect, having built two or three decent houses, sits down to play cards for the rest of his life or hangs about the backstage of a theatre. As soon as a doctor acquires a practice he stops keeping up with science, never reads anything but *Therapeutic News* and by the age of forty is firmly convinced that all diseases come from colds. I have never met a single official who had even the slightest idea of the significance of his work—they usually dig themselves in in the capital, or some provincial town, and invent papers which they dispatch to Zmiyev and Smorgon for fulfilment. And whose freedom of movement is impeded in Zmiyev or Smorgon by these documents the official no more cares than an atheist does about the torments of hell. Having made a name by a successful defense the barrister ceases to bother about the defense of truth and does nothing but defend the rights of property, put money on horses, eat oysters, and pass himself off as a connoisseur of all the arts. An actor, having performed two or three parts with fair success, no longer learns his parts, but puts on a top hat and considers himself a genius. Russia is a land of greedy idlers. People eat and drink enormously, love to sleep in the daytime, and snore in their sleep. They marry for the sake of order in their homes, and take a mistress for the sake of social prestige. Their psychology is a dog's psychology. Beat them and they squeal meekly and sneak off to their kennels. Caress them, and they lie on their backs with their paws up, wagging their tails."

A cold, sorrowful contempt underlay these words. But while despising, he could pity, and when anyone was abused in his presence, Anton Pavlovich was sure to stick up for him.

"Come now! He's an old man, he's seventy. . . ."

Or:

"He's still young, it's just his stupidity. . . ."

And when he spoke like this I could see no signs of disgust in his face. . . .

When one is young, vulgarity seems to be simply amusing and insignificant, but it gradually surrounds the individual, its grey mist creeping into his brains and blood, like poison or charcoal fumes, till he becomes like an old tavern-sign, eaten up with rust—there seems to be something depicted on it, but what, it is impossible to make out.

From the very first Anton Pavlovich managed to reveal, in the grey ocean of vulgarity, its tragically sombre jokes. One only has to read his "humorous" stories carefully, to realize how much that was cruel was seen and shame-facedly concealed by the author in comic narrative and situations.

He had an almost virginal modesty, he could never bring himself to challenge people loudly and openly: "Be more decent—can't you!" vainly trusting that they would themselves realize the urgent necessity for being more decent. Detesting all that was vulgar and unclean, he described the seamy side of life in the lofty language of the poet, with the gentle smile of the humorist, and the bitter inner reproach beneath the polished surface of his stories is scarcely noticeable.

* * *

No one ever understood the tragic nature of life's trifles so clearly and intuitively as Chekhov did, never before has a writer been able to hold up to human beings such a ruthlessly truthful picture of all that was shameful and pitiable in the dingy chaos of middle-class life.

His enemy was vulgarity. All his life he fought against it, held it up to scorn, depicted it with a keen impartial pen, discovering the fungus of vulgarity even where, at first glance, everything seemed to be ordered for the best, the most convenient, and even brilliant. And vulgarity got back on him with an ugly trick when his dead body—the body of a poet—was sent to Moscow in an oyster wagon.

This dingy green wagon strikes me as the broad triumphant grin of vulgarity at its weary foe, and the innumerable "reminiscences" of the yellow press—mere hypocritical grief, behind which I seem to feel the cold, stinking breath of that very vulgarity which secretly rejoiced in the death of its enemy.

* * *

The coffin of the writer, so "tenderly loved" by Moscow, was brought in a green wagon bearing the inscription "Oysters" in big letters on the door. A section of the small crowd which had gathered at the station to meet the writer followed the coffin of General Keller just arrived from Manchuria, and wondered why Chekhov was being carried to his grave to the music of a military band. When the mistake was discovered certain genial persons began laughing and sniggering. Chekhov's coffin was followed by about a hundred people, not more. Two lawyers stand out in my memory, both in new boots and gaily patterned ties, like bridegrooms. Walking behind them I heard one of them, V. A. Maklakov, talking about the cleverness of dogs, and the other, whom I did not know, boasting of the convenience of his summer cottage and the beauty of its environments. And some lady in a purple dress, holding up a lace sunshade, was assuring an old gentleman in horn-rimmed spectacles:

"Oh, he was such a darling, and so witty. . . ."

The old gentleman coughed incredulously. It was a hot, dusty day. The procession was headed by a stout police officer on a stout white horse. All this and much more was disgustingly vulgar and highly inappropriate to the memory of the great and subtle artist.

* * *

He spoke little and reluctantly about his literary work. I had almost said with the same virginal reserve with which he spoke about Lev Tolstoi. Very occasionally, when in spirits, he would relate the plot of a story, chuckling—it was always a humorous story.

"I say, I'm going to write a story about a schoolmistress, an atheist—she adores Darwin, is convinced of the necessity for fighting the prejudices and superstitions of the people, and herself goes to the bath-house at midnight to scald a black cat to get a wishbone for attracting a man and arousing his love—there is such a bone, you know. . . ."

He always spoke of his plays as "amusing," and really seemed to be sincerely convinced that he wrote "amusing plays." No doubt

Savva Morozov was repeating Chekhov's own words when he stub-bornly maintained: "Chekhov's plays must be produced as lyrical comedies."

But to literature in general he always gave the keenest attention, especially touching in the case of "beginners." He read the lengthy manuscripts of B. Lazarevsky, N. Oliger[2] and many others with admirable patience.

"We need more writers," he said. "Literature is still a new thing in our daily life, even for the 'elect.' There is a writer for every two hundred and twenty-six people in Norway, and here only one for every million."

His disease sometimes called into being a hypochondriacal, or even a misanthropic, mood. At such times he would be extremely critical, and very hard to get on with.

One day, lying on the sofa, giving dry coughs, and playing with the thermometer, he said:

"To live simply to die is by no means amusing, but to live with the knowledge that you will die before your time, that really is idiotic. . . ."

Another time, seated at the open window and gazing out into the distance, at the sea, he suddenly said peevishly:

"We are accustomed to live in hopes of good weather, a good harvest, a nice love-affair, hopes of becoming rich or getting the office of chief of police, but I've never noticed anyone hoping to get wiser. We say to ourselves: it'll be better under a new tsar, and in two hundred years it'll be still better, and nobody tries to make this good time come tomorrow. On the whole, life gets more and more complex every day and moves on at its own sweet will, and people get more and more stupid, and get isolated from life in ever-increasing numbers."

After a pause he added, wrinkling up his forehead:

"Like crippled beggars in a religious procession."

He was a doctor, and the illness of a doctor is always worse than the illnesses of his patients. The patients only feel, but the doctor, as well as feeling, has a pretty good idea of the destructive effect of the disease on his constitution. This is a case in which knowledge brings death nearer.

His eyes were very fine when he laughed—there was a feminine gentleness in them then, something soft and tender. And his laugh-ter, almost noiseless, had something particularly attractive about it.

2. B. A. Lazarevsky (1871–1936) and N. F. Oliger (1882–1917), minor writers, were imitators of Chekhov. [*Editor.*]

When he laughed he really enjoyed himself. I have never known anybody who could laugh so "spiritually."

Indecent stories never made him laugh.

* * *

When he spoke about Tolstoi, there was always an almost imperceptible smile, at once tender and shy, in his eyes, and he lowered his voice, as if speaking of something fragile and mysterious, something that must be handled with care and affection.

He constantly deplored the fact that there was no Eckermann[3] by Tolstoi's side, to jot down the keen, unexpected, and frequently contradictory utterances of the old sage.

"*You* ought to do it," he assured Sulerzhitsky. "Tolstoi's so fond of you, he talks such a lot to you, and says such wonderful things."

Of Suler himself, Chekhov said to me:

"He is a wise child."

Very well said.

I once heard Tolstoi praise a story of Chekhov's—*The Darling* I think it was.

"It's like lace woven by a virtuous maiden," he said. "There used to be girl lace-makers in the old days, who, their whole lives long, wove their dreams of happiness into the pattern. They wove their fondest dreams, their lace was saturated with vague, pure aspirations of love." Tolstoi spoke with true emotion, with tears in his eyes.

But that day Chekhov had a temperature, and sat with his head bent, vivid spots of color on his cheeks, carefully wiping his pince-nez. He said nothing for some time, and at last, sighing, said softly and awkwardly: "There are misprints in it."

Much could be written of Chekhov, but this would require close, precise narration, and that is what I'm no good at. He should be written about as he himself wrote *The Steppe*, a fragrant, open-air, very Russian story, pensive and wistful. A story for one's self.

It does one good to remember a man like that, it is like a sudden visitation of cheerfulness, it gives a clear meaning to life again.

Man is the axis of the Universe.

And his vices, you ask, his shortcomings?

We all hunger for the love of our fellow creatures, and when one is hungry, even a half-baked loaf tastes sweet.

3. J. P. Eckermann's *Conversations with Goethe* (published in 1836–48), are a major source for Goethe's opinions in his last years. [*Editor.*]

Criticism

D. S. MIRSKY

Chekhov†

Anton Pavlovich Chekhov (1860–1904) was born at Taganrog, on the sea of Azov. His grandfather had been a serf * * * but had acquired considerable wealth by trade and was able to purchase his freedom and that of all his family. Chekhov's parents were simple, half-educated, very religious people, with a strong family feeling. The family consisted of several sons and a daughter. They were all given a liberal education. Anton, who was the youngest but one, was sent to the gymnasium (secondary school) of Taganrog. But while he was there the prosperity of the Chekhovs came to an end. The building of a railway through the neighboring Rostov was a severe blow to the commerce of Taganrog, and Paul Chekhov soon saw himself forced to close his business. In 1876 he left Taganrog and went to seek employment in Moscow. Anton remained alone in Taganrog. In 1879 he finished his time at the gymnasium and went to Moscow to join his family. He was matriculated as a student of the Faculty of Medicine. After the normal course of five years, he took his degree in 1884. From his arrival in Moscow to his death he never parted from his parents and sister, and as his literary income soon became important, he early became the mainstay of his family. The Chekhovs were an exceptionally united family—a case exceedingly rare among the intelligentsia, and owing, of course, to their peasant and merchant origins.

Chekhov began working in the comic papers the year he came to Moscow, and before he left the university he had become one of their most welcome contributors. So on taking his degree, he did not settle down to practice as a doctor, but fell back on his literary work for subsistence. In 1886 some of his comic stories were collected in book form. The book had an immediate success with the public and was soon followed by another volume of comic stories. The critics, especially the radical critics, took little notice of the book, but it attracted the attention of two influential men of letters —the veteran novelist Grigorovich and Suvorin, editor of the pro-government *New Times*, the largest daily paper of the day. The shrewd and clever Suvorin at once saw the great possibilities of Chekhov and invited him to contribute to his paper, where he even

† From D. S. Mirsky, *A History of Russian Literature* (New York: Knopf, 1949), Vol. II, p. 353–67. This essay originally appeared in 1926.) Titles of stories in the critical essays conform to those in this collection, but quotations may differ.

started a special weekly literary supplement for Chekhov. They became close friends, and in Chekhov's correspondence his letters to Suvorin form undoubtedly the most interesting part. Chekhov had now gained a firm footing in "big literature" and was free from the tyranny of the comic papers. This change in his social position was followed by a change in his work—he abandoned comic writing and developed the style that is most characteristically his. This change is apparent in the stories written by him in 1886–7. At the same time Chekhov wrote his first play, *Ivanov,* which was produced in Moscow in December 1887 and in Petersburg a year later. It is characteristic of this period of transition that Chekhov continued working at these pieces after their first publication; The *Steppe* and *Ivanov* that are now reproduced in his *Works* are very different from what first appeared in 1887. Henceforward Chekhov's life was rather uneventful, and what events there were, are closely connected with his writings. An isolated episode was his journey to Sakhalin, the Russian Botany Bay. He went there in 1890, traveling through Siberia (before the days of the Trans-Siberian) and returning by sea via Ceylon. He made a very thorough investigation of convict life and published the result of it in a separate book (*Sakhalin Island,* 1891). It is remarkable for its thoroughness, objectivity, and impartiality, and is an important historical document. It is supposed to have influenced certain reforms in prison life introduced in 1892. This journey was Chekhov's greatest practical contribution to the humanitarianism that was so near to his heart. In private life he was also very kindhearted and generous. He gave away much of his money. His native town of Taganrog was the recipient of a library and a museum from him.

In 1891 Chekhov was rich enough to buy a piece of land at Melikhovo, some fifty miles south of Moscow. There he settled down with his parents, sister, and younger brother, and lived for six years. He took part in local life and spent much money on local improvements. In 1892–3, during the cholera epidemic, he worked as the head of a sanitary district. Here it was he wrote many of his best and most mature stories. He remained at Melikhovo till 1897, when the state of his health forced him to move. Consumption had set in, and he had to spend the rest of his life mainly between the south coast of the Crimea and foreign—French and German— health resorts. This was not the only change in his life. All his surroundings changed, owing to his new connection with the Moscow Art Theater and his more decided political orientation towards the left. This latter led to his breach with Suvorin, to whom he wrote a very angry letter in connection with the Dreyfus affair (even in Russia the *Affaire* was a hotbed of quarrel!) and to his friendship with the younger generation of writers, headed by Gorky and distinctly revolutionary. During these last years (especially after 1900, when he settled down in Yalta) he saw much of Tolstoy. In the popular opinion of that time, Chekhov, Gorky, and Tolstoy formed a sort of sacred trinity symbolizing all that was best in independent Russia as opposed to the dark forces of Tsarism. Chekhov lived up to his liberal reputation, and when the Academy, following a hint of the government, excluded Gorky from its membership almost immmediately after electing him, Chekhov, like the veteran socialist Korolenko, resigned his membership. But from the literary point of view this phase is hardly of much importance—it introduced no new elements into his work. Far more important is his connection with the Art Theater. After *Ivanov*, Chekhov had written several light one-act comedies that had a considerable success with the public but added little to his intrinsic achievement. In 1895 he turned once more to serious drama and wrote *The Seagull* (as it is called in the English translation, rather absurdly—the Russian *Chayka* means just *Gull*). It was produced at the State Theater of Petersburg in 1896. It was badly understood by the actors and badly acted. The first night was a smashing failure. The play was hissed down, and the author, confounded by his defeat, left the theater after the second act and escaped to Melikhovo, vowing never again to write a play. Meanwhile K. S. Stanislavsky (Alekseyev), a wealthy merchant of Moscow, and the dramatist Vladimir Nemirovich-Danchenko founded the Art Theater, which was to be such an important landmark in the history of the Russian stage. They succeeded in getting *The Seagull* for one of their first productions. The cast worked at it with energy and understanding, and when the play was acted by them in 1898, it proved a triumphant success. Chekhov turned with new energy towards dramatic writing, and wrote his most famous plays with a direct view to Stanislavsky's casts. *Uncle Vanya* (which had been planned as early as 1888) was produced in 1900, *The Three Sisters* in 1901, and *The Cherry Orchard* in January 1904. Each play was a greater triumph than the preceding one. There was complete harmony among playwright, actors, and public. Chekhov's fame was at its height. However, he did not become so rich as to compare with Kipling, or D'Annunzio, or even with Gorky. For like his favorite heroes, he was eminently unpractical: in 1899 he sold all the works he had hitherto written to the publisher Marx for 75,000 rubles ($37,500). It turned out after the transaction that Marx was not aware of the extent of his writings—he had reckoned on four volumes of short stories, and he had unconsciously bought nine! In 1901 Chekhov married an actress of the Art Theater, Olga L. Knipper; so his life became further changed. These last years he lived mostly at Yalta, where he had built a villa. He was constantly besieged by importunate admirers, with whom he was very patient and kind. In June 1904 his illness had so advanced that he was sent by the doctors to Badenweiler, a small health resort in the Black Forest, where he died. His body was brought to Moscow and buried by the side of his father, who had preceded him in 1899.

Chekhov's literary career falls into two distinct periods: before and after 1886.[1] The English reader and the more "literary" Russian public know him by his later work, but it may be safely asserted that a much greater number of Russians know him rather as the author of his early comic stories than as the author of *My Life* and *Three Sisters*. It is a characteristic fact that many of his most popular and typical comic stories, precisely those which are sure to be known to every middle-class or semi-educated Russian (for example, *A Horse Name, Vint, The Complaint Ledger, Surgery*), were not translated into English. It is true that some of these stories are very difficult to translate, so topical and national are the jokes. But it is also evident that the English-speaking admirer of Chekhov has no taste for this buffoonery but looks to Chekhov for commodities of a very different description. The level of the comic papers in which Chekhov wrote was by no means a high one. They were a sanctuary of every kind of vulgarity and bad taste. Their buffoonery was vulgar and meaningless. They lacked the noble gift of nonsense, which of all things elevates man nearest the gods; they lacked wit, restraint, and grace. It was mere trivial buffoonery, and Chekhov's stories stand in no striking contrast to their general background. Except for a higher degree of craftsmanship, they are of a piece with the rest. Their dominant note is an uninspired sneer at the weaknesses and follies of mankind, and it would need a more than lynx-eyed critic to discern in them the note of human sympathy and of the higher humor that is so familiar to the reader of Chekhov's mature work. The great majority of these stories were never reprinted by Chekhov, but still the first and second volumes of his collected edition contain several dozen of the kind. Only a few—and all of them of a less crude variety—have had the honor of an English translation. But even in the crudest, Chekhov stands out as a superior craftsman, and in the economy of his means there is a promise of *Sleepy* and *At Christmas-time*. Before long, Chekhov began to deviate from the straight line imposed on him by the comic papers, and as early as 1886 he could write such a story as *The Chorus Girl*, which may yet be a little primitive and clumsy in its lyrical construction but on the whole stands almost on a level with the best of his mature work. *Parti-colored Stories*, which appeared in 1886 and laid the foundation of Chekhov's reputation in the literary circles, contained, besides many exercises in crude buffoonery, stories of a different kind that presented a gay appearance but were sad

---

1. A great inconvenience of the English edition of Chekhov is that it entirely disregards dates and arranges the tales in an arbitrary order. [Mirsky refers to the edition in thirteen volumes translated by Constance Garnett.—*Editor*.]

in substance—and that answered admirably to the hackneyed phrase of Russian critics, "tears through laughter." Such, for instance, is *Misery*: on a wet winter night a cabman who has just lost his son tries to tell his story to one after another of his fares and does not succeed in kindling their sympathy.

In 1886, as had been said, Chekhov was able to free himself from the comic papers and could now develop a new style that had begun to assert itself somewhat earlier. This style was (and remained) essentially poetical, but it was some time before he finally settled the main lines of what was to be the characteristic Chekhovian story. In his stories of 1886–8 there are many elements that have been yet imperfectly blended—a strain of descriptive journalism (in its most unadulterated form in *Uprooted*); pure anecdote, sometimes just ironical (*The First-Class Passenger*), sometimes poignantly tragicomical (*Vanka*); the lyrical expression of atmosphere (*The Steppe, Happiness*); psychological studies of morbid experience (*Typhus*); parables and moralities laid out in a conventional, un-Russian surrounding (*The Bet, A Story without a Title*). But already one of the favorite and most characteristic themes asserts its domination—the mutual lack of understanding between human beings, the impossibility for one person to feel in tune with another. *The Privy Councilor, The Post, The Name-Day Party, The Princess,* are all based on this idea—which becomes something like the leitmotiv of all Chekhov's later work. The most typical stories of this period are all located in the country of his early life, the steppe between the Sea of Azov and the Donets. These are *The Steppe, Happiness, The Horse-Stealers*. They are planned as lyrical symphonies (though the last one is also an anecdote). Their dominant note is superstition, the vague terror (Chekhov makes it poetical) before the presences that haunt the dark and empty steppe, the profound uninterestingness and poverty of the steppe peasant's life, a vague hope of a happiness that may be discovered, with the help of dark powers, in some ancient treasure mound. *The Steppe*, at which Chekhov worked much and to which he returned again after its publication, is the central thing in this period. It lacks the wonderful architecture of his short stories—it is a lyrical poem, but a poem made out of the substance of trivial, dull, and dusky life. The long, monotonous, uneventful journey of a little boy over the endless steppe from his native village to a distant town is drawn out in a hundred pages to form a languid, melodious, and tedious lullaby. A brighter aspect of Chekhov's lyrical art is in *Easter Eve*. The monk on night duty on the ferryboat tells a passenger about his dead fellow monk, who had the rare gift of writing lauds to the saints. He describes with loving detail the technique of this art, and one discerns Chekhov's sincere sympathy for this unnoticed, unwanted, quiet, and unambitious fellow craftsman. To the same period belongs *Kashtanka*, the delightful history of a dog that was kidnaped by a circus clown to form part of a troupe of performing animals and escaped to her old master in the middle of a performance. The story is a wonderful blend of humor and poetry, and though it certainly sentimentalizes and humanizes its animals, one cannot help recognizing it as a masterpiece. Another little gem is *Sleepy*, a real masterpiece of concentration, economy, and powerful effectiveness.[2]

In some stories of this period we find already the manner that is pre-eminently Chekhovian. The earliest story where it is quite distinctly discernible is *The Name-Day Party* (1887), on which Chekhov himself laid a great value, but which is not yet perfect; he confesses in a letter to Suvorin that he "would gladly have spent six months over *The Name-Day Party*. . . . But what am I to do? I begin a story on September 10th with the thought that I must finish it by October 5th at the latest; if I don't, I shall fail the editor and be left without money. I let myself go at the beginning and write with an easy mind; but by the time I get to the middle, I begin to grow timid and fear that my story will be too long. . . . This is why the beginning of my stories is always very promising . . . the middle is huddled and timid, and the end is, as in a short sketch, like fireworks."[3] But the essential of Chekhov's mature style is unmistakably present. It is the "biography" of a mood developing under the trivial pinpricks of life, but owing in substance to a deep-lying, physiological or psychological cause (in this case the woman's pregnancy). A *Dreary Story*, published in 1889, may be considered the starting point of the mature period. The leitmotiv of mutual isolation is brought out with great power. We may date the meaning that has come to be associated in Russia with the words "Chekhovian state of mind" (*Chekhovskoye nastroyenie*) from A *Dreary Story*. The atmosphere of the story is produced by the professor's deep and growing disillusionment as to himself and the life around him, the gradual loss of faith in his vocation, the gradual drifting apart of people linked together by life. The professor realizes the meaninglessness of his life—and the "giftlessness" (*bezdarnost*, a characteristically Chekhovian word) and dullness of all that surrounds him. His only remaining friend, his former ward Katya, an unsuccessful disillusioned actress, breaks down under an intenser experience of the same feelings. And though his affection for her is sincere and genuine, and though he is suffering from the same causes as she is, he fails to find the necessary language to approach her. An unconquerable inhibition keeps him closed to her, and all he can say to her is:

2. Tolstoy is said to have held this story in high esteem, and one cannot help noticing a certain similarity it bears to his own masterpiece *Alyosha Gorshok*, written eighteen years later.

3. *Letters of Anton Tchehov*, translated by Constance Garnett (London: Chatto & Windus, 1920, p. 101.

"Let us have lunch, Katya."

"No, thank you," she answers coldly.

Another minute passes in silence.

"I don't like Kharkov," I say; "it is so gray here—such a gray town."

"Yes, perhaps. . . . It's ugly. . . . I am here not for long, passing through. I am going on to-day."

"Where?"

"To the Crimea . . . that is, to the Caucasus."

"Oh! For long?"

"I don't know."

"Katya gets up and, with a cold smile, holds out her hand, looking at me. I want to ask her: 'Then you won't be at my funeral?' but she does not look at me; her hand is cold and, as it were, strange. I escort her to the door in silence. She goes out, walks down the long corridor, without looking back. She knows that I am looking after her, and she will look back at the turn. No, she did not look round. I've seen her black dress for the last time; her steps have died away! . . . Farewell, my treasure!"[4]

This ending on a minor note is repeated in all Chekhov's subsequent stories and gives the keynote to his work.

A *Dreary Story* opens the succession of Chekhov's mature masterpieces. Besides the natural growth of his genius, he was now free to work longer over them than he could when he was writing *The Name-Day Party*. So his stories written in the nineties are almost without exception perfect works of art. It is mainly on the work of this period that Chekhov's reputation now rests. The principal stories written after 1889 are, in chronological order, *The Duel, Ward No. 6* (1892), *An Anonymous Story* (1893), *The Black Monk, The Teacher of Literature* (1894), *Three Years, Ariadne, Anna on the Neck, The House with the Mansard, My Life* (1895), *Peasants* (1897), *The Darling, Ionych, The Lady with the Dog* (1898), *The New Villa* (1899), *At Christmas-time, In the Ravine* (1900). After this date (it was the period of *Three Sisters* and *The Cherry Orchard*) he wrote only two stories, *The Bishop* (1902) and *Betrothed* (1903).

Chekhov's art has been called Psychological, but it is psychological in a very different sense from Tolstoy's, Dostoyevsky's, or Marcel Proust's. No writer excels him in conveying the mutual unsurpassable isolation of human beings and the impossibility of understanding each other. This idea forms the core of almost every one of his stories, but, in spite of this, Chekhov's characters are singularly lacking in individual personality. Personality is absent from his stories. His characters all speak (within class limits and apart from the little tricks of catchwords he lends them from time to time) the

4. *The Wife and Other Stories*, translated by Constance Garnett (New York, 1916–22), pp. 218–19.

same language, which is Chekhov's own. They cannot be recognized, as Tolstoy's and Dostoyevsky's can, by the mere *sound of their voices*. They are all alike, all made of the same material—"the common stuff of humanity"—and in this sense Chekhov is the most "democratic," the most "unanimist," of all writers. For of course the similarity of all his men and women is not a sign of weakness— it is the expression of his fundamental intuition of life as a homogeneous matter but cut out into water-tight compartments by the phenomenon of individuality. Like Stendhal and the French classicists, and unlike Tolstoy, Dostoyevsky, and Proust, Chekhov is a student of "man in general." But unlike the classicists, and like Proust, he fixes his attention on the infinitesimals, the "pinpricks" and "straws" of the soul. Stendhal deals in psychological "whole numbers." He traces the major, conscious, creative lines of psychical life. Chekhov concentrates on the "differentials" of mind, its minor, unconscious, involuntary, destructive, and dissolvent forces. As art, Chekhov's method is active—more active than, for instance, Proust's, for it is based on a stricter and a more conscious *choice* of material and a more complicated and elaborate disposition of it. But as "outlook," as "philosophy," it is profoundly passive and "non-resistant," for it is a surrender to the "micro-organisms," of the soul, to its destructive microbes. Hence the general impressions produced by the whole of Chekhov's work that he had a cult for inefficiency and weakness. For Chekhov has no other way of displaying his sympathy with his characters than to show in detail the process of their submission to their microbes. The strong man who does not succumb in this struggle, or who does not experience it, is always treated by Chekhov with less sympathy and comes out as the "villain of the play"—in so far as the word "villain" is at all applicable to the world Chekhov moves in. The strong man in this world of his is merely the insensate brute, with a skin thick enough not to feel the "pinpricks," which are the only important thing in life. Chekhov's art is constructive, But the construction he uses is not a narrative construction—it might rather be called musical; not, however, in the sense that his prose is melodious, for it is not. But his method of constructing a story is akin to the method used in music. His stories are at once fluid and precise. The lines along which he builds them are very complicated curves, but they have been calculated with the utmost precision. A story by him is a series of points marking out with precision the lines discerned by him in the tangled web of consciousness. Chekhov excels in the art of tracing the first stages of an emotional process; in indicating those first symptoms of a deviation when to the general eye, and to the conscious eye of the subject in question, the nascent curve still seems to coincide with a straight line. An infinitesimal touch, which at first hardly arrests the reader's attention, gives a hint at the direction the story is going to take. It is then repeated as a leitmotiv, and at each repetition the true equation of the curve becomes more apparent, and it ends by shooting away in a direction very different from that of the original straight line. Such stories as *The Teacher of Literature, Ionych,* and *The Lady with the Dog* are perfect examples of such emotional curves. The straight line, for instance, in *Ionych* is the doctor's love for Mlle Turkin; the curve, his subsidence into the egoistical complacency of a successful provincial career. In *The Teacher of Literature* the straight line is again the hero's love; the curve, his dormant dissatisfaction with selfish happiness and his intellectual ambition. In *The Lady with the Dog* the straight line is the hero's attitude towards his affair with the lady as a trivial and passing intrigue; the curve, his overwhelming and all-pervading love for her. In most of Chekhov's stories these constructive lines are complicated by a rich and mellow atmosphere, which he produces by the abundance of emotionally significant detail. The effect is poetical, even lyrical: as in a lyric, it is not interest in the development that the reader feels, but "infection" by the poet's mood. Chekhov's stories are lyrical monoliths; they cannot be dissected into episodes, for every episode is strictly conditioned by the whole and is without significance apart from it. In architectural unity Chekhov surpasses all Russian writers of the realistic age. Only in Pushkin and Lermontov do we find an equal or superior gift of design. Chekhov thought Lermontov's *Taman* was the best short story ever written, and this partiality was well founded. *Taman* forestalled Chekhov's method of lyrical construction. Only its air is colder and clearer than the mild and mellow "autumnal" atmosphere of Chekhov's world.

Two of his best stories, *My Life* and *In the Ravine,* stand somewhat apart from the rest of his mature work. *My Life* is the story of a Tolstoyan, and one cannot help thinking that in it Chekhov tried to approach the clearer and more intellectual style of Tolstoy. There are a directness of narrative and a thinness of atmosphere that are otherwise rare in Chekhov. In spite of this relative absence of atmosphere, it is perhaps his most poetically pregnant story. It is convincingly symbolical. The hero, his father, his sister, the Azhogins, and Anyuta Blagovo stand out with the distinctness of morality characters. The very vagueness and generality of its title helps to make it something like an *Everyman.* For poetical grasp and significance *My Life* may be recognized as the masterpiece of Chekhov—unless it is surpassed by *In the Ravine.* This, one of his last stories, is an amazing piece of work. The scene is the Moscow Industrial area—it is the history of a shopkeeper's family. It is remarkably free from all excess of detail, and the atmosphere is produced, with the help of only a few descriptive touches, by the movement of the story. It is infinitely rich in emotional and symbolical significance. What is rare in Chekhov—in both these stories there is an earnestness, a keenness of moral judgment that raises them above the average of his work. All Chekhov's work is symbolical, but in most of his stories the symbolism is less concrete and more vaguely suggestive. It is akin to Maeterlinck's, in spite of the vast difference of style between the Russian realist and the Belgian mystic. *Ward No. 6*, the darkest and most terrible of all Chekhov's stories, is an especially notable example of this suggestive symbolism. It is all the more suggestive for being strictly realistic. (The only time Chekhov attempted to step out of the limits of strict realism was when he wrote the only story that is quite certainly a failure—*The Black Monk*.) But this symbolism reached its full development in his plays, beginning with *The Seagull*.

* * *

Chekhov's English admirers think that everything is perfect in Chekhov. To find weak spots in him will seem blasphemy to them. Still it is only fair to point out these spots. I have already referred to the complete lack of individuality in his characters and in their way of speaking. This is not in itself a fault, for it belongs to his fundamental intuition of life, which recognizes no personality. But it is not a virtue. It is especially noticeable when he makes his characters speak at length on abstract subjects. How different from Dostoyevsky, who "felt ideas" and who made them so splendidly individual! Chekhov did not "feel ideas," and when his characters give expression to theirs, they speak a colorless and monotonous journalese. *The Duel* is especially disfigured by such harangues. This is perhaps Chekhov's tribute to a deep-rooted tradition of Russian intelligentsia literature. Their speeches may have had some emotional significance in their time but certainly have none today. Another serious shortcoming is Chekhov's Russian. It is colorless and lacks individuality. He had no feeling for words. No Russian writer of anything like his significance used a language so devoid of all raciness and nerve. This makes Chekhov (except for topical allusions, technical terms, and occasional catch-words) so easy to translate. Of all Russian writers, he has the least to fear from the treachery of translators.

Chekhov's direct influence on Russian literature was not important. The success of his short stories contributed to the great popularity of that form, which became the predominant form in Russian fiction. But Gorky, Kuprin, and Bunin, to name but the foremost of those who regarded him as their master, can hardly be recognized as his pupils. Certainly no one learned from him the art of constructing his stories. His dramas, which looked so easy to imitate, were imitated, but the style proved a pitfall. Today[1] Russian fiction is

1. Mirsky's essay was first published in 1926. Even then his comments must have seemed outrageously opinionated. Chekhov's stories retain their popularity in Russia as elsewhere. [*Editor.*]

quite free from any trance of Chekhov's influence. Some of the younger writers began, before the Revolution, as his more or less unintelligent imitators, but none of them remained true to him. In Russia, Chekhov has become a thing of the past—of a past remoter than even Turgenev, not to speak of Gogol or Leskov. Abroad, things stand differently. If Chekhov has had a genuine heir to the secrets of his art, it is in England, where Katherine Mansfield did what no Russian has done—learned from Chekhov without imitating him. In England, and to a lesser degree in France, the cult of Chekhov has become the hallmark of the highbrow intellectual. Curiously enough, in Russia, Chekhov was always regarded as a distinctly "lowbrow" writer; the self-conscious intellectual elite was always conspicuously cool to him. The highbrows of the beginning of the century even affected to (or sincerely did) despise him. His real stronghold was in the heart of the honest Philistine in the street. Nowadays Chekhov has of course become the common property of the nation. His place as a classic—a major classic, one of the "ten best"—is not challenged. But he is a classic who has been temporarily shelved.

A. B. DERMAN

Compositional Elements in Chekhov's Poetics†

1

Chekhov stands at the very forefront of those artists of the word who repeatedly proclaimed the principle of creative collaboration between the artist and the scientist, rather than merely using the resources made available by science in his work, resources used by everyone, including those who claim to shun them and to depend entirely on their intuition. As we have seen, in his autobiographical remarks as well, he sharply emphasized the role of science in his work.

There is something scientific in his very approach to the composition of a work. He carefully dissected composition into stages and worked out a methodology for the artistic execution of his conception in each part.

If Chekhov's poetics as a whole is polemical, that is, urges new methods against the old, it is most so particularly in regard to the first stages of composition, "exposition," "opening," the so-called "introduction," "prologue," etc., and its emphasis there is even paradoxical.

† From A. B. Derman, *O Masterstve Chekhova* [On Chekhov's craftsmanship] (Moscow, 1959), pp. 74–88. Translated by Ralph E. Matlaw.

His poetics of "exposition" consists essentially in his insistence that there be no "exposition" at all or that it consists at most of two or three lines. That was, of course, a totally revolutionary approach considering the reigning poetics of the time, Turgenev's—to name it after its strongest representative—who in his main and largest works, that is, in his novels, devoted dozens of pages to a retrospective description of his characters' lives before their appearance on the scene. Perhaps, too, since Chekhov wrote no novels, since the short story and the tale are the main forms of his work, the very character of his formal demands was adapted to the story or the short tale.

Yet unquestionably the main reason for Chekhov's sharp hostility to more or less extended "expositions" was different: they seemed superfluous and unnecessary to Chekhov, and contradicted his conception of the active reader. He supposed that such a reader would reconstruct the main features of the characters' past without the aid of a specific introduction, through the skillful depiction of the present; and even if one thing or another from the past remained unknown to him, another more real danger would be avoided, namely, the diffused impression created by the excessive profusion of details. We shall speak of Chekhov's laconic mode later, in dealing with his style. Here, analyzing the writer's compositional principles, we will limit ourselves to the indication that the "God of brevity's" most ruthless demands were made on the brevity of the "exposition," "introduction," "opening," etc.

This is reported very expressively in the valuable memoirs of the priest S. Shchukin, who had come to Chekhov with the manuscript of his work. Picking up the notebook, Chekhov said:

> "Fledgling authors frequently should do the following: bend the notebook in half and tear off the first half."
>
> "I looked at him in amazement" [Shchukin writes].
>
> "I am speaking seriously," Chekhov said. "Normally beginners try 'to lead into the story,' as they say, and half of what they write is unnecessary. One ought to write so that reader understands what is going on without the author's explanations, from the progress of the story, from the characters' conversations, from their actions. Try to rip out the first half of your story; you'll only have to change the beginning of the second half a little bit and the story will be totally comprehensible. And in general there out to be nothing unnecessary. Everything that has no direct relation to the story must be ruthlessly thrown out. If you write in the first chapter that a rifle hangs on the wall it must without fail fire in the second or third chapter. And if it isn't going to fire, it mustn't hang, either."

Comparable instructions rarely fail to appear in his letters to authors who sent him their works. In his own creative practice he was no less merciless in that respect, and, moreover, his strictness constantly increased with the passage of time. If in his more or less early works one could still find a beginning in the traditional poetic spirit, with some specific flavor of an "introduction," later they disappear without a trace. Chekhov either begins his stories with some single sentence (literally!) which leads into the very essence of the narrative, or manages without even that. The beginning of *Ariadne* is an illustration of the first type: "On the deck of the ship from Odessa to Sevastopol a certain gentleman, quite handsome, with a full beard, came up to me for a match, and said . . ."

That is not only the *entire* introduction to *Ariadne*, but is even more than a mere introduction: the remark on the man's appearance, strictly speaking, belongs to the narrative, since the man who turns out to be the narrator is also an important character in the story. Everything that follows is the body of the work, the narrative itself. Nevertheless, one further point must be noted. Apparently recognizing something unnatural in that sort of beginning, in which a man comes up to a stranger for a match and for no reason tells him a long, complicated, and intimate story, Chekhov was careful later to render this device harmless. Having let the narrator talk first not on the main theme but on something close to it, the author notes in his own person: "It was noticeable that he was disturbed and really wanted to talk about himself rather than about women, and that I could not avoid hearing some long story resembling a confession."

Such a story of course does follow, but as a second "amortizer" of artificiality, the narrator, that is, the gentleman with the full beard, having started the story soon turns again to the auditor-author: " 'Excuse me, I will ask you again: you don't mind listening?' I answered that I did not and he continued," we may add, without further interruption from the author until the end of the story.

As indicated earlier, Chekhov did not stop at that stage of his battle with "introductions" and started to do without them altogether. Here, for example, is the beginning of his long tale *My Life*: "The manager said to me: 'I'm keeping you only out of respect for your honored father, otherwise you'd have been fired long ago.' "

Here we have absolutely nothing of the traditional "opening," "introduction," etc. This is a characteristic piece of the main personage's life, the first of many similar situations of which the life as a whole is made up, and the description of which is therefore even called *My Life*.

In all probability, the primary form of his early work—the obligatory short story—brought about the writer's persistent and long-continued struggle to perfect techniques directed toward the greatest possible curtailing of the "exposition," for there was simply no room for it at his disposal in the newspapers and humorous magazines for which he worked. Having brilliantly mastered the art of the brief opening, Chekhov valued its results, became its champion on principle, and remained true to it even after all sorts of conditions limiting his work disappeared completely.

* * *

3

Of the three classical compositional elements—exposition, development, and conclusion—Chekhov seems to have concerned himself most with the conclusion. Apparently the popular adage "All's well that ends well" was a real principle in the process of his creative work. Considerations of the conclusion occupy the primary place in his remarks on questions of composition. The sharp changes which occurred in Chekhov's poetics over the years may also be observed most clearly in his conclusions: his theory and practice in his early years not only differ from those of the late years but frequently are directly opposed to it.

Chekhov's remarks about his work on conclusions are distinguished by their absolute precision. One of them has become quite popular thanks to its peculiar aphoristic expressiveness, and it is particularly valuable since it applies to the composition of stories as well as plays. Having finished *Ivanov*,[1] he wrote in a letter to his brother Alexander: "It's my first attempt at a play, therefore there will necessarily be mistakes. The subject is complicated and significant. I end each act like a story: I conduct the entire action peacefully and quietly, but at the end I bash the viewer in the snout."

Chekhov doesn't even try to explain to his brother what he means by such an energetic formula, so he must be sure that the addressee won't mistake his meaning. And in actuality, when Chekhov wrote that letter in 1887, the characteristic special quality of the conclusion of his stories was palpably clear: *an effect of the unexpected.*

There is something very noteworthy here, though it is not immediately apparent. First we must note that the effective unexpected ending is firmly associated in our consciousness with the humorous stories of Chekhov's early period, for example *The Orator*, who in his funeral oration commemorates a participant in the service rather than the defunct; *A Horse Name*, only incidentally concerned with horses; *A Mishap*, where a trapped prospective husband escapes because he is blessed with a portrait of the writer Lazhechnikov rather than with the icon; *Drama*, where a writer kills, with his heavy paperweight, a lady who drives him to fury with the reading of her drama, and so on.

---

1. Chekhov's first successful full-length play (performed 1887).

And yet it is clear from Chekhov's letter that he intentionally applies the same sort of ending to a drama without hope! Moreover, in the letter he gives his brother only the most schematic notion of his new literary genre and tries to emphasize that situation: it turns out that he uses the same device for a dramatic work as for a humorous one.

However, the impression of the unexpected is unquestionably misleading here. It is explainable by the unquestioned predominance of humorous works in Chekhov's early period, and, moreover, it is emphasized by the fact that we remember those stories best. Yet among the non-humorous stories of Chekhov's early period unexpected endings play as great a role as in the humorous, and are not immediately taken by the reader to be unexpected only because the unexpected is habitually associated with the amusing, the funny, the humorous; and where there is no laughter the unexpected does not seem to be present either. Yet isn't the ending of *Vanka*, the naïve address on the letter to the grandfather, a typical unexpected conclusion? Or the ending of *Sleepy*? Do we not feel something like a sudden tragic illumination when the coachman Iona in *Misery* turns with his tale of great sorrow to his horse, the only listener he can find? Isn't that the same "bashing the reader in the snout"? In his stories and tales Chekhov successfully creates and develops, and generally canonizes in literature, the ending without resolution. Was it conceivable before Chekhov that a story whose "heroine" has several love affairs could end as his *Darling* does: "She lies down and thinks of Sasha, who is sleeping soundly in the next room and from time to time cries out in his dream: 'I'll show you! Get away! Don't fight!' "?

The very essence of a conclusion contains a hidden danger for the writer. Despite the relative variety possible in an ending, the heightened and rhetorical, a certain saccharine quality, effectiveness, etc., all lead in the end to the same thing: the danger of a specific and commonplace "rounding out." Chekhov had very characteristic devices for combating this danger.

*   *   *

4

The classic example of a Chekhov ending, when he was at the height of his career, exists in *The Lady with the Dog*. It deserves careful attention. Here we have in distinct, clear, and exact words, "audibly" pronounced, the essential, basic components of the endings of almost all Chekhov's works in his mature period, though they appear less openly there, and are at times only hinted at: "And it seemed to them that they were within an inch of arriving at a decision, and that then a new, beautiful life would begin. And they both realized that the end was still far, far away, and that the hardest, the most complicated part was only just beginning."

Even if the words "was beginning" that conclude *The Lady with the Dog* were set down without the author's purposeful intention, it does not prevent us from noting that the same words might have concluded the ending of *The Duel, The House with the Mansard, The Betrothed, My Life,* and a series of other works still read with deep emotion although the concrete details on which they are based have almost entirely disappeared with time. The endings of these stories proclaim that a certain stage has ended in the life he has described—and that is all. The process of life as such continues; a new phase, even more important than the one described, is beginning.

* * *

Chekhov parts from his hero at the moment his hero begins to reflect, or sink into reflection, about what he has experienced in the events that have been described. That, of course, is not merely an accident. The hero's thoughts and reflections are a projection of the reader's most intensive thinking, which occurs at the culmination of the structure, toward the end of the work, when all the figures and events comprising the part of existence that has been described have passed before his eyes. Hence the special attention Chekhov paid to the ending. If in his earlier years he concentrated all his resources in order to create an effect at the end, that is, primarily for the emotional gorging of the reader's reaction, later, without ignoring that aspect of the ending, Chekhov nevertheless moved the center of gravity in order to arouse in the reader the deepest possible thought.

Thus, turning to Chekhov's prose beginning with 1894, that is, for the last decade of his life, we have the following endings:

A Woman's Kingdom: "Now she *thought* that if it were only possible to depict the long day she had passed in a picture, everything bad and vulgar would be the truth, and her dreams would stand out from the whole as false and affected."

In *Rothschild's Fiddle*, Bronze reflects bitterly "Why should the world be so strangely arranged that a man's life, which was given to him only once, must pass without profit?"

The student in the story by the same name "*thought* that beauty and truth . . . evidently were always the main thing in human existence."

In *A Doctor's Visit*, Dr. Korolev, returning early in the morning from his trip to the patient in the country, "*thought* of the time, perhaps already near, when life would be as bright and gay as that peaceful Sunday morning."

In *A New Villa* the peasants *think* about their stupid relations with the villa's owners: "What was the fog that made it impossible to see the main thing?"

The list of Chekhov's works at whose conclusion the hero falls into thought, trying to comprehend everything he has experienced, can be continued to the end of Chekhov's creative career, including his swan song, *Betrothed,* where we read at the end: "She went into Sasha's room and stood there. 'Farewell, dear Sasha!'—she *thought,* and a new, broad, full life appeared to her, and that life, still vague, full of mystery, beckoned and attracted her."

* * * These are the words ["began," "think," "reflected," "thought"] that contain the key to Chekhov's endings as the most important compositional element! Chekhov does not try to strike the reader in any way or to disclose exotic realms of life to him but, on the contrary, merely to lead a "traditional" but "concealed" idea out of darkness into light, to turn it to something ordinary which is constantly before the reader's eyes, to make him open his eyes wider, make him look more deeply into the depths of life, to help him interpret that tedious life "broadly and clearly," *to think.*

RENATO POGGIOLI

Storytelling in a Double Key†

I. A Critique of Six Chekhov Tales

Chekhov's early stories are of some interest to the critic only inasmuch as they anticipate the accomplished master, destined to mature a few years later. Otherwise, their importance is slight, although it would be wrong to despise pieces that are still able to amuse and intrigue the reader. They were written in the early eighties, or about seventy years ago; and it is rare for any kind of writing, especially at the popular level, to survive with any effectiveness for such a long interval. This is even truer when one considers that the writing in question was never taken too seriously by the author himself. Both the critic and the reader should never forget that the young Chekhov wrote to entertain, and to add a little to his own income in the bargain.

The periodicals for which Chekhov wrote his early tales wanted to give their public cheap and easy laughter, rather than rare and thoughtful humor, and Chekhov the budding writer readily complied with his editors' demands. He did so without indulging in vulgarity or coarseness; yet at that stage of his career he dealt only with stock situations, to which he gave, half spontaneously and half mechanically, stock responses. In brief, what distinguishes Che-

† From *The Phoenix and the Spider* (Cambridge, Mass.: Harvard University Press, 1957), pp. 109–30.

khov's literary beginnings from his mature work is their relative lack of quality—the banality of the stuff, the uncouthness of the style, and the conventionality of the outlook. The ideal of the early Chekhov is the commonplace; the muse of his youth is the muse of commonness. Yet shortly afterwards he was able to grow into a genuine and original writer, and to raise his own inspiration, even within an odd and comical framework, to a level of "high seriousness." Many critics and readers have seen in Chekhov the dramatist a more accomplished artist than in Chekhov the storyteller, and, even without sharing such an opinion, one can easily acknowledge the great merits of the dramas he wrote at the end of his life. Yet one must also remember that the artist who ended his career with plays such as *Three Sisters* and *The Cherry Orchard* had started his apprenticeship as a man of the theater by composing the one act play *The Boor*, which is mere vaudeville. His early stories and sketches may be likewise considered as miniature farces in narrative form, and they differ in value from the tales of his mature period as much as *The Boor* differs from the controlled and profound dramas of his late years.

Strangely enough, the vaudeville element was fated to disappear completely from the work of Chekhov the playwright, while remaining a lasting, or at least a recurring, ingredient in his narrative work. It is true that even there the vaudeville element reappears only as an initial presupposition, to be finally discarded or forgotten. This suggests an analogy between his growth as a man and his progress as an artist, as well as between the unconscious workings of his own imagination and his conscious artistic method or creative process. Some of his best tales seem to reproduce *in parvo* the pattern of his career: each one of them ends by changing what at first looks like an unpromising seed into a bitter, and yet ripe, fruit.

Thus, according to the norm of the art and the life of this master, Chekhov's short stories often open in a low key only to close on a higher one. These pages will put this general feature to a detailed test, consisting of a close analysis of some characteristic products of Chekhov's storytelling craft. The examples will be chosen from stories written between the middle and the late eighties, in the transitional period between the writer's youthful apprenticeship and his mature mastery. The closing section will deal, however, with a piece written at the end of the following decade, when Chekhov reached the zenith of his powers and the sunset of his life.

During this transitional period, the new Chekhov slowly unfolds, like a larva, from the old one. This can be seen early in the case of *Vanka* (1886), a story which develops the all too obvious comic theme of the peasant's letter: a theme which will appear again, with varied effects, in the fiction of this master (see, for instance, *The Letter*, 1887, and *At Christmas Time*, 1900). The story at first gives the impression of having been written only to exploit all the fun implied in that situation, as shown by Chekhov's use of the rather worn-out motif of the letter mailed with an address understandable to the sender and perhaps to the addressee, but meaningless to the postmaster. As is to be expected, the greater part of the story is taken by the letter itself, which is supposed to amuse the reader by revealing the ignorance and the naïveté of the writer, and to reach its funny climax at the end, when its full and yet incomplete address, "To Grandfather in the Village," is finally reported.

The usual pattern, however, is completely transformed by the presence of a few very simple, and yet new, elements. First of all, the ignorant letter writer is not an adult, but the child Vanka, who has been apprenticed to a shoemaker in Moscow. In the second place, the letter is not merely a commonplace communication, with the customary inquiries about the health of the correspondent, or with the conventional season's greetings (the message is penned at Christmas time). The letter is far more than this, since it conveys all the anguish and agony of a lonely orphan in the big city, who wants to be rescued from an alien and cruel world, and begs his grandfather to take him back to the country. Furthermore, by punctuating the letter with the intermittent flashbacks of the boy's recollections, full of vain longings for a better and irrevocable past, Chekhov reveals in even starker outline the present plight of the letter writer, and all the misery filling his childish heart.

This undercurrent of pathos gives the story a moral dimension incommensurate with the central anecdote, and destroys it as such. The story operates against those comic traits which are its very roots. The effect is achieved by what could be paradoxically defined as a kind of pathetic relief. Thus, when ultimately submitted, the absurd address no longer amuses us. In a sense, the punch line falls flat; in another, it becomes far too sharp. Instead of provoking a smile on our lips, it stirs a pang in our hearts. The words on the envelope, "To Grandfather in the Village," fail to sound funny as soon as we realize that they will prevent the letter from reaching its destination, thus making all Vanka's efforts futile, and his sorrow fruitless. This example may suffice to prove that Chekhov achieves his creative intent through the technique of a sentimental counterpoint: more precisely, by attuning to each other a few discordant, and even dissonant, strings.

The same contrapuntal technique operates in a story like *Polinka* (1887), where it achieves an effect of suggestive charm, of poetic irony. Polinka, a girl still in her teens, is shopping in a bazaar, and is being served by her favorite salesman, who is also one of her boy friends. During their long and complex business transaction, which is highly comical, since it deals with ladies' things, incongruous for seller and buyer alike, she confesses to the salesman-suitor that she is in love with a student, and asks for his help and advice. This part of their conversation is softspoken, while their more practical exchanges about clothing materials and notions are made aloud. As for the orders passed by the salesman to other sections of the shop, they are shouted at the top of his voice.

The salesman tries to talk Polinka out of her infatuation, but his lower social position, his feeling of awe before the rich young customer, the sense of his own inferiority before an unknown and more glamorous rival, force him to become resigned to the inevitable. All the complexities and perplexities of the young man's mind are made evident by the exaggerated respect he shows to such a young thing as Polinka, whom he addresses very formally as Pelagheya Sergeevna, as well as by his lack of experience, which makes him take her calf love far more seriously than she does herself. His pain is too real for him to realize that Polinka is playing with joyful fun the role of an accomplished lady, in the grand manner of her shopping, as well as in the small talk about the troubles of her heart.

Here the sentimental counterpoint becomes musical as well, by alternating the running *sotto voce* of the private talk, and the resounding *staccato* of the public one. The whole effect of the story derives from the amusing contrast between the sentimental nonsense of the intimate conversation, and the objective, official character of the questions and answers concerning laces and trimmings, buttons and beads. Yet all these solid things become vain trifles when compared to the unsubstantial feelings now agitating their souls, which, however, never meet. The counter is at the same time a bridge and a fence, making for both separation and contact; and as such it symbolizes Chekhov's great theme, which is the failure of communication between human beings, even when they are as close and as friendly as these two. In this case the failure of communication is not due to an external accident, as in "Vanka," where the letter will never reach its destination merely because of a wrong address; but it proceeds from human nature, and is rooted in the inner substance of life itself. Human relations are often based on a misunderstanding, and the misunderstanding is the more tragic when it is neither reciprocal, nor caused by either party's ill will. The young salesman sees the woman in his customer, but Polinka does not see the man in the youth serving her. In itself the contrast is rather comic; its kernel, as usual, is a mere *qui pro quo*. Yet the final effect is one of pathetic irony, precisely because what is happening is far more, and far less, than a business transaction, than an exchange of money and goods. This is what Chekhov has been able to do with a story which perhaps was initially written only to exploit the ridiculous situation of the man serving women in a notion shop.

Among the tales of this period, there are two that stand out: *The Chorus Girl* and *A Gentleman Friend*, both written in 1886. Each one describes a petty and yet painful incident, a "vile tale," to use the term which Dostoevski's fiction offers us ready-made. The protagonists are two prostitutes, both playing a victim's role, and seeing in the incident affecting them an outrageous symbol of their wretched lot. The author, as well as the reader, is aware of the pathetic significance of the grotesque events on which these pieces are centered. Each one of these two "vile tales" becomes what James Joyce would have called an "epiphany," although a negative one, since it reveals not the noble meaning, but the cruel nonsense of life.

In the first of these two tales, the "chorus girl" Pasha is entertaining her current friend, who is a married gentleman, when someone suddenly rings the bell. The gentleman withdraws into the room nearby. The visitor is a lady, the gentleman's wife. She starts by calling Pasha all possible names, and ends her tirade by demanding that the chorus girl return all the presents she has been receiving from her lover, who must pay back the money he has been embezzling from his office. Pasha complies and returns two cheap trinkets. The lady refuses to believe that those trifles are the entire lot. By insulting and threatening Pasha, by moving her to compassion and by humiliating herself, she succeeds in obtaining from the chorus girl all the far more precious jewels and presents she had been given by other, more generous, friends. After the lady has left with her booty, the unfaithful husband, who has overheard everything, runs after her, blaming Pasha, and pitying his wife for having humbled herself before such a "low creature" as the chorus girl.

This marvellous story is, in a certain sense, Chekhov's *Boule de Suif*. But in Maupassant's tale the righteous indignation, on the part of her train companions, toward the prostitute who has saved them from annoyance by complying with the wishes of a Prussian officer, derives from the author's satirical view of the hypocrisy of society in matters of sex. In his story, however, as is usual with him, Chekhov displays little interest in the sex angle as such. His main concern is with the human soul, especially when it is misunderstood, misjudged, mistreated by another soul. The conflict at the base of *The Chorus Girl* revolves not around jealousy and love, but around the bourgeois values of respectability and interest. It is highly significant that the betrayed wife never reproaches Pasha for the alienation of her husband's affection; she blames the chorus girl only for having made him squander his money, thus depriving society and his family of their due.

By the tragic irony of the story, it is not shame or pity, but a sense of awe before the elegant and respectable lady, that forces the chorus girl to surrender all she owns, although she owes nothing to her. And to add insult to injury, the enraged wife calls her a "mercenary hussy" for all that. The tale reaches its climax, both pathetic and absurd, when the lady unknowingly chooses to refuse, among all the things "returned" to her, the pair of baubles her husband had given the chorus girl: "What are you giving me? . . . I am not asking for charity, but for what does not belong to you. . . ."[1]

Unlike the indignant and furious lady, Pasha accepts with dumb resignation her shame, as well as her loss. The tragicomedy of life forces Pasha and her like to behave passively, to undergo what life, or other human beings, *do* to them. But bourgeois wives, even when they are wronged, know how to act, and how to set right their wrongs. The contrast between the parts played by protagonist and antagonist is concretely symbolized by the *physique du rôle* of each one of the two principals. The wife is gaunt and tall, while Pasha, like the heroine of "Boule de Suif," is small and soft. The contrast is further emphasized by their difference in grooming and dress.

The moral superiority of Pasha over the lady is made evident by the very fact that she is the only one of the two women fully aware of the impression she makes on the other. She knows all too well that if she could look differently, she would be treated better, as a human being worthy of love and respect:

> Pasha felt that on this lady in black with angry eyes and white slender fingers she produced the impression of something horrid and unseemly, and she felt ashamed of her chubby red cheeks, the pockmark on her nose, and the fringe on her forehead, which never could be combed back. And it seemed to her that if she had been thin, and had no powder on her face, then she could have disguised the fact that she was not "respectable," and she would not have felt so frightened and ashamed to stand facing the unknown, mysterious lady.

The sad moral of this fable is of course that the Pashas will never change, and will be ever dressed, and treated by men and women alike, as "chorus girls." Yet the tale carries another lesson, perhaps a wiser one, teaching that it is not dress that makes the man, or even the woman, at that. This truth, which applies equally to her rival, to that "mysterious lady" who is hardly mysterious to us, is unconsciously uttered by Pasha herself, in her single complaint or protest. While giving away things rightfully belonging to her, because she had got them, as she says, "from other gentlemen," Pasha

---

1. This, and all quotations from Chekhov's stories, unless indicated otherwise, are taken from Constance Garnett's translation of Chekhov's works, published in several volumes by the Macmillan Company.

bursts out: "Take them and grow rich." We doubt that the lady will grow rich, while knowing all too well that Pasha will grow even poorer than she now is. Yet she is right in what she says, and it is from these words that we realize that the wronged wife is now a wrongdoer, that, even more than the "mercenary hussy" she despises and despoils, she becomes a "gold digger" herself.

The heroine of A *Gentleman Friend*, being a streetwalker, is, at least for bourgeois society, a creature even lower than the chorus girl. We meet her when she is leaving the hospital, and we may easily guess why she has been there. We must not overstress this detail: Chekhov, although more affected by the naturalistic strain than other Russian realists, certainly did not write such a story to point out the dangers of sexual promiscuity, or the horrors of social diseases. Notwithstanding his medical training and the keenness of his social conscience, Chekhov the artist could not but understress a point like this. The writer has no special cause to plead: what interests him is not the sordid side of his case, but its human poignancy and truth.

Thus, at the beginning of the story, he reduces the prostitute's plight to the particular strait she is in: to the immediate practical problems she must face now that she is again on her feet (and *only* on her feet). The poor girl is without shelter, and, even more important, she has no money with which to buy a new dress. She pawns a ring, but she gets only a ruble for it. She is as much aware as Pasha that the role she plays in life depends on how she is groomed and dressed, but while the sad tale of the chorus girl ends with Pasha's realization that her physical and sartorial appearance will never allow her to play any other role but the one fate assigned to her, this sorry story begins with the heroine's frantic attempts to procure the only proper attire for acting and living as she is supposed to. "What can you get for a ruble?" she thinks. "You can't buy for that sum a fashionable short jacket, nor a big hat, nor a pair of bronze-colored shoes, and without those things she had a feeling of being, as it were, undressed. . . ."

All the unconscious irony of the last sentence will be made evident if we consider that this woman, so preoccupied with the clothing she wants to have, is a professional stripteaser, who is paid to undress. The shabbiness of her apparel makes her more ashamed than nudity itself; it makes her feel as if she were nude in the street. In order to buy the trade costume she needs, she decides to visit one of her gentlemen friends, and to borrow from him. She picks a dentist: but while climbing his stairs, and lingering in his waiting room, she loses all her pluck. She thinks that the unfashionable dress she is now wearing makes her look like the beggar she now is, or even worse, like the working girl she is no more. While the chorus girl feels degraded by the sudden appearance of a lady looking respectable, if not in her actions and manners, at least in her aspect and dress, the streetwalker realizes her loss of status merely by drawing an invidious comparison between her present appearance and her former, more glamorous self.

Chekhov dramatizes the conflict between the two opposite self-images within the prostitute's mind, by contrasting her professional name, the fictitious and exotic Vanda, with the prosaic Nastasya, the real and legal one, as testified by her "yellow passport." And Vanda's feeling of humiliation reaches its climax when she suddenly sees her own present image as reflected in the immense mirror by which the writer's provident imagination, with realistic as well as with visionary insight, has furnished the splendid staircase leading to the dentist's office. Here, unknowingly, Chekhov uses the Dantean symbol of "other people's stairs": the climbing and descending of which is such a "bitter path" for the poor and the needy, when they beg for charity and help. To this the author adds the symbol of the looking glass, as if to suggest that the postulant knows all too well that at a given stage of her quest she will sooner or later discover her own wretched likeness on the inward mirror of shame, or on the outward mirror of truth.

Here is the central scene of the story, as the author reports it: "The staircase impressed her as luxurious and magnificent, but of all its splendors what caught her eye most was an immense looking glass, in which she saw a ragged figure without a fashionable jacket, without a big hat, and without bronze-colored shoes." With marvellous intuition, the writer imagines that, at first sight, Vanda fails to recognize herself, because the figure she is looking at is deprived of the objects she longed to see. But when she takes a second look, she identifies in that shabby reflection her own true self. And for a while self-recognition gives place to self-knowledge. With a painful shock, the streetwalker realizes that she has become another person, or rather that she has changed back into the kind of person she once was: "And it seemed strange to Vanda that, now that she was humbly dressed and looked like a laundress or sewing girl, she felt ashamed, and no trace of her usual sauciness remained, and in her own mind she no longer thought of herself as Vanda, but as the Nastasya Kanavkin she used to be in the old days. . . ."

Only a writer endowed with keen psychological and ethical insight could have thought of this: a prostitute ashamed of being ashamed, feeling dishonored for thinking, behaving, and looking again like the better human being she had been before. Nothing is more tragic than such an inverted perspective, such a reversal of values, which the writer, however, sets right without gnashing of teeth, without even lifting a finger to point out the moral of his unadorned tale. Those who lower themselves will be exalted, and the reader glimpses a sign of redemption in the very fact that the prostitute perceives her own indignity when she recovers, if only for a fleeting instant, the sense of her identity.

If such is the climax of the story, its ending cannot be but an anticlimax. When she is admitted into the dentist's office, the girl is taken for a stranger, and treated as if she were not a visitor, but a patient. The dentist obviously fails to recognize in Nastasya the Vanda who, for a full evening, had been his lady friend. Open-mouthed and speechless, the poor streetwalker lets one of her teeth be pulled, and pays the dentist with the only ruble she has left. Like Pasha, she is one of those creatures to whom things are done, and who are done for. But while Pasha is the victim of a foulness masquerading as retributive justice, Nastasya is the victim of something even colder and cruder: of our mechanical indifference to, or perfunctory interest in, not only the suffering but the very being of our fellow men. Thus the incidents reported in these two stories end on the same note of despair. Poor Pasha wails aloud, with her feelings deeply hurt: "She remembered how three years ago a merchant had beaten her for no sort of reason, and she wailed more loudly than ever." As for Nastasya, "she walked along the street, spitting blood, and brooding on her life, and the insults she had endured, and would have to endure tomorrow, and next week, and all her life, up to the very day of her death."

The chorus girl cries because she has no more illusions. She knows that her appearance, as well as the substance of her life, will never change, and that she will be forever wronged by unknown, respectable ladies, and by less respectable gentlemen friends. Nastasya, although equally aware of her fate, fails to weep only because she still hopes to become Vanda again. And at the close of the story she changes again into Vanda, as soon as she is able to buy and wear "an enormous red hat, a fashionable jacket, and bronze-colored shoes." The list of these three pieces of apparel reappears here for the third time in the story (at the beginning, in the middle, and at the end), and this repetition gives those three concrete objects the obsessive quality of an *idée fixe*, which, despite its absurdity, has finally succeeded in materializing.

Chekhov is but one of the many writers who attempt to interpret the comedy of life in pathetic rather than in comic terms. One could say that he tends to reverse Gogol's formula, trying to give us "tears through laughter" instead of "laughter through tears." Yet even so, unlike Gogol, he never changes his laughter into a sneer, or his smile into a grimace. He constantly avoids the temptation of the grotesque, as if he knew that its nemesis is to degrade the comedy of life into a farce. While tragedy is self-sufficient, and can get along quite well even without comic relief, comedy is always a mixed genre, and needs a certain amount of tragic sense to achieve the catharsis of its own pathos and form. Thus, as both *The Chorus Girl* and *A Gentleman Friend* amply prove, Chekhov is quite right in looking for inspiration in what, twisting Maeterlinck's phrase, one may call *le tragicomique quotidien*. And perhaps nothing is as tragicomic in our daily experience as that highly serious comedy of errors, moral and spiritual in character, constantly falsifying social relations and human intercourse.

Chekhov pays great attention to all those mistakes or equivocations that prevent the establishment of a communion of feeling between different human beings. Our own reciprocal misunderstandings are due not to material appearances or optical illusions, but to internal blindness. What Chekhov is primarily interested in is what one might call, perhaps too technically, a failure of communication. Such failure, which takes place mainly on the moral plane, may operate on both sides, although the author attributes it preferably to the party at the receiving end. Thus the comedy of errors becomes pathetic and tragic, deriving from a defective condition which the message sender can hardly improve or correct: in brief, from a fault in the reception. No situation lends itself so well as this one to the contrapuntal technique characteristic of Chekhov's method of presentation and development, and no story brings this point more movingly home than the one entitled, simply and eloquently, *Misery* (1886).

The story opens with a static scene: something like an impressionistic landscape, built around two motionless figures, an animal and a man. The vision gives the eerie feeling of a *tableau vivant*, obviously recapturing a real life experience, which must have vividly caught the imagination of Chekhov, since he reproduced it almost verbatim in the later *Kashtanka*, a tale about a child and a dog. Here is the scene, in Chekhov's words:

> Evening twilight, large flakes of snow are circling lazily about the street lamps which have just been lighted, settling in a thin layer on roofs, horses' backs, people's shoulders, caps. Iona Potapov, the cabby, is all white like a ghost. As hunched as a living body can be, he sits on the box without stirring. . . . His nag, too, is white and motionless. . . .[2]

The inertia of both the man and the horse is suddenly broken by the arrival of Iona's first fare, and Chekhov describes with great artistry the sledge's slow and difficult start. The driving man, the pulling nag, and the dragging sledge seem to be a caricatural replica of such noble visions or figures as the Centaur, or Lohengrin's swan. The human and the animal component of the team act with a

2. Quoted as translated by Avram Yarmolinsky, in his *Portable Chekhov* (Viking Press).

rigid and mechanical parallelism, showing their pain and effort, and become almost as heavy and wooden as the sledge trailing after them: "The driver clucks to the horse, cranes his neck like a swan. . . .The nag, too stretches her neck. . . ."

The aged cabby is a grieving father who has just lost his son. He feels the poignant urge to pour out his sorrow, and wishes to tell somebody of his misery and loss. Only the compassion of a fellow man may console his heart. So "he turns his whole body around to his fare to talk." But the indifference of the customer, as well as the snares of the traffic, prevents him from getting his words and feelings across. The vain attempt repeats itself again and again, and the entire story is punctuated by a series of failures, succeeding each other through the same motions and gestures by driver or horse, or by both: the craning of their necks at the start, Iona's turning around during the ride, the team's return to a deathlike immobility at the ride's end. Then, while waiting for another fare, Iona "sits motionless and hunched on his box."

The last fare is a party of revelers, whom Iona will drive up to "a dark entrance," only to be underpaid by them. One of the riders is a hunchback, bent by nature as cruelly and permanently as Iona by his exposure to the biting cold. The revelers derisively force their crippled friend to stand up in the sledge. To show his indignation at their slow progress, or rather, to vent his resentment on another human being, even more wretched than himself, the hunchback gives Iona a blow on his shoulders. The blow falls on the neck of Iona just when he turns his head forward, after a vain attempt to talk.

The entire story is based, simply and powerfully, on this sort of graphic and dynamic symbolism: on the recurrence of the same tortured gestures by these two creatures, the man and the horse, as well as on the sledge's intermittent jerks. Finally, Iona decides to go back to his yard, where he tries his luck with a young fellow driver, who refuses to listen, and falls asleep. So, in the animal heat of the stable, while feeding his nag, the bereaved father tells his grief to the only living being who seems to lend a willing ear to his tale of woe. The story thus ends almost good-humoredly, relieving the almost unbearable tension, and relaxing the strings of pathos, which were about to snap.

Communication theory takes into account also those failures of understanding which are due to semantic confusions, to wrong assumptions about the agreed or conventional meaning of a given sign, especially a verbal one. Such a confusion is the more frequent and intense when the sign is loaded with an excessive emotional charge, or is one of those "shocking words" which may all too easily become "scandal's stones," or stumbling blocks. Literature generally deals with situations of this sort in a light comic vein, as if impropriety were a matter of misuse rather than of abuse. The usual intention is thus to contrast the outrageous implications of the utterance with the innocence and ignorance of the speaker. The young Chekhov was not above exploiting farcically verbal equivocations of this sort, but in his middle period he wrote at least one noble tale on what in the hands of another writer would have remained a vulgar *double entendre*: the flimsiest of all comical pretexts. Such a story is *The Requiem* (1886), in which the shocking word, like a rock thrown into a pond, suddenly stirs the still waters of our soul.

On a Sunday morning, the shopkeeper Andrey Andreyich leans on a railing in the church. He has just sent a note to the altar, asking that a mass be sung for the repose of the soul of his daughter Maria (or Matushka, as he still calls her). Chekhov characterizes him in a Gogolian manner, that is, by deducing his typical psychological traits from the concrete details of his behavior and aspect. Thus we get to know what kind of man he is as soon as we learn that he wears "the huge clumsy galoshes only seen on the feet of practical and prudent persons of firm religious convictions." While waiting for the requiem mass, the shopkeeper notices that Father Grigori is acting strangely near the altar, and then he realizes that the priest's "twitching eyebrows and beckoning finger might refer to him."

This slight, initial misapprehension prepares the reader for the profound misunderstanding which is the story's central theme. Andrey Andreyich walks toward the altar, tramping with his heavy galoshes, which, although representative of his solid beliefs, still seem incongruous and indecorous in the church. When he reaches the altar, he is harshly reproached by the priest for what he had "dared" to write. At first, he fails to comprehend, but he finally understands that the priest objects to one word he had used in his written request for the mass: "For the soul of the servant of God, the harlot Maria." The word suddenly resounds in the mind of the reader with a more incongruous and indecorous thud than the heavy galoshes on the church's floor. The shopkeeper justifies himself by quoting the lives of the saints, and by citing Mary of Egypt, who had been forgiven by the Lord, and explains that he had added the epithet to the name of his daughter to follow the use of the martyrology, where the martyrs' names are always accompanied by terms designating their station or calling in life. The priest insists that the word is unseemly, reminding the shopkeeper that his daughter had been a "well-known actress," and that her death has been mentioned in the press.

From what Father Grigori tells the old man, the reader understands all too well the ambivalence of the priest's attitude toward the glories and the vanities of the world. He thinks of the dead sinner with an outraged sense of righteousness, but also with a feeling of involuntary respect. After all, through her fall, and even her ruin, she rose high in the eyes of men. It is for this, as well as for the dignity of the church, that he objects to the use of that term. Her guilt must be not only forgiven, but forgotten too. If the veil of the priest's well-meaning hypocrisy is easily lifted, the intention which led the shopkeeper to call his daughter a harlot will forever remain under a cloud of obscurity. The writer fails to solve this ambiguity, leaving in doubt whether Andrey Andreyich really knows what "harlot" means: thus we remain unsure whether by mentioning that word he intends to refer to his daughter's exceptional career, or merely to her sin. We cannot even be sure of his naïveté, and the priest accuses him, not without reason, of being too subtle, and of presuming to read the Holy Writ better than a clergyman. True enough, the old man sticks to his own opinion, and during the mass, he lets drop again the forbidden word from his praying lips.

With his usual method, Chekhov accompanies the audible chant of the rite by the silent antiphony of Andrey Andreyich's reflections, reminiscences, and thoughts. Suddenly the reader relives with him a forgotten episode of his life. The shopkeeper rehearses again in his memory his last walk with his daughter, and suddenly recalls how, at her enraptured enthusiasm for the loveliness of the local landscape, he had replied rather ineptly that farming did not pay on a soil like that. This flashback reveals immediately how and why those two hearts and two minds, with their opposite concerns for beauty and utility, were destined never to meet. Now the problem whether the father did or did not know the real meaning of "harlot" does not matter any longer: the point is that he misunderstood his daughter, to be misunderstood in return. The semantic confusion thus becomes merely a sign of man's inability to know himself, as well as others, including his next of kin. And we see that such inability persists even when we bury our dead. Yet in his last and greatest period, Chekhov was able to find within life, almost unconsciously, that sense of redemption that this somber story fails to find even in death. This is particularly true of the more important of the two stories discussed below.

II. *"Psyche; It's a Fine Subject"*

In Chekhov's canon there are two tales, written at different times, which, starting from the opposite poles of pathos and irony, and following divergent paths, end by giving us parallel transfigurations, in realistic terms, of the same myth. This myth is the ancient story of Psyche, which remained lively and meaningful for the artists and writers of so many centuries, but which our commercial culture has mummified into the everlasting indignity of a soft-drink ad. Chekhov used the Psyche legend not openly, but obliquely, as a furtive hint that even in the profane prose of life there may lie hidden poetry's sacred spark. The grimness or the grayness of our daily lot seems to dominate both of these tales, but the sudden appearance of Psyche redeems their somber or dull view of life with a vivid, and not too unreal, flash. The first tale discloses the vision within the span of a simple image; and the second, of a mere name. That image and that name reduce in their turn the whole legend to a single symbol, hiding, rather than revealing, the myth it transcribes in quasi-hieroglyphic form. The symbol itself, eclipsed by the cloud of the letter, buried under the matter-of-factness of a naturalistic report, has escaped all scrutiny, thus making even less visible the presence of the myth it suggests and for which it stands. Yet in the end the beauty and poetry of the ancient legend triumph over all obtuseness and absurdity, over the obscurity of life and the disguise of art; and Psyche's face shines forth again, in one case through tragedy's, and in the other, through comedy's, mask. It is mainly such a passing and fleeting allusion to Psyche and her story that, beyond all appearance, makes these two tales what they really are; yet a detailed examination of their plainest and lowest level of meaning is required to reinterpret them within the higher, and deeper, frame of reference of both symbol and myth.

The first of these two tales is *Anyuta*, which was written in 1886. The story seems to have been conceived in a mixed mood, half pathetic, half morbid; and it lies halfway, so to speak, between Mürger's *Scènes de la Vie de Bohême*[3] and the most sordid tales of the early Dostoevski. At least at first sight, its protagonists impress us as the conventional seamstress and the conventional student, sharing their poverty and love in the same barely furnished room. Yet, from the very beginning, we surprise them in a highly unconventional situation. The student is preparing himself for one of the examinations he is about to take at the Medical School. In order to get his anatomy straight, he asks Anyuta to take her blouse off, and starts counting her ribs. A while later, a friend drops in. A student at the Academy of Fine Arts, he has come to take Anyuta away, since he needs a model, and wants her to pose for a painting he is working on. Anyuta retires to dress, and in the meanwhile the visitor reproaches his host for his slovenly life. When left alone, the medical student decides that he and the seamstress must part; he tells Anyuta of his decision as soon as she comes back from her sitting, bringing in the sugar she has just bought for the tea of her penniless friend.

---

3. Henri Murger's *Scenes of Bohemian Life* (1948), sketches of life among students and artists, is the basis for Puccini's opera *La Boheme*. [*Editor*.]

Here Chekhov's contrapuntal technique acts, so to speak, negatively: the words and thoughts of the student fail to break the inarticulate silence of the girl. She is the only mute and passive figure of the story, acting with the resigned dumbness of a sacrificial lamb. The author adds his own silence to the silence of the heroine, pretending to look on her from the outside, which is exactly what the other two characters do. Thus all the references to Anyuta, while remaining external and objective, become highly symbolic. This kind of implied, and, so to speak, inert, symbolism grows more and more important in the creations of the late Chekhov. Here it finds expression not only in Anyuta's silence, but also in the parallel indifference of the two students, both of whom treat the seamstress, even if for different ends, as if she were merely an anatomical specimen.

In this story, the obvious love angle is completely overlooked. With unobtrusive but penetrating irony, Chekhov makes Anyuta's body serve the higher purposes of art and science. In reality, she serves, with both her body and soul, the blind selfishness of two human beings who consider her an inferior creature, while she is morally far superior to them. As for the ribs, says the medical student, "they are like the keys of a piano: one must study them in the skeleton and in the living body." Yet in reality he treats her as if she were a corpse on a slab. The art student is even more matter-of-fact: he handles Anyuta as if she were something neither living nor dead, but only a thing, a piece of property of so little value that it is better to borrow than to own it. "Do me a favor," he asks his friend, "lend me your young lady for just a couple of hours! I am painting a picture, you see, and I can't get on without a model." He asks for her as he would ask for a plate of fruit, to be discarded or returned, because he needs it to paint, not to eat. Yet the supreme irony of the story is that the young artist wants to produce something far nobler than a mere study. He is not one of those naïve painters who are satisfied with representing either a nude or a still life. He aims far higher, as we learn from the answer he gives to his friend's question about the theme of the painting he is working on: "Psyche; it's a fine subject."

Neither the students nor, for that matter, Anyuta, will ever realize that the only Psyche of the story is she herself. Yet this is the feeling conveyed to the reader by the tale's closing vision, when the abandoned seamstress returns noiselessly to the corner window of her lonely room, like a Cinderella without beauty, without a prince, and without a magic wand. While treating the *scène de vie de bohême* as if it were a "slice of life," Chekhov succeeds in changing the story into a tragic fable without words. And he does so by projecting on the shabby walls of a bohemian garret, beyond the falsity of a painted image which remains unseen, the true likeness of poor Psyche of old, as she was when she lost her lover, and was left like an orphan alone in the darkness of this world.

The second tale is *The Darling*, which Chekhov wrote more than ten years later, in 1899, at the decline of his years, when his art was gradually changing the tragicomedy of life into something far too noble for pity, and far too pure for contempt. The change is particularly evident in this story, of which one could say, to paraphrase Milton's words, "nothing is here for tears." Nothing is here for laughter either, because *The Darling* ends by "saying yea" to life, by judging it "well and fair." Yet if the critic will go back to the text, so as to recapture the impression of his first reading, he will undoubtedly conclude that the final esthetic outcome transcends the tale's original intent. And he will do so even more confidently if he learns that his conclusion is supported by the authority of Leo Tolstoy, who was a great admirer of this story, as well as of Chekhov in general.

The protagonist, Olenka, is "a gentle, soft-hearted, compassionate girl, with mild, tender eyes, and very good health." Everyone feels captivated by her good nature, and exclaims: "You darling!" at the sight of her pleasant looks. She lives in her father's house, and watches from her back porch the tenant living in a lodge they rent. The tenant, whose name is Ivan Kukin, is thin and no longer young; he manages an open-air theater, and complains constantly about the rain which ruins his business, and about the public which fails to appreciate his shows. By listening to his misfortunes, the "darling" falls in love with him. She marries Kukin, works in his office, and accepts all his views as her own, repeating all he has to say about the theatrical arts. Despite her total identification with her husband, Olenka grows stouter and pinker, while Kukin grows thinner and paler. After a year has passed, he goes to Moscow on business, and within a few days Olenka receives a misspelled telegram informing her of Kukin's sudden death.

The poor widow loses all interest in life, but after a three-month interval she meets at mass Vasili Pustovalov, a dignified gentleman working at a timber merchant's. In a day or two Pustovalov proposes, and Olenka marries again. The "darling" helps her new husband in the shop, and absorbs herself in the timber trade as fully as she had previously done in the theater world. For six years, her husband's ideas become her ideas, but her mind returns to emptiness as soon as her second husband follows the first into the grave. Yet within half a year she finds happiness anew, this time with an army veterinary surgeon, by the name of Vladimir Smirnin, now renting her lodge. Smirnin is married and has a son, but lives separated from his wife and child. Everyone realizes what has happened as soon as Olenka goes around discussing sanitary questions and the dangers of animal epidemics. "It was evident," as Chekhov says, "that she could not live a year without an attachment," and yet nobody thinks ill of the "darling" for this.

But Smirnin is suddenly transferred to a distant place, and Olenka is left alone again. Time passes, and she becomes indifferent, sad, and old: "what is worst of all . . . she had no opinion of any sort." Like all old lonely women, she has a cat, but does not care for her pet. Suddenly her solitude is broken again: Smirnin, looking older and wearing a civilian suit, knocks again at her door. He has left the service and has come back with his family, to start life anew. Olenka yields her house to the newcomers, and retires to the lodge. With this change of perspective, her life seems to take a new turn. And this time she falls in love with the little Sasha, who is ten years old. Soon enough, the father starts working outside, and the mother departs to live elsewhere. Thus Olenka mothers the boy, who calls her auntie, and tells her about his studies, and his school experiences. Now the "darling" goes around discussing teachers and lessons, home assignments and class work. And everybody understands that there is another man in her house and in her life, even if this time he is another woman's child, whom she loves like the mother she was born to be.

This résumé fails to do justice to the story, and to point out the internal contradiction already alluded to. Tolstoy's commentary fulfills, however, both tasks almost perfectly. In the opening of the critique of this piece, which he collected in *Readings for Every Day of the Year*, Tolstoy recalls the biblical story of Balaam (Numbers, 22–24). The King of the Moabites ordered him to curse the people of Israel, and Balaam wanted to comply with this command. But while climbing the mountain, he was warned by an angel, who at first was invisible to him, while being visible to his ass. So, when he reached the altar at the top, Balaam, instead of cursing the Jews, blessed them. "This," Tolstoy concludes, "is just what happened with the true poet and artist Chekhov when he wrote his charming story, *The Darling*." Tolstoy then proceeds to develop his point:

> The author evidently wanted to laugh at this pitiful creature—as he judged her with his intellect, not with his heart—this "Darling," who, after sharing Kukin's troubles about his theater, and then immersing herself in the interests of the timber business, under the influence of the veterinary surgeon considers the struggle against bovine tuberculosis to be the most important matter in the world, and is finally absorbed in questions of grammar and the interests of the little schoolboy in the big cap. Kukin's name is ridiculous, and so even is his illness and the telegram announcing his death. The timber dealer with his sedateness is ridiculous;

but the soul of "Darling," with her capacity for devoting herself with her whole being to the one she loves, is not ridiculous but wonderful and holy.[4]

Nothing could be more exact, or better said: yet one may wonder whether Tolstoy is equally right in identifying the motive that had led the author of *The Darling* to take the pen. "When Chekhov began to write that story," says Tolstoy, "he wanted to show what woman ought not to be." In short, what Chekhov meant to do was to reassert his belief in the ideal of woman's emancipation, in her right and duty to have a mind and a soul of her own. While acknowledging the artistic miracle which had turned a satirical vignette into a noble human image, Tolstoy seems to enjoy as a good joke the implication that the author had to throw his beliefs overboard in the process. Being strongly adverse to the cause of woman's emancipation, Tolstoy speaks here *pro domo sua*,[5] but the reader has no compelling reason to prefer his anti-feminism to Chekhov's feminism. Tolstoy has an axe to grind, and his guess is too shrewd. One could venture to say that Chekhov sat down to write *The Darling* with neither polemical intentions nor ideological pretensions: what he wanted to do was perhaps to exploit again at the lowest level a commonplace type and a stock comic situation, which, however unexpectedly, develops into a vision of beauty and truth. If D. S. Mirsky is right in claiming that each Chekhov story follows a curve, then there is no tale where the curve of his art better overshoots its mark.

What must have attracted Chekhov was the idea of rewriting a half pathetic, half mocking version of the "merry widow" motif: of portraying in his own inimitable way the conventional character of the woman ready and willing to marry a new husband as soon as she has buried the preceding one. That such was the case may still be proved through many eloquent clues. No reader of *The Darling* will fail to notice that Olenka calls her successive mates with almost identical nicknames: Vanichka the first, Vassichka the second, and Volodichka the third. These familiar diminutives, although respectively deriving from such different names as Ivan, Vasili, and Vladimir, sound as if they were practically interchangeable, as if to suggest that the three men are interchangeable too.

This runs true to type, since in the life scheme of the eternal, and eternally remarrying, widow, nothing really changes, while everything recurs: the bridal veil alternates regularly with the veil of mourning, and both may be worn in the same church. It is from this scheme that Chekhov derives the idea of the successive adoption, on Olenka's part, of the opinions and views of each one of her

4. Quoted as translated by Aylmer Maude in his edition of Tolstoy's works (Oxford University Press).   5. "For himself (Latin)." Literally, "about his own house." [*Editor.*]

three men, and this detail is another proof that the story was originally conceived on the merry widow motif. Yet, if we look deeper, we realize that a merry widow does not look for happiness beyond wedded bliss: that she asks for no less than a ring, while offering nothing more than her hand. But Olenka gives and takes other, very different things. She receives her husbands' opinions, and makes them her own, while returning something far more solid and valuable in exchange. And when she loses the person she loves, she has no more use for his views, or for any views at all.

This cracks the merry widow pattern, which begins to break when she joins her third mate, who is a married man, without a wedding ceremony or the blessing of the Church. And the pattern visibly crumbles at the end, when Olenka finds her fourth and last love not in a man, but in a child, who is the son of her last friend. "Of her former attachments," says Chekhov, "not one had been so deep." Now we finally know Olenka for what she really is, and we better appraise in retrospect some of the story's earliest, unconscious hints. Now, for instance, we understand better her girlish infatuations for such unlikely objects as her father, her aunt, or her teacher of French. For her, almost any kind of person or any kind of love can do equally well, and it is because of this, not because of any old-maidish strain, that she fails to reduce love to sex alone.

Chekhov explains this better than we could, at that very point of the tale when the lonely Olenka is about to find her more lasting attachment: "She wanted a love that would absorb her whole being, and whole soul and reason—that could give her ideas and an object in life, and would warm her old blood." For all this one could never say of Olenka, as of Madame Bovary, that she is in love with love: she cares only for living beings like herself, as shown by the ease with which she forgets all her husbands after their deaths. Her brain is never haunted by dreams or ghosts, and this is why it is either empty, or full of other people's thoughts. This does not mean that the "Darling" is a parrot or a monkey in woman's dress, although it is almost certain that Chekhov conceived her initially in such a form. She is more like the ass of Balaam, who sees the angel his master is unable to see. Olenka is poor in spirit and pure in heart, and this is why life curses her three times, only to bless her forever, at the end.

Tolstoy is right when he reminds us that, unlike Olenka, her three men and even her foster-child are slightly ridiculous characters, and one must add that they remain unchangingly so from whatever standpoint we may look. The reminder is necessary: after all, the point of the story is that love is a grace proceeding from the lover's fullness of heart, not from the beloved's attractive qualities or high deserts. In the light of this, the parallel with Balaam's ass must be qualified by saying that Olenka sees angels where others see only men. Thus the double message of the story is that love is a matter of both blindness and insight.

While the whole story seems to emphasize Olenka's "insight," her "blindness" is intimated by a single hint, hidden, of all places, in the title itself. Since the latter is practically untranslatable, the foreign reader cannot help missing the hint. The "Darling" of the English translators is the Russian idiom *Dushechka*, meaning literally "little soul," and used colloquially as a term of endearment, a tribute of personal sympathy, a familiar and good-natured compliment. Chekhov never pays the compliment himself, except by indirection or implication: he merely repeats it again and again, in constant quotations from other people's direct speech. Thus the artist acts as an echo, reiterating that word as if it were a choral refrain, a suggestive *leitmotiv*. Yet, as we already know, everybody addresses Olenka in that way only when she is contented and happy, having someone to love and care for. As soon as she is left without a person on whom to pour the tenderness flowing from her heart, everybody ceases calling her Dushechka, as if she had lost her soul, as if she were no longer a soul.

Thus, even though intermittently used, that term becomes, so to say, Olenka's second name: and the reader finally finds it more right and true than the first. What one witnesses is a sort of transfiguration, both symbolic and literal: by changing into Dushechka, Olenka ends by personifying the very idea of the soul. We are suddenly faced by an allegory and a metamorphosis, turning the story into a fable, which, like all fables, partakes of the nature of myth. With startling awareness, we now realize that Dushechka, after all, is one of the Russian equivalents of the Greek Psyche, and that what Chekhov has written could be but a reinterpretation of the ancient legend about the girl who was named after the word meaning "soul."

The legend, which Apuleius first recorded for us,[6] tells how the youthful Psyche became the loving wife of a great god, who was Eros himself. Eros never showed her his face or person in the daylight; yet Psyche was happy as long as she could take care of her little house in the daytime, and share in night's darkness the bed and love of a husband she could neither know nor see. What the legend means to say is that love is blind, and must remain so, whether the loved one is mortal or an immortal creature. This is the truth which the Greek Psyche had to learn, while the Russian Dushechka seems to have known it, though unconsciously, all the time.

That Chekhov must have thought of this legend while writing *The Darling* may be proved by the fact that the name or word

6. In his *Metamorphoses*, better known under the title of *The Golden Ass*.

Dushechka is but a more popular variant of the literary *Dushenka,* after which Bogdanovich, a minor Russian poet of the eighteenth century, entitled his own imitation of La Fontaine's *Psyché,* which, in its turn, is a rather frivolous version of the same old myth. This slight difference in the endings of what is practically the same noun may have greater significance than we think. Both endings are diminutive suffixes; but while in Bogdanovich's "-enka" there is a connotation of benevolent sympathy, in Chekhov's "-echka" there is an insinuation of pettiness, and a nuance of indulgent scorn. This obviously means that Chekhov's serious tale is as distant from Bogdanovich's light poem as from the original legend itself: the distance may be considered so great as to preclude any relationship. We realize this, and we realize as well that our proof that such a relationship exists may be considered a verbal coincidence and nothing more. In reply to this objection, we could observe that Chekhov testified elsewhere about his knowledge of the legend itself. As we already know, he did so in "Anyuta," by simply stating through the mouth of his student-painter that Psyche is "a fine subject."

The student-painter is right, even if he is fully unconscious of the irony in what he says. Aware as he was of the irony he himself had put in those words, Chekhov must have been equally aware of their truth. Yes, Psyche is a fine subject, even when the artist deals with it so freely as to completely change its background and situation, lowering its fabulous vision to the level of a bourgeois and provincial experience, and transcribing its poetic magic into the plain images and the flat language of modern realism. This does not imply that the tale is deprived of wonder: there is no greater wonder than to make luminous and holy the inner and outer darkness in which we live, even against our will. And there is no greater miracle than to have changed into a new Psyche, with no other sorcery but that of a single word, this heroine of the commonplace, this thrice-married little woman, neither clever nor beautiful, and no longer young.

D. H. Lawrence recommends that we never trust the writer, but only the tale. This is what one should do even with Chekhov, although he is one of the most trustworthy of modern writers, precisely because he builds on a broad moral structure, which compensates for the restrictions of his chosen literary forms. If this is true, then one must reject Leo Shestov's statement that Chekhov's is a creation *ex nihilo,*[7] always returning to the nothingness from

7. In the essay "Tvorchestvo iz nichego" (Creation from nothing), which can be read in English under the title "Creation from the Void," in *Anton Tchekhov, and Other Essays,* by Leo Shestov, translated by S. S. Koteliansky and J. M. Murry (London, 1916).

which it sprang forth. It would be more proper to define it a creation *ex parvo*,[8] producing from humble beginnings a somber and yet beautiful world.

GLEB STRUVE

On Chekhov's Craftsmanship: The Anatomy of a Story†

* * *

The story which Chekhov described[1]—perhaps not without a hint of false modesty—as "rather poor" and scratched in haste is one of the best stories of his middle period, if not one of his best short stories *tout court*.[2] The story, called *Sleepy* (*Spat' khochetsia*) is about a thirteen-year-old girl who works as a nursemaid in a cobbler's household and is so cruelly exploited, and so utterly exhausted from lack of sleep, that in the end, in a state of complete befuddlement she strangles the baby in her charge and, feeling relieved, at last falls sound asleep.

The story is a model of terseness, of a truly compact use of most effective artistic means, and can serve as an excellent illustration of the compositional and stylistic devices which underlie Chekhov's mastery as a short-story writer.

Before discussing those devices, I should like to touch upon what may appear to be one of the secondary aspects of the story—its portrayal of the state on the borderline between waking and sleeping as well as its portrayal of dreams. Though not a story about a dream, dream sequences play an important part in it. Dreams and reality jostle each other, intrude one upon another, merge into one another. There is nothing fantastic about Chekhov's dreams; they are presented realistically; and they are used most ingeniously to broaden the story itself, both spatially and temporally. Although the action of the story is set within twenty-four hours and in the narrow confines of a cobbler's dwelling, Chekhov uses the intervening dream sequences as flashbacks, to show the reader Varka's past and her background. Her father's illness and death, her and her mother's long trudge from the native village to the city in search of work, when they are reduced to begging for alms on the way—all this is seen through Varka's dream.

I repeat: *Sleepy* is not a dream story, but one feels that in writing it Chekhov was very much interested in the portrayal of dreams in

8. "From little" (Latin). [*Editor*.]
† From *Slavic and East European Review*, XX (1961), pp. 465–76. (The author's footnotes have been omitted.)

1. In a letter to A. N. Pleshcheev, January 23, 1888. [*Editor*.]
2. Altogether. [*Editor*.]

literature. I should therefore like to dwell for a while on certain circumstances which I think are related to the genesis of this story.[3] * * *

* * * That Chekhov had dreams, that he was interested in their physiology, in the relation between dream and reality, is demonstrated beyond all doubt by his letter to Grigorovich; it was not often that Chekhov reacted so enthusiastically and spontaneously to another writer's work. Given that interest, it is easy to imagine that sooner or later Chekhov himself would try to introduce dream experience into a story. This he did in *Sleepy*. The two stories are, of course, quite unlike. There are less than six pages in *Sleepy* as against Grigorovich's thirty. There are no social-satirical and philosophical digressions which, as Chekhov rightly pointed out, interfere with Grigorovich's narrative and, one may add, weaken its dreamlike quality. And yet, whatever was the source of Chekhov's little gem of a story (social-minded critics often juxtapose it with another —and much more sentimental one—*Vanka*, as being on the same theme of cruel exploitation of child labor), it is tempting to think that when Chekhov sat down to write it he remembered Grigorovich's attempt to give literary expression to dream sensations, and his own comments upon it, and decided to try his hand at this sort of thing, doing it, of course, in his own way. Little Varka's dreams which are worked into the texture of the story illustrate some of Chekhov's observations in his letter to Grigorovich. Consciously or not, Chekhov was giving Grigorovich an object lesson in the portrayal of dreams in literature.

As Varka falls asleep while rocking the cradle in which the baby cries, she sees dark clouds that chase one another and cry like the baby. Then the wind blows, the clouds disappear

and Varka sees a wide highway covered with watery mud. On the highway, wagon trains stretch, people with bundles on their backs drag themselves along, shadows of sorts flit back and forth; on both sides, through the cold, raw fog, forests can be seen. Suddenly the people with bundles and the shadows fall on the ground into the watery mud. "Why is this?" asks Varka. "To sleep, to sleep," they answer her. And they fall asleep soundly; they sleep sweetly while on the telegraph wires crows and magpies sit, shrilling like the baby and trying to wake her.

Some details here—the cold, raw fog, the watery mud, the dark clouds—recall both Grigorovich's story and Chekhov's letter about his own dreams.

---

3. Professor Struve discusses Grigorovich's story "Karelin's Dream" (January 1887) and Chekhov's letter of February 12, 1887, to Grigorovich. [*Editor.*]

Then Varka relives, in her dream, the sad day when her father was taken ill and was removed at night to the nearby county hospital; and the next morning when her mother went to inquire about him and returned with the news of his death.

> Varka goes into the woods and cries there, but suddenly someone hits her on the back of her head with such force that she bangs her forehead against a birch tree.

This is a transition from the dream to the grim reality; the birch is still part of the dream, but the knock on the head is reality intruding upon the dream:

> She raises her eyes and sees her master, the cobbler, standing before her. "What do you think you're doing, you mangy brat?" he says. "The child is crying and you're asleep?" He jerks her painfully by the ear, and she tosses her head, rocks the cradle, and purrs her song . . .

When she falls asleep again she once more sees, in her dream, the highway covered with watery mud:

> . . . the people with bundles on their backs and the shadows have stretched out and are sound asleep. Looking at them Varka feels a passionate longing for sleep: what a joy it would be for her to lie down, but her mother Pelageia is walking beside her and urging her on. They are both hurrying to town to look for work.

Not long before Chekhov wrote his story, he praised very highly, in a letter to Vladimir Galaktionovich Korolenko, the latter's story *The Sokolinian*. It was, he said, written like a good musical composition, according to all those rules which are suggested to the artist by his instinct. Coming from Chekhov, this was a great compliment. His own short stories, including *Sleepy*, certainly have the qualities of good musical compositions. If closely analyzed, *Sleepy* can be easily broken up into musical phrases. Recurring images and verbal formulas play an important part. The story begins with a masterly description—brief and yet pregnant—of the setting. Small realistic details emphasized by very short sentences (in Russian some of them consist of one or two words) alternate with those impressionistic brush strokes which Tolstoy had in mind when he said:

> Chekhov as an artist cannot even be compared with previous Russian writers—with Turgenev, Dostoevsky, or myself. Chekhov has his own peculiar manner, like the Impressionists. You look and it is as though the man was indiscriminately dabbing on whatever paints came to his hand, and these brush strokes seem to be quite unrelated to each other. But you move some distance away, you look, and you get on the whole an integrated impression. You have, before you, a bright, irresistible picture of nature.

Tolstoy may have thought, in the first place, of Chekhov's descriptions of nature (and in this connection one recalls that Chekhov regarded Turgenev's famous, much-vaunted descriptions as old-fashioned and said that something new was needed). But those words of Tolstoy's are applicable to Chekhov's manner, to his technique, in general.

Here is the beginning of *Sleepy*:

> It is night. Nursemaid Varka, a girl of about thirteen, is rocking a cradle in which a baby lies, and barely audibly purring:

> > "Rockabye, baby,
> > In the treetop . . ."

> Before the ikon a green light is burning; across the room, from corner to corner, stretches a line on which hang diapers and a pair of roomy black trousers. The ikon light throws a large green patch on the ceiling and the trousers cast long shadows on the stove, on the cradle, on Varka. When the light begins to flicker, the patch and the shadows come to life and are set in motion as though by a wind. It is stuffy. There is a smell of cabbage soup and cobbler's ware.

> The baby is shrilling . . .

One should note here the passage about the green patch and the shadows coming to life. In Chekhov's stories of this period (a good example is *The Post*, one of the most "Chekhovian" of Chekhov's short stories) we often find inanimate objects animated. Later Chekhov was to reproach Gorky for his anthropomorphic excesses (Gorky's famous "The sea was laughing . . ." in *Malva*). However, what Chekhov protested against was Gorky's pointless, gratuitous anthropomorphism—anthropomorphism for its own sake. In Chekhov's stories these animated objects have their own compositional and stylistic functions to perform, and in *Sleepy* the green patch and the shadows return again and again and play an important part. They serve as musical refrains and at the same time form part of Varka's sleepy obsession, of her hallucination.

> The ikon light flickers. The green patch and the shadows are set in motion, they force their way into Varka's half-open, staring eyes, and in her half-dormant brain form into hazy dreams. She sees dark clouds which chase each other across the sky and shrill like the baby.

When her employer hits her for dozing instead of minding the baby she tosses her head, and

> the green patch and the shadows from the trousers and diapers waver, wink at her, and soon again take possession of her brain.

One important detail here can be easily lost in translation. In Russian the verbs "to flicker" or "blink" (of the light) and "to wink" are closely related. So when Chekhov speaks of the green light flickering and the green patch winking at Varka he uses different forms of the same Russian verb. It is a surprisingly modern device that we constantly find in Chekhov. One of Chekhov's Russian critics called it "verbal suggestion." Another striking example of it in *Sleepy* is Varka's dream that she and her mother are begging for alms on the road: here the words "Give us . . ." are echoed by the mistress's angry command to *give* her the baby. Its function here is dual, however, for it also serves as a link between dream and reality.

Another recurrent image is the cricket which chirps in the stove, its chirping becoming in Varka's sleepy, befuddled mind identified with the crying of the baby. Here in translating the story into English one must at all cost find one verb which will do both for the crying of the baby and the sound produced by the cricket; that is why I have used the verb "to shrill." The same verb is used before for the cawing of crows and magpies, which is also a link connecting the dream with the crying of the baby. Just before the story ends, those images—the green patch, the shadows, and the cricket —return in combination:

> In the stove the cricket shrills. The green patch and the shadows from the trousers and diapers on the ceiling force their way into Varka's half-open eyes, flicker and befuddle her brain.
> "Rockabye, baby," she purrs.
> And the baby shrills and is exhausted with shrilling. Varka again sees the muddy highway, the people with bundles, Pelageia, her father Efim.

The description of Varka's pastime between the morning, when the baby is fed, and the next evening, when she goes back to her nocturnal watch over it, is also musically organized with the aid of oral staccato orders which progress crescendo and punctuate the narrative into a series of brief realistic descriptions of Varka's typically dreary and exhausting day: "Varka, light the stove!" "Varka, get the samovar ready!" "Varka, clean the master's overshoes!" "Varka, wash the staircase outside!" "Varka, get the samovar ready!" "Varka, run and buy three bottles of beer!" "Varka, run for some vodka!" "Varka, where is the corkscrew? Varka, clean the herring!" Without describing the life of Varka's employers, Chekhov gives us a complete picture of their daily routine. Note the double order for the samovar. The final order is: "Varka, rock the baby!"

The story has come round full circle; it has returned to its initial point: the last order can easily be imagined as preceding the beginning of the story. The circle begins to repeat itself:

> In the stove the cricket shrills. The green patch and the shadows on the ceiling from the trousers and diapers again force their way into Varka's half-open eyes, flicker and befuddle her brain.
> "Rockabye, baby,
> In the treetop," she purrs.
> And the baby shrills and is exhausted with shrilling. Varka again sees the muddy highway, the people with bundles, Pelageia, her father Efim.

But this time the vicious circle is broken. Chekhov has in store for us one of his most effective and dramatic surprise endings. About a dozen lines are given to the preparation and motivation of the denouement:

> She [Varka] understands everything, she recognizes everyone, but through her dozing she just cannot understand this force which shackles her hand and foot, weighs down on her, and interferes with her life. She turns round, looks for this force in order to rid herself of it, but cannot find it. At last exhausted, she strains all her strength and vision, looks up at the blinking [flickering] green patch and, after listening intently to the shrilling, finds the enemy that interferes with her life. That enemy is the child. She laughs. She is surprised. How is it that until now she could not understand such a simple thing? The green patch, the shadows and the cricket, too, seem to laugh and to be surprised.
> A false notion takes hold of Varka. She gets up from her stool and, smiling a wide smile, without blinking her eyes, walks about the room. She is pleasantly tickled by the thought that presently she will be rid of the baby which shackles her hand and foot. . . . To kill the baby and then sleep, sleep, sleep . . .

These words "sleep, sleep, sleep" very effectively echo the answer which the people with bundles and shadows give to Varka's question at the beginning of her dream. There is, perhaps, in this passage just one false note: the sentence about "false notion" seems superfluous, un-Chekhovian. On the other hand, one should not, perhaps, translate it that way; Chekhov may have used this expression instead of the medical term "hallucination."

The denouement itself is quite short. Its dispassionate terseness and banality contrasts with some of the endings in earlier stories of this middle period, which are either overmuffled or not free from a somewhat obtrusive didacticism (e.g., in the story *The Enemies*, 1887, otherwise a most effective story on the subject of mutual unintelligibility and isolation of human beings).

In the final paragraph of the story the green patch and the

shadows which, as we have just seen, seemed to share Varka's joyful surprise, reappear again, acquiring a new significance (and remember what has been said about the near-identity of the verbs "to flicker" and "to wink" in Russian):

> Laughing, winking at the green patch and shaking her fingers at it, Varka steals up to the cradle and bends over the baby. Having strangled it, she quickly lies down on the floor, laughing with joy now that she can sleep, and a minute later is sleeping already as soundly as if she were dead.

This ending is the very limit of the detachment which Chekhov prized so highly in a writer, and which made Mikhailovsky so indignant (in referring to the callous indifference with which Chekhov chose his subjects, he mentioned, among other stories, *Sleepy*). It is strange to think now that in the story as printed originally in the newspaper the last sentence ("Having strangled, etc.") was absent. It occurs first in the version—otherwise almost unrevised—included in the volume *Khmurye liudi*[4] (1890). Whether the sentence was an afterthought, or whether Chekhov had it in mind from the very outset but had decided to spare the susceptibilities of the readers of the *Petersburg Gazette*, we do not know; its manuscript does not seem to have been preserved. There exists also a remote possibility that this final sentence was struck out by the editor, but if this had been the case it would probably have become known. Although Chekhov sometimes attained excellent effects by leaving things unsaid (this was part of his "Impressionism"), it seems to me that here, by spelling things out, he enhanced the effect of the story, without making it in the least melodramatic.

Sleepy is said to have been very highly regarded by Leo Tolstoy. It is certainly a very good confirmation of Tolstoy's opinion of Chekhov as an impressionist artist. It may be worth mentioning that Chekhov's impressionism was noted, even before Tolstoy, by the same Grigorovich, though he did not use the word; in one of his letters to Chekhov he discussed Chekhov's impressionistic technique in the story *Agatha*. The same impressionistic technique is skillfully and effectively applied by Chekhov in a number of stories written between 1886 and 1889, in which pictures gradually acquire breadth and depth and result of similar brush strokes, seemingly laid at random but actually contrived very cleverly. To name only two, such stories as *The Post* and *Typhus*, which usually are not considered among Chekhov's best, would repay a close compositional and stylistic analysis in this light. Such an analysis would confirm the impression of Chekhov's exquisite mastery even in this early middle period. There is much to be said for preferring those

---

4. *Gloomy People.* [*Editor.*]

stories, and certainly *Sleepy*, to such more famous ones as *A Dreary Story*, *The Duel*, or *Ward No. 6*.

DONALD RAYFIELD

[The Student] †

* * *

The mystic side of Chekhov—his irrational intuition that there is meaning and beauty in the cosmos, which aligns him more to Leskov than to Tolstoy in the Russian literary tradition—is very nearly suppressed in the Melikhovo phase, preoccupied as it is with the objective and concrete. But there is one work of 1894, *The Student*, which Chekhov insisted to Bunin was his favorite and most optimistic piece. It is the only story of the Melikhovo period which links the lyricism of *Steppe* with the late prose of *The Bishop*, and almost the only story of Chekhov's which can be read as a parable about art. Lyrical praise of nature brings about fusion of love and reflection. For the first time Chekhov shows that he has found out what makes art of crucial importance to humanity, and, as always when dealing with poetry or music, he sees it as its purest in an ecclesiastical setting. A seminary student is walking home on a wintry day just before Easter; the wind and the desolate landscape arouse the romantic thought that this cold and wind are something perpetual that Ivan the Terrible and Christ too experienced. Misery and oppression are the essence of human life and will always be so. Debilitated by this insight, the student stops to talk to two peasant widows and finds himself clumsily retelling the story of Peter's betrayal of Christ, mixing half-intelligible Church-Slavonisms with the utmost simplification of the story. To his amazement, the women burst into tears, and the student discovers the inexplicable magic of narrative that has nothing to do with the person of the narrator, and the affinity that the suffering and oppressed have with all the suffering and oppression in history. Time and space are bridged in an instant. The story ends with the student filled with a joy at this sudden collapse of time and space as powerful as the depression which the oneness of the world evoked in the beginning. He has touched 'both ends of a chain'. This is Chekhov's only image for describing what art does. The student understands that the misery and horror of life engender truth and beauty in those who suffer from it. His joy may be conditional, for Chekhov breaks in as a narrator when he says 'he was only twenty-two', but faith in human

† From Donald Rayfield, *Chekhov: The Evolution of His Art* (London: Paul Elek, 1975), pp. 152–55.

response to a hostile universe is to be the strongest strand in the late prose.

The Student is an oddity among the Melikhovo works, but technically it is among the most representative in Chekhov's *oeuvre*. At the outset Chekhov very precisely establishes time and place, the visual and auditory impressions on the hero, and leaves vague all the traditional details of his face and gait. Nature is given predominance. Even in such a brief work, changes of mood are initiated by nature: the weather suddenly becomes wintry, thrushes and snipe call, something croaks in the marshes, slivers of ice appear in the river. These images lead to a series of apparently unrelated phenomena: a shot, a sound like someone blowing over an empty bottle, all bring a sense of desolation and hollowness to the hero, whose name, like all those in late Chekhov, is perfectly convincing and yet also links him with the open countryside through which he is passing: he is Velikopol'sky, 'great fields'. The fragmentary background given—the coughing father, the bare-footed mother, the student's hunger—integrates him all the more closely into the scene. As he approaches the two widows to whom he is to tell the story of Peter's betrayal, the verbs of the narrative already prefigure tension, conflict: the verb *dulo, dul* (blew) shows the disturbance in nature and in the hero; the paradox of the hero's fingers frozen stiff (*zakocheneli*) while his face is burnt (*razgorelos'*) by the wind anticipates the strange mixture of misery and joy in his story and the reaction to it.

The most striking element of the structure is its cyclic shape: all the details of the scene are mirrored in the story of Peter's betrayal, which in turn is mirrored in the final page of narrative. The workmen on the other side of the river correspond to the workmen warming themselves by the fire in the story of Peter: the calling of the birds in the opening phrases corresponds to the triple crowing of the cock; the description of the younger widow as *zabitaya* (beaten down) corresponds to the description of Christ, beaten and tormented (*bili, zamuchennyy*); the weeping of Peter (*zaplakal* and the Church Slavonic *plakasya*) leads to the weeping of Vasilisa. The campfire in the story of Peter is echoed by a campfire in the background of the last scene; the dawn of Peter's betrayal corresponds to the sunset into which the student walks. On one level, this structure merely shows how a natural scene—desolate spring, a camp-fire, two windows—provokes a narrative which embodies its mood and its details. But two paragraphs, at the beginning and the end of the story, show us how Velikopol'sky's thoughts make more of the connection. The word *dul* (blew) inspires the student with the thought that 'now' is part of eternity, that this scene of poverty is, like the wind, timeless. From that idea of dejection spring the narrative and the final joy of the whole story: if want and wind are timeless, so are the great moments of human suffering. And if these moments are meaningful to later generations, then art, the narration of suffering, like religion, is meaningful. Rarely was Chekhov's integrated imagery so economically effective. The final paragraph of the story is typical in its symbolism of his ecclesiastical works. The overjoyed student crosses the river by the ferry: as in *On Easter Eve* of 1886 and elsewhere, the river symbolises the division of two worlds. He climbs a hill and looks down on his village—a moment of transfiguration, of escape from the prison of environment, again to be seen in *In the Ravine* when Lipa walks on the hillside above her village. The images of sunset and daybreak, with their blood-red coloring, remain ominous, but in *The Student* the association of Peter and the present day makes the 'coldness' insignificant: the final impressions are of truth, beauty and happiness.

The rhythm of the language brings out the joy of the student's narration. The first part of the story is harsh and laconic; when the student begins to speak, the style becomes rich and gentle. Some of his language is childlike: his double adjectives, *tikhiy-tikhiy*, *tyomnyy-tyomnyy*, *gor'ko-gor'ko* (quiet, dark, bitter). Some is exotic, his Church Slavonic *petel* (cock), *vecherya* (last supper), *plakasya* (he wept), mingling the past with the present in the very texture of the prose. The last part of the story has a verbal rhythm that follows the movement of the characters. 'Vasilisa suddenly sobbed [*vskhlipnula*], tears, big, copious' is punctuated to show the convulsions of tears. The third paragraph from the end of the story is cast as a Tolstoyan series of syllogisms, slow, firm and dry: 'If Vasilisa cried . . . then clearly, what he had just been relating . . . was relevant to the present . . . and probably to this empty village, to himself, to everyone. If . . . then not because . . . but because . . . and because . . . in what had been happening.' Almost without concrete imagery, with a stringent syntax unlike that of the rest of the story, this paragraph mimics the tortuous, even clumsy cerebral reaction in Velikopol'sky. If we compare this 'cerebral' passage, with its conjunctions and its parallel constructions, with the last paragraph, we can see the difference between thought and intuition. The last paragraph is one long sentence of a hundred words, one flow of images concrete and abstract, moving from 'the ferry . . . river . . . hill . . . village . . . sunset' to 'truth . . . beauty . . . youth . . . health . . . strength . . . joy . . . sense'. There is no 'because': the construction is parenthetic, not logical, and is made when 'when', 'where', 'he thought about how'; with dashes, with 'and's, leading not to an elucidation, but to a climax. The third paragraph from the close explains what has happened; the last paragraph is a subjective ending. For Chekhov the illusion of an imminent break-through of happiness was in his last words more important than the verifiable observations on the present. *The Student* is a perfect example in miniature of Chekhov's art, and it bridges the gap between the ecstatic mood of the ecclesiastical and steppe stories of 1886 and 1887 and the lyricism of the prose of the 1900s.

KARL KRAMER

Stories of Ambiguity†

One could, with respect to terminology, talk about either ambiguity or paradox in describing that particular aspect of Chekhov's work which involves the concept of meaning in the later stories. If the term 'ambiguity' ordinarily denotes situations in which two or more interpretations can coexist, then it refers to a "both-and" type of relationship. The term 'paradox' normally indicates contradictory meanings, and thus refers to an "either-or" situation. The difficulty in regard to Chekhov is that the two or more meanings of a given story are ordinarily opposed to each other. However, there is some precedent for calling this relationship ambiguous: William Empson's last two categories of ambiguity involve contradictory meanings,[1] and Edmund Wilson's initial example of ambiguity in Henry James' work is *The Turn of the Screw*, where a choice of interpretations hinges on two opposed suppositions: the governess does see the ghosts; she does not see the ghosts.[2] On the other hand, as Cleanth Brooks defines paradox in "The Language of Paradox"[3] the contradictory situations which he cites are invariably reconciled. Thus, one could define the type of ambiguity we usually find in Chekhov's later stories as unresolved paradox. In the following collection of alternative readings one interpretation may appear considerably more plausible than another for a given story; however, my primary intention is to indicate that no single reading will adequately account for the whole fabric in any of these stories. This in itself is sufficient to establish their ambiguity.

Inasmuch as Empson and Brooks confine their discussions to poetry, they are using ambiguity and paradox in reference to particular words and phrases. Assuming that the semantic unit is correspondingly larger in artistic prose, we shall ordinarily be talking about ambiguity engendered by what Tolstoy called 'the labyrinth of linkages' of prose fiction.[4] In short, Chekhov's ambiguity frequently emerges from the reader's perception of contradictions in parallel passages throughout a given story.

† Chapter IX of Karl Kramer, *The Chameleon and the Dream* (The Hague: Mouton, 1970), pp. 153–73.
1. William Empson, *Seven Types of Ambiguity* (New York, 1955), pp. 199–264.
2. Edmund Wilson, *The Triple Thinkers* (New York, 1948), pp. 88–95.
3. Cleanth Brooks, *The Well Wrought Urn* (New York, 1947), pp. 3–22.
4. See Victor Erlich, *Russian Formalism* (The Hague, 1955), p. 209.

One of the clearest examples of Chekhov's ambiguity is his last short story, *Betrothed* (*Nevesta*, 1903). It is useful for two reasons to begin here—because the ambiguity is closely related to the problem of time discussed in the last chapter and because *Betrothed* offers the reader his only opportunity to watch Chekhov in the process of constructing a story which can be equally well interpreted in several different ways. This is made possible through the existence of a different, earlier version of the manuscript.[5] The ambiguity is related to the question of human progress versus the monotonous appearance of constant change which moves mankind neither forward nor backward—the ladder versus the treadmill. Framed after the manner of the announcer in a radio soap opera, the question in *Betrothed* is this: does the heroine, Nadya, escape the confines of her parents' narrow provincialism and will she eventually find a better life, or is she condemned to a constant flitting from one passion to another, each of which is essentially meaningless in its relation to all the others? The commonly accepted interpretation of the story is the first one, both in the West and in the Soviet Union.[6] In this reading Nadya gradually becomes aware of the *poshlost'* [7] in life at home, aware too of the fact that nothing in her family's way of life has changed during the past twenty years. Under the influence of a friend studying at the university, Sasha, she realizes that her forthcoming marriage would condemn her to just such a life forever. Therefore, she takes Sasha's advice, breaks off her engagement, and leaves her family to study. After a year at the university she returns home on a visit and finds that she has definitely outgrown her earlier life and confidently looks forward to a much better and more interesting one in the future. This interpretation starts running into difficulties when one notices that of all the Chekhov characters who discuss the future only Nadya and possibly Trofimov in *The Cherry Orchard* are so unreservedly committed to their faith in a better future.

5. There are actually three complete versions of the manuscript in existence: the rough draft (IX, 505–528), the fair copy submitted to Mirolzhubov, the editor of the *Journal for Everybody* (*Zhurnal dlya vsekh*), where it was first published, and the final version, which appeared in the 1906 edition of Chekhov's collected works and also in the 1944–51 Soviet edition (IX, 432–453). The magazine version is available in *Literaturnoe nasledstvo: Chekhov*, ed. V. V. Vinogradov *et al.* (Moscow, 1960), LXVIII, 87–109. Although most of the crucial changes had already been incorporated in the magazine version, for the sake of simplicity my references are limited to the rough draft and the story in its final form, as it appeared in the 1906 edition. [The volume numbers referred to in the text of this essay are those of the 1944–51 Soviet edition of Chekhov's works.—*Editor*.]

6. See in particular, Ronald Hingley, *Chekhov: A Biographical and Critical Study* (London, 1950), pp. 170–171; V. Ermilov, *Chekhov* (Moscow, 1949), p. 414; and Zinovii Papernyi, *A. P. Chekhov: Ocherk tvorchestva* (Moscow, 1960,) pp. 280–291. From my own experience I should like to add that during the 1960 centennial celebrations of Chekhov's birth, educational institutions in Moscow were deluged with posters describing what was purported to be Chekhov's formula for a better life in the future, such as this quotation from *Betrothed*: "Oh, if only that new, bright life would come more quickly—that life in which one will be able to face one's fate boldly and directly, to know that one is right, to be lighthearted and free! And sooner or later such a life will come" (IX, 449).

7. Triviality, vulgarity. [*Editor*.]

The second possible interpretation would see Nadya going through a series of awakenings and a process in which each new stage implies a rejection of the previous one. We see such a process in her disillusionment with the people who guide her. At the beginning of the story she believes that her mother is an extraordinary person, but as Sasha comes to have more influence over Nadya, the mother becomes increasingly ordinary until finally Nadya can no longer understand why her mother ever struck her as remarkable.

Even before she leaves home, the process of disillusionment with Sasha gets under way: " 'He is a strange, naïve man', thought Nadya, 'and in his dreams, in all these wonderful gardens, unusual fountains, one feels something absurd', but for some reason in his naïveté, even in this absurdity there was so much beauty that scarcely had she thought about going away to study when a cold feeling would pour through her heart and her bosom and she was filled with a feeling of joy and delight" (IX, 439).

When she tells Sasha that she has made up her mind to leave, he is delighted: "But she looked at him, not blinking, with large, adoring eyes, as though spellbound, expecting him to say to her immediately something significant, limitless in its importance; he hadn't yet told her anything, but already it seemed to her that something new and broad was opening before her, something she hadn't known about earlier, and already she was looking at him full of expectation, ready for everything, even death" (IX, 444). But instead of saying something significant Sasha immediately plunges into talking about the details of their departure.

These hints at disillusionment with Sasha are not fully realized until she sees him again after a year of study, when he appears to her "gray, provincial" (IX, 446). As she sits in his room looking at him, ". . . for some reason Andrei Andreich rose up in her imagination and the naked lady with the vase [an earlier image of the *poshlost'* she associated with her prospective marriage to Andrei] and all her past which seemed to her now so far away, like childhood. And she started crying because Sasha already seemed to her not so new, intellectual, interesting as he had been last year" (IX, 446–447). She comes to the conclusion that "from Sasha, from his words, from his smile, and from his whole figure came something out of date, old fashioned, done with long ago, and, perhaps, already departed for the grave" (IX, 447). Sasha is dying of tuberculosis, but in context obviously this speech points to something more than a premonition of his death.

In the final scene she is at home again on a visit. She reaffirms her faith in a better future and receives a telegram announcing Sasha's death. The last paragraph reads: "She went up to her room to pack, and the next morning said goodbye to her own, and vibrant, joyful left the town—as she supposed, forever" (IX, 450). These words convey several facts about the present but say nothing really about the future. We know for certain only that Nadya thought she would never return. It is equally possible that she is right and that she is wrong. If we keep in mind the fact that we have twice observed her going through this process of excited explanation followed by disillusionment, the last phrase suggests the possibility that the whole process is beginning all over again. Therefore, the question remains: has Nadya escaped a narrowly provincial life and will she find some kind of more exalted existence, or is she condemned to an endless repetition of these awakenings and disillusionments? It seems to me both interpretations are equally tenable and this, of course, is at the heart of the story's ambiguity.

The original version was considerably less susceptible to the latter reading. In the rough draft there is no doubt that Nadya is moving forward to a better life; the concept of an endless series of illusions is simply not there. Probably the most important changes from this point of view concern the presentation of Sasha's character, particularly as it appears in several of the scenes just discussed. When Nadya announces to Sasha that she is going away to study, she does not await something significant from his lips. She has no expectation for him to disappoint; instead, he makes just the kind of speech that Nadya in the finished version hopes to hear:

> "Listen to me. We will speak seriously," he began, frowning. "I am convinced, believe deeply that Russia needs only two sorts of people: the holy and the enlightened. I deeply believe in this and consider it my duty to convince others, such as you. We live in rude, ignorant time, we must go for a minority. I swear to you, you will not regret it, will not swerve, and you'll marry, and your bridegroom will be a remarkable man," again he started laughing. "Go away to study and there let fate carry you where it will. And so shall we go tomorrow?" (IX, 521).

In short, by dropping this speech Chekhov reversed the conception of Sasha's character in this scene. Indeed, Sasha deteriorates at several points in the revision; thus, originally, when Nadya visits him after her year of study, she does not classify him with those elements of her old life which she had rejected.

When she returns home for a visit, she makes this observation on her life—an observation subsequently dropped: " 'I am satisfied, mama. Naturally, when I began my courses, I thought I would attain everything and that I'd want nothing more, but as I went to school and studied, new plans opened out, and then again new plans, and always broader and broader, and it seems there isn't and never will be an end to either work or anxiety' " (IX, 525). This speech causes the reader to set more store by Nadya's understanding of herself than he can in the finished story. The final paragraph was also rewritten. Here is first the original and then the revised version:

> She went up to her room to pack and the next morning she left; before her she pictured a broad, pure life of labor (IX, 527).

> "Goodbye, dear Sasha!" she thought, and before her she pictured a new life, broad and vast, and this life, still not clear, full of mysteries, attracted her and beckoned her to it.
> She went up to her room to pack, and the next morning she said goodbye to her own, and vibrant, joyful, left the town—as she supposed, forever (IX, 450).

This rearrangement of the elements obviously indicates, it seems to me, an effort to make Nadya's future considerably less certain, to cast a final doubt on her outcome.

If there is a deliberate effort to plant ambiguity at the very core of the story, then what is the significance of this effort? As in the great majority of the last stories, the point of the ambiguity is to highlight the precarious relationship between actuality and one's consciousness of it. Chekhov's ambiguity is always a reflection of the ambiguity inherent in the character's realtionship to his existence: he can never be certain just what that relationship is, and finally, in one of the very last stories, *The Bishop*, there is some doubt whether a relationship exists at all.[8]

* * *

* * * In *Betrothed* and *The Black Monk* the ambiguity hinges on the question, what has happened to the characters? In *The Darling* (*Dushechka*, 1898) it hinges rather on the question, what does the central character herself represent? The traditional interpretation sees Olenka as completely passive. This is the view taken by Renato Poggioli,[9] for instance, when he quotes with approval and accepts as a proper summation of Olenka's character this line from the story: "She wanted a love that would absorb her whole being, her soul, her mind, that would give her ideas, a purpose in life, that would warm her aging blood" (IX, 323). But there is another side to Olenka's life; there are hints that it so dominates the loved one that it eventually destroys him. At any rate, she completely takes over the opinions of her first two husbands, Kukin and Pustovalov, both of whom die. Describing her absorption of Kukin's opinions,

---

8. Dmitrii Merezhkovskii wrote: Chekhov heroes have no life, there is only the daily routine without any event, or with only one event: death, the end of the daily routine, the end of being. Daily routine and death: these are the two fixed poles of Chekhov's world." See "Chekhov i Gorky" in *Gryadushchii kham* (St. Petersburg, 1906), p. 50. I would say rather that the first pole— daily routine—has ultimately a dubious kind of being, or at least one is never exactly certain just what the nature of it is.

9. See Renato Poggioli, "Storytelling in a Double Key" in *The Phoenix and the Spider* (Cambridge, Massachusetts, 1957), pp. 109–131. [The essay is reprinted in this volume.—*Editor*.]

Chekhov writes: "Olenka was filling out and beamed with satisfaction, but Kukin was getting thinner and more sallow..." (IX, 317). The syntactical arrangement of the sentence hints at a direct relationship between Olenka's vigor and Kukin's languor. Though it does not necessarily mean this, it could be taken to imply that as Olenka emotionally feeds on her husband, she saps him of his vitality. Her third attachment is with the veterinarian, Vladimir Platonich. Her relationship with him differs in two respects from that with Kukin and Pustovalov. In the first place, the veterinarian is the only man to resent her parroting his opinions: " 'I've asked you before not to talk about things you don't understand! When veterinarians are speaking among themselves, please don't butt in! It's really annoying' " (IX, 322). In the second place, the veterinarian does not die; he finally deserts Olenka to return to his wife. Now it could be more than coincidence that these two sets of conditions occur in just these combinations.

Olenka's final encounter is with Sasha, a young boy. It is a mother's love she shows here, but like the veterinarian, Sasha deeply resents her fondling attentions. The final lines read: "... She goes back to bed and thinks of Sasha who is fast asleep in the next room and sometimes shouts in his sleep: 'I'll give it to you! Scram! No fighting!' " (IX, 327). Obviously, Sasha is having a dream in which he is talking with his schoolmates, but in view of the pattern established in Olenka's relation to those she loves, and in view of Sasha's open resistance to her attentions, the final line may apply to Olenka as well. If not, then the ending appears considerably less relevant to the story than Chekhov's endings normally are.

* * *

In several of the major stories written during this period the ambiguity crystallizes in the narrator's uncertain attitude toward the people and events he describes. In *The House with a Mansard* (*Dom s mezoninom*, 1896) the ambiguity in Lida's character becomes a reflection of the narrator's personality. Soviet interpretation, for which there is solid evidence, sees the story as a melodrama in which Lida, the older sister, is the villainess, destroying the romance between her younger sister, Missuse, and the painter-narrator, as well as exerting her will in local government affairs at every turn.[1] Certainly she displays a despotic nature: she tyrannizes over Missuse and her mother; she seeks power in the local *zemstvo* organization; there are hints that her instruction of peasants appeals to her mainly as an outlet for her tyrannical tendencies; and she crushes the beginnings of love in Missuse and the narrator.

However, to view the narrator and Missuse as innocent victims of

1. Once again, the "model" Soviet inter-   *Chekhov*, pp. 266–277.
pretation is to be found in Ermilov,

Lida's cruelty leaves a number of incidents and remarks unexplained. We must keep in mind the fact that we see Lida only through the narrator's eyes and that he himself vacillates in his attitude toward her. He begins by describing his life in the country: "Condemned by destiny to perpetual idleness, I did absolutely nothing" (IX, 86). Describing his impression of the two sisters, he observes: "And everything seemed to me young and pure, thanks to the presence of Lida and Missuse, and there was an atmosphere of refinement over everything" (IX, 89). He makes this remark at a time when he had already seen enough of Lida to know her character and interests. He continues: "As a rule I sat on the lower step of the terrace; I was tormented by dissatisfaction with myself, grieved by the thought that my life was passing so rapidly and uninterestingly . . ." (IX, 90). This observation could refer equally well to either the romance beginning to develop between him and Missuse, or, in view of the artist's indolent life, it could also refer to his frustration at the contrast between his own inactivity and Lida's absorption in her work. As a matter of fact, in a later scene when Lida and the artist attack one another's social ideas, she accuses him of criticizing her to cover his own indifference. And he himself confesses to a friend that: "From my earliest days I've been wrung by envy, self-dissatisfaction, and distrust in my work" (IX, 94). Viewed in this light, the relationship between Lida and the narrator is ambiguous through its vagueness.

Unlike her sister, Missuse is an extremely passive personality. She does everything her sister tells her, and certainly one reason Lida resents the artist's presence is that she fears he will disrupt her influence over her sister. The artist accepts a peculiar role in his relationship with Missuse also: he becomes her spiritual guide for a short time, only because she expects this of him. The possessor is also the possessed: "Zhenia [Missuse] thought that as an artist I must know a great deal and that I can accurately guess at what I don't know. She wished I would lead her into the region of the eternal and the beautiful, to that higher world in which, according to her, I was my own master, and she talked with me of God, eternal life, miracles. And I, who had not admitted that myself and my imagination would perish forever after death, answered, 'yes, man is immortal,' 'yes, eternal life awaits us,' while she listened, believed and did not demand proof" (IX, 92). He indicates his passive nature again when he bows before Lida's decision that the romance must come to an end. At the real center of the story, then, stands the narrator, who vacillates between the extreme character types of Missuse and Lida, who leads and is led by Missuse, who admires and abhors the strength of Lida's personality.

Nikitin, the central character in *The Teacher of Literature* (*Uchitel' slovesnosti*, 1894), if not ambivalent, is certainly shifty in his attitude toward his environment. D. S. Mirsky is the spokesman for the standard interpretation of the story:

> Chekhov excels in the art of tracing the first stages of an emotional process; in indicating those first symptoms of a deviation when to the general eye, and to the conscious eye of the subject in question, the nascent curve still seems to coincide with a straight line. An infinitesimal touch, which at first hardly arrests the reader's attention, gives a hint at the direction the story is going to take. It is then repeated as a leit-motiv, and at each repetition the true equation of the curve becomes more apparent, and it ends by shooting away in a direction very different from that of the original straight line. . . . In *The Teacher of Literature* the straight line is again the hero's love; the curve, his dormant dissatisfaction with selfish happiness and his intellectual ambition.[1]

Mirsky assumes that Nikitin comes to a real awareness of the false values in his life, but there remains a nagging doubt about whether such an awareness ever actually occurs. Nikitin's peculiarity is that mood alone governs his reactions to the world. His inner attitude determines the nature of the external world, as if the latter were dependent on the former. We are introduced to a man whose emotional response bears no direct relationship to the stimulus. Therefore, we have no means of knowing whether his feelings are in any way permanent or simply the result of a combination of factors which make up his mood: "Since Nikitin had been in love with Masha, everything at the Shelestovs pleased him: the house, the garden, and the evening tea, and the wickerwork chairs and the old nurse, and even the word 'loutishness' which the old man was fond of using" (VIII, 352). Here he is clearly reacting not to the Shelestov family, but to his love for Masha.

After their marriage he tells Masha: " 'But I don't look upon my happiness as on something that has come to me by accident, as if from heaven. This happiness is a perfectly natural, consistent, logically probable occurrence. I believe that man is the creator of his own happiness and I am now taking precisely that which I have created' " (VIII, 367). Nikitin is probably right in what he says, but ironically for the wrong reason. He believes his happiness is something real which he has created, but it exists only in his own imagination. It cannot operate independently of his mood; thus it has no real foundation.

Here is Nikitin's 'awakening': in bed one night he thinks that there is "another world. . . . And he had a passionate poignant longing to be in that other world, to work himself at some factory or big workshop, to speak with authority, to write, to publish, to raise a

1. D. S. Mirsky, *A History of Russian Literature* (New York, 1949), p. 362.

stir, to exhaust himself, to suffer . . ." (VIII, 369–370). But this other world is another product of Nikitin's imagination; it bears no direct relation to his experience.

The weather, a detail from actual experience, is a revealing reference point in the story. Just after his marriage Nikitin writes in his diary: "I recalled our first meetings, our rides into the country, my declaration of love, and the weather, which as though on purpose had been exquisitely fine all summer" (VIII, 364). But the weather which Nikitin thought so delightful when it fitted his own concept of the world, has no influence over him when his mood changes. One year later, "Spring was beginning as exquisitely as last year, and it promised the same joys . . ." (VIII, 371). But now Nikitin notes in his diary: "There is nothing more terrible than vulgarity. I must escape from here, I must escape today, or I shall go out of my mind!" (VIII, 372). Frequently during the course of the story Chekhov permits us to read passages from Nikitin's diary. Certainly this device increases our sense of direct contact with Nikitin, but as a way of representing the world to which he responds it is far from direct. It blurs our perception of external reality to a point where we have no basis for judging the appropriateness of Nikitin's responses. Thus, we are left not quite certain whether this is an awakening to the actual world around him, or whether it is another of his moods, no more accurate a reflection of actuality than his previous one. Chekhov offers us no way of knowing for sure, and herein lies the ambiguity.

By way of contrast, James Joyce's "Araby" is another story of disillusionment, but it contains no ambiguity whatsoever. The hero's romantic concept of a village fair is violently shattered by the conventionality and crudeness of the real thing, but in Joyce the hero's realization is of secondary importance. His preconception and the stark reality are the two focuses for the story. The reader knows what the hero thought the fair would be like and he knows what it is actually like, while Chekhov limits our perception of the real to Nikitin's impressions of it.

In the trilogy of stories from 1898, *The Man in a Case* (*Chelovek v futliare*), *Gooseberries* (*Kryzhovnik*), and *About Love* (*O liubvi*), there is a problem in the way the narrator understands his own story and in the extent of his commitment to the principles he espouses. In this series the 'labyrinth of linkages' extends from one story into the next. In the first there are two central characters, Burkin and Ivan Ivanych, who are joined by a third figure in the next two, Alekhin. All three stories focus on the theme of *futliarnost'*,[2] as the title of the first pointedly reminds us. In *The Man in a*

2. Encasing oneself physically, psychologically, morally, and spiritually in order to reduce the points of contact between oneself and the rest of the world. [As defined by Kramer later— *Editor.*]

Case Burkin, the narrator, apparently comprehends that *futliarnost'*, retreat and escape from life, is not a peculiarity of Belikov alone. He observes at the end of his narrative that within a week of Belikov's death life in the town had slipped back into its familiar pattern and he asks how many "such men in shells were left, how many more of them there will be" (IX, 264). Then Burkin and Ivan Ivanych step outside to look at the night:

> It was already midnight. On the right could be seen the whole village, a long street stretching far away for some three miles. Everything was sunk in deep, silent slumber; not a movement, not a sound; one could hardly believe that nature could be so still. When on a moonlit night you see a wide village street, with its cottages, its haystacks, and its willows that have dropped off to sleep, a feeling of serenity comes over the soul; as it rests thus, hidden from toil, care, and sorrow by the nocturnal shadows, the street is gentle, sad, beautiful, and it seems as though the stars look down upon it kindly and tenderly, and as if there were no more evil on earth, and all were well. On the left, where the village ended, the open country began; the fields could be seen stretching far away to the horizon, and there was no movement, no sound in that whole expanse drenched with moonlight (IX, 264).

The earth itself is enveloped in a shell which lulls one; the spirit of *futliarnost'* spreads over the entire world. Burkin apparently succumbs to its spell as he falls asleep. Ivan Ivanych, on the other hand, becomes extremely agitated and extends the implications of his friend's story: " 'And isn't the fact that we live in the stifling, crowded city, write useless documents, play whist—isn't this a shell? And that we spend our whole life among loafers, petty quarrelers, stupid, lazy women, speak and hear various inanities—isn't this a shell? Now if you like, I'll tell you a very instructive story' " (IX, 265).

When Ivan Ivanych does tell his story in *Gooseberries* the confusions multiply because his behavior and even his words contradict his narrative. The two friends visit Alekhin's estate in the country, where their first action is to bathe. Ivan Ivanych is especially taken with his bath in the open air and continues to splash about rapturously long after his companions have finished. The image that emerges is of a man who deeply loves the country from which he has long been cut off by life in the city. But his story concerns his brother, who retreats from city to country, to retire in the shell of a small estate. When Ivan Ivanych observes, " '. . . I never sympathized with his desire to lock himself up for his whole life on his own country estate' " (IX, 269), his words fail to jibe with his obvious delight in the country life.

After explaining that his brother's cramped style of living made him realize that his own life was no less shell-like, Ivan Ivanych says: " 'I then left my brother's place early in the morning, and since then living in the city has become unendurable for me. Peace and quiet oppress me . . .' " (IX, 274). It is unclear whether Ivan Ivanych realizes that at this point he is talking about both city and country. There is also the possibility that his behavior in the bath contradicts these words.

There is a further contradiction in his statement that his brother's way of life showed him the inadequacy of his own behavior: he subsequently rejects the implications of this awareness for his own life when he pleads that he is now old, and instead implores Alekhin, who is younger, to live in a way which he himself refuses to do. Alekhin, incidentally, is unmoved, seeing no connection between Ivan Ivanych's story and his own life.

When the three men retire for the night, Ivan Ivanych falls asleep instantly, as if he is no longer troubled by his own agitation. This time it is Burkin who cannot fall asleep, irritated by the smell of tobacco still burning in Ivan Ivanych's last pipe. It may be that Burkin is aware of the implications in the tale and that the smell of the pipe is a vague reminder of Ivan Ivanych's plea, or it may be that Burkin is aroused, ironically, by the irritating smell to a far greater degree than he was by Ivan Ivanych's stirring message, or it may be, as Mark Schorer has suggested, that the smell of the pipe is "the smell of some lingering falsehood, of Ivan's story, in fact, which tried at once to prove and disprove its point".[3]

About Love is Alekhin's story of how he and a young woman sacrificed their love for the happiness of others; the young woman already had a husband and children. His point is that he and the woman made a mistake, that now he feels everything should have been sacrificed for the only real love he would ever know. Alekhin's story is a protest against the concealment of real feeling under the protective cloak of social convention. It is also an answer to Ivan Ivanych's appeal at the end of *Gooseberries*: " 'There is no happiness and there shouldn't be, but if there is a meaning and purpose in life, then this meaning and purpose lie not in our happiness but in something more rational and greater. Do good!' " (IX, 274). In effect this is what Alekhin has done, and the result is his own brand of *futliarnost'*.

The story ends on an irrelevance as Burkin and Ivan Ivanych recall having met the woman whom Alekhin loved: "Burkin was even acquainted with her and found her beautiful" (IX, 285). The irrelevance points up the failure of both men to comprehend the correlation between Alekhin's experience and theirs. The series of stories possesses its own inner intensity as it moves from Burkin's

3. *The Story: A Critical Anthology*, ed. Mark Schorer (Englewood Cliffs, N.J., 1950), p. 64.

account of an acquaintance to Ivan Ivanych's account of his brother to Alekhin's account of himself, while at the same time the sense of the characters' commitment to their principles becomes increasingly hazy. There is a final parallel between Burkin in the first tale and Alekhin in the last. Each man's *futliarnost'* has taken the form of a rejection of love, and there may be a further hint at Alekhin's resemblance to Belikov in the image of a squirrel in its cage which is used twice to describe Alekhin in *About Love*. Thus, for all the intensity of conviction which these characters exhibit there is a strong sense that they fail to cómprehend the nature of their own commitment—a sense which is reinforced by the disparity between their convictions and their acts.

In *The Lady with the Dog* (*Dama s sobachkoi*, 1899) the hero's inability to understand his own feelings infects the entire story to a point where the reader is unsure what has happened. Perhaps in Anna, Gurov has found the only real love of his entire life. As they wonder what they should do about their love, the story ends: "And it seemed that it would be a little while longer—and the solution would be found, and then would begin a new beautiful life" (IX, 372). It *seemed* that way, but on the other hand we know that Gurov has had a long history of self-deception:

> Oft-repeated experience, actually bitter experience, had taught him long ago that every intimacy which at the beginning so pleasantly diversifies life and seems to be a sweet and easy adventure, among decent people, especially among Muscovites, who are sluggish and indecisive, inevitably grows into a real problem, extraordinarily complicated, and the situation finally becomes painful. But at every new meeting with an interesting woman this experience somehow slipped from his memory, and he felt a desire to live, and everything seemed simple and amusing (IX, 358).

The fundamental question which lies before Gurov at the end of the story is not what he and Anna will do in the future, but rather precisely what kind of relationship exists between them. Is this a new experience for Gurov, or is it merely a repetition of the emotional tangle he has been in so often before? Gurov himself is unable to answer and thus the narrative which describes their relationship is itself ambiguous.

The final story to be considered here, *The Bishop* (*Arkhierei*, 1902), casts some doubt on the central character's mode of existence. The bishop is himself so uncertain that what he sees and feels in the present really exists, or that his past ever really existed, that his own actuality becomes tenuous at best. It is in this story, incidentally, that the word 'seems' comes close to replacing the verb 'to be'. It 'seems' to the bishop "as though in a dream or delirium" that he sees his mother for the first time in nine years standing among the crowd in church (IX, 416). Thinking on his younger days, he is confused, ". . . and all the past had left for somewhere far away into the mist, as if it had been dreamed" (IX, 423) ". . . and now that past rose up before him—living, fair, and joyful, as in all likelihood it had never been" (IX, 425). Curiously, he thinks of his life in the past in a foreign country as more real than his present life in his native country. The bishop does exist and he accurately perceives reality (his mother was standing there in church), but there is a serious disparity between reality and the bishop's perception of it, and this disparity becomes most acute when he is faced with those to whom he should be closest. We stand in a peculiar relationship to reality when we refuse to accept our principal means of confirming that reality—the evidence of our own senses.

At one point there is a kind of double doubting as to the bishop's existence. Katya, his niece, "gazed without blinking at her uncle, his holiness, as though trying to discover what sort of a person he was" (IX, 421). We are not told that Katya tried to discover what sort of person he was; rather, it is *as though* she tried to discover this. One possible implication is that if he does not really exist, then there is nothing to discover.

The bishop dies and his existence is quickly forgotten by everyone except his mother, who would sometimes tell acquaintances "about her children, her grandchildren, and about how she had had a bishop son (*syn arkhierei*), and here she would speak timidly, fearing that they wouldn't believe her. . . . And as a matter of fact not everyone did believe her" (IX, 431). For sheer vague suggestiveness this is one of Chekhov's finest passages. It may mean that some did not believe that one of her sons became a bishop, though the existence of a hypothetical son is not doubted; but the odd coupling of *syn arkhierei* could carry a lingering doubt about the existence of the son himself, even of a hypothetical one. Her timid speech when referring to the bishop may imply her own doubt about his existence (either as son or bishop); even if she is sure she had a son and that son was a bishop, she has no faith in her ability to attest to such a reality before others. In short, an aura of doubt about existence itself hangs over the ending of *The Bishop*.

Ambiguity is a concomitant of Chekhov's impressionism; whenever our focus shifts from what is to what it seems to us to be, we have opened the floodgates to a deluge of possibilities, none of which can ever be certainties. In addition, Chekhov's ambiguity forms one of the literary paths which move distinctly away from realism toward symbolism. His splintering of meaning within a character's perception of the external world forms a bridge between the realist's single-plane view of actuality and the symbolist's conception of heterogenous levels of actuality encompassed by a single image.[4] *The Bishop* is an appropriate story with which to end an account of Chekhov's studies in the tenuous and uncertain nature of man's existence in a world whose exact proportions he is incapable of ascertaining, and where all truths are relative. Although this vision of life was not a consciously thought out and formulated philosophic conception, nevertheless it is a fundamental theme, which both in its presence and in the attempt at its denial, runs from the very earliest through the final stories that Chekhov wrote. The last ten years represent the ultimate, though subdued, triumph of the chameleon over the dream.

VIRGINIA LLEWELLYN SMITH

The Lady with the Dog†

* * * Chekhov was to write two further stories on the theme of lovers who cannot marry: *About Love* (1898) and *The Lady with the Dog* (1899).

The plots of these two stories are rather similar, and as in *Neighbors* the block to happiness lies in the fact of previous marriages—of the woman in *About Love*, of both lovers in *The Lady with the Dog*. But in tone they differ sharply from the earlier story. There is no humor in them, only pathos and bitterness towards the fate that has brought about this situation. The emotional climax of *About Love* is reached as the hero, Alekhin, parts with his beloved for ever: 'oh, how wretched she and I were! I confessed my love to her, and with a searing pain in my heart I realized that everything that stood in the way of our love was irrelevant, petty, and false.' A similar, if more restrained, emotion is expressed in *The Lady with the Dog*. Gurov and Anna Sergeevna have fallen in love for the first time in their lives: 'they felt that fate itself had predestined them one for the other', but in reality fate has brought about the incomprehensible fact of their being married to different people, so that 'it was as if they were two migrant birds . . . which had been caught and made to inhabit separate cages.' The image is a good example of Chekhov's narrative style at its most restrained and moving.

It has been shown that the theme of love being destroyed by a cruel fate did not always have for Chekhov the appeal of the tragic:

---

4. For an excellent discussion of the homogeneous nature of the realist's conception of reality versus the symbolist's renovation of heterogeneous, intertwining layers see Dmitrii Chizhevskii, *Outline of Comparative Slavic Literature*, Survey of Slavic Civilization, I (Boston, 1952),

pp. 104–130, esp. pp. 105 and 123–124.
† From Virginia Llewellyn Smith, *Anton Chekhov and the Lady with the Dog* (London: Oxford University Press, 1973), pp. 96–97, 212–18. (Some of the author's footnotes have been omitted or abridged.)

that it could also serve him as a good framework on which to build farce. Nor could one claim that the theme of illicit passion found its source in Chekhov's own imagination, let alone experience: Tolstoy's *Anna Karenina* had been published in the later 1870s, before any of Chekhov's work. None the less the coincidence of plot and emotion found in *About Love* and *The Lady with the Dog*, together with the fact that the theme occupied Chekhov chiefly in the 1890s, has given rise to some speculation as to whether in fact Chekhov's own love-life during those years suffered as one critic puts it from the interference of a *force majeure*.[1] Since in this period Chekhov's private life is no longer a closed book (although many pages are indecipherable) the search for the romantic heroine becomes more complex. It becomes feasible to try to connect with her image certain women whose relations with Chekhov are at least partially illuminated and illuminating. Of Chekhov's female friends three in particular must now claim our attention.

* * *

It will by now be apparent that Anna Sergeevna, the lady with the dog, can be considered symbolic of the ideal love that Chekhov could envisage but not embrace—that remained, so to speak, behind a pane of glass, as in Heifitz's film.[2] But the significance of the whole story is much greater than that comprised in Anna Sergeevna alone.

No other single work of Chekhov's fiction constitutes a more meaningful comment on Chekhov's attitude to women and to love than does *The Lady with the Dog*. So many threads of Chekhov's thought and experience appear to have been woven together into this succinct story that it may be regarded as something in the nature of a summary of the entire topic.

Gurov, the hero of the story, may at first appear no more closely identifiable with Chekhov himself than are many other sympathetic male characters in Chekhov's fiction: he has a post in a bank and is a married man with three children. It is because he has this wife and family that his love-affair with Anna Sergeevna leads him into an *impasse*. And the affair itself, involving Gurov's desperate trip to Anna's home town, has no obvious feature in common with anything we know of Chekhov's amorous liaisons.

And yet Chekhov's own attitudes and experience have clearly shaped Gurov's character and fate. The reader is told that Gurov 'was not yet forty': Chekhov was thirty-nine when he wrote *The Lady with the Dog*. Gurov 'was married young' (*ego zhenili rano*):

1. A force beyond one's control. [*Editor.*]
2. Dr. Llewellyn Smith earlier (p. 8) says of Heifitz's film: "In the last scene Anna Sergeevna, the 'lady with the dog', weeps and gesticulates inaudibly behind a window as she watches her lover Gurov walk away. The blatantly tear-jerking quality of this scene is alien to Chekhov; but the pane of glass separating us from the lady is, however crudely, symbolically accurate." [*Editor.*]

there is a faint implication in the phrase that an element of coercion played some part in his taking this step—a step which Chekhov, when he was young, managed to avoid. As in general with early marriages in Chekhov's fiction, Gurov's has not proved a success. His wife seems 'much older than he' and imagines herself to be an intellectual: familiar danger-signals. She is summed-up in three words: 'stiff, pompous, dignified' (*pryamaya, vazhnaya, solidnaya*) which epitomize a type of woman (and man) that Chekhov heartily disliked.

Gurov's wife treats sex as something more complicated than it is, and spoils it for him; and it is also spoilt for him by those mistresses of whom he soon tires: beautiful, cold women with a 'predatory' expression who are determined to snatch what they can from life. 'When Gurov grew cold to them, their beauty aroused hatred in him and the lace on their linen reminded him of scales.' * * *

Gurov has had, however, liaisons that were, for him, enjoyable— and these we note, were brief: as was Chekhov's liaison with Yavorskaya and indeed, so far as we know, all the sexual relationships that he had before he met Olga Knipper.

'Frequent experience and indeed bitter experience had long since taught [Gurov] that every liaison which to begin with makes such a pleasant change . . . inevitably evolves into a real and extremely complex problem, and the situation eventually becomes a burden.' That his friendships with, for instance, Lika and Avilova should evolve into a situation of this kind seems to have been exactly what Chekhov himself feared: he backed out of these friendships as soon as there appeared to be a danger of close involvement.

Gurov cannot do without the company of women, and yet he describes them as an 'inferior breed': his experience of intimacy with women is limited to casual affairs and an unsatisfactory marriage. Chekhov also enjoyed the company of women and had many female friends and admirers: but he failed, or was unwilling, to involve himself deeply or lastingly with them. That in his work he should suggest that women are an inferior breed can be to some extent explained by the limited knowledge of women his self-contained attitude brought him—and perhaps, to some extent, by a sense of guilt concerning his inability to feel involved.

Gurov's behaviour to Anna Sergeevna at the beginning of their love-affair is characterized by an absence of emotional involvement, just such as appears in Chekhov's attitude towards certain women. There is a scene in *The Lady with the Dog* where, after they have been to bed together, Gurov eats a watermelon while Anna Sergeevna weeps over her corruption. It is not difficult to imagine Chekhov doing something similarly prosaic—weeding his garden, perhaps—while Lika poured out her emotional troubles to him.

Gurov's egocentricity is dispelled, however, by the potent influence of love, because Anna Sergeevna turns out to be the ideal type of woman: pitiable, defenseless, childlike, capable of offering Gurov an unquestioning love. Love is seen to operate as a force for good: under its influence Gurov feels revulsion for the philistinism of his normal life and associates. Soviet interpreters have made much of the theme of regeneration,[3] of the idea implicit in the story that 'a profound love experienced by ordinary people has become an enormous moral force'.[4] In fact, although some idea of this sort is certainly implicit in the story, Chekhov is surely attempting above all to evoke what love meant to his protagonists as they themselves saw their situation. Chekhov originally wrote in the conclusion of *The Lady with the Dog* that the love of Gurov and Anna Sergeevna had 'made them both better'. He altered this subsequently to 'changed them both for the better'; but still dissatisfied, finally he altered this once more to 'had changed them both', and thus avoided any overt suggestion of pointing a moral.

The point is that we are not seeing the lovers changed in relation to society, but in relation to their own inner lives. Gurov is shaken out of his romantic dreaming by a sudden recognition of the grossness of others in his stratum of society: but he does not give up his job or abandon his social life. Instead, he leads a double existence, and imagines that every man's 'real, most interesting life' goes on in secret. It is this life that Chekhov is interested in, not in Gurov as a representative of his class or his time.

That Gurov and Anna Sergeevna are alone amongst their fellow-men does not point a moral: but it is where the pathos of their initial situation lies. We are not impressed by their moral superiority, but moved by their loneliness. Love is the answer to this loneliness, and there is no need to bring morality into it. Chekhov, where love was concerned, wrote from the heart, not the head.

---

3. **B. S.** Meilakh in his article 'Dva resheniya odnoi temy' states that in *The Lady with the Dog* Chekhov was seeking to present in terms of everyday people (i.e. not the nobility) the problem Tolstoy had posed in *Anna Karenina*: how can there be happiness in the false society that has made it possible for two such dissimilar people as Anna and Karenin to be united? Meilakh writes: Anna Karenina 'perishes as the victim of the cruel mores which constituted the norm of existence for a person of her milieu'. Chekhov, he holds, was showing his lovers to be in virtually the same predicament; but by not resolving the problem in death, Chekhov was suggesting that the more the situation seems impossible, the more one should intensify the search for an exit. In fact, Tolstoy was if anything more concerned with doing away with the evils of the old order than Chekhov: in *The Lady with the Dog* the lovers blame fate, not society, for their predicament, and the way in which they confront their situation probably only means that Chekhov preferred less dramatic effects and positive statements than Tolstoy, and did not wish to copy the latter too closely.

4. K. M. Vinogradova, 'Stranitsa iz chernovoi rukopisi rasskaza "Dama s sobachkoi"': Vinogradova maintains that Chekhov's alterations to the first-published text of *The Lady with the Dog* were made to underline the theme of Gurov's regeneration. However, the changes she adduces seem rather to have been dictated by artistic considerations, and with the aim of making both lovers appear more ordinary, less wholly good, less wholly bad. Chekhov cuts out, for example, a series of coarse rejoinders that Gurov makes to Anna Sergeevna in the bedroom scene: which would have been better left in, had Chekhov wished to point up the change in Gurov's character to the utmost.

Chekhov wrote *The Lady with the Dog* in Yalta in the autumn of 1899, not long after he and Olga were there together (although they were not, as yet, lovers) and had made the trip back to Moscow together. In the Kokkoz valley, it will be remembered, they apparently agreed to marry: and so by then, we may presume, Chekhov knew what it was to love.

How do Gurov and Anna Sergeevna love one another? Not unnaturally, Chekhov describes the affair from the man's point of view. As one might expect, Gurov's love for Anna Sergeevna has its romantic side. It is associated with the beauty of nature, for it is helped into existence by the view of the sea at Oreanda. When, back in Moscow, Gurov thinks of Anna, he poeticizes her: the whole affair becomes the subject of a daydream, and ultimately an obsession. So, perhaps, did Chekhov's thoughts dwell on Olga Knipper when she was in Moscow and he recalled their time in Yalta and journey through an area of great natural beauty.

Olga Knipper, however, was no dream. And Anna Sergeevna is not seen solely in terms of 'poetry', even by Gurov. Forced to seek Anna out in her home town, from this point Gurov is back in reality. At the theatre he—and the reader—see her as a 'small woman who was in no way remarkable, with a cheap-looking lorgnette in her hand'. But this does not detract from her appeal for him (and it enhances her appeal for the reader). The romantic heroine has become a creature of flesh and blood, and Gurov still loves her: 'she . . . now filled his whole life, she was his joy and his grief, the sole happiness that he now desired; and to the sound of the bad orchestra, the wretched philistine violins, he mused on how fine she was. He mused and dreamed dreams.'

Gurov dreams—but dreaming is not enough for him. He has tasted happiness: the affair in Yalta was happy, in spite of Anna's sense of guilt. His love there developed from when, after Anna's self-recrimination and his irritation, they suddenly laughed together. This laugh denotes the beginning of communication: the tension relaxes and they behave normally, and find enjoyment in each other's company as well as in 'love'. Love, in fact, has come down to earth. Sex, communication, and simple companionship all play their part in it, in addition to 'poetry'.

And there the problem lies: the love-affair being rooted in reality, Anna and Gurov have to face the world's problems. Gurov, unlike Laevsky and Laptev,[5] has found romantic love: but he also wants the companionship that Laevsky and Laptev had, and because he and Anna Sergeevna are already married, he cannot have it.

The situation, indeed the entire plot of 'The Lady with the Dog', is obvious, even banal, and its merit as a work of art lies in the artis-

5. In *The Duel* and *Three Years*, respectively. [*Editor.*]

try with which Chekhov has preserved in the story a balance between the poetic and the prosaic, and in the careful characterization, dependent upon the use of half-tones. Soviet critics have a valid point when they regard Gurov as a sort of Everyman; *The Lady with the Dog* is an essentially simple exposition of a commonplace theme. Unlike in *The Duel* and *Three Years*, in *The Lady with the Dog* Chekhov has made no attempt to investigate the problems of love: the conclusion of *The Lady with the Dog* is left really and truly open: there is no suggestion, nor have we any inkling, of what the future may bring: 'And it seemed that in a very little while an answer would be found, and a new and beautiful life would begin. And to both it was evident that the end was far, far away, and that the hardest, most complicated part was only just beginning.'

There can be no doubt but that the policy of expounding questions without presuming to answer them—that policy which Chekhov had declared to be the writer's task[6]—suited his style best. A full appreciation of Chekhov's work requires of the reader a certain degree of involvement, a response intellectual, or, as in the case of his love-stories, emotional, that Chekhov invites rather than commandeers. Ultimately, all depends on how Chekhov is read; but much depends on his striking the delicate balance between sentimentality and flatness.

All must surely agree that the right balance has been achieved in the final scene of *The Lady with the Dog*, which is as direct an appeal to the heart as can be found in Chekhov's fiction:

> His hair was already beginning to turn gray. And it struck him as strange that he had aged so in the last few years, and lost his good looks. Her shoulders, on which he had lain his hands, were warm and shook slightly. He felt a pang of compassion for this life that was still warm and beautiful, but which would probably soon begin to fade and wither, like his own life. Why did she love him so? He had always appeared to women as something which he was not, and they had loved in him not him himself, but a creature of their own imagination, which they had sought again and again in their own lives; and then, when they perceived their mistake, they loved him all the same. And not one of them had been happy with him. Time passed, he would strike up an acquaintance, have an affair, and part, but never once had he loved; he had had everything he might wish for, only not love.
>
> And only now, when his hair had gone gray, he had fallen in love properly, genuinely—for the first time in his life.

This passage, read in the light of what we know of the author, gains a new dimension of pathos. The history of Gurov's relation-

6. See letter to A. S. Suvorin, 27 October 1888, where Chekhov wrote: '. . . you are confusing two things: solving the problem and the correct exposition of the problem. In *Anna Karenina* and [*Evgeny*] *Onegin* not a single problem is solved, but they are wholly satisfying, just because all the problems in them are correctly set out.'

ships with women is a transmutation of Chekhov's history, and the essential point of the fiction was reality for him: true love had come too late, and complete happiness—poetry and communication and companionship—was impossible.

Chekhov wrote that Gurov and Anna Sergeevna 'loved one another . . . as husband and wife'. But how are we to explain the incongruity of this bland phrase 'as husband and wife' in the context of Chekhov's entire *œuvre*, in which the love of husband and wife is thwarted and cheapened—virtually never, in fact, seen to exist? Gurov and Anna are, after all, husband and wife, and he does not love his wife, nor she her husband. The irony here, whether conscious or unconscious, finds its origin in Chekhov's apparently unshakeable belief that an ideal love somewhere, somehow could exist.

NILS ÅKE NILSSON

The Bishop: Its Theme†

The Bishop is Chekhov's last story but one. It was written in 1901–2 and published in the April issue of *Journal for All* in 1902. According to one of his letters, however, the subject was not a new one; it was something "which I have had in my head for about fifteen years already".[1]

The story tells of the illness and death of the Right Reverend Bishop Pyotr. It begins with the midnight mass on the eve of Palm Sunday, and by the time the bells call the people to the Easter Day Service the bishop is already dead. His mother and his niece have come to see him because of the holiday, and it is together with them that he spends his last days, recalling his childhood, his whole life. Finally, we are told that a new bishop has been appointed and—though bishop Pyotr apparently discharged his duties better than many of his colleagues—people are quick to forget him. His mother returns to her small provincial town, and she is the only one who still remembers him. Sometimes she tells the other women that she had a son who was a bishop, but this she does cautiously, fearing that they will not believe her. And—so ends the story—not everybody in fact does so.

† From Nils Åke Nilsson, *Studies in Čechov's Narrative Technique: "The Steppe" and "The Bishop,"* Stockholm Slavic Studies, 2 (Stockholm, 1968), pp. 62–75. (Some of the author's footnotes have been omitted or abridged. Literal translations have been provided for the texts from which Professor Nilsson quotes in Russian.)

1. Shchukin says in his *Recollections of Chekhov* that Chekhov told him that *The Bishop* was an old story which he had rewritten (Chekhov, *Polnoe sobranie sochineniia* (Works), IX, 616 (Moscow, 1944–51).

The Bishop has often been called one of Chekhov's best stories. It is not difficult to understand why. The subject is simple, human and moving. It is told without any sentimentality, with Chekhov's usual sense of balance and economy, and yet with an emotional tone contributing very much to the powerful impression we get from it. Even so, the story has attracted little attention as an object of study.[2] The reason may very well be that it has been considered merely simple and clear, not involving any complicated problems. It might appear difficult to say more than what is usually said about it: that it is one of his best stories. Nevertheless, it seems to me that *The Bishop* raises certain interesting questions as to subject, style and structure. My purpose here is to discuss some of them.

On first reading, the most natural reaction is to connect the story with Chekhov's biography. It was, after all, one of the last efforts of a writer approaching death, of a man who knew only too well that his days were numbered. It is a story of break-up and departure, a frequent theme in the plays and stories of his last years. But here the theme is no departure "for Moscow" but a breaking up from life. There is a tone of restrained sadness in the story, corroborated —as it seems—by the special twist at the end: the bishop dies, and soon he and all his good work will be forgotten. It sounds like a final pessimistic chord on the vanity of all human endeavor.

But should we actually read the story in this way? Is it really as pessimistic as this synopsis would have us believe? A closer look at the structure gives a different answer; the story is in point of fact more ambiguous.

It is not difficult, in the first place, to see that Chekhov has been very careful not to let the tone of pessimism dominate. And this he did in spite of—or, with our knowledge of Chekhov's art, we might even prefer to say exactly because of—the subject. We recognize a technique used in other stories and in his plays: to work with change and contrast, with a rhythmical play of bright and subdued light, with a balance of trivial and serious scenes.

This interplay of rhythms is emphasized by something which could be called an impressionistic or a 'bloc technique'. Such a technique, a result of Chekhov's demand for economy and objectivity, consists in placing small complete scenes next to each other without any comments. There is still a clear chronological scheme and logical development from one scene to another, but the reader should never feel that there is a narrator guiding him, anxious to

2. See, however, especially the article by Bicilli (in *Godoshnik na sofijskija universitet. Istoriko-filologicheski fakultet*, T. XXXVIII; German translation: *A. P. Chekhov. Werk und Stil*, München 1966, which contains some interesting views on the story. G. Berdnikov in his *A. P. Chekhov*, pp. 451–53, has paid less attention to it, but he gives the story its proper place among Chekhov's later works; on the whole the Soviet critics seem to be rather reluctant to mention the story, apparently because it is a sympathetic portrait of a priest.

explain everything. Most of the conclusions should be drawn by the reader himself. The content and significance of the scenes will be clear by their contrast with the preceeding or following scene, or by their place in the story as a whole. *The Bishop* is, among other things, an interesting example of the application of such a technique.

The first scene touches a powerful emotional note. It reaches a climax when the bishop bursts into tears during the midnight mass and the whole congregation begins to sob and cry with him: "And for some reason tears flowed down his face. . . . Tears glistened on his face, on his beard. Nearby someone else started to weep, then, further away, someone else, then more and more, and little by little the church was filled with soft weeping."

The bishop's tears seem to be explained by his fatigue and irritation. But the whole episode is connected to the preceding sentence by an "and". In this preceding sentence the bishop believes that he sees the face of his old mother in the crowd. The conjunction seems to tell us that it is the image of his mother that provokes his tears. The mother vision takes his thoughts back to his childhood; by this he also understands that he is now an old man, his life is over and done with, and he is soon going to die. The inexplicable tears are a presage of what is going to happen in the story: the bishop's death. But all this is only implied, it is there behind the lines, in the "subtext", and we shall not fully understand the meaning of this scene until we have read further in the story.

In fact, the author tries to assure us that it is difficult to find any reason for the bishop's tears. This is said by the "for some reason", which seems to belong to the bishop rather than to the narrator: it is the bishop who cannot explain his own tears, who is surprised by them.[3] This is further stressed in the next sentence: "There was peace in his heart, everything was felicitous, but he kept gazing fixedly at the left choir, where prayers were being read, where it was no longer possible to recognize a single person in the evening dusk, and—he wept."

It is interesting to note that in the original plan, as told by N. S. Shchukin, it was explicitly stated that the bishop cried because, while reading the story of Christ's passion, he applied it to the fate of every human being, and to himself in particular, knowing that he was ill and that he was going to die. In the final version all these explanations were left out. The reason might have been that Chekhov did not want to reveal the action of the story from the very beginning. Further, this introductory scene has a powerful emotional tone, skilfully conveyed by various stylistic devices. There

3. Cf. the use of 'for some reason' (pochemu-to) in *The Betrothed*, Chekhov's last story; there it is very clear that it is used to stress the point of view of the heroine.

was always the danger that such a scene might become sentimental; even as it is now, we can see how Chekhov has tried to tone things down and balance the emotional pitch by "for some reason", the markedly neutral phrases ending the first two paragraphs, etc.

Now follows a scene set in a different key, yet quite clearly connected with the first. The bishop returns to his monastery. It is midnight, the moon is shining. It would have been very easy here to continue the sad tone of the introduction by simply allowing the night landscape and the moon to do their work. It is true that Nature is said to live her own incomprehensible, mysterious life, but at the same time a different atmosphere is evoked: gay light and colours clearly dominate, the bells resound joyfully. In the air there is a hint of spring and everything seems close and friendly: "... everything around was inviting, youthful, so akin, everything—the trees and the sky, and even the moon, and one wanted to think that it would always be so." When the bishop reaches his monastery he is told that his mother has come to see him, and by now all sense of sadness is dispelled.

The arrival of his mother inevitably leads his thoughts back to his childhood. A new scene ensues. An emotional evocation of a kind we recognize from Chekhov's plays ("Dear, precious, unforgettable childhood!") is followed by memories of mostly unsentimental and even joyous character: "... and it seemed to the bishop that joy trembled in the air, and he followed the icon (he was called Pavlusha then) without a hat, barefoot, with simple faith, with a simple smile, infinitely happy!"

The bishop's thoughts are then interrupted by a short description of the night outside: "The moon shone in the window, the floor was lit, and shadows lay on it. A cricket chirped." As we see, just a few simple details, familiar enough from many another description of a moonlit night, but here they appear brief and naked, with the particular economy Chekhov so liked. In fact, the economy has its obvious explanation. The two simple sentences hark back to the description of the bishop's return journey from the midnight mass. The night atmosphere was already evoked there, a few sentences are now enough to bring it back to mind. This is a characteristic means whereby Chekhov recalls an underlying mood merely by hinting at images conjured up before.

The sentences also serve as a transition to the next scene, where Father Sisoi is introduced, and with him a new key—Father Sisoi with his snoring, his yawns and his "I don't like it" ("ne ndravitsia"). He brings the bishop back from the past with its many pleasant memories, back to the present, a trivial, petty present.

As we see, the first chapter consists of a series of small scenes, each set in a different key and introducing the persons and the themes that will appear in the chapters to come. The changing mood is connected with what constitutes the main principle of structure of the story: the blending of time. The story lives on all three levels of time: the bishop looks back on his life—the verb 'remember' is used frequently, and it is worth noting how Chekhov varies it all the time. These forms occur twice: '*vspominat*',' '*vspomnit*',' '*vspominal*,' '*vspomnil*,' '*vspomnilos*' (to remember, to recollect, kept remembering, recollected, was remembered). The following are used only once: '*vspomnilas*',' '*vspomnilsia*,' '*vspominalas*',' '*pomnil*,' '*pomnila*,' '*pripomnilsia*' (was remembered, was reminded, kept being remembered, remembered, (she) remembered, was reminded.

But he also looks ahead, to the future (symbolized by approaching spring). His memories of the past and his dreams of the future are contrasted with the present. From this emerges a re-evaluation of his life and of himself. In the first chapter all this is still not clear to himself or to the reader, but it will become increasingly evident from chapter to chapter as the contrast is given ever-increasing stress.[4]

The second chapter takes up the same themes as the first, i.e. there is a new combination of time levels. In the first chapter they were simply introduced, now they begin to work together, unveiling the idea of the story. The second chapter opens with a bright note, the promise of spring, already met with in the first chapter in the description of the night landscape: "All during dinner the spring sunshine shone in the window from the courtyard and gaily shone on the white tablecloth, and on Katya's reddish hair. Through the double windows they could hear the noise of the rooks and the song of the starlings in the garden."

But this mood is soon toned down; the focus moves from the future to the present. The meeting and dinner with his mother does not, however, bring the bishop the joy and pleasure he had been looking forward to. They have nothing to say to each other, her small-talk irritates him, and it is characteristic that she finds a sympathetic haven in Father Sisoi. In the middle of the chapter the shift of humour is underlined: "His mood somehow changed suddenly . . . he became sad, vexed." He flies back again to his memories; in the first chapter there was the childhood, now we come to know of his life and career as a priest.

The second chapter also introduces a new theme. The beginning of the chapter runs: "The following day, Palm Sunday, the bishop celebrated mass in the cathedral in town, then visited the archbishop of the diocese, visited a very sick old general's wife, and, finally, drove home. After one o'clock dear guests dined with him, his old

---

4. Bicilli recognizes only a present and a past, which influences his view on the idea of the story (Bicilli p. 110). Instead, Berdnikov stresses the importance of this line of spring and future (Berdnikov p. 452).

mother, and Katya, his niece, a girl of eight." There are quite a few such passages in the story, written in a pronounced objective style, having almost the character of a report. They are, for that matter, easy enough to find in other stories by Chekhov, occurring particularly in descriptions or at the beginning of a chapter, clearly being a part of his programme of objectivity and economy. But here, in *The Bishop*, they serve a further function. They record briefly and swiftly what the bishop is doing during the last days of his life: he goes to the church, he visits various people, he receives others: "After dinner two rich ladies arrived, landowners, who sat for an hour and a half in silence, with drawn faces; the archimandrite, a silent man, hard of hearing, came on business. And then they began to ring for vespers; the sun set behind the woods and the day was over. Returning from church, the bishop hurriedly said his offices, got into bed, and covered himself as warmly as he could. . . . On Tuesday after mass the bishop was at the archbishop's house and heard petitioners there, got excited and angry, then went home."

This is his duty, part of the routine he has performed day after day all through his life and which has to be done even now, in spite of his illness (cf. the use of an expression like *"nado bylo"*: *"nado bylo itti v tserkov'*," *"nado bylo prinyat' ego"* ["had to": "he had to go to church," "he had to see him"]. Such passages stand as stylistic contrasts to the more emotional, lyrical passages. But they also have another function. They mark the rhythmic interplay of rest and movement in the story: they themselves give us the movement, the point of rest being the bishop's recollections. They tell us that time passes, that the bishop's fate is sealed, that it is approaching inexorably. They also constitute a present tense (from the point of view of the story), a present tense as against the bishop's looking back to the past or ahead to the future.

His illness strengthens his sense of the negative sides of the life around him. As often happens with the sick, he becomes irritated and nervous. He sees people around him in a new way, naked, petty, egoistic, uneducated. But this is more than a sick man's irritation. Step by step, from chapter to chapter, we learn to understand that this is deep suppressed dissatisfaction with life, coming to surface for the first time now that approaching death has given him a new perspective on what is essential in life.

This direction is already intimated in the first chapter with Father Sisoi's snoring and his "I don't like it" ("ne ndravitsia"). In the second chapter it is the main theme. Here again we have Father Sisoi with his silly remarks about the Japanese ("The Japanese are the same as Montenegrins, Mother, they're the same race. They were under the Turkish yoke together.") But not only is Father Sisoi involved: the bishop's own mother too belongs to this short-sighted, petty world, his own mother with her constantly repeated "and then we had a cup of tea": "and right away 'we had a cup of tea' or 'we drunk a cup of tea,' and it seemed as if in her whole life all she knew was that she drank tea."

It is worth noting how Chekhov uses Father Sisoi's and the mother's conversation as inserts in the bishop's recollections. The bishop has retired to bed, and, while he is lying there, his thoughts once again focus on memories of the past. In the other room Father Sisoi and his mother sit chatting; their trivial exchanges intermingle with the pictures of the past. What Chekhov is applying here is a technique designed for the stage; as we know, his plays often contain two kinds of dialogue going on in different parts of the stage (cf. the first scene of *Three Sisters*). Here, in the story, there are no comments from the narrator, but it is easy to understand the function of his contrast between the pair of unwitting chatterboxes and the lonely bishop trying to discover some meaning behind his life.

In the third chapter the notes of triviality and pettiness appear in a more intense form. The bishop is struck by this when he has to receive visitors and listen to their little requests and complaints: "And now, when he was ill, he was struck by the emptiness, the triviality of everything that was asked for and was wept about; the ignorance and timidity angered him; and all of this petty and unnecessary business oppressed him with its mass, and it seemed to him that he now understood the diocesan archbishop who had once in his younger years written *Doctrines of Free Will* but now, apparently, was completely lost in triviality, forgot everything, and didn't think about God."

People are backward and uncultured; the bishop is able to make comparisons on this point because he has lived outside Russia for several years—a detail which Chekhov apparently has added as a further explanation of the bishop's critical view: "While abroad the bishop must have lost touch with Russian life, it wasn't easy for him; the people seemed coarse to him, the women petititioners boring and stupid, the seminarians and their teachers uneducated and at times savages."

His nervous irritation eventually reaches its peak in the fourth chapter and manifests itself as hatred of the whole environment that is threatening to suffocate him, of a way of life that is unendurable: "When he got under the blanket, he suddenly longed to be abroad, longed unbearably! It seemed that he would give his life not to see these pitiful, cheap shutters, low ceilings, not to smell that heavy monastery smell. If there were only one person to whom he could speak, to whom he could open his heart!"

But along with the levels of past and present there is also the level of the future. To begin with it appears only indirectly, in the first and the second chapter: the bright scenery, the feeling of spring in the air. In the third chapter it appears in the bishop's thoughts, mingling with his recollections of the past. This is an emotional scene again, reminding us of the introduction. Tears flow down his cheeks now as then, but this time he is already aware of the reason: he understands that he is going to die, and he thinks he is not yet ready for it. There is still something missing in his life, and he is sure that there must be an answer to all his questions in the future: "He thought that here he had attained everything that a man in his position could attain, he had faith, but nevertheless it was not all clear, something was still lacking, he did not want to die; and it still seemed to him that he lacked something that was the most important thing, that he had dimly dreamed of in the past, and that at present he was moved by the same hope for the future that he had had in his childhood, and in the Academy, and abroad."

At the end of the story this theme is brought to a climax in the joy of Easter Day. The mood and even the details from the second scene of the introduction return, now fortified and stressed. Again the bells ring out merrily ("The joyous pealing of the bells hung over the town from morning till night without ceasing, stirring the spring air"), there is spring in the air, and, instead of a bright moon, there is bright sunshine ("Birds sang, the sun shone brightly"). In the marketplace people are enjoying themselves: "The big marketplace was noisy, swings were swinging, barrel organs were playing, an accordion was squeaking, drunken voices were heard."

What we have here is a characteristic application of Chekhov's 'bloc technique': scene is added to scene—the bishop's death, the boisterous market scene and, at the very end, the mother in her provincial town—but there are no clear transitions, no comments. The scenes are connected, and yet they contrast with each other in an effective way at the same time.

The contrasting of life and death [of death and the indifference of nature] in the way done here is a device rather frequently used by various prose writers and even poets * * * (not) just for the sake of effect. Behind them is a personal view on these questions, and a view which has much in common with the concluding scene of *The Bishop* and with the whole idea of that story.

To understand the meaning of this scene, let us now first see what happens to the bishop during the last days of his illness. While sitting in the church listening to the choir (in the third chapter) he does not want to die. There is, he thinks, something missing, there are certain things still not clear to him, a truth he has been looking for all his life. But before dying, the realization that the past is gone for ever and will never come back is thrust home to him. His recollections, the review of his whole life, are finally brought to an end. His only comment is "how wonderful". When the past is put aside he becomes a changed man, a different man, a man of truly humble dimensions: "It already seemed to him that he was thinner and weaker, more insignificant than anyone."

Now we understand the function that the arrival of his mother performs in the story. He becomes like a child again, a long-lost child returning to its mother; the immediate contact, lost during the years of service to the Church, is renewed. To his mother he is no longer an imposing and venerable bishop but simply her son of old: "And for some reason it seemed to her too that he was thinner, weaker, and more insignificant than anyone, and she no longer remembered that he was an archbishop, and kissed him as if he were a little child, very dear and very close."

What happens to the bishop before he dies is that responsibility and duty are lifted from him, the pressure that prevented him from being simple and human, prevented him from achieving personal contact with his congregation, is released. In his way he too was one of those "men in a case" whom Chekhov depicted in several stories from the late eighties; contrary to those, the bishop realizes what has been wrong, even if it is too late.

Easter Day and its mystery of resurrection has its special significance in the context. It is connected with the bishop's new environmental attitude, with the feeling of freedom that comes to him just before he dies. This, too, seems to be a form of resurrection. But what kind of resurrection is it and how are we then to understand the end, which could promise the bishop nothing but oblivion?

It would, I think, be rather interesting at this stage to compare Chekhov's story with another very well-known story on a similar theme: Tolstoi's *The Death of Ivan Ilich*. This Ivan, as Tolstoi emphasizes, is a very ordinary man living a very ordinary and, as he himself thinks, normal, honest and true life. When he is told by his doctor that his time is up he realizes that this was all wrong. He starts reviewing his life and arrives at a new understanding of what is essential to man. When he finally dies, death is no longer any threat to him; he has accepted and overcome it, and he looks forward to a new life, to a resurrection:

> "It is finished!" someone said above him.
> He heard these words and repeated them in his heart.
> "Death is finished," he said to himself. "It no longer exists"
> He drew a breath into himself, stopped in the middle of his breathing, stretched out, and died.

It seems that Tolstoi's and Chekhov's stories are different. Ivan Ilich is an ordinary man, while the bishop is definitely not. The bishop, as he himself realizes when looking back on his life, has come so far and attained all that was possible for a man with his background and qualifications. Ivan Ilich has lived a dull common-place existence, unconscious of the essentials of life. The bishop, on the other hand, has lived a life of righteousness and truth, at least in the eyes of the Church and the general public. And still, at the end, what awaits him is not resurrection, as for Ivan Ilich, but oblivion.

The difference between the stories is a difference between the authors: Chekhov the agnostic, and Tolstoi the believer. Yet the stories have a great deal in common. Facing death, the bishop also comes to the conclusion that there has been something amiss with his life. His journey into the past does not have the same character of self-criticism, of showdown, as we find with Tolstoi's hero. The bishop feels that something has been missing from his life, but he is unable to put a finger on it with the ease of Ivan Ilich. His irritation first turns against his immediate environment, the people round him, the poor, dull, ugly life of the world at hand as symbolized by the fence, the low ceilings, the peculiar smell of the monastery. But before dying he understands that the fault was also in part his own, that he never allowed himself to be a simple, straightforward human being. He does not face resurrection as Ivan Ilich does, but still a promise of freedom and rest suddenly opens itself to him.

And now the theme of oblivion. Tolstoi's story also stresses peo-ple's indifference to death. This is the main idea underlying the introductory chapter. Ivan Petrovich visits the widow to pay his respects to the deceased, but it does not prevent him from going directly from the scene of mourning to the card table. We also learn that the widow's thoughts gravitate towards very practical things, above all how to get as much money as possible from her husband's employers. All these details are part of Tolstoi's purpose to unmask people, to show them naked in all their egotism, to present the other side, the true face of such an official function as a funeral, to stress the contrast between appearance and reality. The whole episode is given with the clear, hard and merciless strokes of a moralist with a purpose and a plan—all so different from Chekhov's lyrical tone, his comprehension of human weakness and abstinence from com-ment.

In *The Bishop* the theme of human indifference only appears in clear-cut form at the end. It is true that the story has already hinted at people's pettiness, egotism and ignorance. In a way, then, the conclusion has been prepared for, but it comes as a surprise never-theless. It has the character of a moral. The whole story has en-deavoured to evoke our sympathy for the aged bishop, but death is brought to him, and, instead of words of consolation, all we are told is that he was quickly forgotten.

We might call this an unsentimental agnostic's calm and simple view of death. It was needed for the purpose of precluding any direct religious interpretation of the bishop's death, but also as a counterbalance to the nostalgic atmosphere brought to its peak in the death scene. But further, hidden in this special twist at the end, there is an idea of apparently much importance to Chekhov, one which we can find in many another of his stories. If we scrutinize it, the meaning of the final scene will stand out more clearly and we shall find that it is not so pessimistic after all.

A main theme of the story is, of course, the contrast between time and eternity. It is easy to understand that the bishop as a young man thinks that he will live for ever: "life was then so simple, pleasant, it seemed to go on and on, with no end in sight." Now, as an old man, he knows that there is an end. But he also knows that, in contrast to his temporal life, there is something eternal, something that will go on living after he is dead and forgotten. When he returns from the midnight mass he looks at the landscape and feels that "everything around was inviting, youthful, so akin, everything—the trees and the sky, and even the moon, and one wanted to think that it would always be so."

But it is not only nature that can prove the existence of eternity. While officiating at the service in the cathedral the bishop sees before him the congregation like a sea of lights: "and it seemed that they would be the same every year, and for how long—only God knew."

There will always be a congregation, the cathedral will always be filled by the same people or people who appear to be the same. And outside the church, too, the holiday will be celebrated in the same way, with barrel-organs and accordians and drunkenness, "in short, it was gay, everything was fine, just as it was last year and as in all probability it would be next year."

From the point of view of the congregation the bishop himself is a link in a chain, a tradition, which seems to be without end. When looking back on the past, he recalls that there has always been a priest in the family, "His father had been a deacon, his grandfather a priest, his great-grandfather a deacon, and his whole family, perhaps, from the days Russia became Christian, had belonged to the clergy." We are not told if the bishop had a son to carry on the tradition, but this is not important. There will always be a successor; the chain will not be broken: "A month later a new suffragan bishop was appointed, and no one remembered Bishop Peter any longer."

Individual man is mortal, but life is eternal as mankind is eternal; every individual is a mortal link in an immortal chain, a member of an unbroken tradition. Placing the last part of the story in such a context, we are better able to understand that the seemingly pessimistic note at the end is not so pessimistic after all. And this is not an isolated example in Chekhov's works. If we go through them we shall find many other examples proving that this was, in fact, a favorite twist.

* * *

Selected Bibliography

The books from which essays in this volume were derived are not listed.

BIBLIOGRAPHICAL WORKS

Heifetz, Anna, ed. *Chekhov in English*. New York, 1947.
Yachnin, Rissa, ed. *The Chekhov Centennial Chekhov in English: A Selective List of Works by and about Him, 1947–1960*. New York, 1960.

CHEKHOV'S WRITINGS

Anton Chekhov's Life and Thought: Selected Letters and Commentary. Edited by Simon Karlinsky. Translated by Henry Heim and Simon Karlinsky. New York, 1973.
Anton Chekhov's Plays: A Norton Critical Edition. Translated and edited by Eugene K. Bristow. New York, 1977.
The Oxford Chekhov. Translated and edited by Ronald Hingley. 9 vols. London, 1964–75.

STUDIES OF CHEKHOV

Avilova, Lidiia. *Chekhov in My Life*. Translated with an introduction by David Magarshack. Illustrations by Lynton Lamb. New York, 1950.
Bruford, W. H. *Chekhov and His Russia: A Sociological Study*. London, 1947.
T. Eekman, ed. *Anton Cechov, 1860–1960: Some Essays*. Leiden, 1960.
Ehrenburg, Ilya. *Chekhov, Stendhal, and Other Essays*. New York, 1963.
Garnett, Edward. *Chekhov and His Art*. London, 1929.
Gerhardi, William. Anton Chehov: *A Critical Study*. London, 1923; reprinted New York, 1975.
Hingley, Ronald. *Chekhov: A Biographical and Critical Study*. London, 1950.
———. *A New Life of Anton Chekhov*. New York, 1976.
Robert Louis Jackson, ed. *Chekhov: A Collection of Critical Essays*. Englewood Cliffs, N.J., 1967.
J. Katzer, ed. *Anton Chekhov: 1860–1960*. Moscow, 1960.
S. S. Koteliansky, ed. and tr. *Anton Tchekhov: Literary and Theatrical Reminiscences*. London, 1927; reprinted New York, 1974.
Magarshack, David. *Chekhov: A Life*. New York, 1952.
Mann, Thomas. "Chekhov." In *Last Essays*. New York, 1959.
Shestov, Leon. *Chekhov and Other Essays*. Ann Arbor, Mich., 1966.
Simmons, Ernest J. *Chekhov: A Biography*. Boston, 1962.
Struve, Gleb. "Chekhov in Communist Censorship." *Slavonic and East European Review*, XXXII (1955).
Toumanova, N. N. *Anton Chekhov: The Voice of Twilight Russia*. New York, 1937.
Triolet, Elsa. *L'Histoire d'Anton Tchékhov: Sa vie—son oeuvre*. Paris. 1954.
Winner, Thomas G. *Chekhov and His Prose*. New York, 1966.
Yermilov, V. *Anton Chekhov*. Moscow, 1956.